OTHER GHOST BOOKS BY TROY TAYLOR

HAUNTED ILLINOIS is a generous introduction to the resident wraiths of one of the nation's most haunted states, from its most prolific ghost writer. This book is a must for natives, ghost hunters and aficionados of Americana and holds captive anyone with an interest in the wonderful experiences so often omitted from the "proper" historical record.
URSULA BIELSKI, author of CHICAGO HAUNTS

Historians and cavers alike will find a wealth of information contained in DOWN IN THE DARKNESS and Taylor, a caver himself, also recounts stories of lost treasure caves and disputed civilizations underground. There is nothing better than a good cave book when you just can't get underground. This book should help you through those desperate times. Put on your helmet, turn down the lights and enjoy a unique journey into the dark, ghost-infested underworld.
PAUL STEWARD - NATIONAL SPELOGICAL SOCIETY NEWS

Troy Taylor has brought a new level of professionalism to the field with the GHOST HUNTER'S GUIDEBOOK, which stands as the best and most authoritative book written to date on ghost investigation. Both beginners and experienced investigators alike should make this book their bible... it gives the straight savvy... the material is grounded, practical and informative. It comes as no surprise that Taylor's book has received international praise!
ROSEMARY ELLEN GUILEY, author of ENCYCLOPEDIA OF GHOSTS & SPIRITS

SEASON OF THE WITCH is not a book for the faint of heart! Through his tireless research and mastery of the art of storytelling, Troy Taylor transports the reader back in time and into the frightening world of the creature known as the Bell Witch ... it's a legend that only Troy Taylor can bring to life!"
DAVID GOODWIN, author of GHOSTS OF JEFFERSON BARRACKS

GHOST BOOKS BY TROY TAYLOR

HAUNTED DECATUR (1995)
MORE HAUNTED DECATUR (1996)
GHOSTS OF MILLIKIN (1996 / 2001)
WHERE THE DEAD WALK (1997 / 2002)
DARK HARVEST (1997)
HAUNTED DECATUR REVISITED (2000)
FLICKERING IMAGES (2001)

GHOSTS OF SPRINGFIELD (1997)
THE GHOST HUNTER'S HANDBOOK (1997)
THE NEW GHOST HUNTER'S HANDBOOK (1998)
GHOSTS OF LITTLE EGYPT (1998)

HAUNTED ILLINOIS (1999 / 2001)
SPIRITS OF THE CIVIL WAR (1999)
THE GHOST HUNTER'S GUIDEBOOK (1999 / 2001)
SEASON OF THE WITCH (1999/ 2002)
HAUNTED ALTON (2000 / 2003)
HAUNTED NEW ORLEANS (2000)
BEYOND THE GRAVE (2001)
NO REST FOR THE WICKED (2001)
THE HAUNTING OF AMERICA (2001)
HAUNTED ST. LOUIS (2002)
INTO THE SHADOWS (2002)
CONFESSIONS OF A GHOST HUNTER (2002)
HAUNTED CHICAGO (2003)
DOWN IN THE DARKNESS (2003)
FIELD GUIDE TO HAUNTED GRAVEYARDS (2003)
OUT PAST THE CAMPFIRE LIGHT (2004)

GHOST TOURS
HAUNTED DECATUR, ILLINOIS TOURS (1994 - 2003)
HISTORY & HAUNTINGS TOURS OF GRAFTON, ILLINOIS (FROM 1999)
HISTORY & HAUNTINGS TOURS OF ST. CHARLES, MISSOURI (FROM 2000)
HISTORY & HAUNTINGS TOURS OF ST. LOUIS, MISSOURI (FROM 2002)
HISTORY & HAUNTINGS TOURS OF ALTON, ILLINOIS (FROM 1998)

- HISTORY & HAUNTINGS SERIES -

OUT PAST THE CAMPFIRE LIGHT

HAUNTINGS, HORRORS & UNSOLVED MYSTERIES OF THE GREAT OUTDOORS

- A WHITECHAPEL PRODUCTIONS PRESS PUBLICATION -

This book is dedicated to two men who are no longer with us -- to my Uncle Bud Hawkins, who gave me my first copy of "Call of the Wild" and who taught me about cowboys and to my Uncle Don Hawkins, who took me to my first ghost town and showed me how to "shoot at the Indians". They were an important part of my childhood and I never really got to tell them just how important they were.

And of course, to Amy -- who makes sure that I never get lost in the wilderness and keeps me always coming back home.

Original Cover Artwork Designed by

Michael Schwab, M & S Graphics & Troy Taylor
Visit M & S Graphics at www.msgrfx.com

THIS BOOK IS PUBLISHED BY

- Whitechapel Productions Press -

A Division of the History & Hauntings Book Co.
515 East Third Street - Alton, Illinois -62002
(618) 465-1086 / 1-888-GHOSTLY
Visit us on the Internet at www.historyandhauntings.com

First Edition - March 2004
ISBN: 1-892523-35-3

Printed in the United States of America

THE HISTORY & HAUNTINGS SERIES

Welcome to the fourth book in my "History & Hauntings Series". The series was first conceived a few years ago as a way to combine my two greatest literary interests. I have long been of the belief that no great ghost story can exist without a rich history to back it up. The events of yesterday truly give birth to the hauntings of today.

The book that you now hold in your hands is but another installment in an ongoing series of ghostly titles. In future volumes, I hope to continue to delve into the darker side of American history and to take you along on a continuing journey into the haunted corners of our country and to the farthest reaches of your imagination!

Happy Hauntings!

TABLE OF CONTENTS

INTRODUCTION

Dark spruce forest frowned on either side of the frozen waterway. The trees had been stripped by a recent wind of their white covering of frost, and they seemed to lean toward each other, black and ominous, in the fading light. A vast silence resigned over the land. The land itself was desolation, lifeless, without movement, so lone and cold that the spirit of it was not even that of sadness. There was a hint in it of laughter, but of a laughter more terrible than sadness --- a laughter that was as mirthless as the smile of the Sphinx, a laughter as cold as the frost and partaking of the grimness of infallibility. It was the masterful and incommunicable wisdom of eternity laughing at the futility of life and the effort of life. It was the Wild, the savage, frozen-hearted Northland wild.

JACK LONDON
WHITE FANG

I have always had a love of the "wild". As a kid, I think that I spent more time outdoors than in. My brother and I practically lived in the woods near our home in rural central Illinois and during the summer months we would vanish with our packed lunches and not return again until dark. My family has always had an affinity for nature and the outdoors. We could often be found on lakes, fishing, traveling and exploring the natural regions of the west, like Yellowstone and the Tetons. My first camping trip came when I was just nine months old and my mother recalls that she convinced me to stop taking the bottle so that we could journey to the Rocky Mountains in July of 1967. Growing up, we summered in northern Minnesota for many years and readers of my last book in this series, *Down in the*

Darkness, might recall my love of caves and my search for ghost towns and lost mines in Utah. I have never been able to get enough of being outside.

Somewhere, around age 16 or so, I discovered author Peter Jenkin's books about his walk across America in the 1970's and I was hooked on that vagabond sense of travel. For a short time, I was even able to experience it for myself but eventually, it lost its luster for me. And whatever dreams of it that I still had came to a crashing end in 1993 when I read an article by Jon Krakauer about a young man named Christopher McCandless who died a tragic death in the wilds of Alaska.

McCandless was living just the sort of life that I dreamed of, wandering about the American west, working when he needed to and exploring the world outside of the normalcy of everyday life. In April 1992, he headed off into the Alaskan wilderness, determined to live off the land. As anyone who has ever read Jack London knows, Alaska is the last great American wilderness and there are few of us who thirst for outdoor adventure who have not wanted to travel there. For McCandless though, it would be his final journey. Four months after he left civilization, hunters found him dead in an abandoned bus that had been used for shelter, just outside Denali National Park. It's likely that Chris died of starvation. His journal entries for this time tell of him getting weaker and weaker – possibly after eating the poisonous seeds of a wild sweet pea – and finally, becoming too sick to look for food. It remains a mystery as to what really happened to McCandless. Was he simply lacking the knowledge to survive in the woods, or did he have some sort of death wish? No one knows. "If this adventure proves fatal and you don't hear from me again," he wrote to a friend before he departed for Alaska, "I want you to know that you're a great man. I now walk into the wild."

Something about McCandless' story chilled me to the bone and not long after, I sold off most of my camping equipment and outdoor gear. I still enjoy the outdoors and remain an avid hiker, caver and explorer but I rarely ever return to the woods for an overnight excursion. I am still not sure what it was that bothered me so much about the fate of Christopher McCandless but whatever it was, I have never forgotten it. Perhaps this is why I chose to write this particular book – as a way of getting back in touch with the outdoor side of my own nature and maybe even confronting my own fears of vanishing into the wild.

One thing that I do know is that there has long been a need for a book to deal with the darker side of the outdoors – the hauntings, the horrors and the unexplained mysteries of the "things that go bump in the wild", so to speak. God knows, I have had my own brushes with eeriness in the outdoors and I am sure that many other nature enthusiasts have too. Let's face it, it's human nature to be unnerved by the wilderness. As children, many of us indulged in the ultimate terror experience, which consisted of camping out in a tent in the backyard for the night, telling ghost stories. With each horrific tale, the distance between the tent and the back door of the house grew by leaps and bounds. The stories seem silly to us now, as they would have then, if we had been sitting around the brightly lit kitchen table as we told them. Instead, we huddled around the flashlight and spoke in breathless tones while the wind howled outside and every crack of a stick or rustle of leaves undoubtedly became some graveyard ghoul approaching the thin barrier of canvas that separated the inside of the tent from the terror in the night.

I was reminded of these old childhood fears (and, in fact, inspired to begin this book) by a conversation that I had with a man named Jim Lombard, who lives in the wild regions of New Hampshire. Jim recalled an experience that he had with a friend named Tom back in the middle 1980's. They were scouting for the upcoming hunting season near Ossipe, New Hampshire, south of the White Mountain region. They walked back to an old logging road that vanished into the woods and by mid-day, had stumbled onto an overgrown orchard that was well-marked with deer sign. Jim and Tom looked around, thinking that it would make a great location for a deer stand, and then walked on. As they traveled a short distance further into the forest, they somehow got turned around and ended up in a place that had clearly once been a crossroads of sorts. They saw 10 or 15 old stone foundations, an abandoned well and debris from a wagon at the side of the leaf-strewn path. The orchard they had discovered had apparently once belonged to a settler who had lived here but the village had been gone for quite some time and the site had since been reclaimed by the forest.

Curious, Jim and Tom decided that they would eat lunch here and then they walked around to explore the ruins of the settlement. Behind one of the larger foundations, they discovered a small cemetery, where only a dozen or so tombstones remained, still fighting back against time and the elements. After that, they headed back to the orchard and scouted around the area for more deer sign.

Late in the October afternoon, it started to get dark and so Jim and Tom decided to sit down on one of the old stone walls from the village and watch for any deer to appear. In an hour or so, the light began to get murky and it became very hard to see. As darkness began to descend on the clearing in the woods, Jim began to get very uneasy. He couldn't put his finger on where the feelings were coming from either. He was an experienced outdoorsman and had spent many nights out in the woods by himself. There was something eating at him though, and then he realized what it was – he was being watched. Just as Jim was starting to consider hiking out of the area before it became too dark to see at all, he suddenly felt Tom stiffen up beside him and heard his breath hiss in a sharp intake of air. By unspoken agreement, they decided to leave and hike back to where they had left their vehicle.

They were within about a half mile of the van when Jim spoke up. It was now completely dark but the logging road was wide enough by then so that they could see a light from a house that bordered the woods. Jim spoke to his friend. "Tom, when we were back there sitting on that stone wall... I had the weirdest feeling that we were being watched," he said.

Tom stopped in the roadway and turned to Jim. "It's strange that you should say that because do you remember when I sort of stiffened up when we were there?" Jim said that he did and Tom continued. "I was just sitting there and it was pretty dark but I saw something out of the corner of my eye. I looked and just then saw an old woman, dressed in white, step into the glade and walk right across in front of me. She just disappeared into the woods."

Jim was stunned, remembering the uneasy sensation of being watched that he had felt while sitting on the wall. He thought that perhaps it had been an animal out there in the woods – but a ghost? He would have laughed if he had not realized how serious Tom was about it. He was not a practical joker and if he said that he saw a ghostly old woman in white, then he really had.

"Tom never said another word about that day," Jim told me years later. "I continued to ask him questions but he never spoke about it again. We walked pretty quickly on that final bit back to the van and I can tell you that it was a pretty nice feeling to get back home that night!"

What happened to the two men out there that afternoon? Did they really encounter a ghost in the dark reaches of the forest? There is no way that we can know for sure one way or another but such an account begs us to realize that we may not be as alone out there in the wild as we think. Sometimes when we feel that someone may be watching us – someone actually is!

The reader may or may not care to believe this but it was a statement considered to be fact by the early pioneers and settlers of this country. How many of us have dreamed of seeing the American continent before it was overwhelmed by civilization? Imagine seeing the Great Lakes before they were polluted, the Appalachian Mountains before strip mining, the Great Plains before the railroads, the rolling prairies when they were still black with the herds of buffalo and so on. This has become a common dream for many in the years since most of the real American wilderness has vanished but it is a dream that has been conjured up in recent times. For the most part, the early settlers of this country did not look at the unbroken landscape with awe, but rather with terror. Most did not see the wonder of nature but instead looked at the dark tree line that waited on the border of their stump-filled clearings and were afraid of what might be waiting out there.

The unknown wilderness could be filled with anything, from strange creatures to a boundless waste where devils and demons waited for the unlucky and the daring. Many of the settlers would not even admit to a shared humanity with the only other inhabitants of the country in those days, the American Indians. To them, the Native Americans were not even human, they were, in the words of the Puritan minister Cotton Mather, "tawney serpents". The horrors of the unknown wilderness took physical form in the shape of these "wild men". The Indians would sometimes descend on the frontier settlements in a bloody rage and after a dreadful destruction, would disappear into the woods with captives of whom no trace would ever be found, save for a torn dress, a piece of ribbon, or the blue eyes of a half-Indian child met at a trading post years later.

As the frontiersmen, explorers and adventurers began to travel into the new regions, and away from the safe shores of the ocean, they began to find that America was indeed a strange and haunted place. They began to discover things that the Native Americans who explored before them were already aware and these adventurers and indigenous peoples left behind evidence of their weird discoveries in the names they gave certain locations. As the explorers started to roam the vast reaches of the rugged land, they discovered areas that the Native Americans had already discovered centuries before. The Indians treated these locations as sacred spots and also sometimes as terrifying places that were better left untouched. These "mystery sites" became the first "haunted" places in America, places where the explorers, settlers and the Indians witnessed strange sights and sounds like unexplained balls of light, apparitions, screams in the night and various other unsettling types of phenomena.

The idea that such locations were linked to the "Devil" was the first thought that crossed the minds of the bible-reading, God-fearing folks and they promptly set about to do two things. They learned to avoid these strange and haunted places and secondly, they gave names to the spots to alert other visitors and settlers of the dangers of the area. Such places, they believed, were best shunned or at least entered with caution.

Some of these locations will be visited within the pages of this book, as their legends still linger today. Near Lawrence, Indiana is a place called the Devil's Backbone, where a woman's disembodied screams are sometimes heard in the night. In Illinois, there is another Devil's Backbone (and an accompanying Bake Oven) that has long been the scene of hauntings and horror. There is also Devil's Track Lake, near Cook, Minnesota. The lake was long considered a haunted site by the Indians of the region as they believed that evil spirits lurked in the water. There is a Devil's Hole located in California and it was believed by the Indians to be the literal "home of a devil". This demon was controlled, the legends said, by the local shaman and their stories had it that it helped the Indians against the Spanish in the 1700's. Another Devil's Hole can be found in Niagara, New York. This hole is a twenty-foot cave that gained its name from Indian legends. Their lore insisted that an evil presence dwelt there and has been the scene of much in the way of death and tragedy over the past three centuries. British troops were massacred here by Indians in 1763 and by the 1850's, countless people had lost their lives in nearby freak accidents. Even today, hardly a year goes by without someone being killed or drowning in the haunted cave. And the list goes on and on …

But those were days gone by. Mysteries can terrify us, especially mysteries that extend all of the way up to the lighted doorsteps of the closest town. It is human nature for us to fear what we cannot explain and what we cannot understand. The progress of new arrivals in the country has been a persistent attempt to stamp out the mysteries and bury them under parking lots, shopping malls and housing editions. For some reason, people can accept the worst mishaps and violence in cities and towns but yet become electric with fear at the thought of bumping into some wild creature in a place without roads, electric lights and air conditioning. Ordinary fears, even bad ones – fear of your husband leaving, of news from the doctor, of financial problems – can seem manageable when compared to the unspecified fears that await us in the unknown. There is nothing to be afraid of, we tell ourselves, and we do not have to be frightened of that which is not easily understood.

Or do we?

Centuries after man cowered from what might be out behind the lantern light, and named terrifying places in honor of the Devil, we are still afraid of what might be out there in the woods. Witness the popularity of such horror films as the *Blair Witch Project*, about three students who vanish into the wilderness and are never seen again, if you have any doubt that we are still terrified by the what lies out in the woods. And that brings us to this book...

When people have asked me what this book is about, I have had a hard time putting my finger on it. Unlike other books that I have written, which I can say are about a haunted house or a haunted place, this book is different. It is filled with mystery – mysteries of haunted places, lost and vanished treasure, missing people and mysterious creatures for which no explanation exists – but most of all, it is about the "wild". For me, the "wild" is that elusive mystery that can be found in the beyond regions, the woods, lakes, rivers and forests of America. This is not a book that is all about ghosts and hauntings, although they will find their place here and often where you least expect it, but simply about the unknown. There will be mysterious tales here of monsters, missing people and lost mines that will not have a ghostly element at all but were simply too strange – and to "wild" – not to be included in these pages.

I hope that you will enjoy delving into these strange tales and often amazing stories and perhaps might even want to seek out some of the lost people and places on your own. But if you do, be sure to pack plenty of supplies, your warmest clothing and take along your sense of adventure. There is a great mystery waiting for us out there – out past the campfire light – and it constantly works to undermine the rational world that we live in. There really is something lurking out there in the woods, let me assure you of that, and to find it, you need to only start walking.

And to set off "into the wild".

Troy Taylor
Winter 2004

1. WITHOUT A TRACE

Those Who Walked into the Wild and Never Returned

When I was growing up, my family had a vacation cabin in the woods of northern Minnesota. There, on the shores of a place called Pelican Lake, we swam, fished and explored the islands that were spread out on the water and hiked through the forests that pressed up against the shoreline. It was a place far removed from cable television, fast food restaurants, shopping malls and even radio stations. We were so far away from everything that we could get only one clear signal on the radio dial, a local pirate operation run by a crazy family of hippies who would play relentless hours of the Grateful Dead between hallucinogenic rants about politics and the evils of Ronald Reagan. By the time that we were teenagers, we had learned to record hours of cassette tapes of WLS in Chicago (back when it was still a rock-n-roll station) and then we would play them on the stereo. It provided the illusion of listening to a radio station and it didn't matter to us that by the end of the summer the news was old and the weather forecast was for a place hundreds of miles away and several months before.

Take a look at a map of Minnesota some time and search for Pelican Lake, and the little town of Orr, in the north-central part of the state. We were only an hour or so from the Canadian border during those summers and what seemed like years away from reality. As you run your finger across the map, you'll see just how much blank space there is around the lake, with only small towns dotting the white area between the Superior National Forest and the nearby Indian reservations. Don't let the map fool you though. Those white spaces on the map were not actually white – they were green. It is an area of heavy, shrouded forest, a wilderness area where you have to chain down your garbage cans at night to keep the bears from knocking them over.

We used to roam those miles of green space, searching for forgotten paths, lost lakes and patches of blueberries that were so big you could fill bucket after bucket and still never reach the other side of the clearing. We walked and we wandered but one thing that we never did was to get off of the trail – at least more than once. I used to like to lose myself in those forests, spending hours hiking along the shaded trails, never meeting anyone else, lost in the solitude and the silence. There came one afternoon when my walk was not so peaceful though and in fact, was downright eerie. I became overwhelmed by a feeling of dread and foreboding like nothing that I had experienced before in my life. It was caused by something as simple as taking a wrong turn.

As I walked one afternoon, I decided to follow a new trail that I had never journeyed down before. I traveled deeper and deeper into the woods but I was not worried. All of the trails that I had followed in the past all had ended up somewhere, usually at the lake, a highway or at one of the resorts that were scattered along the water. This trail kept on going though, winding back and forth through the woods so much that I eventually lost my sense of direction. Eventually, the path itself even faded out. At this point, I was so far along that I thought it best to keep going. I did have some experience in the woods and most of my experiences had taught me that trails always lead somewhere. I would keep going, I told myself, and the trail will start back up again. I assured myself that this area was simply overgrown. The path was seldom used but I was convinced that I would find it again a little further ahead. But I didn't…

After another half hour or so, I realized that I was lost. I did not panic but rather just tried to re-trace my steps and find the section of trail that had ended. I looked and looked for it, likely walking in circles, for at least an hour but I never saw it again. Now, I was starting to get worried and I began to realize just how much wilderness was really up here. Yes, it was the 1980's but it might as well have been the 1880's because human occupants in these north woods were few and far between. If my directions were off, I could walk for days and never run into anyone else. I could simply vanish, I realized, and never be seen again.

I think that it was this final thought that put me up onto the edge. The woods were no longer a place of refuge but had become foreign territory, filled with danger and perhaps even death. As I continued blindly stumbling through the gloomy woods, I caught a case of the "creeps". In the outdoors, when you are far from anywhere, they can get you any time. There are stories told of people who wander out into a blizzard and then die from exposure just ten feet from their house and it's always because a case of the "creeps" unhinged their mind. We are all subject to the "creeps" because in some places, the things that we do know are greatly outnumbered by the things that we don't. Panic is always waiting to set in. All it requires to take over is a flicker of disorientation or an encounter with something that is too spooky to explain. Our rational mind wants to control us but it has to do battle with the "creeps" first. They can get you anywhere – it doesn't have to be in the woods – but anyone who has spent time outdoors can tell you that if you let your imagination run away with you, you are in deep trouble.

On that afternoon, the "creeps" ran up my back and put my legs into motion. I'm not ashamed to admit that I started to run. I likely would have ran all of the way to Canada if I had not finally stopped and shook off my case of the "creeps". After taking a deep breath, I came to the conclusion that just by turning north, I could walk until I hit the edge of Pelican Lake, or if I had gone too far, the Indian reservation to the west of it. Once I realized this, and started calmly walking again, I was well on my way. Within an hour, I had reached the lakeshore and by following the line of the water, I made it back to our cabin. I never told anyone about my brief moment of being lost in the Minnesota woods but I certainly never forgot about it.

After that day, I realized how easy it would be for someone to vanish without a trace into the "wild". A good case of the "creeps" was all that would be required. I think this realization was what cemented my fascination with those who one day just walked into the woods – or flew off into the sky, or set out into the jungle – and just never came back.

It has been written that in America, about 10 million people are reported missing during the course of a single year. The vast majority of them return home within hours or days, but a very small percentage of them vanish forever. It is not easy to disappear without a trace but it is a common occurrence. There are many people who have done so and each account of such a vanishing have all of the ingredients to a mystery story – except for the ending, which can only be left to speculation. The circumstances surrounding these disappearances are bizarre, sometimes ridiculous, but in the end, are inexplicable. And while often they occur in such mundane locations as from a ship, a train, an airplane, or even crossing a street, many more of them take place in the outdoors. When ordinary people walk into the "wild" and never come back again.

America's most famous case of vanishing into the wilderness occurred long before our country was ever established when the haunting colony of Roanoke, founded in 1587 by more than 100 English men and women, disappeared with barely a trace. The colony was settled on the Virginia coastline (now North Carolina) and it was intended for the colonists to farm and to pay for supplies from home with the cultivation of wild sassafras, an import that was prized for medicinal purposes in England. The governor of the colony, John White, sailed back to England for supplies to get the settlers through the winter but detained there by a war with Spain, he did not return to America until 1591. When he arrived at Roanoke, he found that the entire colony had vanished, including his daughter and her infant, Virginia Dare, the first white child born in America. The buildings, stockade and settlement had been utterly abandoned and the only clue left behind was the word "Croatan", the name of a nearby island and Indian tribe, that had been carved into a post. A number of search parties were sent out to look for the colonists but bad weather eventually forced White to return to England. The colonists were abandoned to their mysterious fate, but were not forgotten. Years later, John Smith would launch several expeditions from the Jamestown Colony to try and determine the fate of those who went missing at Roanoke. He never learned what happened to them and neither have the scores of historians, archaeologists and curiosity-seekers who have followed in his footsteps.

Throughout the early years of American exploration, one of the "holy grails" of the expeditions was to find a Northwest Passage that could take ships from the Great Lakes to the waters of the Pacific Ocean. Many searched for it and failed but perhaps the greatest of these failures can be attributed to British explorer Sir John Franklin, whose arrogance and shortsightedness led to some 140 deaths, including his own. In 1819, Franklin, a British naval officer, was sent to the wilderness of northwestern Canada to lead an expedition in search of the passage. Winter overtook his small party as they tracked across a section of icy tundra that is so vast they christened it the Barrens, the name by which it is still known. Their food and supplies ran out and game was so scarce that Franklin and his men were forced to eat lichen scraped from boulders, deer hide, scavenged animal bones, their own boot leather and eventually, one another's flesh. Before the ordeal was over, at least two men had been murdered and eaten, the suspected murderer had been executed and eight others were dead from sickness and starvation. Franklin himself was likely within days of his own death when he and the other survivors were rescued by a band of Indians.

Franklin was known as a good-natured bumbler who had been woefully ill-prepared to lead an Arctic expedition and when he returned to England, he became known as the Man Who Ate His Shoes and yet this was uttered more in praise than in ridicule. He was hailed as a national hero, promoted to the rank of captain by the Admiralty, paid handsomely to write an account of the ordeal, and in 1825, given command of a second expedition.

This trip was relatively uneventful but in 1845, still searching for the elusive Northwest Passage, Franklin made the fatal mistake of returning to the Arctic for a third time. He and the 128 men under his command were never heard from again. The Admiralty posted a huge reward for any trace of the men and more than 40 different expeditions were launched to search for them. The first evidence of their fate was discovered in 1851 but would come in gradually over time in the form of journals, pieces of clothing and ice-covered skeletons. It was eventually established that they had all perished, the victims of scurvy, starvation and unspeakable suffering.

Another expedition, which was likely just as fatal but inevitably more mysterious, journeyed into the wilds of South America in April 1925. It was led by Colonel Percy Fawcett, an archaeologist, geographer and adventurer, who went into Brazil's little-known Mato Grosso region in search of a lost city of gold. The search led to Fawcett, his son, Jack, and their friend, Raleigh Rimell, meeting an unknown fate in a dangerous and forbidding land.

Fawcett had served in England's Indian Army in Ceylon during the twilight years of the British Empire, spending his leisure time searching for ancient tombs and treasures. When his service ended, he traveled to South America in 1906 and spent the next three years surveying "a long and excessively unhealthy sector of the Brazilian-Bolivian frontier". During this time, he carefully studied an old Portuguese account of a great city that lay in ruins in the jungle, purportedly laden with gold and rare gems. Convinced that the city did indeed exist, Fawcett and his party started out from Cuyaba on April 20, traveling light and planning to live off the country. His last dispatch, which spoke of swimming and fording small streams, climbing rocky hills and being eaten by bugs, was received on May 30 – and after that, the expedition vanished without a trace.

No one would ever hear from Fawcett again and because he had warned that he was likely to be gone for as long as two years, no search party was sent out until May 1928. By then, the trail was more than just a little cold. Indians from several of the hostile tribes in the area accused each other of killing the explorers, while others told of seeing the Englishmen near death from disease and exhaustion. For more than a decade, travelers returned from the jungle with stories that Fawcett had "gone native" and was now a half-mad old man who was living among the Indians but no convincing evidence ever emerged to support this or to explain what had happened in the dark reaches of the region.

The annals of mysterious history are filled with instances of people who have simply walked away one day and have vanished without a trace – but what about an entire village of people? Could such a thing really happen? According to reliable and thoroughly investigated reports, this is exactly what occurred in November 1930. One cold and blustery day, a Canadian fur trapper named Joe Labelle snowshoed into a thriving Eskimo fishing village on the shores of Lake Anjikuni. Labelle was greeted by an eerie silence, which was strange because the village was usually a noisy, bustling settlement of more than 2,000 inhabitants. As he shuffled down the street though, he saw not a single soul in sight. Labelle visited many of the homes and fish storehouses, some of which belonged to close friends, but no one in the village was anywhere to be seen. The only sign of life that he found was one burning fire, which had a pot of blackened stew now smoldering over it. Even stranger, he reportedly did not find even a single footprint in the fresh snow on the village streets.

Labelle immediately left the village and went straight to the nearest telegraph office to send a message to the Royal Canadian Mounted Police. Investigators turned up a few hours later and they too were baffled by the disappearance. An enormous search party was organized to try and find some clue as to where the inhabitants had gone but what they found only added to the mystery. All of the sled dogs that belonged to the Eskimos were found buried under a huge snowdrift at the edge of the village – they had starved to death. As would the villagers, wherever they had gone, because they had left all of their food and provisions in their homes when they had vanished. Most chilling of all though was that all of the ancestral graves in the village's cemetery had been unearthed and the bodies had been removed.

The Mounties and many volunteers searched throughout the region for weeks after the discovery of the empty village but none of the inhabitants were ever found.

But most wilderness disappearances aren't nearly as dramatic as lost colonies, disappearing villages or vanished expeditions. In October 1964, a retired paint contractor named Charles F. Holden from Oakland, California disappeared while on a hunting trip with his son and brother-in-law. While the other men planned to hunt, Holden merely wanted to paint and sketch in the woods. The three men stopped on the highway east of Crescent City, California in the middle of the afternoon on October 11. While the two younger men went to scout the area for game, Holden set up his sketching board. Albert, his son, glanced back at him as he started up the trail and saw his father sketching away, lost in thought. This was the last time that he would ever see him...

When the two men returned, about 45 minutes later, they found absolutely no trace of Charles Holden. He had left no footprints, discarded sketch paper or cigarette butts behind – he was simply gone. Sheriff's deputies and forestry officials conducted an extensive search of the area and found no evidence that Holden had ever been there at all. Deputy David Brenbemer was quoted as saying: "It is physically impossible for him to be up there. If he had fallen into the brush or had wandered away – any distance – we would have found him."

Another tragic disappearance occurred near Lander, Wyoming in July 1997. It was on July 24 that 24 year-old runner and Olympic marathon hopeful Amy Wroe Bechtel inexplicably vanished into the woods near town. On the morning of her disappearance, Amy said good bye to her husband, climber Steve Bechtel, and drove into Lander. The last verifiable sighting of her took place in a local art gallery around 2:30 that afternoon. She was wearing a yellow shirt, black shorts and running shoes. When she did not return home by 10:00 P.M., Steve called her parents to see if she was with them. She wasn't and so he immediately called the sheriff's office. Amy's car was found about three hours later on Loop Road, which runs through the mountains of the Shoshone National Forest outside of town. The car was unlocked and the keys were found under Amy's to-do list, which had been left on the passenger seat. She had been planning a 10k race in the area and it was believed that she was out checking the course.

Before dawn, a group of the couple's friends began scouring the nearby woods but turned up nothing. Searches continued, involving horses, dogs, helicopters, the National Guard and even the FBI, but continued to come up empty. Many theories were advanced, including that Amy had been the victim of a hit and run accident and the driver had buried her body or had dropped it into a nearby lake; that she had run away; or that she had been attacked by a mountain lion or a bear. The authorities, faced with few plausible options, began to focus the investigation on Steve Bechtel. But her husband stated that he had been rock-climbing with a friend, 75 miles north of town, on the day of the disappearance. The friend backed up the alibi but some, including Amy's mother, continue to suspect that he might be involved. To this day though, Steve has steadfastly maintained his innocence and has remained active in ongoing efforts to find Amy. No real clues as to her whereabouts have ever been discovered.

There are stretches of wilderness across our land that just seem to swallow people up and to never let them be found. Mount Rainier in Washington state is just one of those places. In July 1999, the 65th person in history to vanish on Rainier walked into the wild and did not return. His name was Joe Wood and the Bronx born journalist, who worked as an editor for a New York book publisher, was in Seattle attending a minority journalist's conference. On July 8, he decided to hike up Mount Rainier National Park's Mildred Point Trail – and walked into oblivion. Wood was no novice in the outdoors, having been an Eagle Scout, but he may not have been prepared for the conditions in the park that day. Rainier had received its fifth heaviest snowfall in its history and the six-mile hike was made treacherous by ice and was lined with tree wells and dangerous snow bridges. On the trail, Wood ran into Bruce Gaummond, a retired Boeing aircraft employee who came forward after Joe was reported missing. Gaummond told the National Park Service that the two of them had chatted briefly about birds, the length of the trail and a slippery creek crossing ahead. After that, Wood was never seen again.

The Park Service believes that the journalist may have fallen into the creek or may have slipped off a snowy cliff but others, like Wood's mother Elizabeth, remain haunted by the possibility of foul play. Searchers scoured the area for five days after Joe was last seen but a warm spell had melted all of the snow, erasing Wood's tracks. A final search was conducted in September 1999 and after that, Joe Wood was added to the list of those who walked away – and never came back.

NEMO 1934
THE MYSTERIOUS DISAPPEARANCE OF EVERETT RUESS

Although he vanished without a trace into the vast canyonlands of Utah in 1934, Everett Ruess has never been proclaimed dead. He lives on as a legend – a western myth that is the embodiment of finding beauty and freedom in nature. Little that is of the physical world still remains of this charismatic young man, save for an inscription on the wall of stone in southern Utah's David Gulch. It reads "Nemo 1934", an enigmatic reminder from Ruess that we are "no one" in the greater scheme of things.

Everett Ruess

Everett Ruess was born in Oakland, California in 1914, the younger of two sons raised by Christopher and Stella Ruess. Christopher was a graduate of Harvard Divinity School and was a poet, philosopher and Unitarian minister. To feed his family though, he worked as a bureaucrat in the California penal system. Stella was a headstrong woman with artistic ambitions for both herself and her family. She published a literary journal, the *Ruess Quartette*, with the family motto emblazoned on the cover: "Glorify the Hour". The Ruess family was a tight knit bunch and a nomadic one. They moved from Oakland to Fresno to Los Angeles to Boston to Brooklyn to New Jersey to Indiana to finally settling in southern California when Everett was 14. One can understand where Everett got his wandering ways.

Living in Los Angeles, Everett attended the Otis Art School and Hollywood High School. He embarked on his first solo journey at age 16, spending the summer of 1930 hitchhiking and roaming through Yosemite and Big Sur, eventually winding up in Carmel. Two days after he arrived, he knocked on the door of Edward Weston, the famous photographer, who was charmed enough by the young man to humor him. Over the next two months, he encouraged Everett's uneven but promising efforts at painting and block printing and permitted him to hang around the studio with his sons, Neil and Cole.

At the end of the summer, he returned home long enough to earn a high school diploma, which he received in January 1931. Less than a month later, he was on the road again, tramping alone through the sparsely populated lands of Utah, Arizona and New Mexico. Except for a single semester at UCLA, two extended visits with his parents, a winter in San Francisco – which he managed to spend in the company of Dorothea Lange, Ansel Adams and painter Maynard Dixon – Everett spent the rest of his life constantly on the move. He lived on little money, right out of his backpack, sleeping on the ground and going hungry for days at a time. He could not have been happier.

Ruess kept a diary and wrote numerous letters to his friends and family, telling them of his "serene and tempestuous days" scaling cliffs, wandering through canyons and walking across the desert. He befriended many of those he met. He learned to speak Navajo and once sang with a medicine man at the beside of a sick girl. Hopi Indians painted Ruess and allowed him to participate in their traditional Antelope Dance, which was a high honor.

One day in June 1931, Randolph "Pat" Jenks and Tad Nichols were driving from Cameron, Arizona to Flagstaff when they came upon Everett and his burro, Pegasus. Ruess was badly sunburned, half-starved and dehydrated. They stopped and asked him if he wanted a drink. But Everett, thinking that they had asked him for water, started to unleash one of the two canteens that he had on the side of the burro. "He had only a small amount of water left, but was immediately willing to share it," Nichols recalled many years later.

Jenks and Nichols drove Everett to Flagstaff and the young artists stayed at Jenks' ranch under the San Francisco Peaks for several weeks, painting the aspens. Then, just as suddenly as he had come, he vanished.

For a time, Everett reportedly worked with archaeologists from the University of California who were excavating ruins near Kayenta, Arizona. His lack of regard for his own safety terrified some of them. "One time in camp he stood on the edge of a 400-foot cliff in a rainstorm and did a water-color sketch of a waterfall," archaeologist H.C. Lockett told *Desert Magazine* in 1939. I remember this clearly because I personally was scared to death just watching him perched on the edge of the cliff".

Ruess financed his wanderings buy selling his block prints and paintings but he never stayed in the same place for long. "There is always an undercurrent of restlessness and wild longing," he once wrote. "The wind is in my hair, there is a fire in my heels and I shall always be a rover, I know."

Everett continued to roam the southwest until the age of 20, when he was gone. The last letters anyone received from him were posted from the Mormon settlement of Escalante, 57 miles north of a place called Davis Gulch, on November 11, 1934. The letters were addressed to his parents and brother and he advised them that he would be incommunicado for "a month or two". Eight days after mailing them,

Ruess encountered two sheepherders about a mile from the gulch and spent two nights at their camp. These men were the last people known to have seen Everett alive. He did leave one last marker in his wake however. Later, discovered carved into the sandstone of the gulch, Everett twice etched the name "Nemo" – Latin for "nobody" – and then vanished.

Some three months after Ruess departed Escalante, his parents received a bundle of unopened mail that had been forwarded from the postmaster at Marble Canyon, Arizona, where Everett was long overdue. Worried, Christopher and Stella contacted the authorities in Escalante, who organized a search party in March 1935. Starting from the sheep camp where he was last seen, they began combing the surrounding region and soon found Everett's two burros at the bottom of Davis Gulch, peacefully grazing behind a corral that had been fashioned from brush and tree branches. The burros were confined in the upper canyon and nearby, under a large natural arch, they found Everett's "Nemo 1934" inscription. Four pieces of Anasazi pottery, which Everett had likely discovered, were neatly arranged a few feet away. Three months later, searchers came across another "Nemo" inscription a little deeper into the gulch, although both have long since disappeared under the waters of Lake Powell. Except for the burros and their tack, none of Everett's possessions, including his camping gear, journals and paintings, were ever found. Everett was simply gone and the question of what happened to him has produced many theories, but no answers.

Given the rough area where he was camping, Everett likely fell to his death while scrambling up or down one of the canyon walls but no search ever turned up any human remains. His parents came to believe that he was murdered for his belongings and likely based their belief on the confession of an outlaw Navajo named Jack Crank. His story was inconsistent and no body was ever discovered where he said that it would be, despite several intense searches.

If he was not killed, some say, there is the mystery as to why Everett would have left the gulch with a heavy load of gear but without his pack animals. This bewildering puzzle has led some to conclude that he was murdered by a band of cattle rustlers known to have been in the area, who then stole his belongings and buried his remains or threw them into the Colorado River. This is plausible but no evidence exists to prove or disprove it.

Many of the people that Everett met on his wilderness sojourns were so taken with the young man that they contacted his parents in with offers to help in the search. Reporters from Los Angeles, San Francisco and Salt Lake City covered the searches and their dispatches provoked interest and leads from around the country. In the first few month after he vanished, Ruess was "spotted" in all sorts of places, from a transient camp in Florida to a mine in Moab, Utah and even hitchhiking on a Mexican highway. None of these false leads panned out though and the search continued.

In early 1935, a California placer miner named Neil Johnson heard about Everett's disappearance and he offered to help look for him. He was accompanied on the search by a report from the *Salt Lake Tribune*, John Terrell. When the two men reached the desert region in the southern part of Utah, they found it nearly impossible to get an Indian guide to sign on with the search party. At a desert trading post, Johnson and Terrell announced that the man they were looking for might be dead and the Indians scattered. They explained that they feared the search might be successful but instead of finding Ruess, they might find his ghost! Finally, an expert tracker, a half-Ute, half-Navajo named Dougeye, agreed to lead the men but only if they left behind their camera. The guide wanted no part of the "winking-eye box."

In August 1935, Douglas and Terrell journeyed through miles of wild country. They swam the Colorado and then continued north to Davis Gulch. At this point, their Indian guide became puzzled and spent two days thoroughly searching the area for any sign of Everett. He finally concluded that the boy had gone into the canyon but had not come out.

Interest in the fate of Everett Ruess continued and in the summer of 1941, two Paiute Indians told Toney Richardson, a trading post owner at Tonalea, Arizona, that a white man had been found "sleeping" in the sand across the Colorado River in Utah. At the same time, Richardson heard wild rumors from the Navajo reservation about medicine men holding squaw dances using the scalp of a white man. A tiny piece of it was sliced off for each dance and afterward, it was buried to kill his spirit. The scalp was said to be from a "sleeping" man, who was blond. Everett had been fair-skinned but not quite blond. The identity of the dead man was never determined.

For the most part, friends and searchers came to believe that Everett was murdered and if not by rustlers, then by Indians in the area. Pat Jenks feels that he ran into a group of Paiute Indians who were on their way to Escalante for winter supplies and they killed him and stole his gear. Tad Nichols though disagreed. "I don't believe he was killed by Indians," he said back in 1997. "He got along well with them. Maybe they didn't like him poking into caves, and through their ceremonial material, but I don't think they were responsible." He believed that Everett likely died in a flash flood or fell off a cliff.

To this day though, no one really knows. And while Everett vanished from the region in 1934, he has never really been gone. Nearly 30 years after he was last seen, archaeologists digging at what it now Arizona's Lake Powell found his canteen and some other gear, including a box of razor blades from the Owl Drug Company of Los Angeles. They were Everett's brand.

In 1976, when Colorado River boatman and Grand Canyon legend Emory Kolb died, friends searching through his belongings found a human skeleton inside a skiff in his garage. The skull had a hole behind the right ear and rattling around inside of it was a .32-caliber slug. Some speculated that it was Ruess. Coconino County sent the remains to University of Arizona's human identification lab and Forensic Anthropologist Walter Birkby stated that the cause of death was certainly murder. However, the bones had belonged to a man that was well over six feet tall and Everett had only stood 5-foot-8.

In 1983, another "Nemo" inscription turned up on a canyon wall along the San Juan River and rumors persisted that Navajo medicine men were continuing to have visions of Everett – alive and well. Some believe that Everett Ruess never died at all but simply vanished. One man told author Jon Krakauer that he knew a man who had "definitely bumped into Ruess" in the late 1960's at a remote hogan on the Navajo Indian reservation. According to the man, Everett had married a Navajo woman, with whom he had raised at least one child. Some even believe that, although now quite elderly, he continues to live today.

So, what really happened to Everett Ruess? It's likely that we will never know for sure but regardless of whether he died here in the Utah canyonlands, his legend lives on. Author Wallace Stegner described Everett as an artistic athlete, a callow romantic, and an atavistic wanderer of the wastelands. "But one who died – if he died – with the dream intact."

DOWN THE RIVER
THE VANISHING OF GLEN AND BESSIE HYDE

The magnificent and breathtaking Grand Canyon has been a place of wonder and mystery since the first Spanish explorers looked down from the rim at the Colorado River far below. The canyon was conquered first by John Wesley Powell in the 1860's but has been the scene of both triumph and tragedy ever since. Perhaps the most famous unsolved disappearance in the Grand Canyon was that of a young couple named Glen and Bessie Hyde, who vanished without a trace in 1929. But they were not the only ones to do so...

In the early 1800's, the Grand Canyon was an enigma so deep and so wide that it was commonly believed that no bird smaller than an eagle could fly across it. It was also believed that no one could possibly ride through the canyon in a boat and survive the journey. If the canyon itself is awe-inspiring than the rampaging river that courses through it is utterly intimidating. There were rumors of waterfalls as deadly as Niagara and whirlpools that could swallow a boat of any size. There were even claims that the river went underground at one point and came rushing back up again several miles downstream. It was certain that no one in his right mind would dare to challenge the mighty Colorado River. Even running the river today, with maps and a real knowledge of what dangers lie ahead, can be death-defying but a century and a half ago, it was tantamount to suicide and certainly something that would not be undertaken for pure thrills.

Lieutenant Joseph C. Ives was the first to attempt it in the spring of 1858 and had been ordered to do so by his superiors in Washington, who had organized and authorized the expedition. These bureaucrats, having never been west of the Mississippi, believed the best type of craft to make the voyage up the Colorado was a paddlewheel steamer. Ives was less than impressed with the canyon. "This region is altogether valueless," he told a group of surveyors, geologists and artists, while looking down from the rim. "Ours will doubtless be the last party of whites to visit this profitless locality. It seems intended by nature that the Colorado River, along the greater part of its lonely and majestic way, shall be forever unvisited and undisturbed. There is nothing to do but leave, and probably none will follow us."

Lieutenant Ives, faced with the prospect of navigating the river, supervised the construction of the steamer, a bright red, 54-foor craft that he tested on the peaceful Delaware River. He christened the boat *Explorer* and had it shipped in sections to Panama. The crated sections were then sent by rail to the Pacific Ocean and then around the southern tip of the Baja California until it reached the muddy delta of the Colorado. By this time, December 1, 1857, the *Explorer* had traveled more than 8,000 miles without ever touching water.

With considerable difficulty, Ives and his men assembled and launched the fragile boat. The first leg of the journey, from Fort Yuma to the mouth of the canyon, was arduous and slow but it had been attempted before. On January 30, the vessel passed the previous points of exploration and paddled into the unknown. It would be 24 hours later when the expedition would come to a halt. Ives got no further than the juncture of Black Canyon and Grand Canyon before the *Explorer*'s bow was split by a huge submerged rock. The collision was so strong that everyone on deck was thrown into the water, the wheelhouse was ripped off and the boiler came loose from its support bolts and caused the smokestack to pitch sideways.

Although badly damaged and taking on water, Ives refused to give up. He had already gone deeper into the canyon than anyone ever had before and he was determined to continue on. He nursed the craft on upstream until he reached what he believed was the Virgin River and there, he abandoned the *Explorer* on a sandbar. He and his men climbed up out of the canyon, having done their best, and never knowing that death would have surely awaited them ahead if they had tried to take the unwieldy vessel through the rapids.

A decade passed before another expedition was established to try and explore the Colorado River through the canyon. The man who headed this excursion was a stubborn, tenacious and brilliant explorer named John Wesley Powell. He had been born the son of a Methodist minister, who was also an avowed abolitionist. Powell was never afraid to settle arguments with his fists as a young man and was constantly called upon to defend his family's view on slavery. His fighting eventually led to his being thrown out of public school and so he had to be privately tutored. At the age of 18, he became a teacher and a few years later, married his cousin, Emma Dean, against the objections of both of their families.

John Wesley Powell

The wedding took place in 1861, when Powell was already enrolled in the military as a second lieutenant under General Ulysses S. Grant. During the battle of Shiloh, Powell's right arm was shattered by a bullet and it had to be amputated just below the shoulder. Such an injury would have ended the military career of a lesser man, but Powell returned to combat and rose to the rank of major. He commanded an artillery battalion until the end of the war.

After the fighting ended, the discharged veteran found that he had too much time on his hands and found teaching to be too settled for his restless nature. The west beckoned to him and in the summer of 1867, with the equally adventurous Emma at his side, he led an expedition into the Rocky Mountains to collect geologic and botanic specimens for universities in the east. It was here that Powell first encountered the waters of the Colorado River – and when a plan began to grow in his mind that would assure him a place in history beside the other great explorers of the American west. He became determined to be the first to take an expedition down the river – from the headwaters to the Gulf of California – and it would be the grandest river run of all time.

Powell spent the better part of the next year seeking financial backing for the expedition and with the help of his friend and fellow officer, then President Grant, he managed to outfit the journey. On May 24, 1869, he and a crew of nine men launched four, specially-built boats at Green River, Wyoming. As the local folks cheered, the sturdy, round-bottomed boats started off downstream. Each of the boats had been double-ribbed with cured oak and each was loaded with two tons of supplies and equipment in waterproof bulkheads. Powell led the group in the first boat, the *Emma Dean*, scouting the way and giving names to the side canyons and mountains they passed.

The expedition hit its first rough water at Ladore Canyon in Utah. The peaceful Green River became a raging torrent and Powell, from his vantage point, signaled the other boats to go into shore. But the boat called *No Name* responded too slowly and spun like a top before exploding into shards and kindling against the rocks. All three of the crew members were washed away but managed to make it to a tiny island, where they were rescued. The accident was a sobering experience and as the men were going to find out, the river was unforgiving to those who made mistakes. Powell named the rapids "Disaster Falls" and they moved on.

The flotilla reached the confluence of the Colorado and the Green Rivers on June 16 and from there, raced through 64 rapids in Cataract Canyon, passed Lee's Ferry and entered the Grand Canyon. Powell's journals (which I highly recommend) eloquently described the expeditions plunge through "the great Unknown" and spoke of the deep river, narrow canyons and the steady flow of a stream that rolled, boiled and would drag the boats into rapids and whirlpools. The breakers often rolled over them, capsizing the boats and making it impossible for them to steer or to land. About halfway through the wild and unpredictable canyon, three of the crewmen decided that they had had enough. They bid goodbye to Powell and hiked out of the canyon – only to die in the empty country to the south.

The rest of the expedition plunged ahead, riding the rapids and then coasting through the calm stretches, singing loud tunes that echoed back at them from the towering cliffs. At the end of August, they reached the Mormon town of Callville, where Lake Mead now rests, and came ashore in triumph. Powell became a national hero as newspapers across the land told of the one-armed man who was the first to successfully take a boat through the Grand Canyon.

Almost immediately though, his claim was challenged. Many people claimed that Powell was not the first and that there had been another before him. This man, all by himself, had survived a run through the canyon. The people of Callville remembered a day back in September 1867 when a crude raft was sighted coming out of the canyon. The pathetic figure clinging to it was half-naked, starved and delirious from exposure to the sun and water. Several days passed before he could tell his rescuers what he had been through. His name was James White and what he told them would be argued about for years to come.

White was an unsuccessful prospector who was working the wild and unexplored country between the San Juan Mountains and the Colorado River. With two companions, Captain Baker and George Strole, he had followed the San Juan River for what he thought was about 200 miles over a period of three weeks. When they reached the Colorado, they made camp at the top of a side canyon that has never been determined. Most believe today that it was in the Glen Canyon area. While encamped, the men were attacked by Indians and Baker was killed. The remaining prospectors managed to escape into the night with their horses and a few supplies but fearful that they were being pursued, they built a small raft by tying three cottonwood trees together and pushed off into the rushing waters of the river. The raft was about ten feet long and two feet wide and the men soon ran into trouble. Strole was washed off during a series of rapids, leaving White alone. He tied a rope around his waist and then tied the other end to the raft, hoping that he would survive any other calamities as he plunged down into the Grand Canyon.

As it was, the raft turned over several times each day and White was so afraid of losing the raft, and being stranded at the bottom of the canyon, that he would tie it to the rocks each night and sleep on it. His supplies were all gone, save for a few beans, but he managed to subsist on a few small lizards that he was able to kill and eat. By the end of the first week, he was so hungry that he cut his leather knife scabbard into pieces and ate it. His problems on the river went from bad to worse. As he raced through some violent rapids, the raft broke apart but White managed to hold onto the logs until he could wash onto a sandbar, He somehow managed to untangle the ropes, tie them together again and continue on down the river.

Two weeks into his journey, White met up with some Indians and he traded his pistols for some food. He then continued on down the river to Callville, where he was assisted by the Mormons and then resumed his life as a drifting prospector. His story was often told in and around Callville but it did not attract much attention outside of the region until Powell's expedition made its successful run through the canyon. When the newspapers heralded Powell's accomplishment, White's brother took a letter that the prospector had written to him, describing his ordeal, to the press. It was published in several newspapers and a journalist from Denver managed to track down White and conduct an interview with him. White stuck to his original story but admitted that he didn't know precisely where he had entered the canyon, or how many days that he traveled down the Colorado River.

Powell scoffed at the story when he heard, knowing from personal experience that no one could survive a journey through the canyon in the manner that White described. According to Powell, the prospector was "a monumental prevaricator, the biggest liar that ever told a tale about the Colorado River."

And perhaps he was, but he had been seen coming out of the canyon and he had obviously been in it for a number of days. The real question seemed to be whether or not he had traveled the full length of the Grand Canyon or just a portion of it. Powell insisted that, under no circumstances, could the journey take only two weeks. It had taken his expedition 27 days and they had been experienced and well-equipped. White's defenders countered by pointing out that White had plummeted down the river, hanging on for dear life, and that he had not been exploring side canyons and collecting scientific data.

The controversy refused to be resolved as White's account could neither be verified nor disproved. However, it was an undisputed fact that Powell did make it down the canyon and the vast majority of the public accepted him as the conqueror of the Grand Canyon. After the canyon was granted national park status in 1919, a monument was erected to honor him on the west rim and to commemorate his achievement. By then, James White had long since died in obscurity.

This would not be the end of the controversy about Powell's expedition though.

In 1932, Herbert Gregory, a professor at the University of Utah, announced that he had discovered the identity of someone who may have gone through the Grand Canyon at least 30 years before both White and Powell.

During the summer of 1931, Gregory had been hiking along Utah's Uintah River and was exploring a vertical sandstone slab that was commonly referred to as Fur Trader's Rock. Here, in the 1830's, mountain men, trappers and hunters had often carved their names as they passed through the region. As a historian, Gregory had always wanted to see the rock and to record the names that had been inscribed on it. He was surprised when he found an inscription that was marked "Denis Julien". He was familiar with the name "D. Julien", as it had been mentioned in two books that had been written by early Grand Canyon explorers. Frederick Dellenbaugh, a member of Powell's second expedition through the canyon in 1872, reported seeing the name carved on a rock in Labyrinth Canyon near the river, dated 1836. Robert Brewster Stanton discovered D. Julien's signature twice while surveying the canyon in 1889 for the proposed, but preposterous, Colorado Canyon Railway. Two different parties of prospectors also told of seeing the name in two different locations, each close to the river.

The most interesting aspect of the inscriptions was the second one that Stanton had found. It was high on a sandstone wall and in reach of someone who might have been in a boat during high water. The name of "D. Julien" had been marked with the year 1836 and beside the signature was a picture of a boat with a mast. Below the boat was a drawing of a winged sun but no one could understand what it represented. But they did realize that their original ideas about Julien exploring the canyon on foot could be wrong. It now appeared that he had been trying to travel down the river itself. Since none of his signatures had ever been found in the lower part of the canyon, it was now thought that he might have perished in the attempt.

Gregory was so excited about his discovery of the signature at Fur Trader's Rock because he now had a first name for the mysterious explorer. Assuming that Julien had been a fur trapper, he contacted the Missouri Historical Society in St. Louis to see if there was any information in their records about a Denis Julien. In the 1830's, during the heyday of the American fur trade, St. Louis had been the headquarters for the fur companies of the west and the historical society maintains an extensive library of their records today.

Gregory soon learned that there were records of a Denis Julien, a French-Canadian who had come to the Louisiana Territory in the late 1700's. Baptismal records showed that he had three children who were born in St. Louis in the 1790's and after they were grown, Julien went west and started working for Antoine Robidoux's fur company in Utah in 1831.

Professor Gregory now began making inquiries and found that Julien's signature had been found in other locations as well – including below the junction of the Green and Grand Rivers. This inscription had been dated 1844, which seemed to prove that Julien did not die in the Grand Canyon in 1836, as had been suspected. This later inscription raised the possibility that he made it all of the way through but as with James White, it will never be proven.

If either Julien or White did run the river ahead of Powell though, it still does not take away from his amazing and historic accomplishment. He and his crew had braved danger and death and then three years later, went back and did it all over again. By that same token, Powell's adventures take no glory away from those who came after him.

In 1937, Haldane Holdstrom made the first officially acknowledged solo run of the river, following Powell's route from Green River, Wyoming to the Boulder Dam. At that time, it was firmly believed that running the Grand Canyon was strictly an undertaking for a man. If a stout-hearted man could barely survive the experience, it was certainly well beyond the capabilities of a woman. But in 1938, Dr. Elzada Clover and Lois Jotter destroyed this misconception when they became the first women to successfully raft down the canyon.

Journeys through the Grand Canyon, until recently, stood a very good chance of being fatal encounters with this merciless river. As mentioned earlier, a disturbing number of people have entered the canyon over the years and have never come out the other end. A death in the Grand Canyon would be a lonely one, vanishing under circumstances that would remain forever mysterious.

One of the most horrific of these deaths was discovered by Stanton's expedition in June 1889. A skeleton was found crushed inside the wreckage of a wooden wagon, more than 150 miles downstream from the closest river crossing. Stanton surmised that someone had misjudged the depth of the river and had tried to cross it, only to be swept downstream and crushed by the Colorado's fury.

Even veteran river runners from the early days were sometimes lost to the river. The disappearance of Albert "Bert" Loper is a perfect example of this. Loper was born on July 31, 1869, the exact day that Powell and his crew found their way out of the rapids of Cataract Canyon, which seemed to make him destined to live and die on the Colorado River, some would later say. In the early 1890's, Loper frequently ran the San Juan River as a prospector but it was not until 1907 that he decided to try the Colorado. That summer, he and three companions set out in three steel boats. The first of them was lost at Cataract Canyon, the second was wrecked by the Hance Rapid and the third was damaged so badly at Hermit Rapid that it was a miracle that it made it the rest of the way down. Loper's friends thought the trip was miserable and terrifying but for Loper himself, it was the most exciting experience of his life and he was hooked on river running.

He ran the river again and again, later becoming a guide and boatman for a number of scientific expeditions. Over a period of 40 years, he earned the title "Grand Old Man of the Colorado". In 1949, with his 80th birthday approaching, he decided to celebrate by going down the river one last time. He pushed off from Lee's

Ferry on July 7 and planned to emerge from the canyon on July 31, his birthday and the anniversary of the Powell Expedition. Loper was accompanied by a passenger, Wayne Nichol, two other boats and a neoprene raft. Tragically though, the boat capsized at Unnamed Rapid the following day and Loper was last seen swirling into the water ahead of it. Wayne Nichol managed to make it to shore and joined others in a desperate search for the old man. The boat was found jammed into the rocks 17 miles from where it capsized but Bert Loper was gone for good.

Then, in 1975, a hiker stumbled across a few of his bones that had washed ashore just below Lava Falls Rapid. After the bones were positively identified, they were buried beside his wife's grave in Sandy, Utah. Bert's remains are gone from the Grand Canyon but many believe that his spirit is still there. They swear that they have seen him in his boat on the river at night and whenever a camper's coffee pot overturns, or a piece of gear is mysteriously lost, Bert always gets the blame.

The most tragic river disappearance though, occurred in 1928. In October of that year, a young, honeymooning couple named Glen and Bessie Hyde came to the Grand Canyon with plans to run the river.

Glen & Bessie Hyde, the young honeymooning couple who vanished in the Grand Canyon.

(Left) A High School photograph of Bessie.

(Right) Glen on the river, shortly before they disappeared

Glen Hyde had been born in Spokane, Washington in 1888, the middle child of Rollin and Mary Hyde. He was raised in Washington, California, Canada and Idaho and after attending college, he worked with his father on their family farm in Hansen, Idaho, in the southern part of the state. In 1928, he married Bessie Haley in Twin Falls. Bessie had been born in Takoma Park, Maryland, just north of Washington, D.C., and had attended Marshall College in West Virginia. She left school after a brief marriage to Earl Helmick, then left for San Francisco, where she studied art in 1926 and 1927. Glen and Bessie met aboard a steamship in 1927 and after Bessie divorced Helmick, she married Glen. They worked the Hyde farms together through the summer of 1928 and that fall, set off on their honeymoon. They planned an adventure of a lifetime – running the rapids of the Grand Canyon in a homemade scow. Several newspapers even carried the story of Bessie being the first woman to attempt to ride the river.

One day in November, they came hiking up from the river on the Bright Angel Trail and knocked on the door of the Kolb brothers' photographic studio, which at that time, was located at the top of the trail. Emory and Ellsworth Kolb were the foremost photographers of the Grand Canyon of their time. Between 1901 and 1941, they captured the magnificence of the canyon in a way that no one has done, before or since. The Kolb's literally moved onto the rim of the canyon to photograph and film the area, constructing a combination of a home and a studio into the side of the cliff. They posted a sign outside that read "Bright Angel Toll Road. Riding Animals, Pack Animals, Loose Animals.. $1.00 each".

By 1928, a steady stream of tourists were handing dollar bills to the Kolb's for the privilege of straddling a burro from a nearby stable and heading down into the canyon. They kept a pretty close eye on everyone who came and went on the canyon trail, so they were surprised one day when the Hyde's hiked in from the canyon down below. They introduced themselves to the Kolb's and explained that they were honeymooners who had spent the past 26 days rafting on the treacherous river. They expected to

Emory & Ellsworth Kolb during their days of exploration in the Grand Canyon

conclude their journey within another week or two. They asked the Kolb's to take their photograph standing on the rim of the canyon. They would come back to get the photo after their trip.

After doing so, Emory Kolb asked them about their boat and they explained that they had built it themselves in Idaho and they planned to navigate the canyon with it. Despite the rapids, they did not have life preservers. Kolb was shocked and warned against such foolhardiness. Glen Hyde laughed off the warnings but Kolb could see that Bessie was nervous about the journey ahead. He told himself that the girl did not want to go back on the river. He later stated that he saw a look of fear in her eyes.

As the couple prepared to depart, Kolb's daughter Emily came out of the studio to greet the young couple. Emily was very neatly dressed and Bessie Hyde took one look at her own weary clothing and then spoke aloud. "I wonder if I shall ever wear pretty shoes again," she said. Then, she turned and followed her husband down Bright Angel Trail.

The night was November 16 and none of the Kolb's slept well that night, worried about the haunted young woman named Bessie Hyde. Both Emory and Emily kept thinking about the girl's parting words. By early December, there was still no sign of the Hyde's. Finally, Kolb initiated a search of the, area which included a small plane that flew down through the inner gorge of the canyon. This was the first time that such a flight had been attempted. The pilot spotted the Hyde's boat snagged in the rocks of the river.

Emory Kolb joined the rescue party and hiked down from the rim. When they reached the boat, they found everything packed and secure. The food, clothing and even the couple's books were neatly put into place. All that was missing were the Hyde's themselves. The search party combed the area, but they were nowhere to be found. If they had made it down the river, Bessie would have been the first woman to successfully navigate the canyon. As it was, she had disappeared -- vanished without a trace.

When the couple failed to turn up, Glen's father and Bessie's father, William, launched search after search into the canyon. Hyde kept searching sporadically for another year but to no avail. He died in Twin Falls in 1945 after being hit by a potato truck and after all of these years, not trace of Glen or Bessie Hyde has ever been found.

But this has not stopped the theories, and often wild stores, from being circulated about their fates. Several theories have emerged as to what happened to Glen and Bessie. The most likely scenario is that the couple drowned and that their boat managed to remain intact when it was scuttled. Given their lack of experience with rivers like the Colorado, this seems very possible.

Others believe that Bessie may have murdered Glen and then left the canyon to start a new life. This theory was first proposed back in 1971 when an elderly woman named Liz Cutler "confessed" to a group in the Grand Canyon that she was Bessie Hyde and that she had stabbed Glen after a disagreement that they had. Cutler later recanted her story but it did get some people thinking. Glen had been described as controlling and domineering and it was said that Bessie was afraid of him.

In 1976, after the death of Emory Kolb, friends going through his belongings discovered a skeleton inside of a skiff in his garage. Rumors abounded that the body might be Glen's (or Everett Ruess'!). The victim apparently died as the result of a bullet wound to the head. Laboratory tests conducted in 1985 concluded that the remains were not Glen's. The man had been much too young and a belt buckle found with the body did not match one that Glen was known to wear. Of course, this begs an answer to yet another unsolved mystery – who did the skeleton belong to and why did Emory Kolb have it?

In addition to these theories, another man and woman claimed to be Bessie and Glen in the years after the skeleton's discovery. Bessie's brother said that her first husband, Earl Helmick, had a violent temper and mentioned that some people thought he might be involved in the couple's disappearance. No evidence has ever been discovered to support any of these claims however.

The most intriguing of the theories as to "what happened to Bessie" is that a famous river runner, Georgie White Clark, was Bessie Hyde. Clark was an unconventional river guide and her penchant for leopard-print swimsuits, canned food cookouts and amazing daring made her the stuff of legend at the Grand Canyon. She and her "Royal River Rats" raft trips were featured in magazines such as *Life*, television shows like the "Tonight Show" with Johnny Carson and countless newspaper stories. She became the first woman to swim the Grand Canyon and the first woman outfitter to run expeditions for tourists.

After her 15 year-old daughter was killed in an accident in 1944, Clark began hiking in Arizona and Utah with a friend, Harry Aleson, to ease her grief. Donning life jackets, the pair swam and floated the lower portion of the canyon in 1945. The next year, they floated the river on a driftwood raft and then in 1947, became the first to navigate the rapids of the Green and Colorado Rivers in war-surplus inflatable rafts. Clark began tying two and three rafts together to make a floating island of passengers in the 1950's and eventually invented the "g-rig", a raft of three pontoons lashed together and powered by an outdoor motor. These "thrill rigs", as she called them, helped to create the modern-day river outfitting business. But Clark paid little attention to the pampering that other outfitters were known to provide for their customers. She told guests, "If you want to eat, go to a restaurant; if you want to see the canyon, come with me." Meals on her raft trips usually consisted of canned good that Georgie would drop into a pot of boiling water. The labels would come off and no one would ever know what they were opening.

Clark died from cancer at age 81 in 1992 and soon after, her already larger than life legend took another turn. Evidence discovered at her home on the day of her funeral raised the possibility that Clark fabricated portions of her past and led many to believe that she was actually Bessie Hyde. The speculations began when friends began going through her personal effects at her home in Las Vegas. Those who had known her for decades, and even those who considered themselves close friends, had never been invited into her home.

Bill George, of Salt Lake City, whose Western River Expeditions bought Clark's company at her request when she became too ill to run raft trips, conducted her funeral. Afterwards, he got a call from Clark's good friend and nurse, Lee McCurry, and told him, "Bill, we don't know who we are burying today." She told George that she had gone over to Georgie's trailer and that "you're never going to believe the stuff that I've found."

For starters, Clark's birth certificate showed that her real name was Bessie DeRoss, not Georgie. Clark, as well as another surname she sometimes used, White, were the last names of two divorced husbands. In her 1977 autobiography, she had written about her childhood in Chicago but she was actually born in Oklahoma and raised in Colorado. Lee also presented Bill with a marriage certificate, which was notarized, for Glen R. Hyde and Bessie Haley, and showed him a pistol that she kept in her lingerie drawer. "If you match it up to one of the pictures of Glen and Bessie Hyde in the canyon, it looks like the same pistol," Bill George said. "I'm not saying that Georgie was Bessie Hyde, but the whole thing is a little spooky."

Once this information started to get around, others began to point out additional oddities. Georgie had developed the triple rig – an assemblage of three rafts tied to each other and run with one oar downstream and one upstream – similar to the manner that Glen and Bessie had operated their scow. She also claimed to hate Emory Kolb when he was alive and if she would go into a meeting and he was there, she would turn around and leave. It was later speculated that perhaps she did not hate Kolb at all but avoided him because he was one of the few people who might have recognized her as Bessie.

While many have been willing to entertain the fact that Bessie and Georgie were one and the same person, there are just as many others who dispute the idea. They maintain that while some of the connections are "inexplicable", they believe that photographs of the two women show marked differences. Clark's biographer, Richard Westwood, added that he found little to substantiate the theory that she and Bessie were the same person but he wouldn't put it past her to leave behind the Hyde clues just to keep people guessing. Georgie, he said, always loved a good story.

So, if Georgie White Clark was not Bessie Hyde, then what happened to Bessie and her luckless husband? Did she really kill him and then vanish to start a new life? Or did they both perish in the furious waters of the canyon? And if they did, what became of their bodies? These questions will never be answered and only the Grand Canyon, and the river, knows what finally befell this ill-fated couple.

FOREST OF DISAPPEARING CHILDREN

One of the most eerie, unsolved mysteries in the history of southern California centers around the forbidding Angeles National Forest, which occupies over 690,000 acres of rugged territory. It is a sprawling wilderness that in the late 1950's and early 1960's was given the tragic nickname of the "Forest of Disappearing Children". It was here that four children vanished utterly without a trace, creating a horrifying and tragic mystery that has never been explained.

The Angeles National Forest embraces a quarter of the area of Los Angeles County and rests beyond the communities of Pasadena, Altadena, Azusa and San Gabriel. It contains some of the region's highest peaks, including Mount Wilson, site of the famous observatory, and has become known as one of southern California's most popular recreation areas. But over what should be a place of relaxation and enjoyment hangs an ominous shadow – and a dark past. Between August 1956 and July 1960, four young children vanished in the forest, leaving absolutely no clues behind. Despite the efforts of hundreds of highly skilled forest officials, sheriff's deputies, outdoorsmen, helicopter pilots and scores of volunteers familiar with the area, nothing ever turned up to reveal the ultimate fate of these children.

The first dark chapter in the story began on the Sunday morning of August 5, 1956. Donald Baker, 13, who lived on Rockvale Avenue in Azusa, called next door for his new friend, Brenda Howell, 11, who, on vacation from Fort Bragg, California, was visiting her married sister, Mary Edwards. The two children set off on their bicycles for a ride along the trails in the nearby forest and around the San Gabriel Reservoir below the Morris Dam. Helen Baker, Donald's mother, told her son to be back home by 8:30 A.M. so that they could attend morning church services and that was the last time that she ever saw him alive.

By evening, with no word from the children, Mrs. Baker, along with her husband, Jesse, a chemical plant foreman, became very alarmed and with Mary Edwards, contacted the authorities. Searchers soon found Brenda's bicycle and Donald's jacket in the brush near the reservoir, leading many to believe that they might have fallen in. As Navy divers began searching the water, deputies from the San Dimas Station, police officers from Azusa and hundreds of volunteers began combing the area. A woman motorist reported seeing them with only one bike around 4:30 that afternoon and two hours later, a County Flood Control worker said that he had seen them on one of the trails. In addition, an Azusa service station attendant identified them as having passed his station at around 8:30 on the evening of their disappearance. The police were ruling out nothing at this point but were inclined at first to think that the vanishing was voluntary. The children had become very fond of one another, even though they had been acquainted just a few weeks, and as the time got closer for Brenda to return home, it was surmised that they might have "run away" together. The search was widened but no further sightings were reported.

As nothing turned up, Brenda's frantic parents, Edna and Fay Howell, rushed to the scene from Fort Bragg and arrived the next morning, as volunteers were returning to the woods and the Los Angeles County Sheriff was issuing an all-points bulletin on them. The search continued but after more than a week with no further leads, the authorities called off the search. The grief-stricken parents refused to give up though and pushed on. On October 23, the search was renewed once more when

Donald Baker's bike turned up in a rack at the Glendora Elementary School. One of the students, Robert Lee West, readily admitted that he had ridden the bike since finding it, in some brush by the reservoir, on August 6 – the date of the children's disappearance.

While reports of sighting them in Ventura County, as far north as Washington and Oregon, and even as far off as Texas and New York, continued to be received for years afterward, Donald and Brenda were never heard from again. No clues were ever uncovered as to their fate and each and every report was thoroughly investigated and checked out. The two of them just vanished into the woods and the case remains open and unsolved to this day.

Unfortunately, they would not be the last to vanish...

On March 23, 1957, a young boy named Tommy Bowman, 8, was hiking along one of the many trails near the Devil's Gate Reservoir. The dry, brush-filled channel is above the city of Altadena and not far from the Arroyo Seco Ranger Station. With Tommy in the woods that day were his sister Janice, 5, his brother John, 4, Eldon Bowman, his father, Gordon Wicks, his uncle, and his two cousins, Christine, 8, and Maureen, 5. The Bowman family was visiting from their home in Redondo Beach and the two parents thought the children would enjoy a day out in the forest. Tommy was described as an energetic youngster and he ran ahead of the others to beat them down the trail to the clearing. He was only a few yards away from the others when he rounded a curve in the trail – and disappeared.

Eldon Bowman, a Northrop Aircraft researcher, did not become too concerned about not seeing Tommy directly ahead of them. He assumed that the boy would meet up with them down the path. When the party reached the clearing though and did not see or hear him anywhere nearby, everyone began calling his name and searching through the surrounding brush. Only minutes passed before they contacted the police.

Within two hours, the area was swarming with search teams. Over 400 volunteers turned out and the sheriff's department brought in helicopters, dogs and mounted patrols. They scoured the area for an entire week, hacking through chaparral and delving into holes and crevices near the trail but finally the search was called off. The disappearance prompted the L.A. County Sheriff, Eugene Biscailuz, to issue strong warnings to the public about safety precautions in the rugged forest. The possibility of sex criminals being active in the area was stressed and the idea that Tommy might have been the victim of some deviant was not discounted, especially in light of a later report. According to a woman in Arroyo Seco Canyon, she had seen a child that matched Tommy's description walking by her house crying on the evening that he vanished. He was being followed by an unshaven man. Further investigation unearthed this man in the forest area but no connection could be found between him and the missing boy and with no evidence to show that he was involved, the police had to let him go.

Northrop Aircraft posted a $1,000 reward for information on the case and subsequently, the usual number of ransom notes and crank calls were received by the Bowman's. Each and every one of them was checked out by detectives but the trail soon grew cold. Tommy Bowman became the third child to vanish forever into the forest.

Another child followed Donald, Brenda and Tommy into oblivion just three years later. On July 13, 1960, Bruce Kremen, 6, mysteriously vanished in the same general area. He was within 300 yards of and within full sight of his Y.M.C.A camp at the time he disappeared.

Bruce, the son of Mr. and Mrs. Joseph Kremen of Granada Hills, a community in the San Fernando Valley, had just arrived at the camp. He was on his first visit to the Forest and was on a hike with a group leader and a number of other boys. The group leader noticed that Bruce was getting tired and falling behind and realized that, since it was his first day out, the altitude might be bothering him. Since they were still within sight of the camp, he told Bruce that maybe he had better return instead of continuing on with the hike. He could always come out with them again another day. He stopped the group and walked back a few paces with Bruce along the plainly marked and cleared trail and then stood watching as the boy sauntered on back to camp. Assured that he was now within a few yards of it, the group leader rejoined the other children.

Bruce Kremen was never seen again.

For the next 12 days, an army of more than 300 searchers combed through the heavily wooded, 10 square miles of forest around the camp. Temperatures soared in the afternoon hours, leaving the volunteers exhausted and soaked with sweat. Finally, they gave up, defeated. Bruce's parents never once gave up hope that Bruce was trying to walk back home. If this was his intention though, he never made it. Like the other three children, he too vanished and left no clues, no suspects, no remains – and no solution to the case.

The disappearance of the four children remains one of the strangest unsolved mysteries of the region. To this day, no trace of them has ever been found. And police, rangers and others are still at a loss as to how Tommy Bowman could vanish while within a few feet of his family or what happened to Bruce Kremen in the short distance between his hiking companions and the camp. Perhaps someday, we may find out what happened in the "Forest of Disappearing Children" but for now, the baffling cases remain in the active, unsolved files of the Los Angeles County Sheriff.

MYSTERY OF THE LONG TRAIL

The historic Green Mountains of Vermont have been described as being part of the most beautiful stretch of wilderness in New England. The warm weather months make this a place of tranquil shade, soaked in a warm array of greens and browns. In the autumn, the hills come alive with a symphony of breath-taking color. But at other times, a darker side emerges from these rugged mountains, when the shadows grow long and the snow starts to fall, finally covering the landscape in a monotonous blanket of white. There are places, like this place some say, where the fabric of time and space is stretched a little bit thinner. Places where things that aren't supposed to do so slip through into our world. And occasionally things from our world sometimes slip out...

This is one of the treacherous secrets of the Green Mountains near Bennington, Vermont. The area has always had a reputation for strangeness. It is a spot that is almost inaccessible and remote and since colonial days, it has been plagued with reports of mysterious lights and sounds, ghostly tales and unknown creatures. The local Native Americans shunned the place and according to tradition, used it as a place to bury the dead.

And while stories of spook lights and Indian curses may stretch the limits of the imagination, there is no denying that nearby Glastonbury Mountain, and its scenic Long Trail, has been the site of a great American mystery. This unsolved puzzle involves the disappearance of a number of people who have never been found. Thousands of hours were spent searching for them, but not a single clue was ever discovered.

The bizarre disappearances began on November 12, 1945 with the vanishing of Middie Rivers, a 74 year-old hunting and fishing guide. He was reportedly in perfect health and knew the area well, having been a native of the region for most of his life. The day that he disappeared was unusually mild for late fall and Rivers led four hunters up onto the mountain. After spending the day away from camp, they packed up to return with Rivers leading the way. He got a little bit ahead of them and literally vanished around a bend in the trail. One minute he was there and the next he wasn't! The old man simply disappeared.

The hunters searched frantically and then notified the authorities. State police, soldiers, boy scouts and local residents combed the woods for hours. They refused to lose hope, knowing that Rivers was an experienced outdoorsman and could survive in the woods, even under icy cold conditions. When no sign of him turned up, efforts were expanded and the search continued for a month. It was eventually called off though and Middie Rivers was never seen again.

On December 1, 1946, the second person vanished from the Long Trail. Her name was Paula Welden from Stamford, Connecticut and she was a sophomore at Bennington College. Paula was the daughter of Archibald Welden, an industrial engineer who was employed by Revere Copper & Brass Co. and had come to Bennington College because of the excellent reputation that the school had for progressive teaching. Paula was described as blue-eyed, blond and pretty and usually wore her hair pulled back from her pleasant face. Her features were "regular and slightly heavy and she had a clean, well-scrubbed look." Paula stood 5-foot-5 and weighed about 123 pounds. Descriptions of her from 1946 speak of her being soft-spoken, polite and well-behaved, like the average girl of her background. She was a fair student whose favorite subject was botany. Her interest in trees and plants gave her an excuse for solitary walks along the local forest trails.

On the afternoon of Sunday December 1, she announced to her roommate, Elizabeth Johnson, that she was going out for a short afternoon hike. Paula changed into outdoor clothing – blue jeans, white sneakers and a red parka with a fur-trimmed hood – but failed to take into account the miserable conditions outside. It was a particularly gloomy day, her roommate later recalled, and a cold rain had make the ground slippery and muddy and it seemed a much better day to stay indoors and study than to go out. Elizabeth, knowing her friend's affinity for being outside though, made no effort to dissuade her from going.

Paula Welden's actions from the moment that she left Elizabeth Johnson cannot be traced exactly. Against the drab December day though, she made a conspicuous figure with her bright red coat but only a handful of people were out to notice her. An attendant at a gas station across Route 67A from the Bennington College gates saw her hitchhiking a short distance from the gas station at around 3:15 in the afternoon.

Shortly, a car appeared on the highway driven by Louis Knapp, a contractor who lived about 15 miles east of the college in the direction of Glastonbury Mountain and the beginning of the Long Trail. The trail was Paula's goal that day and during the summer, the picturesque trail was one of the area's greatest attractions, with thriving tourist cottages and cabins lining it. In the winter though, it was barren and neglected. Only four families lived along it in the winter months, which made Paula's choice for her hike that day a strange one. Nevertheless, Knapp agreed to take her up the highway as far as to where he lived in Woodford Hollow, just three miles from the start of the Long Trail. When Knapp stopped the car at his driveway, Paula asked him the distance to the trail and then she got out and started walking. She soon vanished into the mist that had replaced the cold rain of the early afternoon.

About an hour later, close to 5:00, she encountered another resident of the area, Ernest Whitman, a night watchman for the *Bennington Banner* newspaper. Whitman was surprised to see a young girl sloshing along the desolate and now growing dark road. He spoke with her for a few minutes and gave her directions. After that, other witnesses spotted her on the trail itself and remembered her distinctly because she had been wearing a bright red parka. It was very visible, even though the sun was setting by this time. He would be the last person to see her alive...

Paula did not return to wait on tables at the Commons, the Bennington College dining hall, that evening, nor had she appeared by her usual bedtime. Although worried, Elizabeth Johnson decided to wait until morning to report her absence. After a sleepless night, she left her room at dawn and made her way to the Dean's residence. The Dean offered the opinion that Paula might have made a last minute application to stay away from the college all night but a quick check of the sign-out records showed that this was not the case. The two of them hurried across campus to the home of Bennington president Lewis Webster Jones. He had no solution to the problem, except to make a careful telephone call to the Welden home in Stamford to see if Paula had unexpectedly turned up there. She had not and so Jones next called the local Sheriff Clyde W. Peck, who came straight to the college. He was later joined by Vermont State Police detective Almo Fronzoni, a veteran of more than 25 years with the department.

Fronzoni took charge of the investigation and started by questioning Elizabeth Johnson. He accompanied her to the dorm room that she shared with Paula and saw that there was no sign that she had taken any clothing with her. Nor, apparently, had she taken any extra money either. He found $8.26 on her bureau, along with an uncashed check for $10. Elizabeth told him that Paula rarely ever had more cash than that on hand.

Fronzoni next drove to the local bus and railroad stations. Here, he ran into a taxi driver who told him that he had driven a Bennington girl to the bus station that day but this later turned out to be untrue. At the railway station, Fronzoni mentioned Stamford, Connecticut and the ticket seller perked up. On Sunday afternoon, three hunters had purchased tickets to New York and then at the last minute, had changed their destination to Stamford instead. The ticket seller remembered this because it required quite a bit of adjustment on his part. No matter how Fronzoni tried though, he was unable to see a connection, other than coincidence, between the three hunters and Paula. All it did was, like the false statement from the taxi driver, slow down the investigation and lessen his chances of finding the missing girl.

The detective returned to the Bennington campus and began questioning other students who knew Paula. Since she had not told anyone where she was going that day, only that she was going for a hike, no one knew where she was headed when she left campus. However, several of her friends mentioned her fondness for a place called Everett's Cave on Mount Anthony. It was three miles south of the college. If Paula had hiked there, it was suggested, she might have fallen and been injured. Fronzoni, Sheriff Peck and several deputies immediately drove to Everett's Cave but Paula, injured or otherwise, was not to be found there.

By this time, word was beginning to spread of the disappearance and when newspaper reporters from the *Bennington Banner* picked up the story, night watchman Ernest Whitman heard about the missing student. He immediately reported to Fronzoni that he had met Paula near the entrance to the Long Trail. After the story hit the newspapers on Tuesday, the authorities would hear from the gas station attendant who saw Paula hitchhiking and from local resident Louis Knapp as well. The officials now realized that Paul had been heading for the Long Trail when she vanished and an immediate search was started. It was feared that the young woman had met with an accident while hiking on the trail in the dark and not being dressed for the bitterly cold nighttime temperatures, she could be dead or badly injured. There was hope that, injured or lost, she could have broken into one of the empty summer cottages on the trail and that she could have found food or at least a fire.

The search commenced on Monday afternoon, headed by Bennington game warden Jesse Wilson. He was assisted by five other game wardens, some sheriff's deputies and several search dogs. It was hurriedly put together and badly organized but they believed that if Paula was injured, time was crucial. Besides that, many of the men in the area were expert woodsmen and they had the best chance of finding her quickly.

As they searched along the trail, Detective Fronzoni questioned members of the families who lived on Long Trail all year long. He found two leads. One person stated that he had seen a half-ton truck driving along the trail late Sunday evening at a time when Paula might have been on it. The other lead was more definite. A woman in one of the resident families had been walking along the trail on Sunday and had been forced to step aside to permit a maroon colored car to pass by. She saw a young couple inside and the girl had been a blonde. She had not looked very closely at the couple but it did raise the question as to whether or not someone had given Paula a lift. If they had though, what had happened to her?

On Tuesday, December 3, a more comprehensive search for Paula Welden was organized. Classes at Bennington College were suspended and nearly 400 students took part in the effort. Faculty members, students from Williams College, Boy Scouts, trappers, woodsmen, local residents and search dogs joined deputies and law enforcement officials as they scoured the area. The group had been joined by a number of employees from Revere Copper & Brass and the huge contingent was organized into smaller search teams by expert mountain climbers from the National Guard. The United States Navy also sent nine Marine search planes from the air base at Squantam and a helicopter was brought in to fly low over isolated areas.

As the National Guard climbers worked their way up Glastonbury Mountain, the army of searchers sloshed in long lines up and down the foothills. The weather was drab and drizzling, soaking everyone to the skin. It was cold, wearying work along the trail and elsewhere, other work was being accomplished too. The Bennington student body and friends of the Welden family had started a reward-for-information fund, which soon made it to $5,000. The offer of a reward brought in even more volunteers and the search continued for two full days. On December 5 though, it was called off thanks to overhanging clouds that had grounded the search planes, followed by several inches of snow that obliterated the landscape.

By this time, the Welden family and most of the volunteers were exhausted. The fact that Paula had written no farewell note and that no ransom letters had been received indicated that whatever happened to her must have been spontaneous – she was either a victim of amnesia, an accident or someone's murderous madness. Many feared that Paula was now dead but her parents refused to give up hope, insisting that their daughter had been kidnapped. With no evidence of this though, the FBI refused to get involved. When the official refusal became public knowledge, well-known novelist Dorothy Canfield Fisher, a Bennington College trustee, wrote letters to J. Edgar Hoover and several political figures in Washington. "Paula is not in these hills," she stated. "She was taken away against her will."

Others felt the same way and made determined appeals but all were turned down. The governor appealed to both New York and Connecticut for skilled investigators to assist them but only Connecticut responded, sending two state detectives who had proven expert at missing persons cases in the past. Their laborious investigations still failed to produce the missing girl. One of the investigators, Robert Rundle, agreed with Detective Fronzoni when he had declared Paula's case to be the most perplexing of his career. "We have not a single clue," Rundle admitted.

Paula was simply gone. They found not a single clue – no blood, no clothing, nothing. In the end, helicopters, aircraft, bloodhounds and as many as 1,000 people combed the mountain for the young woman but no evidence was found that she ever existed at all.

On December 16, the Welden's returned to Connecticut and took all of Paula's belongings from her dorm room with them. Even they had given up hope of seeing their daughter alive again. Classes resumed at Bennington College and after the shock of Paula's disappearance passed, students began to think more of going home for the holidays than about the missing girl. The townspeople still talked and speculated but few were still willing to spend time combing the hills for her. Detective Fronzoni moved on to other cases and Paula Welden began to become a part of Bennington's past.

But over the next fine months, Archibald Welden urged a second organized search, once the winter snows had thawed. On May 23, several hundred volunteers assembled and spent two days in the rain, crisscrossing more than 24 square miles between Glastonbury and Bald Mountains. When the search ended, it had accomplished nothing, for no trace of Paula was ever found.

When Bennington College reconvened again the following autumn, Paula Welden seemed a forgotten, shadowy figure. People still walked the Long Trail and wondered about her sometimes but few spoke of her again – until the next person vanished into the mountains.

On December 1, 1949, three years to the day of Paula Welden's disappearance, an elderly man named James E. Tetford also vanished near Bennington. Tetford had been visiting relatives in northern Vermont and his family had placed him on a bus in St. Albans for the journey back to where he lived, the Bennington Soldier's Home.

For some reason though, he never arrived. Where he actually disappeared is just part of the mystery. Witnesses recalled him getting on the bus and several were sure that he was still on board at the stop before Bennington. At some point though, he apparently got off along the road. He left no clues behind. No one saw him disappear (including the bus driver) and he was never seen again.

Another disappearance took place near Bennington in October 1950. An eight year-old boy named Paul Jepson vanished from the town dump, where his parents were caretakers. Paul was waiting in the family's truck while his mother relocated some pigs. She was gone for only a moment but when she looked up, the boy was gone. It was between 3:00 and 4:00 in the afternoon and was a sunny day. Paul was wearing a bright red jacket and should have been easily spotted – but he was nowhere to be seen. Mrs. Jepson searched frantically and called for him and after a little while, went for help.

Volunteers assembled to start another search and hundreds of local residents joined police officers in combing through the dump, walking the roads and hunting in the mountains. They even instituted a "double check" system so that after one group checked an area, another would follow them and check it again. But even with the search parties and aircraft brought in by the Coast Guard, there was no sign of the boy.

The only clues came from a group of bloodhounds that were borrowed from the New Hampshire State Police. The dogs managed to follow Paul's scent, only to lose it at the junction of East and Chapel Roads, just west of Glastonbury Mountain. According to locals, this was the same spot where Paula Welden had last been seen. The search was eventually called off and another person was lost to the mountains.

About two weeks later, on October 28, the mountain claimed another victim. Her name was Freida Langer and she was on a hike that day with her cousin, Herbert Elsner. The 53 year-old Langer was described as a rugged outdoor person with long experience in the woods and a skill with firearms. She was also very familiar with the region and like Middie Rivers before her, was an unlikely person to simply get lost or to wander off the trail. Somehow though, she managed to disappear.

At about 3:45 that afternoon, Freida slipped and fell into the edge of a stream, soaking her boots and pants. Since she and her cousin were only about a half-mile from camp, she said that she would run back and change clothes and then catch up with him. Elsner sat down to wait but after Frieda had been gone for awhile, he began to grow concerned. After an hour or so, he started back up the trail to their camp. When he got there, he discovered that no one had seen her come back and from the looks of her gear, she had never returned to change her wet clothing. He immediately contacted the authorities.

Alarmed by another disappearance in the same area, local officials quickly launched another massive search. Again, hundreds of volunteers combed the woods, tracing and re-tracing what should have been Frieda's footsteps between the stream where she had fallen and the camp.

On November 1, General Merritt Edson, the state director of public safety, started a second search. He vowed that they would find Frieda, dead or alive, and he ordered his men to keep searching around the clock. More helicopters, aircraft, officers and volunteers were brought in, but once again, they found no clues. Another search was started on November 5 and the volunteers divided up into groups of 30. They lined up and marched side by side along trails and through the forest, scanning every inch of ground. There was still no sign of the missing woman.

On November 11, the largest search so far was organized. Over 300 people joined police officers, fire fighters and military units as they scoured the woods. A few days later, Frieda's family gave up hope and the search was called off.

Strangely though, Frieda Langer would be the only person to go missing here that would later be found. On May 12, 1951, seven months after she had vanished, the body of Frieda Langer was discovered lying in some tall grass near the flood dam of the Somerset Reservoir. It was nowhere near the spot where she had vanished and impossibly, this site had been thoroughly searched while the hunt for the missing woman was being carried out. The volunteers swore that the body had not been there during the initial search! The site where the corpse was found was an open and visible area and it was simply impossible that the searchers could have missed it. And unfortunately, no clues could be gathered from Frieda's body and no cause of death could ever be determined by the medical examiner. Her remains were too decomposed and the newspaper stated they were in "gruesome condition".

Could someone have placed the body there much later? Rumors swirled about a killer who was hiding on Glastonbury Mountain, claiming victims that were chosen from those who vanished into the woods. In those days, the term "serial killer" had not come to public attention and later examinations of each case do suggest that a killer might have been at work. The disappearances occurred over a limited length of time (five years) and all in one central area, around the mountain and the Long Trail. Perhaps the killer was someone who came to Vermont each fall, committed his crimes, and than left. That might explain why no one ever became a suspect in the vanishings but why was no body, save for that of Frieda Langer, ever found?

What happened in the mountains near Bennington, Vermont between 1945 and 1950? Was a madman preying on lone hikers or were darker and more mysterious forces at work? Could these people have simply gotten lost or were they carried off against their will, to a place that none of us can imagine? Hopefully, no one else will ever discover the answers to those questions.

THE VILLAGE THAT VANISHED

In the far reaches of northwestern Connecticut, in the shadows of the mountains and lost in the pages of time, rests the remains of a small village called Dudleytown. The homes of this once thriving community are long gone, but the land where the town once stood is far from empty. Amidst the forest and rocks are tales of ghosts, demons, unexplained mysteries, curses and a rich history that dates back to the very beginnings of America.

On the road to Dudleytown
(Courtesy Carrie Reiss)

Today, only the cellar holes and a few stone foundations remain. The roads that once traversed to this place are now little more than narrow trails where only a few adventurous hikers, and the occasional ghost hunter, dare to wander. Although it is forbidden, the most hardened curiosity-seekers still dare to venture down Dark Entry Road and into these shadowy woods at night.

Dudleytown, or at least the area where it was located, was first owned by a man named Thomas Griffis, one of the first to settle in this region, in the early 1740's. There are no records to say that he ever lived where Dudleytown later stood but he did own half of the land in 1741. A few years later, with the arrival of Gideon Dudley in 1747, the village would be named. Gideon was followed to the region by two brothers and Dudley's have become known over the years as the men who brought a curse to this small town – a curse that has allegedly plagued the region ever since.

According to what have turned out to be both recent and fanciful accounts, the "curse" had its beginnings in England in 1510. At that time, Edmund Dudley was beheaded for being involved in a plot to overthrow King Henry VIII. Supposedly, a curse was placed on the family at this time, which stated that all of the Dudley descendants would be surrounded by horror and death. Proponents of the curse claim that the Dudley's then began to experience a rather disquieting run of bad luck.

Edmund's son, John Dudley, also attempted to control the British throne by arranging for his son, Guilford, to marry Lady Jane Grey, next in line for the crown. After Edward VI died, Lady Jane became the queen for a short time before the plan failed, ending with the execution of Lady Jane and the two Dudley's. To make matters worse, Guilford's brother returned from France, and being a military officer, brought home a plague that he spread to his officers and troops. The sickness wiped out massive numbers of British soldiers and eventually spread throughout the country, killing thousands.

John Dudley's third son, Robert, Earl of Leicester, a favorite of Elizabeth I, wisely decided to leave England and travel to the New World. It would be his somewhat luckier descendant, William, who would settle in Guilford, Connecticut. Three of William's descendants, Abiel, Barzallai and Gideon, would later buy a plot of land in Cornwall township.

While there are undoubtedly some grim events that surrounded the Dudley family in England and France, questions have been raised as whether or not any "curse" really followed them to America. The question has been raised because in order for the curse to have been passed along to account for the haunting of Dudleytown, then William Dudley would have had to have been the son of Robert, Earl of Leicester – but he wasn't. Robert Dudley had only two sons and one of them died while still a child. The other went to Italy and while he had children, all of them remained in that country. This means that there was no link between William, his sons who founded Dudleytown, and any so-called "curse".

But while we may have established the fact that Dudleytown was never "cursed", this does not mean that it was not "tainted" in some other way. There are many places across the country where odd things happen and where the land does not seem quite right. Records indicate that the land around Dudleytown was once Mohawk Indian tribal grounds but tell us little else before the coming of the first settlers. This region has gained a chilling reputation over the years. Could the weird stories and strange disappearances here be connected to the past in some way – or are they nothing more than just coincidence and imagination?

In the early 1740's, the mentioned Thomas Griffis bought a parcel of land that would later be considered the first lot in Dudleytown. The land today looks much as it did when Griffis first came here. It is covered in thick forest and the ground is strewn with rocks. The nearby mountains also heavily shadow the area, so it receives little sunlight. The woods were later dubbed with the rather ominous name of "Dark Entry Forest".

In 1747, Gideon Dudley bought some land from Griffis to start a small farm. By 1753, Gideon's two brothers, Barzallai and Abiel Dudley, from Guilford, Connecticut, also purchased land nearby. A few years later, a Martin Dudley from Massachusetts also moved to the area but was from a different line of the family. He later married Gideon's daughter.

One thing that should be mentioned was that Dudleytown was never an actual town. It was a more isolated part of Cornwall. The village rested in the middle of three large hills, which accounts for the recollections of it being nearly dark at noon time. The Cornwall township was never a good area for farming, as is apparent by the rocks that were used to build the foundations and stone walls that still stand today. In spite of this though, settlers began to trickle into the area. The Tanner family, the Jones', the Patterson's, the Dibble's and the Porter's all took up residence here. The community grew even larger after iron ore was discovered nearby and farming became a secondary concern. However, there were never any stores, shops , schools or churches in Dudleytown. Provisions had to be purchased in nearby towns and when one died, a trip to Cornwall was necessary because, in addition to there being no church in town, there was no cemetery either. The population of Dudleytown was never large and according to an 1854 map, the peak number of families who lived here only reached 26.

In spite of all of these things, the town did thrive for a time. Dudleytown was noted for its timber, which was burned and used to make wood coal for the nearby Litchfield County Iron Furnaces in Cornwall and other towns. The furnaces later moved closer to the railroads and the more industrial towns though and the lumber was no longer needed. Iron ore was used from the area for a time and there were three water-powered mills in Dudleytown as well. Most of the mills eventually closed because of the long trip down the mountain to deliver their goods.

Despite the outward signs of prosperity though, there were strange deaths and bizarre occurrences at Dudleytown from the start. Some historians have attempted to downplay the unusual events in recent years. They will debunk the legends of the town by first stating how few people there ever were who lived here and then will try and downplay the disappearances, cases of insanity and weird deaths, as if such things happen all of the time. And perhaps they do – but why so many unusual happenings in such an isolated area with so few people living in it? The number of deaths that have occurred here would not be such a high number in a larger town but in this small community, one can't help but wonder what exactly was taking place. There are also, I believe, an inordinate number of people who went insane in this area, as well as people who simply vanished that are in addition to those who are documented here. It's no wonder – bogus or not – that a story started about a Dudleytown "curse".

Three of the Dudley's moved out of the region and lived long and full lives, dying of natural causes and forever diminishing any possibilities of a curse. Only

Abiel Dudley remained in town and after a series of reverses, lost his entire fortune – and his mind. Abiel died in 1799 at the age of 90 and when he was no longer able to pay his debts, the town took his property, sold it and then made him a ward of the town. Toward the end, Abiel was senile and insane and would not be the last to suffer from this affliction.

In 1792, seven years before Abiel Dudley passed away, his good friend and neighbor, Gershon Hollister, was killed while building a barn at the home of William Tanner, Abiel's closest neighbor. Tanner was also said to have gone insane, although likely from old age and senility rather than from supernatural influences. He lived to the age of 104 and according to records was "slightly demented" at the time of his death. There have been stories that have circulated claiming that Tanner told other villages of "strange creatures" that came out of the woods at night. If this is true, there is no way for us to know if these "creatures" were products of the unexplained or products of Tanner's feeble mind.

The Nathaniel Carter family moved to Dudleytown in 1759 and lived in a house once owned by Abiel Dudley before he was made a ward of the town. A mysterious plague swept through Dudleytown and Cornwall and took the lives of the Adoniram Carter family, relatives of Nathaniel, and saddened by the loss, they moved to Binghampton, New York from Dudleytown in 1763. Those who believe in the "curse" say that the taint of Dudleytown followed after them but their tragic fate was actually far too common during the early days of the frontier. The Carter's moved to the "Delaware wilderness", in the heart of Indian territory, and during an attack, Indians slaughtered Nathaniel, his wife and an infant child. The Carter's other three children were abducted and taken to Canada, where two daughters were ransomed. The son, David Carter, remained with his captors, married an Indian girl and later returned to the United States for his education. He went on to edit a newspaper and became a justice on the Supreme Court.

Another bizarre tragedy affected one of the most famous residents of the region, General Herman Swift, who had served in the Revolutionary War under George Washington. In 1804, his wife, Sarah Faye, was struck by lightning while standing on the front porch of their home near Dudleytown. She was killed instantly. The General went insane and died soon after. Many have dismissed this incident as not being connected to the other unusual events, saying that Swift did not actually live in Dudleytown but on Bald Mountain Road (where his house remains today) and that he only went insane when he became old and senile. But in an area this sparsely populated, the records indicated three people to have gone insane in the space of less than a half century – could this be mere coincidence? And does a person being struck by lightning while standing on their front porch qualify as being "unusual"? I would say that it does and our story is not yet complete.

Another famous personage allegedly connected to Dudleytown was Horace Greeley, the editor and founder of the *New York Tribune* – or so the stories of the "curse" go. In this case, the story deserves to be debunked. Greeley married a young woman named Mary Young Cheney, who the stories of the "curse" say was born in Dudleytown. In truth, Mary was born and raised in nearby Litchfield and never lived in Dudleytown. She left the area as early as 1833 and went to live in a vegetarian boarding house that was owned by Dr. Graham (of "Graham Cracker" fame) and became involved in the popular "wellness" movement of the time. While there, she met and later married Horace Greeley. In 1872, Greeley ran for president against Ulysses S. Grant and lost the election. A short time before it, Mary suffered from an attack of "lung disease" and died. Her death occurred in New York City with her husband and two daughters, Ida and Gabrielle, in attendance. She was buried in Greenwood Cemetery. The legends claim that she committed suicide but this was not the case. Greeley himself died one month later and the electoral votes that he received in the election were distributed to minor candidates.

After the Civil War, Dudleytown began to die and many of the villagers simply packed up and moved away. The demise of the town itself is hardly surprising, whether you believe in the so-called "curse" or not. Its geographical location was foolhardy at best. Surrounded by hills and at elevations of more than 1500 feet, there was little chance that a good crop would ever grow and sustain life in the village. The winters were harsh here and even the hardy apple trees were stunted from months of cold. As mentioned already, the soil was rocky and the area was plagued by almost too much water. It pooled into tepid swamps and seeped into the earth, creating a damp morass.

But even if you overlook the idea of an actual "curse" and admit that the location of the town must have had a hand in its undoing, the sheer number of unusual deaths (leaving out that of Mary Greeley) and mental conditions in such an isolated area more than suggests that something out of the ordinary was occurring in the little town. And no matter how hard the debunkers try to disregard the next mysterious event to occur in Dudleytown, their efforts fall short.

This event occurred in 1901, at a time when the population of Dudleytown had dwindled away to almost nothing. One of the last residents of the town was a man named John Patrick Brophy. Tragedy visited swiftly and in several blows. First, his wife died of consumption, which was not uncommon in those days and there was nothing strange about her ailment, as she had been suffering from it for years. This did not lessen Brophy's grief however, but he was soon further stricken when his two children vanished into the forest just a short time after the funeral. And while their disappearance could have been voluntary (they had been accused of stealing sleigh blankets, a minor offense), there is nothing to indicate that it was. They vanished and were never found. Shortly after, the Brophy's house burned to the ground in an unexplained fire and not long after, Brophy himself vanished into the forest. He was never seen again.

By the early 1900's, Dudleytown was completely deserted. The remaining homes began to fall into disrepair and ruin, and soon, the forest began to reclaim the village that had been carved out of it. But there was still one other death that proponents of the "curse" have connected to Dudleytown and while the curse may be unlikely, it does mark one additional case of insanity for an isolated region that was already riddled with them.

Around 1900, Dr. William Clarke came to Cornwall and fell in love with the forest and the quiet country life. Clarke had been born in 1877 and grew up on a farm in Tenafly, New Jersey. He later became a professor of surgery and taught at Columbia College of Physicians and Surgeons, as well as earning a reputation as the leading cancer specialist in New York. He purchased 1,000 acres of land in the wilds of Connecticut, which included Dudleytown, and began construction of a summer and vacation home here. Over the next number of years, he and his wife, Harriet Bank Clarke, visited the house on weekends and during the summer until it was completed. After that, it became mostly a holiday house for short trips in the summer and for Thanksgiving. Together, they maintained an idyllic second life near Dudleytown until 1918.

One summer weekend, Dr. Clarke was called away to New York on an emergency. His wife stayed behind and according to the story, he returned 36 hours later to find that she had gone insane, just as a number of previous residents of the village had done. The story also claims that she told of strange creatures that came out of the forest and attacked her. She committed suicide soon after. But how much truth is there to this tale? Perhaps more than some would like you to believe. It has been recorded that for several years before her suicide, Mrs. Clarke suffered from a "chronic illness". There is nothing to indicate what this ailment might have been or whether it was a physical or mental one. I think that it is safe to say though that mentally stable individuals do not ordinarily take their own lives. As far as whether or not she saw "strange creatures in the woods" – well, we will never really know for sure but even if we disregard this, we still have one more suicide that occurred to a resident of the nearly nonexistent village of Dudleytown.

While undoubtedly shattered by his wife's suicide, Dr. Clarke continued to maintain his house in Dudleytown and continued to visit. A number of years later, he remarried and returned to stay at his summer house until a larger home was completed nearby in 1930. In 1924, he and his wife, Carita, as well as other doctors, friends and interested landowners formed the "Dark Entry Forest Association". It was designed to act as forest preserve so that the land around Dudleytown would remain "forever wild". They held their first meeting in 1926 with 41 members. Dr. Clarke died in Cornwall Bridge in February 1943 and Carita passed away five years later. A number of their children and family members still reside in the area.

Today, Dudleytown is mostly deserted, except for the curiosity-seekers and tourists, who come looking for thrills. The Dark Forest Entry Association still owns most of the land the village once stood on. There are a group of homes on Bald Mountain Road that are very secluded from the main roads and they belong to the closest residents. These locals maintain that nothing supernatural takes place in this region and perhaps they are right. It seems unlikely that the "curse" on Dudleytown ever really existed but on the other hand, there is something strange about such a small area with so many disappearances, unusual deaths, suicides and cases of insanity. The stories of a "curse" had to have gotten started for some reason and perhaps this was why.

As far as we know, the ghostly tales began to surface in the 1940's. It was at this time that visitors to the ruins of the village began to speak of strange incidents and wispy apparitions in the woods. Even today, those who have visited the place boast of paranormal photographs, overwhelming feelings of terror, mysterious lights, sights and sounds and even of being touched, pushed and scratched by unseen hands. Some researchers refer to the area as a "negative power spot", or a place where entities enter this world from the other side. They say this may explain the strange events in Dudleytown's history, like the eerie reports, the strange creatures and perhaps even the outbreaks of insanity and madness. The place is often thought of as "tainted" in some way, as if the ground has somehow spoiled here, or perhaps was sour all along.

Some historians and debunkers dismiss such reports and theories and maintain that just because the so-called "Curse of Dudleytown" doesn't exist, then nothing strange has ever occurred here either. However, an open-minded look at some of the things that have happened do seem to show this is a strange place and one that has been an enigma from the earliest days of its history. Whether or not there is any truth to the accounts of people who have come here since the days when the village was abandoned is up to the reader to decide.

I should warn you though that trying to visit Dudleytown today can be hazardous – and not because of ghosts. It should be noted that the planners for the Dark Forest Entry Association have forbidden trespassing on their property. In 1999, they announced that they would no longer allow hikers on the land. In spite of this, many still go – now daring not only the spirits, but the authorities as well. Unfortunately, the ruins of Dudleytown have been vandalized in recent years and the constant streams of trespassers have had a negative effect on the ecology of the area. Just as unfortunate is the fact that the forbidden quality of Dudleytown is what brings so many curiosity-seekers to the vicinity. However, this author advises readers to refrain from visiting this area until methods can be devised to better preserve the wilderness here and until this unsettled corner of New England has been opened to the public again.

11. MYSTERY LEFT BEHIND

LOST TREASURE AND HIDDEN GOLD IN AMERICA'S WILD REGIONS

In a previous book of mine, I wrote about some of the adventures that I had while living in Utah back around 1990. In that book, *Down in the Darkness*, I wrote of the tales of hauntings, ghost towns and lost mines that can be found spread out through the beautiful and haunted state. While working in Utah, I spent much of my free time tracking down ghost towns and ghost stories and mentioned in passing my half-hearted search for lost treasure. But really, how half-hearted was that search? Perhaps it was not as reluctant as my story sounded. For who among us, with a taste for the outdoors and for the "wild", has not dreamed of that lost cache of gold, that mysterious trove of silver that was inadvertently left behind by some miner or bandit in the past?

One of the searches for lost treasure that I had the chance to experience in Utah took me out along the old Overland Trail, a famed stage route that had its beginnings not long after the Mormons settled into the valley of the Great Salt Lake. Almost immediately, they ran into problems with communication and mail delivery from the east, so in 1850, a mail contract was awarded to Colonel Samuel Woodson to carry mail from Independence, Missouri to Salt Lake City. Under Woodson's control, the mail came slowly and uncertainly and after several years of this, his contract was canceled. In 1854, another service was started but this one was also canceled almost as soon as it began.

In 1856, a little-known mail service was started by the Mormon Church called the Brigham Young Express & Carrying Company, commonly referred to as the "Y-X Company". It became the forerunner of both the Overland Stage and the Pony

Express. The company was planned as "a swift pony express to carry the mail" and also would establish "a coach line for passengers." Way stations, which were settlements, farms and business buildings, were established at regular intervals between Independence and Salt Lake City. Most of them were later used by the Overland Stage and the Pony Express. With the outbreak of the Mormon wars in Utah in August 1858, the Y-X Company was shut down, making it a complete loss to the Mormon Church.

Later in 1858, another contract was granted to Hockaday & Leggett and the company improved on the stations started by the Y-X Company and outfitted them with supplies, livestock and express riders. Unfortunately, they went bankrupt before they could start service and sold out to Russell, Majors & Waddell, the company that soon became famous for its short-lived Pony Express.

Mail service from Salt Lake City to the west coast began as early as May 1851, when Absalom Woodward and Major George Chorpenning began operations. Major Chorpenning was the famous trail blazer who had pioneered the Chorpenning Trail, which would be used by the Overland Stage, Pony Express and the Overland Telegraph Company. Although the two men were unable to maintain their service on a regular basis (Woodward was killed by Indians a few months after they started), they continued to carry the mail under great hardship until May 1860, when the line was taken over by Russell, Majors & Waddell. The now legendary Pony Express stretched all of the way from Independence to Sacramento and carried the mail until October 1861, when the Overland Telegraph made the service obsolete.

Nearly all of the Pony Express stations were used by the Overland Stage Company and were set up alternately as mail and express stations. The mail stations were operated by five or six employees, while the express stations only had a company agent and a relief rider. The riders were all young men, weighing between 125 and 135 pounds, and each was armed with a revolver and a Bowie knife. The combined weight of their saddle and gear had to be less than 14 pounds and the mail pouch was never allowed to exceed 20 pounds. Although the Pony Express has been greatly glorified, it was a financial disaster for its owners. When the service was started, postage cost the user $5 an ounce and when the company began losing $60,000 each month, they cut the price in half in hopes that business would improve. The volume of mail increased but they still lost money, even after cutting the price again to just $1 for an ounce of mail. Profits continued to elude them until finally, in March 1862, Russell, Majors & Waddell filed for bankruptcy with debts of more than $1 million. The firm was taken over by the Holloday Stage Company, its largest creditor.

Ben Holloday, known as the "Stagecoach King", changed the name of the company to the Overland Stage and turned it into the west's largest transportation company. It was operated by Holloday until November 1866, when it was purchased by Wells Fargo & Company. Wells Fargo continued Holloday's far-flung stage empire until 1869, when the rails of the Central and Union Pacific Railroads met at Promontory, Utah.

From the 1850's, Salt Lake City was the central point along the Overland route and much of the history of the Overland Trail occurred at seldom remembered stations strung out across the mountains and deserts of Utah. Today, not much remains of any of these spots but a number of years ago, I followed tales of lost treasure to the easternmost Overland Stage station in Utah, Needle Rock. Within a short distance of the Wyoming border, Needle Rock was named for a prominent landmark that was used as a guide point for the early pioneers. Captain Albert Tracy, an officer with Johnston's army during the Utah War, wrote in his journal, "Very peculiar rocks are the Needles, strange, massive obelisks, paired in twins, projecting themselves high into the sky." The station was a regular stop on the stage line, where teams were changed and meals and lodging could be had by travelers. Few chose to stay any longer than necessary though, as the food was plain, the summers hot and the winter winds blew cold from the barren hills.

From Needle Rock Station, the trail passed through an open, sage-covered flat and down a grassy draw near Cache Cave, which was just off the trail to the north. The cave had been home to Indians before the coming of the white man and was later used by mountain men, explorers and travelers. During the Utah War, Mormon military leaders used it as a headquarters and under the leadership of Lot Smith, burned Fort Bridger and Fort Supply and barricaded Echo Canyon against the approach of the U.S. Army. The cave still contains the names of more than 150 trappers, explorers and pioneers, some dating back to 1820.

It was Cache Cave that had brought me to the former stage stop. The cave was once exactly what the name of it suggests - a place where mountain men cached their furs, caches of supplies were hidden here and later, it became a cache for outlaw loot, secreted away by the infamous Ike Potter Gang. Few people today have ever heard of Ike Potter and his gang of outlaws but they terrorized small settlements throughout northern Utah during the 1860's. Allied with army deserters from Camp Floyd and renegade Indians, Potter's gang attacked lone travelers, ambushed wagon trains and raided small and isolated settlements. They hid out at Cache Cave and it was common knowledge that Potter hid his loot somewhere nearby. His Indian compatriots kept all of the horses and livestock but Potter kept the gold, money and other valuables.

In July 1867, a letter written by Potter went astray and from it, the residents of Coalville learned that Potter and his men planned to attack their town. The settlers were prepared when the attack came on July 28, 1867 and the gang was met by armed citizens and Sheriff J.C. Roundy and 15 deputies. Potter and his two lieutenants were taken by surprise and captured and the rest of the outlaws were driven from town.

R.H. "Ike" Potter, Charley Wilson and John Walker were held at the town's stone schoolhouse until midnight, when a group of armed men entered and marched the prisoner's to the edge of town. Potter was killed instantly by a single blast of a shotgun but Walker and Wilson tried to escape. Wilson was caught and killed alongside Weber River and Walker managed to escape, even though he was shot at from such close range that his shirt caught fire. He was captured again several days later in the mountains near Fort Douglas. He was left with his throat cut and his body as food for the wolves.

With Potter, Walker and Wilson all dead, there was no one left who knew the location where the gang had hidden their gold. Many have speculated that it contained everything from gold coins to pistols, watches, wedding rings and perhaps even rare Mormon coins, which were in use in those days. It is strongly believed that this loot is hidden either in, or nearby, Cache Cave.

In all honesty, I had little chance of stumbling onto the loot by accident, but it didn't stop me from joining the legion of other treasure hunters who have sought out the cave over the years in hopes that they too might get lucky. When I arrived at the cave, I was disappointed to find that it was closed off from the road by a gate. The land now belongs to an oil company, I believe, but I hiked back there anyway for a look. The history of this small cave - it only goes back a very short distance into the hills - is simply amazing and, treasure or not, it's worth a look just for the names of adventurers who came before.

I never found any gold or lost treasure that day but in truth, that didn't make me all that much different than most of the unlucky adventurers, miners and ordinary folks that you will read about in the pages ahead. Searching for treasure in America is as old as the discovery of the New World itself, from the famed Seven Cities of Gold to the little known lost mines of the west. We have long searched for wealth and for the shining gold and silver that remains hidden beneath the earth, rocks and sand. Our search is often a fruitless one, filled with danger, hardship and often death and usually ends in defeat, leaving only legends, and sometimes ghosts, behind.

I have collected in the pages to come some of the greatest tales of the search for lost treasure in America. Some of them, the reader may be familiar with and others will have never have been seen before but they all have several things in common - a great story, a rich history, the promise of fortune and the lure of the unsolved. You are even likely to find bizarre deaths, mysterious disappearances and ghostly tales lurking in the mix but in each one of them, you will find the story of men who ventured into the "wild" and in many cases, never returned.

MYSTERY OF THE LOST DUTCHMAN

There has been much written over the years, including in my own hand, about the strange history of Arizona's legendary Lost Dutchman Mine. The mine is said to be located east of Phoenix in a rugged, mountainous region that is a place of mystery and lore called Superstition Mountain. It is the west's most celebrated lost mine and while there is a great mythology that surrounds it, there is much truth too. Many have gone in search of it over the years, only to vanish into the rocks and desert - never to be seen again. The history of the mine is filled with danger, death, horror and misconception and thanks to its mysterious location, it has been the quest of many adventurers and has turned out to be a place of doom for countless others.

Superstition Mountain with Weaver's Needle in the background. This is the starting off point for nearly every expedition in search of the Dutchman's Gold.

What has caused dozens of people who seek the mine to vanish without a trace? Is the answer really as the Apache Indians say- that the "Thunder God" protects this mine, bringing death to those who attempt to pillage it? Or can the deaths be linked to other causes? Are they caused, as some have claimed, by the spirits of those who have died seeking the mine before? The pages that follow will delve into these questions but be prepared - there are far more mysteries here than there are solutions.

Superstition Mountain is actually a collection of rough terrain that has gained the name of a single mountain. The contour of the region takes in thousands of cliffs, peaks, plateaus and mesas and even today, much of it remains largely unexplored. Despite the tendency by many to call this a range of mountains, it is, in reality, only one. It is certainly not the highest mountain in the region, but it has the reputation of being the deadliest. Over the course of several centuries, it has taken the lives of many men and women and has perhaps caused a madness in them that has encouraged them to kill one another.

The first inhabitants of the region to set eyes on the mountain were likely the Hohokams, a tribe of ancient Native Americans whose culture and way of life was more advanced than many of the tribes who came after them. The Hohokams numbered in the thousands and the center of their civilization was the Salt River Valley, which is adjacent to Superstition Mountain. They lived in adobe and stone homes and built elaborate irrigation systems to raise crops. They also carried out mining operations and centuries later, some of their burial grounds have been excavated and have been found to contain ornaments made of gold. This means that they were likely the first to discover the rich vein of gold that is hidden in Superstition Mountain.

The Hohokams are believed to have remained in this region for about 2,000 years but exactly when they disappeared is unknown, as is their fate. Some say that they were wiped out by disease, war or some other disaster or for inexplicable reasons, simply migrated from the area. What is known is that when the Spanish first came here from Mexico in the 1500's, there was nothing left of the Hohokams civilization but ruins.

In the wake of the Hohokams came the Pima and Maricopa Indians. Their origin has not been definitively established but it is believed they came from the north, although some maintain that they are the descendants of the Hohokams. If so, they were a much more primitive people than their ancestors, growing few crops and existing on what meager rations came from the desert. When they came to the region is unknown but when the Apache came in the early 1400's, the Pima and Maricopa were firmly established and already held Superstition Mountain in great awe and refused to enter the treacherous peaks and mesas.

The Apaches, according to their tradition, came to the area from Mexico. They had a fierce hatred for the Spanish, who had conquered the lands to the south, and for years had migrated further and further north to escape the bonds of slavery. The Apache were very different from the Pima and Maricopa, being nomadic and war-like and having no interest in farming. When they needed food and supplies, they simply raided the villages and dwellings of other tribes. They also had no fear of the Superstition - at least not at first - and used the massive tangle of rocks as a fortress. They would launch their raiding parties from the mountain and then vanish back into the valleys, where they knew no other Indians would follow them.

According to legend, there was an event that occurred before the Spanish came to the region that changed the attitude of the Apache toward the Superstition. The account has it that the raiding parties of the Apache finally became so unacceptable to the Maricopa that they eventually overcame their fear of the fierce tribe and decided to fight back. They set a trap, which worked well at first. The Apaches were turned back and retreated to the mountain, with the Maricopa in pursuit. Their determination to rid themselves of their enemy was even greater than what they feared awaited them on the mountain. However, the Apache outwitted them and ambushed them in the midst of the crags and gulches of the Superstition. Many Apache were killed but the Maricopa were effectively slaughtered. Even so, it was the greatest loss that the Apache had ever suffered. They held council after the battle and decided that the mountain was indeed inhabited by gods who became angry over the battle held in their domain and caused many Apache warriors to die as punishment. In repentance, they set aside the portion of the mountain where the battle occurred as home to their gods - sacred ground. From that time on, this portion of the mountain was home to the Apache "Thunder God" and was forbidden to any intruders.

The Spanish conquistadors were the first white men to come to the region, led by Francisco Vasquez de Coronado. He came north from Mexico in 1540 seeking the legendary "Seven Golden Cities of Cibola". When he reached the region, the local Indians told him that the mountain held much gold, although they refused to help the Spaniard explore it. They were in too much fear of the "Thunder God", who was said to dwell there, and who would destroy them if they dared to trespass upon his sacred ground.

When the Spaniards tried to explore the mountain on their own, they discovered that men began to vanish mysteriously. It was said that if one of them strayed more than a few feet from his companions, he was never seen alive again. The bodies of the men who were found were discovered to be mutilated and with their heads cut off. The terrified survivors refused to return to the mountain and so Coronado dubbed the collection of peaks Monte Superstition, which explains the origin of the infamous name. The mountain became a legendary spot to the Spanish explorers who followed and it was regarded as an evil place.

The first man to discover the gold of the Indians on Superstition Mountain was Don Miguel Peralta, a member of a prominent family who owned a ranch near Sonora, Mexico. Peralta came to the Superstitions looking for a new source of income for his family. In the 1600's, his ancestors had been given a huge land grant by the Spanish court, which included a few profitable silver mines and the Superstition Mountains. After two centuries of pillaging, the silver mines began to show less and less profit and so Peralta decided to see if there was anything to the stories of gold in the mysterious mountains to the north.

In 1845, he journeyed to the Superstitions and began prospecting for gold. Within six months, he discovered a rich vein of ore and made a map of the area so that he could return to Mexico and come back with men and supplies to begin his excavations. As he mapped out the area, he memorized the surrounding territory. He described the mountain's most outstanding landmark as looking like a "sombrero" and so he named the cache of gold the "Sombrero Mine". To others, the peak, or spire, looked more like a finger pointing upwards and it has also been referred to as the "Finger of God" - except to early white explorer Pauline Weaver. He used the rock as a place to etch his name with a knife and subsequent prospectors discovered the etching and dubbed the landmark "Weaver's Needle". The name stuck and nearly every reference to what would become the lost mine uses the Needle as a point of origin.

Peralta returned to Mexico and gathered men and material to work the mine. Soon, he was shipping millions of pesos in pure gold back to Sonora. It was obvious that this was a gold strike like no other. He worked for three years and as time passed, the Apache began to grow angry about the Spanish presence on the mountain. In 1848, the Indians, encouraged by their charismatic leader Cochise, raised a large force to drive Peralta and his men from the area. Peralta soon got word of the impending fight and withdrew his men from the mine. They would pack up all of the available burros and wagons with the already mined ore and return home. Because he planned to return someday, Peralta took elaborate precautions to conceal the entrance to the mine and to wipe out any trace that they had ever worked there.

Early the next day, he assembled his men and prepared to move out - but they never had a chance. Taking the Spaniards by surprise, the Apache warriors attacked and massacred the entire company of Spaniards. The pack mules were scattered in all directions, spilling the gold and taking it with them as they plunged over cliffs and into ravines.

In the late 1850's, two prospectors known as Hurley and O'Connor accidentally found a dead Spanish mule while trying to backtrack from the field where Peralta's men had been killed. They were hoping to find the entrance to the mine, but stumbled onto the crumbling remains of the burro instead. Strapped to the animal was a leather pack that was filled with gold ore. Over the course of the next few weeks, they managed to find several other mules and stuffed the gold into their own rucksacks as they continued to search. Then, instead of going to the nearest town to cash in the ore, they made the long journey to the U.S. Government Assay Office in San Francisco and were given $50,000 for it. Needless to say, they returned to the Superstitions many times over the next several years and retired very wealthy men. Most would agree that they managed to get out just in time for they narrowly avoided the wrath of the Apaches in the area and the desperation of other treasure hunters, who were sure they had found the location of Peralta's lost mine.

Once they retired, they spilled the story of where the gold had come from and the area where the Spaniards were killed was dubbed "Gold Field". It became a favorite place for outlaws and get-rich-quick schemers, who spent days and months searching for the lost gold. The last case of anyone finding the bones of a Peralta mule was in 1914. A man named C.H. Silverlocke showed up in Phoenix one day with a few pieces of badly decayed leather, some pieces of Spanish saddle silver and about $18,000 in gold concentrate.

The next man to profit from the Peralta mine was a man named Dr. Abraham Thorne. He was born in East St. Louis, Illinois and all of his life, he longed to be a doctor to the Indians in the western states. Early in his life, he was befriended by the frontier legend, Kit Carson, and when Fort McDowell was founded in Arizona in 1865, Carson arranged for Thorne to become an army doctor with an officer's rank.

At this time, fighting between the whites and the Apache was often fierce. The Indians were being besieged by the Army but it would not be long before cooler heads would prevail and President Abraham Lincoln would create a compromise in the area. He proposed a reservation along the Verde River, near Fort McDowell, which could serve as a sanctuary for the Apache. It was here, in an area known unofficially as the "Strip", where Thorne came to live and work amongst the Indians. He soon made many friends and earned respect from the tribal leaders, caring for the sick and injured, delivering babies and teaching hygiene and waste disposal.

In 1870, a strange incident took place in Dr. Thorne's career. Several of the elders in the tribe came to him with a proposal. Because he was considered a good man and a friend of the Apache, they would take him to a place where he could find gold. The only condition would be that he was to be blindfolded during the journey of roughly 20 miles.

Dr. Thorne agreed and the Indians placed a cloth around his head and over his eyes. They led him away on horseback and at the end of the journey, the cloth was removed and he found himself in an unknown canyon. He would later write that he saw a sharp pinnacle of rock about a mile to the south of him. Treasure hunters believe this was most likely Weaver's Needle. There was no sign of a mine, but piled near the base of the canyon wall (as if placed there for him) was a stack of almost pure gold nuggets. He picked up as much of it as he could carry and returned home. He later sold the ore for $6,000 and became another strange link in the mystery of the mine's location.

Of course, the most famous person associated with the lost Peralta mine (and the man who has given the mine its popular name) is a man who has come to be known as "The Dutchman".

First of all, I should clear up one popular misconception about Jacob Walz (or Waltz, or Walzer depending on the story you hear) and it's that he was not a "Dutchman". He was actually from Germany and born there in the early 1800's. He came to America in 1845 and soon heard about the riches and adventures that were waiting in the frontier beyond New York. His first gold seeking took him to a strike in North Carolina and from there he traveled to Mississippi, California and Nevada - always looking for his elusive fortune.

Walz worked the gold field of the Sierra Nevada foothills for more than ten years, never getting rich, but turning up enough gold to get along. By 1868, he was in his fifties and wondering if he was ever going to find his proverbial "mother lode". The Indians had nicknamed him "Snowbeard" because of his long, white whiskers and it isn't hard to picture him as one of those grizzled old prospectors who were so common in western films.

That same year, Walz began homesteading in the Rio Satillo Valley, which is on the northern side of Superstition Mountain. Soon after he arrived, he began to hear stories from the local Indians about supernatural doings around the mountain, about a fierce god -- and about vast deposits of gold.

After coming to Arizona, Walz took up with a young Indian woman and they lived together on the Dutchman's homestead. At that time, Walz was working at the Vulture Gold Mine and rumors say that he was skimming gold from the mine. And he was not the only miner who was doing so either. Things eventually got so bad that the mine operators hired men to raid the homes of the workers who were believed to be stealing. Walz was the only one of them not arrested, but he did lose his job. He had managed to put away enough gold over time though that he didn't seem to care. He worked aimlessly at other men's mines and sites and continued to pocket enough wages to keep him going while he searched for his own fortune.

Around 1870, Walz was working a mining claim and he struck up an acquaintance with a fellow German immigrant named Jacob Weiser. Soon, the two "Dutchmen" struck out on their own and vanished into the land around Superstition Mountain. Not long after, they were seen in Phoenix paying for drinks and supplies with gold nuggets. Some claimed this gold was the stolen loot from the Vulture Mine, while others said that it was of much higher quality and had to have come from somewhere else. Regardless of where it came from, the two men would spend the gold around town for the next two decades.

There have been a number of stories about how the men found the "lost" mine. According to some, they stumbled upon it by accident. Others say they killed two Mexican miners, who they mistook for Indians, and then realized the men were mining gold. But the most accepted version of the story is that they were given a map to the mine by a Mexican don whose life they saved.

The man was said to have been Don Miguel Peralta, the son of a rich landowner in Sonora, Mexico and a descendant of the original discoverer of the mine. The Dutchmen saved Peralta from certain death in a knife fight and as a reward, he gave them a look at the map to the mine. He was later said to have been bought out of the mine by Walz and Weiser.

At some point in the years that followed, Jacob Weiser disappeared without a trace. Some say that the Apaches killed him, while others maintain that Walz actually did him in. As the reader can see, there is a lot of speculation to the legend.

But Walz was always around, at least part of the time. Long periods would go by when no one would see him and then he would show up in Phoenix again, buying drinks with gold nuggets. It was said that Walz had the richest gold ore that anyone had ever seen and for the rest of his life, he vanished back and forth to his secret mine, always bringing back saddlebags filled with gold. Whenever anyone tried to get information out of him, he would always give contradictory directions as to where the mine was located. On many occasions, men tried to follow him when he left town, but Walz would always shake his pursuers in the rugged region around the mountain.

By the winter of 1891, an old Mexican widow named Julia Elena Thomas, who owned a small bakery in Phoenix, befriended the aged miner. Apparently, they became romantically involved and Walz promised to take her to his secret mine "in the spring" - but she never saw it. He did manage to gasp out some rough directions to her while on his deathbed though. According to his story, "the mine can be found at the spot on which the shadow of the tip of Weaver's Needle rests at four in the afternoon. The mine faces west. Near the mine is a hideout cave. One mile from the cave is a rock with a natural face looking east. To the south is Weaver's Needle. Follow to the right of the canyons, but not very far." Walz also went on to tell her that the mine was shaped like an upside down funnel with ledges cut into the sides. The Spaniards also built a tunnel through the hill to remove the gold from the bottom of the shaft.

These vague directions were all that he managed to give her. The Dutchman died on October 25, 1891 with a sack of rich gold ore beneath his bed.

On two separate occasions, Julia Thomas attempted to find the mine but failed. She probably now reasoned that there was no harm in making Walz's story public and there was always the possibility that someone would find the lode and reward her for the information. An article appeared in the November 17, 1894 edition of the *Saturday Evening Review* that claimed to contain the detailed directions that Walz had given to Julia. As soon as word of the article spread, the hunt for the gold, which had already been fierce after the Dutchman's death, soon became frenzied. A number of men who had heard Walz speak about the mine for years rode out for the mountain in search of the mystery.

In the description of the site that Julia gave to the newspaper, she told of a gulch where certain landmarks were located. "There is a two-room house," the report stated, "in the mouth of a cave on the side of the slope near the gulch. Just across the gulch.. opposite this house in the cave, is a tunnel, well covered up and concealed in the bushes. Here is the mine … the richest in the world." One prospector, P.C. Bicknell, found the cave with the house in it but failed, after a persistent effort, to find the mine. The house was a key landmark in Julia's story, although she failed to find it, and it was said to be in direct line with the mine entrance. After Bicknell found the cave, the search became concentrated in this area and it seemed like it would be only a matter of time before the mine was found - but it never was. Two prospectors, who owned ranches in the area, Jim Bark and Huse Ward, spent the next 25 years searching in vain for what they called "The Lost Dutchman Mine".

The search has since fueled well more than a century of speculation. Theories as to the mine's location have filled dozens of books and pamphlets. Literally hundreds of would-be prospectors have searched the Superstition Mountain region and most have come home with little more than sunburns.

But there are also many who have not come home at all.

There is no way to guess just how many people have died in pursuit of the Lost Dutchman Mine. Some who have disappeared may have just quietly slipped away, unwilling to admit that they failed to find the treasure, while others may have gone in secretly and never came out, their names recorded as a missing persons case somewhere else.

The death toll of the legendary Peralta Massacre varies between 100 to 400, plus there are the murders attributed to the Dutchman, Jacob Walz himself. He is alleged to have killed at least two men who found his treasure trove and is blamed for the death of his partner, Jacob Weiser, and others.

There are also a number of people who were slain by the Apaches after they were found searching the mountain for the mine. These deaths, like the victims of the massacre and those killed by the Dutchman, are easy to document and understand.

But there are others that are not so easy to explain.

In the summer of 1880, two young soldiers appeared in the town of Pinal. They had recently been discharged from Fort McDowell and were looking for work at the Silver King Mine, operated by Aaron Mason. They also asked him to take a look at some gold ore they had found while crossing Superstition Mountain. Mason was stunned to see a bag of extremely rich gold ore. Where had they found it? The soldiers explained that they had been on the mountain and had flushed a deer into one of the canyons. On their way out, they found the remains of an old tunnel and mine. This small bag of gold was only a little of what could be found there.

Mason asked them if they could find the place again and they believed they could, having been scouts for the Army and very conscious of the details of the landscape. They remembered the mine being in the northerly direction of a sharp peak (which Mason was sure was Weaver's Needle) and in very rough country. A narrow trail had led from the peak and into the valley where they found the mine.

The soldiers admitted however, that they knew little about mining. Would Mason go into partnership with them? He agreed and purchased the ore they brought with them for $700, then helped them get outfitted for their return to the mine. They left Pinal the next day - and never returned.

Mason waited two weeks and then sent out a search party. The nude body of one of the soldiers was found beside a trail leading to the mountain. He had been shot in the head. The other man was found the next day and had been killed in the same manner. Apaches? No one would ever find out.

A year later, a prospector named Joe Dearing showed up in Pinal. After hearing about the death of the two soldiers, he began to make searches of the Superstition, looking for the mysterious mine. He was more successful in his search than most, although I don't think I would go as far as to say his luck was any better.

Dearing soon returned to Pinal, seeking a temporary job while he waited for a partner to arrive in the region. He looked for work at the Silver King Mine but since they weren't hiring, he took a job as a bartender instead. He put in his time at a local saloon that was owned by a man named Brown and within a short time, the two men became friends. Dearing confided in Brown that he was anxious for his partner to arrive because he had discovered a mine in the nearby mountains that "was kind of a pit, shaped like a funnel and with a large opening at the top". He said that the pit had been partially filled in by debris and there was a tunnel that had been walled over with rocks. Dearing planned to work until he could make enough money to excavate his find. He did not reveal the location to Brown but his description of the site matched that of Jacob Walz almost exactly - ten years before the Dutchman's death and the public record of the mine. He had found the place after hearing the story of the two soldiers and only told Brown that it was located in an area of extremely rough terrain.

Dearing later went to work at the Silver King Mine, still intent on saving his earnings, and after making friends with his foreman, John Chewning, he told him virtually the same story that he had told to Brown. However, he also produced a piece of mine ore for the foreman that validated his claims. He also added that he had found the mine by following an old trail and remarked that before reaching the mine, the trail became somewhat tricky and that it was necessary to go through a hole. Exactly what he meant by this, no one has been able to discover.

Unfortunately, Dearing never made it back to the mine for he was killed in a cave-in just one week after his conversation with Chewning. If he really knew the location of the mine, then he took the secret with him to the grave.

Another story that coincides with the tale of the two soldiers is one reportedly related by an aging Mexican woman named Maria Robles. In her story, she related that when she was a young girl, she went with a lover, Juan Gonzales, from Sonora to a very rich gold mine on Superstition Mountain. To reach the mine, she said that they had followed an inclining trail past a tall peak and from the top, the trail went down over a slope and to the mine. According to Maria, the gold could be taken in small pieces from a deep, vertical, cone-shaped digging.

Not only does Maria's description of the mine match that of the Dutchman and Dearing, but the character of Juan Gonzales shows up elsewhere in Lost Dutchman lore. This story was supposed to have taken place in 1874 and includes the information that he was also known as Juan Peralta Gonzales and that he came to Arizona in search of someone to outfit an expedition into the Superstition. He met up with the man who owned the local telegraph office and told his prospective partner that he had a map to a gold mine that had been given to him by his father, Manuel Peralta, just before his death. His father told him of much gold that had been taken from "Canyon Fresco", which was located in the mountains south of Four Peak - mountains that included La Sombrero - and that he now had a map to the spot.

After much haggling, the telegrapher was allowed to see the map briefly and to ascertain that the canyon in question drained from the mountains, northwest into the river. An undetermined distance from the river, the canyon forked to the east and to the south. At this fork on the map, was where the mine was marked . If this story is true, then Canyon Fresco is likely Tortilla Creek. It is the only remarkable tributary that runs from Superstition Mountain and forks in the manner described. This was the first clue as to the location of this elusive canyon.

Gonzales was able to get his grubstake and after buying supplies, he is said to have traveled up the south bank of the Salt River toward Canyon Fresco. But he never got that far. The story has it that he stumbled on the site of the old Spanish massacre and found several decaying bags filled with gold. Rather than continue the arduous search for the mine, he decided to make due with the bags that he found and abandoning the quest, returned home to Mexico.

Another prospector connected to the Lost Dutchman Mine and its mysterious deaths was Elisha Reavis, better known as the "Madman of the Superstitions". From 1872 until his death in 1896, he resided in a remote area on the mountain and raised vegetables. The local Apaches never bothered him because they were afraid of him. The Indians held those who were mad in superstitious awe and Reavis certainly seemed to fit the bill. It was said that he ran naked through the canyons at night and fired his pistol at the stars.

In April of 1896, a friend of Reavis realized that he was overdue for his periodic trip into town and went in search of him. His badly decomposed body was found near his home. Coyotes had eaten him and his head had been severed from his body (much like the Spanish conquistadors). It was found lying several feet away.

The same year that Reavis was found murdered, two Easterners went looking for the mine. They were never seen again.

Around 1900, two prospectors, remembered only as Silverlock and Malm, began an excavation on the northern edge of the Superstition. They found some of the gold remaining from the Peralta Massacre, but little else. For some reason though, they remained working the area for years after, sinking dozens of shafts and finding nothing.

Then, in 1910, Malm appeared at the Mormon cooperative in Mesa. He was babbling incoherently that Silverlock had tried to kill him. Deputies brought the other man in and he was judged insane and committed to the territorial asylum. Malm was later sent to the county poor farm, none too steady himself, and both men died within two years. What was it about the Superstition that unbalanced these men?

Also in 1910, the skeleton of a woman was found in a cave, high up on Superstition Mountain. Several gold nuggets were found with the remains. The coroner judged the death to be of recent date, although no further information about her was ever found. And the gold nuggets were never explained.

In 1927, a New Jersey man and his sons were hiking on the mountain when someone began rolling rocks down on them from the cliffs above. A boulder ended up crushing the legs of one of the boys. The following year, a person rolling huge rocks down at them also drove two deer hunters off the mountain.

In June of 1931, a government employee named Adolph Ruth from Washington, D.C. left for the Superstition foothills with what he claimed was an old Peralta map to the mine. The map had allegedly been given to his son, Erwin, by a prominent Mexican official. The map - which may have been authentic - will turn up again later in this narrative. As it turned out, the map was likely Ruth's undoing, as he told nearly everyone that he met about it. He also made the mistake of going onto the mountain alone and at one of the worst times of the year.

After making local inquiries as to the location of a tall peak and being advised that it was likely Weaver's Needle, Ruth was packed into the mountains by a couple of local cowboys. They helped him set up a camp near a water hole in West Boulder Canyon and then left him alone in his search. That was the last time that Adolph Ruth was ever seen alive.

A search party went out looking for him after Ruth had not been heard from in some time but while they found his campsite to be intact, the old man was nowhere to be found. Six months later, in December, his skull was found on Black Top Mountain with two holes in it. The rest of his skeleton was found a month later, about three-quarters of a mile away. In his clothing was a cryptic note that read "About 200 feet across from cave" and "Veni, Vidi, Vici" (I came, I saw, I conquered).The message was written inside of a small notebook, along with other material that, had part of it not been missing, might have solved the mystery of the Lost Dutchman years ago.

The notebook implied that "it" was located just over two miles from Weaver's Needle (no direction was given) in a formation of basalt at approximately 2,500 feet elevation. There was also said to be a "monumented" trail located in the westernmost gorge on the south side of the mountain. It further stated that "they" followed this trail north and were led over a ridge and down past Sombrero Butte and into a canyon. From this point, they hiked into a side canyon that was dense with brush. At one time, there had been more to the message, but it was at that point where a portion of the page had been destroyed. At the bottom of the page, in Ruth's handwriting, were the mysterious lines mentioned earlier "... about 200 feet across from cave..." and the Latin notation. Although nothing exists to prove it, it seems that Adolph Ruth must have found the Lost Dutchman Mine about 200 feet away from a cave entrance.

There was no trace of the treasure map that Ruth had taken into the mountains with him. It was not found on his body, nor had it turned up in the earlier search of his camp. It is common knowledge that Ruth had the map with him when he made the ill-fated trip onto the mountain but unless he hid it somewhere that has not been discovered, his killer must have taken it. It is an accepted theory that he was murdered for the map or that the killer watched and waited until Ruth found the map and then after murdering him, took the map so that no one else could get their hands on it.

Since Ruth's death, there have been a number of people who have claimed to have the map, or at least a copy of it. It seems unlikely that any of them have the original though, unless they are also claiming to be Ruth's killer. The crime has remained unsolved over the years.

Ruth is one of the most famous deaths connected to the Lost Dutchman in the last century but he was far from the only one who was killed or murdered .In December 1936, Roman O'Hal, a broker's clerk from New York City, died from a fall while searching for the mine. It was believed to have been an accident.

In 1937, an old prospector named Guy "Hematite" Frink came down from the mountain with some rich gold samples. That following November, he was found shot in the stomach on the side of a trail. A small sack of gold ore was discovered beside him. His death was also ruled to be an accident.

In June 1947, a prospector named James A. Cravey made a much-publicized trip into the Superstition canyons by helicopter, searching for the Lost Dutchman Mine. The pilot set him down in La Barge Canyon, close to Weaver's Needle. When Cravey failed to hike out as planned, a search was started and although his camp was found, Cravey was not. The following February, his body was finally found under mysterious circumstances. Two men were hiking on the mountain when they came upon a rope that had been stretched across the trail in front of them. One end of the rope led into the dense brush at the side of the trail and when they investigated, they found a headless body that was wrapped in a blanket and bound with the end of the rope. Nearby, they found a jacket and in one of the pockets was a wallet that still held money and identification papers with the name James Cravey on them.

Strangely, the trail had been widely traveled during the seven months between when Cravey had vanished and the corpse had been found. It would have been impossible for anyone to have missed the rope that had been stretched across it, which begs the question as to who killed Cravey - and where had his body been during the time when he was missing?

In February 1951, Dr. John Burns, a physician from Oregon, was found shot to death on the Superstition. It was said to have been an accidental death.

In early 1952, Joseph Kelley of Dayton, Ohio began his own search for the mine. He had been intrigued by the mystery of the Lost Dutchman for years and came to believe that he had stumbled across the solution. After selling his car, he purchased a gun at a Mesa sporting goods store and then went onto the mountain on foot. He left word with a Mesa motor hotel operator to call his wife and the police in case he did not return within ten days. The calls were placed because Kelley never returned and was never heard from again. He was never seen again - until his skeleton was discovered near Weaver's Needle in May of 1954. He had been shot directly from above and according to the coroner's jury, "by accident".

Two California boys hiked onto Superstition Mountain the same year as Kelley. Nothing further was ever seen of them. Some have suggested that they met the same fate as the three Texas boys who had also disappeared a few years before.

Bernardo Flores, a prospector from Coolidge, also went onto the mountain in search of the mine. According to his relatives, he left one summer day and just never returned. His headless skeleton was found nearly a year later.

Charles Massey came from Tucson to do some javelina hunting with friends in 1954 but while on the mountain, he became separated from the others and was never seen alive again. His skeleton was found in February 1955 at the bottom of a cliff and he had been shot directly between the eyes. A coroner's jury later ruled that it was an accident.

In January 1956, a Brooklyn man reported to police that his brother had been missing for several weeks. It was believed that he had gone in search of the mine. The body of Martin Zywotho was discovered with a bullet hole above his right temple. A coroner's jury was undecided as to whether it was the result of accident or suicide.

In April 1958, a deserted campsite was found on the northern edge of the mountain. There was a bloodstained blanket, a Geiger counter, cooking utensils, a gun-cleaning kit, but no gun, and some letters from which the names and addresses had been torn. No trace of the camp's occupant was ever found.

In April 1959, two friends traveled to Arizona from Hawaii in a search for the mine. They came equipped with a map of dubious origins and were eager to search for the gold. However, they did not hunt for long. One night, as he lay in his sleeping bag, Stanley Fernandez was shot and killed by his companion and best friend, Benjamin Ferreira. The accused later took a guilty plea to a manslaughter charge and was sentenced to serve time in Florence, Arizona. No explanation was ever given as to why he killed his friend. After he was released on parole, he headed back to Hawaii and after a brief time at home, shot his mother-in-law.

In November 1959, Robert St. Marie was shot and killed on Superstition Mountain. His killing was not mysterious and stemmed from another case of senseless madness, the kind that has long plagued the mountain. He had been murdered by a prospector named Ed Piper, who had gotten into a disagreement over "claim jumping" with St. Marie. The dead man had been part of a group led by a singer named Celeste Marie Jones, who had come seeking the Lost Dutchman on a tip from a Los Angeles astrologer. The two parties ran into one another on the mountain and got involved in a shoot-out over who had the right to be there. Norman Teason, the justice of the peace at Apache Junction, ordered all of the rifles from both parties confiscated. Despite the order, Piper later testified that he saw St.

Marie approach him with a rifle in his hand so Piper shot and killed him. Piper was released after the judge agreed that it had been a shooting in self defense.

In October 1960, a group of hikers found a headless skeleton near the foot of a cliff. The skull was found four days later and it was determined that it belonged to an Austrian student named Franz Harrier. Five days later, another skeleton was found and in November, police identified the body as William Richard Harvey, a painter from San Francisco. His cause of death was unknown.

In January 1961, a family picnicking near the edge of the mountain discovered the body of Hilmer Charles Bohen buried beneath the sand. He was a Utah prospector who had been shot in the back. Two months later, another prospector, Walter J. Mowry from Denver, was found shot to death in Needle Canyon. That same year, the body of Charles Bohen, a Salt Lake City man, was also found. He had been shot through the heart,

That fall, police began searching for Jay Clapp, a prospector who had been working on the Superstition on and off for about 15 years. He had last been seen in July and after several weeks, the search was eventually called off. His headless skeleton was finally discovered three years later. He was identified by two cameras with the initials "JC" scratched on them.

And with that, my personal record of mysterious deaths comes to an end, although the death of Jay Clapp was reportedly far from the last. I have been told there have been many others who have sought the gold of the Dutchman and who have never returned.

There have been many who have searched for it and according to their reports, many who have "found" the mine as well. In fact, the Lost Dutchman may just qualify as the most "found" lost mine in the world! The "finding" of the Lost Dutchman just might constitute an entire saga of disappointment, fraud and disillusionment all its own. Most of the time the perpetuation of the mine's "discovery" can be blamed on the press and its search for a good story and the mine has been allegedly found many times in the past and undoubtedly will be "found" many times in the future. These stories have become almost as an important a part of the story as Jacob Walz himself. Arizona newspapers, from the 1800's to the present, contain many stories of "finding" the Lost Dutchman Mine but no one ever has. It is still out there somewhere in the rugged hills of Arizona, just waiting for someone to return and claim its prize.

The first public acknowledgment of the mine's discovery though came right after the turn of the last century, in September 1901, when it was thought to have been found by Charlie Woolf, a prospector and cowboy, who accidentally stumbled onto an 80-foot shaft that was surrounded by abandoned mining equipment and human skeletons. The paper soon retracted the story, stating that the mine that Woolf supposedly found was not in the right area to have been the Lost Dutchman.

The famous mine was "discovered" again in 1920 and according to a publicity report from Dr. R.A. Ailton, the secretary and treasurer of the "Lost Dutchman Mine", it was the greatest gold strike in Arizona history. The story was carried in many regional newspapers but to many, the wording of the "publicity release" was little more than a phony scheme to bilk investors in the new mine out of their money. The public wanted to believe that the mine had been found and many readers simply couldn't wait to become a part of the company.

Using the newspaper's thirst for a good story, the new owners of the Lost Dutchman neatly laid out their snare. They spoke of the many "prominent men" who had approved of the company and their plans without really saying who these men actually were. And it also happened that the Lost Dutchman company planned to set up offices in downtown Phoenix and conveniently planned to offer stock to the public. On the company's application for stock, they even stressed their "90 day credit plan". Hundreds of people invested but not surprisingly, the company vanished and the subsequent development of the "mine" never took place.

In January 1935, sheriff's deputies in Phoenix were puzzled over a note that had been found in a bottle floating in the Salt River. It read: "Lost up Salt River. Broken Leg. I've found the Lost Dutchman Mine, I think. Come up and I'll reward you. By Blue Point. Please come quick. Jake Lee." Since no one believed the writer had actually found the mine, no one bothered to go up onto the mountain to look for the supposedly injured "Jake Lee". He was never heard from again.

Another of the stranger "findings" of the mine came in 1936 but in this case, the man who claimed it did not get rich - it actually cost him money. One day, a man stumbled down from the Superstition with a sack of pure gold, claiming that it had come from the lost mine. The gold was very fine and pure - too pure in fact - and it aroused the suspicions of the authorities. Police investigators launched an investigation and it was discovered that the gold was actually manufactured from gold meant to be used to fill teeth. The gold, worth about $5,000, turned out to be stolen and it was confiscated by the United States Mint authorities.

Years later, according to Frank Edward's 1961 book *Strange People*, the well-known psychic Peter Hurkos also reportedly found the mine. He and several associates came to Arizona without the amount of fanfare that usually accompanied the psychic's outings. It was announced that he planned to find the Lost Dutchman using ESP. Little was heard about his progress until a somewhat belated report appeared to say that he had found the mine and was now very rich. The report added that it had not been found where the stories normally claimed it would be. There was no fanfare and no fuss and not much more was learned about the search. The statement was made and after a brief flurry of interest - as well as denials by everyone not involved - it was dismissed as another eccentric tale.

When Edwards reported the find in his book, he wrote of Peter Hurkos: "Today he lives in Milwaukee, happily married and with a substantial income assured, for Hurkos used his weird talents to locate for himself and a small group of associates the fabulous Lost Dutchman gold mine in Arizona, one of the legendary treasures of the west."

But did he really? It's true that Hurkos had established an excellent reputation for himself, especially among law enforcement professionals, for having fabulous psychic powers but was he able to use them to find the mine, as he had done for missing and murdered people? Only Hurkos can answer that for sure but there were many claims of finding the mine that came after him, so most have to wonder.

Some 45 years after the demise of the Lost Dutchman Mining Corporation in 1920, another company formed with an amazingly similar name - the Lost Dutchman Exploration Company. Except this time, it was for real as the Lost Dutchman really had been found. Glenn Magill, a private investigator from Oklahoma City, and a group of associates had laid claim to Jacob Walz's mine. They had incorporated and were in the process of developing it. The publicity ran rampant and included not only newspaper and magazine reports but also a book by Curt Gentry called *The Killer Mountains*. Wild statements by Magill flashed across the newswires. "We don't think we have the right mine, we know we do," he stated without hesitation.

A Tucson radio station, learning of the discovery, received permission from Magill to do live broadcasts from the site. Adding more credence to the "discovery" was a statement from Sidney Brinkerhoof of the Arizona Historical Society in Tucson. The statement said in effect that Magill's mine certainly matched the legendary aspects of the story and that the "significance of this discovery is in a close parallel with descriptions of the mine left to us in years past. If in the weeks ahead, they are to hit pay dirt, it will be because they have gone at this project with a conscientious and scientific approach, Certainly they've put a lot of hard work into the project. And in the end they will probably come closer to the truth than any group in the past."

Brinkerhoff had been careful to make his statement so that it was not an outright confirmation of Magill's claims and this was likely for the best because something here was not right. Brinkerhoff had said that ... "if in the weeks ahead, they are to hit pay dirt.." but Magill was already claiming that they had hit "pay dirt". He confirmed in press releases that he had discovered the Lost Dutchman Mine and had even talked of gold being taken out. But if this was the case, where was the gold?

Not everyone, including some newspapers, were taken in by Magill's claims. His filing of a claim that included the location of the mine was met with skepticism by locals who were long familiar with the stories of the mine. They also noted the absence of any hard evidence to corroborate the discovery, namely the gold. Magill claimed to find nuggets of pure gold in the mine and yet he had not produced them, or even produced photographs of the mine that he claimed to have showing his men removing a seal on the entrance that had been placed there by the Apache.

It later turned out that Magill had "found" the mine using maps that had originally belonged to Erwin Ruth, whose father, Adolph Ruth, had been killed looking for the mine in 1931. This would cause many to wonder what may have gone wrong as Adolph Ruth remains one of the only people in the history of the mine to have ever really discovered its location.

Perhaps Magill read them wrong, who knows? The Lost Dutchman "find" never turned up any gold. A few pieces of quartz, flecked with gold - a common find for even amateur prospectors - was the extent of the so-called fabulous bonanza. After being questioned, Magill finally admitted that perhaps some of his previous statements had been premature. Maybe the mine was a little more to the east or west and perhaps if he continued to look ...

On June 7, 1967, the Oklahoma Securities Commission filed a "cease and desist" order against the Lost Dutchman Exploration Company. The officers had been selling stock in the company and failed to first register it with the Securities Commission. Magill abandoned Superstition Mountain and went back to Oklahoma.

In April 1975, Robert "Crazy Jake" Jacob held a press conference to announce to the world that he and another prospector had found the Lost Dutchman. It was on Superstition Mountain and within view of Weaver's Needle, as the legends had always stated. Jacob reported that the entrance to the mine was covered by "only 18 inches of dirt and some two by fours and rocks." The article from the Associated Press added one more ingredient, which seems to be common on all Dutchman "discovery" stories - that Jacob failed to present any gold at the press conference to substantiate their claim of finding the mine."

Two more Dutchman "discoveries" were announced within weeks of one another in 1980. In January of that year, Charles Kentworthy, head of a treasure hunting corporation said that he had his group had found a number of gold and silver "glory holes" on Superstition Mountain. He said that they had used aerial photography, the infamous "Peralta Stone Maps" (a set of carvings later shown to be phony carved stone markers), a proton magnetometer and an optical sensing device to find the mine. In this case, Kentworthy was a bit more cautious than some of his predecessors about claiming outright that it was Walz's mine. When asked by a reporter if he thought it was the Lost Dutchman, he replied "Who can tell? Nobody ever put a sign on it." A Tonto National Forest spokesperson only gave one comment on the validity of the Kentworthy claim. "There have been many claims and none of them have ever borne out." This may be one of the greatest understatements in the history of the Lost Dutchman!

A few weeks after the Kentworthy "discovery", Charles Crawford announced that he had found the Lost Dutchman mine. He added a new twist by confessing that he had found it by dowsing. He told reporters that this time, "there was no doubt about it." He had found the mine in La Barge Canyon, exactly where the old maps said it would be, but Crawford claimed he was the first to interpret these maps correctly. The mine had been sealed by tons of rock and an old tailing dump nearby, Crawford said, had assayed at three ounces of gold per ton. By his estimate, this pile alone would contain more than $20 million in gold and he had not even gotten into the mine yet.

What happened to it though? As opposed to most Lost Dutchman claimants - who vanished within days and weeks of achieving publicity - Crawford remained in the area until 1982, giving slide presentations about his "find" for $5 per person. He also conducted horseback tours to the "mine", where visitors were allowed to pan for gold. These seem to be unusual activities for someone who claimed just two years before to have found the "richest mine in the world".

And so it continues today...

Although prospectors who come looking for the Dutchman's gold today find a much different place than most who came before. Superstition Mountain is now a part of the great Tonto National Forest and falls within an area that has been designated as the Superstition Wilderness Area. Most of the land, with Weaver's Needle as its center, was set aside as a public landmark and recreation area and mining claims are no longer allowed. There are no roads permitted here, which is unchanged from the past, but Forest Service trails now beckon to the adventurous and are so clearly marked that one can navigate to as far as Weaver's Needle without hesitation. Thousands of people come here every year, lured by the mystery, but the days of lost mines - at least here - are now largely forgotten.

The legends of the place remain strong though, at least for as long as we want to remember them and they keep the link to the past alive and well. There is a mine out there somewhere, still waiting to be found and perhaps the prospector named Joe Dearing said it best when he described the mine as "the most God-awful rough place you can imagine... a ghostly place."

What brought so many to it, to fight and die for an enigma? Was it merely the lure of wealth or a madness they could not explain? That answer is as mysterious as the location of the Lost Dutchman Mine itself.

PEGLEG SMITH'S LOST GOLD

For well over a hundred years, prospectors have roamed the desolate outback regions of California's Borrego Badlands in search of Pegleg Smith's fabulous treasure. As one of America's most famous lost mines, the legendary Lost Pegleg has lured countless miners, dreamers and fools into the desert, each one of them sure that he could locate Smith's fabled cache of black-stained gold nuggets. To this day, no one has succeeded, although a crude memorial has stood for years northeast of Borrego Springs as a tribute to these adventurers.

The search for Pegleg's mysterious treasure has been unlike the quest for the gold of the Lost Dutchman and others because it has been impossible to nail it down to one region. No one was sure where it actually was and men have looked for it from the San Ysidro Mountains in the west to the Colorado River in the east. But time and time again, the gold hunters return to the Borrego Badlands. It is here, the voices whisper, where vast fortunes await and where many go and never return...

The Borrego Badlands of California

The Borrego Badlands are tucked into the southeastern corner of California and is one of the most hostile, desolate and scorching locations in America. During the summer months, temperatures here can reach as high as 125 degrees. The land was discovered by the Spanish several centuries ago. The explorer Juan Batista de Anza came through this region leading a band of men, women and mules northward to Monterey. The trail that he forged through the desert followed the San Felipe Wash. Father Pedro Font, who served as the chaplain and official observer for Anza's 1775 expedition, described the Borrego Badlands, later named for Anza, as the "sweepings of the earth."

It's uncertain when the Borrego region and Pegleg Smith became so utterly intertwined. Because of this, and the far reaching claims as to where the source of Smith's gold actually was, many have come to doubt the fact that Borrego is where the strange "black-stained" gold could be found. It was doubted for years that such gold could even be found here but in more recent times, geologists have admitted that it is possible. In addition to that, small samples of ore have also appeared to lead many to wonder about the existence of a mine, or at least of a vein of gold in the badlands. But are the samples real - or are they the same type of "fool's gold" that Pegleg Smith so often produced that ruined his reputation in the first place?

Thomas Smith, who would later become the "Pegleg Smith" of legend, was born at Crab Orchard, Kentucky in October 1801. While still in his teens, he left home and headed west to St. Louis. He worked for several years for the fur trader Antoine Robedaux, and became acquainted with such frontier notables as Jim Bridger, Kit Carson, Ceran St. Vrain and others. When Alexander Le Grand organized his first expedition to Santa Fe, Smith went along and got his first taste of the wild, free life in the West. He did not return. He became a trapper, married a Shoshone woman and settled down with the Indians on the Green River. During the 1820's, he acted as an agent for the St. Louis Fur Company and learned to speak several Native

American languages. He also gained prestige among the Shoshone by leading them to victory in a battle against the Ute.

Smith gained his infamous nickname in the late 1820's. While trapping for beaver, he and some of his party met up with some hostile Indians. Smith was shot and the bullet shattered the bones in his leg just above his ankle. The wound was so bad that he insisted that his companions amputate the limb but having no experience, they refused. Finally, Smith asked the camp cook to bring him a large knife and he amputated it himself, with assistance from the famous Milton Sublette. Smith was then carried by stretcher to his winter quarters on the Green River and used various herbs to heal the stump. In the spring of 1828, he made a rough wooden leg and from that point on was known as "Pegleg" to the whites and "We-he-to-ca" to the Indians.

Smith was still a young man at this time and while largely unimpaired by his injury, he found that his range as a trapper had been shortened. He temporarily began trading whiskey to the Shoshone, Snakes and the Utah to earn money and by doing this, he did not lose face with the other mountain men, who had engaged in the same business on occasion when trapping seasons were poor.

In 1829, he was with a large party of trappers under the leadership of Ewing Young, who would later play a large part in the settlement of Oregon, on the Virgin River near its junction with the Colorado. They were so successful that when the season was half over, Young dispatched Smith and Maurice LeDuc to Santa Fe, the nearest market, with a load of pelts. Instead of going to Santa Fe though, they crossed the Colorado at the future site of Fort Yuma and headed west to Los Angeles instead. The reason for this was unknown, other than that Smith had decided to steal the furs that had been entrusted to him and keep the money from them, which he proceeded to do. It was the turning point of his rather remarkable career and it placed on stigma on him from which he never recovered.

No one has ever been able to recreate the route that was taken by LeDuc and Smith as they crossed the desert. Mounted on mules and leading their pack animals, they encountered an unknown land of hills, craggy rocks and mountains and day after day of drifting sand. There was no water here, no trees and no trail to follow. At some point, according to Smith, they cached part of the furs in order to travel faster and in the desert, he claimed to see "three golden hills" and picked up his nuggets of "black gold". It is on this gold - an odd vein of very rich ore that appears to have a black paint or stain on it - and the three hills, that the foundation of the Pegleg legend has been built.

In 1829, Los Angeles, or the Pueblo de Nuestra Senora de los Angeles, was still a small Mexican village. Smith and LeDuc disposed of the furs to a sea captain to sell in China and now quite wealthy, Smith went on a protracted drunk. He was involved in one fight after another and at one point, even beat the proprietor of the Bella Union Hotel with his wooden leg. He and LeDuc were run out of town but they took several hundred head of horses with them when they went. They managed to make it to Taos with most of the horses and sold them off when they arrived.

For the next decade or so, Smith had no other business in California than stealing horses. He lived with the Indians and befriended Old Bill Williams, the mountain man and scout and Jim Beckwourth, the mulatto trader and frontiersman. Between them, they worked out a plan for horse-stealing in California that would surpass anything that had been attempted before. They arranged to rendezvous at Resting Springs, not far outside of Death Valley, on May 1, 1840 and brought a contingent of Indians with them. They slipped over the Cajon Pass without incident and on May 14, Juan Perez, the Administrator at the San Gabriel Mission, startled the authorities by announcing that every ranch in the valley from San Gabriel to San Bernardino had been stripped of its horses. A search was organized at once but the thieves had vanished. It was not until five days later that Governor Jose Antonio Carillo and 75 armed men set off on the trail. A battle occurred at Resting Springs a short time later and the California men were driven back. Smith lost only a few horses and the remainder of the herd, estimated to have been as many as 1,200 head of stock, was sold in Utah to traders and ranchers.

It was at this point in his life that many historians and treasure hunters believe Smith invented the "lost mine", a get-rich-quick scheme that used small bits of gold ore to lure investors into giving him money to develop the mine that he supposedly found. Most of these scholars believe that this is the reason that no one has ever found the Lost Pegleg Mine - because it doesn't really exist. But if this is the case, what about the black-stained gold that Smith brought to Los Angeles and what about the similar gold that has turned up in Borrego?

Whether the mine is truth or fiction, it is known that Smith engaged in some unsavory activities in the late 1840's and 1850's. By this time, the great Gold Rush of 1849 had passed him by and he had taken to hanging around San Francisco, a crippled drunk, cadging drinks and looking for handouts with promises of gold mines and vast amounts of wealth. Once, he tried to organize an expedition to recover the lost treasure in the desert but the plan failed before it even got started. He returned to San Francisco and died there in the county hospital in 1866. He was friendless, beaten and discredited and died in shame. But the Lost Pegleg Mine lived on without him and by 1875, it was one of the great lost mine stories of the southwest.

But this new interest in the mine came about in a strange way - it was discovered that there were actually two "Pegleg Smith's". This complicated the situation considerably and those who had discarded the story of the lost mine as nothing more than an old drunk's tall tale now had to re-examine the facts once again. Those who believed in the story were quick to point out how things had gotten so confused. Smith was a common name, they said, and many men had lost a limb in the Civil War, only to have it replaced with a wooden peg. This second

Pegleg had to have a beginning and it was soon agreed that Fort Yuma was the place.

The most popular version of the story has it that Pegleg was a civilian worker at the fort, since his missing leg would have prevented him from being an army deserter, so some stories have it. Supposedly, Smith stole a wagon, loaded with provisions, and drove north along the Colorado River to past Castle Dome, where he swam his mules across, pulled his wagon over and then hid out at a waterhole in the mountains. It was here that he discovered a ledge of dark, gold-bearing quartz. From time to time, he sold small quantities of the gold and bought supplies in San Bernardino.

In the summer of 1871, a deserter from Fort Yuma staggered into San Bernardino clutching a small bag of gold. He was put to bed in the local hospital and when he had recovered enough to talk, he told a doctor and a fellow patient that he had found a dead man in the desert with the gold beside him. The description of the dead man matched that of Pegleg Smith and everyone assumed that it was him. The soldier was unable to tell of where he found the body, since he knew no place names, but he was sure that he could find the place again once he recovered his health. The doctor soon organized a search party, in hopes that the body might lead them to the discovery of the mine, but the soldier died before he could provide any directions. The search went on without him but no dead man - and no lost mine - was ever found.

The lack of any discovery at all is likely what causes adventurers and desert rats, year after year, to roam the Borrego Badlands, searching for Pegleg's "three hills" and his lost mine. The stories have continued to be told over the years and the search continues on as well. Interestingly, it has been the search for the gold that has sparked other tales to be told over the years as well.

In the early 1900's, when the search for the Pegleg Mine was at a frenzy, another curious story began to be told around Borrego. It seemed that a terrifying ghost was chasing would-be prospectors out of the Badlands, the most popular area in southern California to search for the treasure.

The first man to see the phantom was Charley Arizona, an old desert hand who had seen pretty much everything that there was to see in the Badlands - or so he thought. One night, Charley was camping out on the western edge of the desert and something startled his burros into making a racket. Walking over to investigate, he spotted what he later described as an "eight-foot skeleton" lurching along about 200 yards to his east. The skeleton had a lantern-like flickering light coming from between its ribs and Charlie swore that he could hear its bones rattling as it disappeared over a ridge. This would be the first sighting of the mysterious apparition but it would not be the last.

The phantom showed up again about two years later, when several prospectors saw it shambling though some hills to the south of where Charlie Arizona's sighting had occurred. They forgot about the incident until a year afterwards, when another prospector spoke of seeing a giant skeleton with a light in its chest crossing the Badlands.

Soon, many of the Borrego prospectors knew of the skeleton and stories and speculations made the rounds for years. Eventually, two of the men decided to set out and see if they could track down the creature for themselves. On the third night of the hunt, they spotted an eerie light bobbing along the desert floor. As they approached it, they saw that it was the skeleton that they had heard about, running across the sand. They took off after it, chasing the apparition across the hills and down through arroyos. One of the men even fired several shots at it but after three miles, the skeleton lost its pursuers in the darkness.

The skeleton was seen infrequently after that, usually in the Badlands, and a story came to be told about it. It was, the stories recalled, the spirit of a man who prospected and died out on the desert. His body had been reduced to bones by the scavengers and the heat and now his ghost, in skeleton form, wanders the night on his old claim, chasing away the intruders.

Although the skeleton has not been reported in recent years, one has to wonder if perhaps he is still out there, watching over the lost mine that is said to exist in the Badlands. Could he be the ghost of Pegleg Smith himself? The soldier who died in San Bernardino claimed that the body of the dead man that he found looked like old Pegleg, so perhaps it is his ghost that chases miners away from the lost bonanza that awaits out there in the desert.

THE LOST GUNSIGHT MINE OF DEATH VALLEY

There are a number of stories concerning lost mines in the Death Valley region of California but none are as famous as the tales of the legendary Lost Gunsight. Hundreds of men have searched for the mine over the years but it has never been found. And during those years, many of the searchers have vanished into the land where it supposedly lies, never to be seen again. There were many sunken mounds on lonely mesas, some men claimed, which an old-timer would explain away tersely as "he was lookin' for the Gunsight" and offer little else.

The mine has been largely forgotten over the years, except to diehard treasure buffs, and so have the men who died for it. Death Valley is a lonely, brutal region and one that does not take trespassers - or prospectors - lightly.

The story of the Lost Gunsight began in 1849, when Captain Jefferson Hunt led a long and well-provisioned wagon train out of Salt Lake City and down the Old Spanish Trail to California. It was largely composed of Mormons who planned to colonize the San Bernardino Valley but among them were two parties of Gentiles, bound for the California gold fields. The parties became known in history as the Forty-Niners and the Jayhawkers and there were 46 of them in all, with most being of the Jayhawkers party. Oddly, the Jayhawkers, who had organized at Westport, Missouri, were not from Kansas, as most would think the nickname implies. The men had come mostly from Illinois, Georgia and Mississippi but perhaps the name had a different meaning at that time than it does now. It had first been used by Texas cattlemen from the 1840's to the days of the Civil War to signify border ruffians that they met while driving herds up the trail, but who knows why it was used for this group of prospectors?

By the time that Captain Hunt's wagon train reached Mountain Meadows, Utah, traveling south from the Great Salt Lake, the gold seekers were so unhappy with the continued southerly trek that they threatened to change direction on their own if the train did not change direction. They wanted to get to the gold fields in the west and Hunt was taking them too far out of the way towards southern California. But Hunt had seen Death Valley to the west and he warned the miners of the suffering and disaster that awaited them if they left. They knew nothing of the country through which they would have to pass but the men refused to heed his warnings.

On November 1, 1849, they parted company with the wagon train but they found the travel so bad that some of them turned back after a few days and rejoined Hunt. However, all of the Jayhawkers continued on, as did the men from the Wade, Brier and Bennett-Arcane parties, who came with the Forty-Niners. They pushed on but soon found it impossible to stay on course. Mountains turned them aside, as did the search for water, but they went on. They crossed Emigrant Valley, turned south around the Spotted Mountains and reached what was later to be known as Frenchman Flat.

Out ahead of the expedition was the dreaded Amargosa Desert and while already tired and weary, the men were determined, believing that the worst was behind them. They were wrong - but started off across the desert and spent days getting through the bleak Funeral Mountains that blocked the trail ahead of them. Finally, they looked down on the utter hell that Captain Hunt had warned they would have to cross - Death Valley. It is the lowest spot on the American continent, a parched wasteland with swirling winds, a scorching sun and blistering temperatures. The prospectors were no longer thinking of gold. They only wanted to escape from the terrible trap their foolishness and disregard had plunged them into.

To get their wagons through the miles of sand that stretched out in front of them was impossible. Even though it meant going it on foot, they burned their wagons and saved only their food, oxen and most important supplies. During the early morning hours, they set out and soon crossed a warm but palatable stream. It was the only running water they were going to see. Days of agony, thirst and despair awaited them and soon strife and dissension made matters worse when a group of the Forty-Niners, led by Captain Towne and Jim Martin, split away from the main group when they faced the towering barrier of the Panamint Mountains. They decided that rather than try to walk around the mountains, and spend even more time, they would scale them instead. After three days of trying to work their way through the precipices and chasms of Tucki Mountain, the party rejoined the Jayhawkers on what came to be known as White Sage Flats.

This was the final time when those who survived the Death Valley crossing were together at one time. They had come up from the desert by way of what was later called Emigrant Wash and proceeded through unnamed canyons to White Sage Flats. They were without water and food by the time they arrived there, having butchered and eaten the last of their oxen. As it happened, one of the men was able to kill a deer but the meat did not go far divided among so many. They took the killing of the animal as a sign though, believing that they might live to get out of the mountains and to cross the desert beyond. Even better, fortune smiled on them at White Sage Flats when it began to snow. They melted it and the skies gave them water to drink.

But good fortune did not last long. They were weak and undernourished, on the verge of starvation. To lighten their weight, they had stripped themselves of everything but their guns, canteens and the clothes on their backs. But winter had come to the high places and without their blankets, they suffered from the cold at night. The best these weakened men could manage was three or four miles each day and thankfully, they were unaware they had more than 70 miles to go. They only knew that for some of them, it would be too far, so to better their chances, they decided to split up into smaller groups of twos and threes.

After the first day of travel, they lost track of one another. Some were lucky and others were not. Those who made it across the desert assumed that the others had died and while they mourned their brethren, they celebrated their own success. After they had recuperated, they began the long trek north to the gold fields.

All though the diggings, stories were told of California-bound miners who had perished in the wastes of Death Valley. If the stories varied it was because they were told by widely separated survivors who still believed that only a few had come out alive. As it happened, the majority of them made it through and at least a year passed before this fact became common knowledge. By that time, only those who had survived the journey cared, for Californians had been swept up in the fury of the gold fields.

If the Forty-Niners and the Jayhawkers expedition was forgotten though, White Sage Flats was not. It was here where the legend of the Lost Gunsight was born. It came about on New Year's Day 1850 but at the time, the men who discovered it could not have cared less. They were half dead and starving and faced with a brutal ordeal - treasure was the last thing on their mind. Silver would be of no interest to them then, or even gold, but they would remember the occurrence years after.

There are several different versions of what took place. The most commonly told involves the deer that was killed by a prospector named Ash Bennett. As he was trying to shoot the animal, he raised his rifle and noticed that the gun sight had been lost. Picking up what he thought was a thin piece of shale, he wedged it in the sight slot and fired. Later, at White Sage Flats, he removed the makeshift sight to improve it and discovered that it was not shale at all, but pure silver. Half a dozen of the men handled it and asked where he had picked it up. "On the mesa a bit below," he told them. "The ground was black with the stuff."

Another version of the Bennett story says that he did not discover that his rifle site was a piece of silver until he took the weapon to a gunsmith at the Mariposa Mines to have a new sight made. The gunsmith recognized the metal at once and when he asked Bennett where it had come from, the miner is supposed to have said, "where I picked it up, there was a mountain of the stuff."

A third version of the story places the discovery of the silver in the hands of Captain Towne and claims that it occurred somewhere between the camp where the Towne-Martin party split away from the Jayhawkers and White Sage Flats. He was said to have been seated at the campfire making a new sight for his gun when someone asked him what he was making it from. "It's silver," he was reputed to say. "I could have picked up a carload from the mesa I was crossing."

In truth, it was the younger of two brothers named Turner was who killed the deer that was eaten at White Sage Flats but discrepancies in the stories soon vanished and they merged into one. Somewhere in the vicinity of the flats, it was believed, there was a great surface deposit of almost pure silver. With such a prospect, it was inevitable that a search for the Lost Gunsight would eventually be under way. Within a year after the last of the survivors had emerged from the desert, and had told of their adventure, an expedition was organized by one of the Turners in an effort to find the site. They promptly got lost and were not only unsuccessful but nearly starved to death as they made their way to Fort Tejon. Three or four of the men wanted to try again and so they enlisted the support of Dr. E. Darwin French, who financed a new expedition and left with it in September. They had an Indian to guide them and he got them as far as Darwin Falls and Darwin Wash (both later named for the doctor) and then refused to go any further, asserting that this was the last water they would find. After prospecting on the adjacent mesa, they turned back without finding the mesa that was "black with silver".

While this expedition had failed, the promise of wealth lured hundreds of others into the Panamints and the furnace of Death Valley. Many of these would-be miners actually found a few small outcrops of silver and managed to become wealthy, while many others left their bones where they fell, to whiten and bleach in the merciless sun. The ones who were successful contributed to the mining districts that led to silver strikes in the Panamints, Slate Range and Telescope Peak but they did not find the fabulous mesa where native silver could be "picked up by the carload."

Dr. Darwin French, from the second quest to find the Lost Gunsight, later left his Fort Tejon ranch and established a home at Oroville, in northern California, but he was not finished with the Lost Gunsight. He waited ten years before launching another expedition to try and find it and became the most acclaimed of the searchers who looked for the silver lode. More than any other, he explored the sun-baked sink of Death Valley and gave names to places that remain today like Darwin Wash, Darwin Falls, Bennett's Well, Towne's Pass, Furnace Creek and others. While living in Oroville, he had dreamed of finding the mesa and when the Comstock Lode, just across the border in Nevada, began disgorging huge amounts of silver, he could wait no longer. He knew the Lost Gunsight was out there, just waiting to be found.

Dr. French organized an expedition that would be prepared to spend months, not weeks, searching for it and he recruited his friend, Dr. Samuel G. George, to assist him. Together, they carefully chose 12 men and in the early spring of 1860, set out down the Sacramento Valley and the San Joaquin. When they reached Visalia, they turned up the south fork of the Kern River and then southwest to Walker's Pass. From there, they doubled back north to Indian Spring and Little Owens Lake and then northeast to Hot Mud Springs, across the Argus Mountains and on to what is now known as Darwin Canyon and Darwin Spring. After they explored the surrounding country, they crossed the head of the Panamint Valley, went over the Panamint Mountains through Towne's Pass and descended into Death Valley as far as Furnace Creek.

The expedition made a gallant effort to find the silver mesa, exploring more of the valley than any white men ever had before, but there was no sign of it. As they turned back, they searched the region around White Sage Flats with exhausting patience but the mesa could not be found.

Dr. French returned again the following year and was now no longer looking for just the silver mesa but also for a tribe of Indians who were reputed to be making their bullets from gold. He found neither. In the meantime though, his friend, Dr. George, had come back for another try with his own expedition. He crossed the Panamint Valley and reached Telescope Creek, the highest spot in Death Valley. With him was a young man named Dennis Searles, who with his brother, John, would make considerable history in Death Valley in years to come. Dr. George staked some claims in the valley but as far as the Lost Gunsight was concerned, his second try was no more successful than his first. He returned to Oroville and disappeared from the lore of the region.

The search was continued by others. Late in 1860, another doctor, Dr. Hugh McCormack, was in Panamint Valley and is believed to have crossed Death Valley as well. He turned up later with silver that he claimed had come from a "mountain that was seamed with silver" but was met with skepticism.

Better received were the attempts of three of the original Forty-Niners to find the Lost Gunsight. Ash Bennett led a small party in from near San Bernardino in 1861 but turned back before he got very far. J.W. Brier, a minister and one of the leaders of the Bennett-Arcane faction, took a small group in for a search in 1865 but returned in failure. In 1869, Bill Rhodes led another expedition to White Sage Flats but after weeks of searching, returned empty-handed.

William Lewis Manly, another of the original Forty-Niners, also came back to search for the Lost Gunsight. He later wrote that he came much closer to losing his life searching for the mine than he did making his way across Death Valley on the first journey. "Lost and without water and beaten to my knees," he wrote, "I was deserted by my companions and escaped death by a miracle."

Needless to say, Manly never found the Gunsight and neither has anyone else. If the great silver lode was ever there, it still is, for no one has ever loaded up a carload of it and carried it off. No other "lost mine" has ever fueled the imaginations of so many men over so long a period of time with no better evidence of its existence than a small piece of silver that was no bigger than the sight on a rifle. Regardless, this mine, real or not, was responsible for other strikes in the region. It's likely that they would never have been found if the hunt for the Lost Gunsight had not drawn scores of prospectors and developers into the deadly and dehydrated region where a bucket of water left in the sun will evaporate in an hour.

It is certain that the search for the mine hastened the discovery of Death Valley's multimillion dollar borax industry and made it world famous. Borax is a naturally occurring mineral made from sodium, boron, oxygen and water and was widely used in cleaning powders that were popular for decades. It was not until recently that it began to fall out of fashion. Years ago, almost everyone kept a box of borax around the house and all were familiar with popular advertising icons like the "20 Mule Team".

John Searles came to Death Valley with Dr. George's expedition in 1860 and got his first look at the country. He and his brother, Dennis, returned together later and began developing some gold and silver claims in the Slate Range that overlooked a marsh, from which they boiled water for drinking purposes. They remained here until 1880, taking a comfortable living from the ground.

For nearly a dozen years, they often sat in front of their cabin in the evening and gazed without interest at the muck-filled swamp before them without ever suspecting that a fortune lay at the bottom of the slope. In 1875, Isadore Daunet had discovered borax in Death Valley but it was not until Aaron Winters found borax on Furnace Creek and sold his claim to the Pacific Coast Borax Company for $20,000 that Daunet returned from Arizona, filed on a number of claims and began a refining plant that he called Eagle Borax Works.

It was only then that John Searles began to wonder if the rim of crystals on the pots that he and his brother boiled swamp water in might be borax. Tests showed that it was and he and Dennis filed mineral claims on what they named Borax Lake, later to be known as Searles lake. They were soon shipping borax to Mojave by wagon and this was only the beginning. The American Potash and Chemical Co. moved in and established the town of Trona (coined from natron, the scientific name of sodium carbonate) to house its processing plants and workers. The products that have their origin here kept the region thriving for years after.

Like all of the others, Dennis and John Searles did not find the Lost Gunsight but had they not searched for it, they likely would not have found themselves at the edge of Death Valley. In their case, the Lost Gunsight paid off after all - even though they never found a single piece of its silver.

THE LOST SAN SABA AND BOWIE MINES OF TEXAS

The legends of Texas are filled with accounts of lost mines and mysterious piles of buried silver and most of these accounts begin in antiquity when Spain, and later Mexico, held sovereignty in the region. The stories are filled with history and much in the way of lore as well. Of all of these mines though, none has engaged the attention of as many men, and been as desperately sought, as the Lost San Saba. It is not only a mine but a cave in which a fortune in silver bars lies buried. In Texas, it is as equally well known as the Lost Bowie Mine, which some believe may be one and the same.

The stories of these two lost treasures are drenched in blood - Mexican, Spanish and American alike - and remain a great mystery to this day.

The legend of the land where the San Saba treasure is believed to be - between the Almagres Hills and the Mission San Saba de la Santa Cruz, on the south bank of the San Saba River - has its beginnings in February 1756. It was at this time that Don Bernardo de Miranda, lieutenant general of the province of Texas, accompanied by a small company of soldiers, five civilians of consequence, an interpreter and a few laborers, set out from the small settlement of San Fernando (San Antonio) "with orders from the governor to investigate thoroughly the mineral riches so long rumored on the Llano River". They traveled for eight days to the northwest until they reached the Arroyo San Miguel, known today as Honey Creek, a tributary of the Llano. From the camp they erected, the Cerro del Almagres were less than a mile to the north.

A cave was opened into the mountain that revealed traces of silver. It was explored thoroughly and prospected and with unwarranted optimism, Miranda wrote, after his return to San Fernando three weeks later, and told the Viceroy at Mexico City that the mines "are so rich that I guarantee to give every settler in the province of Texas a full claim." He stated that the vein of silver appeared to be of immeasurable thickness and that everything was on hand for conducting mining operations, including good pasture for livestock, land for crops and an abundance of wood and water. He recommended that an outpost of 30 men be established there to "guarantee the protection of the miners against the Indians."

With his report, he sent several pounds of ore to be assayed but he heard nothing in reply. After waiting two months, Miranda journeyed to Mexico City and presented his petition again, this time in person, to the Viceroy. His samples of ore had been assayed by Manuel de Aldaco, a wealthy mine owner, and had been found to be of considerable value. But Aldaco pointed out to the Viceroy that three pounds of handpicked ore did not provide any proof of a large deposit. He suggested that 30 loads of ore be transported to the nearest smelter, which just happened to be over 700 miles away from Texas, and that the cost of the transportation be covered by Miranda and his partners. The partners were the five civilians who had accompanied Miranda on his expedition. They came to Mexico City with him and protested the cost of bringing the silver to Mexico, insisting that it should be financed by the Crown. In the end, they agreed to underwrite the operation and in November 1757, the Viceroy accepted their offer.

But there was more to the slow and time-consuming problems than Miranda and his associates suspected. The Viceroy has used his wealthy friend Aldaco to discourage Miranda for he had no intention of building a fort at Honey Creek. At the same time that Miranda and his men were waiting in Mexico City, the Spanish government, without their knowledge, had established an outpost called San Luis de las Amarillas on the north bank of the San Saba River. It was completed in June 1757, months before Miranda was given permission to have his ore tested at his own expense.

With high hopes, Miranda returned to Texas, only to be dispatched on urgent business to the eastern part of the province - before he ever learned that someone else was going to be mining his discovery. After that, he disappears from the story of the Lost San Saba Mine.

A month or so after the fort was established, Captain Diego Ortiz de Parrilla, the commander of San Luis de las Amarillas, asked permission to move his garrison to the Llano River, closer to where Spanish settlers were, but this was denied. Some have speculated that the authorities in Mexico City wanted to keep the soldiers closer to the silver deposit, although history has recorded that this garrison was actually established to provide a buffer between settlers and the Comanche Indians.

The outpost had been constructed from the recently abandoned San Xavier Mission on the San Gabriel River. Two other missions were also closed at this time because of, in the words of the church "internal disorder", and were consolidated into a new mission on the San Saba. It was called Mission San Saba de la Santa Cruz with Padre Alonso Giralde de Terreres as the superior.

The shifting of the missions hints of further intrigue involving the silver deposits. It becomes more clear when it is learned that Pedro Romero de Terreres, a wealthy and experienced mining man and cousin to the mission priest, was in charge of the removal and the building of the Mission San Saba de la Santa Cruz. It was located just three miles downriver from the military outpost on the south side of the river. Later, a second mission was built four miles below the first. Of course, the main purpose of the mission was to convert the Apache and Comanche Indians to Christianity but this concentration of power in so small an area suggests that something else was at stake here that needed to be developed and protected. However, nothing was ever developed for after 12 years of almost incessant raids and warfare with the Indians, they were forced to leave San Saba in 1769. The year after the second mission was built, it was attacked and destroyed by the Comanche.

Prior to this, three of the six Franciscans who had been stationed on the San Saba were ordered to return to Mexico and the three who remained attempted to till their irrigated fields with assistance from their converts. However, the Comanche attacked again and again. Captain Parrilla would always appear with his soldiers and drive them off but after camping in the mission yard for a few days, he would return to his fort. He would no sooner be gone before the Comanche would return, killing and driving off livestock and destroying the fields.

Parrilla felt helpless and unable to defend the mission, he ordered the priests to close it and return to Mexico. Knowing he had no authority over them, they defied him until March 1758, when the Comanche settled the dispute for them. Several hundred warriors attacked the mission and burned it down, slaughtering everyone inside except for the few who managed to make it upriver. This inflated the population of the fort, which now housed nearly 400 people, including soldiers, priests, laborers, traders and others. The Indians, rallied by their success, attacked the outpost but were cut down by the soldier's guns. Before darkness fell, the Comanche had lost more than 300 warriors. During the night, they removed their dead and wounded and then renewed the attack at dawn. The fort managed to put up such a defense that they were forced to leave.

Parrilla seized the opportunity to rid himself of the three troublesome Franciscans from the second mission and he sent them south to Mexico with a load of bullion along what came to be called the Silver Trail. The expedition struck southward to the Llano River and on to the Frio and the Nueces. The tracks from what became a well-used trail were cut so deep that they were still visible into the middle part of the last century.

After destroying the mission, the Indians were more determined to burn the outpost and drive the Spanish from the region. They ran off livestock, destroyed crops and interfered as much as possible with the smelting and transportation of the silver bars that were being produced on the San Saba. The decade that followed brought no peace and little security to the inhabitants of the fort and by the spring and summer of 1768, the Presidio San Luis de las Amarillas was practically under siege. The only lull in the fighting came when the Comanche left to follow the buffalo herds and to secure meat for the winter. Captain Parrilla seized the opportunity to send his entire horse herd across the Rio Grande and into the province of Coahuilla for safety. The horses were returned in the spring and by this time, preparations of the evacuation of the fort were complete.

In April 1769, the outpost was abandoned and the long march to the Rio Grande began. This marked the end of any Spanish involvement with the Lost San Saba Mine and the cavern of buried silver bars. Whether the Spaniards spent the winter months concealing the mine and the rich cache they were leaving behind or whether it was done by the Comanche when they destroyed the fort, remains uncertain. Someone hid the cave so that anyone who came looking for it would be thwarted and whoever it was, their methods were clever. Author J. Frank Dobie wrote of three old men who lived in Menard, Texas and who claimed that, as boys, they played in a water hole below the fort and often stood on a cannon barrel that was beneath the surface. When the water was drained in 1927, no cannon was found. Earlier than this, according to Dobie, a man named Burnum had lost $1,500 in pumping dry a cave north of the old fort and had emptied a lake in Menard with no better luck at finding the treasure. It seems possible that whoever hid the mine managed to divert the river in order to conceal it. In this case, it was likely the Spaniards who did it but regardless, whoever erased all 12 years of mining along the little San Saba River did so to such an extent that the Lost San Saba still remains a mystery.

Following the withdrawal of the Spanish from the region, the tales of the old mine had a wide circulation among the Spanish-speaking residents of Texas. They often talked and dreamed about it but it was not until the first American adventurers appeared in the area between 1810 and 1812 that efforts started to be made to find it. Using what was left of the Presidio San Luis de las Amarillas to guide them, several expeditions were launched.

It is generally agreed that the first of the Americans to see the Lost San Saba was Harp Perry, a former member of a small army of Americans who had ridden into Texas with the purpose of freeing it from Spanish rule and establishing an independent state. This was actually the second attempt to do this. The first, led by Phillip Nolan in 1799, had been poorly supported and was crushed. The second, led by Augustus Magee and aided by Mexican revolutionaries, captured San Antonio and defeated the Royalists in several small engagements. They were ultimately overpowered and dispersed though and the surviving remnants found safely in the wild regions north of the city.

One of these groups, led by Harp Perry and another American whose name has been forgotten, struck west up the Llano River and made it to the fort on the San Saba. They continued on as far as the Little Llano and found evidence of mining that was probably the first diggings started by Miranda in 1756. Giving up any thought of looking for the Lost San Saba, they settled here instead and built what Perry later called a "furnace" in which to smelt ore, some gold and mostly silver. They fashioned the metal into crude bars and buried, Perry claimed, over 1,000 pounds of gold and silver under the ground. Soon after, the expedition was slaughtered by Comanche and only Perry and the other American escaped with their lives.

Perry's story of the years that followed is largely a mystery. He claims to have made his way to Mexico and lived there through the Mexican Revolution, the Mexican-Texas struggle, the Mexican War and the Civil War. Wherever he was, and many believe that he was in St. Louis for an extended period, he was back in Texas in 1865, looking for the treasure that he had helped to bury. He soon discovered that he had waited too long to come back. Out on the Llano River, the Indians were still a menace but this was the only thing that had not changed. Soil erosion and thickets of brush had altered the country and after a year of being unable to orient himself, he gave up. He was too old to continue and catching on with a trail outfit that was heading north towards Kansas, he started back to St. Louis. He was never to reach it however, for somewhere north of Red River Station, he was killed by an accidental discharge of his own pistol.

If any other expeditions took place between the time when the mines were hidden and the massacre of Harp Perry's party, history has not recorded them. But the mines were not forgotten. In November 1831, James Bowie was to touch them with his own fame and to give them immortality in the legends of Texas.

There is no question that James Bowie is a larger than life character in the history of Texas, although much of what has been written about him is little more than folklore. No one ever saw him ride alligators, spear wild cattle or fight deadly duels in dark rooms with his fearsome Bowie knife. In truth, Bowie and his brother, Rezin, trafficked illegal slaves with pirate Jean Lafitte and was widely considered to be arrogant, pompous and always ready to face death in his search for great wealth - which never came his way. On the other hand, he was also a remarkable man, who was courageous and brave to the point of foolhardiness and he gave his life in glory at the Alamo.

Bowie had been born in the hills of Tennessee and he drifted west with his brother into Arkansas and Louisiana. When they came west to Texas in 1828, they prospected for gold and silver far beyond the last settlements on the upper Nueces and Frio Rivers. He lived with the Apache for a time and it was during this period that he learned of the Comanche and the old Spanish mine at San Saba.

When Jim Bowie set out from San Antonio for the Indian country in November 1831, it was with the intention of finding the mine. His brother was with him and they were accompanied by nine carefully chosen men. One of these was Cephas Ham, who would later contradict much of Bowie's account of the expedition and after Bowie's death at the Alamo, would claim to have complete knowledge of what came to be called the Lost Bowie Mine. Ham flatly denied the widely believed story that Bowie was living with the Apache and they had shown him the cave where Spanish treasure was stored with "silver bars so high that a man on horseback could not look over them." Instead, he claimed that it had been he (Ham) who had been adopted by the Comanche and that he often heard them taking about a great Spanish treasure that was near the old fort. He also insisted that it was Rezin Bowie who was the only white men so see the lost treasure. Ham said that Rezin had made a previous trip to San Saba and had not only seen where the silver was stored but had found the mine and, with his tomahawk, had hacked off samples of ore to be assayed. The report that came back said that the ore was very rich and James Bowie organized an expedition and set out at once. Ham said that Bowie had pretended to befriend him but really only wanted to trick him into coming along the expedition because of his prior knowledge of the lost mine.

There was little truth in what Ham would go on to claim. There is no record that Rezin Bowie ever previously visited the site and if he had, then the expedition would have likely known where it was going when it left San Antonio. As it was, it took them three weeks to travel a distance that should have taken only a few days. Bowie would later say that they took so long because they "were examining the nature of the country." He does not say what they were "examining" during that time but it appears that neither he nor his brother knew how to find the old fort.

It's likely that the nearest that the Bowie party got to the Spanish fort was Calf Creek, in today's McCulloch County, about 20 miles east of San Luis de las Amarillas. There, at dawn on November 19, their camp was attacked by several hundred Comanche. They were taken by surprise, even though they had believed that a group of Indians were approaching them for several days. Luckily, their camp had been chosen for its defensive position. They had a thicket in front of them that ran down to the creek and a cave in the hillside at their back, where they hid the horses. The fight lasted all day and the Indians were badly beaten. Several of Bowie's men were wounded and one, a man named Buchanan, was shot in the leg and wounded so badly that he could not ride. The party waited on Calf Creek for a week, waiting on their friend to mend, and then returned to San Antonio no richer than when they had left.

After returning to San Antonio, Bowie claimed that he had found the cached silver of the Spanish. He offered no proof of it but his name was enough to enable him to put together a second expedition in the spring and head for San Saba. He reached the ruins of the San Luis de las Amarillas without difficulty but told his men that rain or the Indians had erased all sign of the cave that he had claimed to find. Some said that he only "pretended" not to be able to find it and that he took his bearings and planned to return a third time with a smaller party and less men with whom to divide the spoils. When he returned empty-handed to San Antonio this time though, the Texas War for Independence was at hand. The part that Bowie played in that has become history.

After the war had ended, the site of the battle between the Bowie expedition and the Comanche began to be questioned. Fire had burned off the thickets along Calf Creek but the hill and the cave were still there, as well as a hastily built cover that had been used so that the men could fire from shelter. In spite of this, Ham insisted that the battle had taken place on Jackson Creek, six miles east of the old fort. To the surprise of many, Rezin Bowie agreed with him. Searchers even managed to find a location with a hill and a cave, and even a stone fortification, that matched the account. Ham and Rezin may have even been right, for if the party had been heading for San Luis de las Amarillas, then the battle could have logically taken place within six miles of the outpost instead of almost 20.

As it has turned out though, it did not matter, since the whole area soon came to be regarded as the site of the Old Spanish Mine and it was even given a new name. It was no longer referred to as the Lost San Saba Mine but became the Lost Bowie Mine instead.

Bowie's name was enough to keep interest alive in the lost treasure until the Comanche and the Kiowa lost their hold on the country. Cattlemen were moving into the region and as the cattle came, the Indians were driven out. Once they ceased to be a menace on the San Saba, the search for the Lost Bowie began in earnest. Anything that looked like a walled-up cave was opened and explored. The man who found an old ax head or a piece of broken bit of stirrup was convinced that he was close to the bonanza. The stories were told and re-told and became more incredible as the years passed. Many of the tales were printed in newspapers as true stories and as a result, the Lost Bowie was repeatedly "found". Some of the tales that sent a continuing and ever increasing number of treasure seekers into the San Saba hills were the creation of entertaining liars - but not all of them. A justice of the Texas Supreme Court, successful lawyers and ranchers, men of wealth, took time off from their regular occupations to join the adventure of the missing Spanish silver.

The last best chance for finding the mine likely died many years ago. A piece of vital information was discovered by a man named Moses Grumble, an old Indian fighter, who had a ranch on the San Saba River. He lived about 75 miles below the old fort but it was not quite far enough away for him to not have an interest in the Lost Bowie Mine. From some unknown source, Grumble learned that a Mexican woman, who had been a captive of the Comanche for years until a comanchero had purchased her freedom, was living in San Antonio. She was quite elderly now but he went to see her in hopes that she might be able to shed some light on what happened to the Spanish silver.

The woman talked freely but she could not tell him where the silver was taken from the ground. She said that it was very near to the old fort and that the Comanche went there four or five times a year to take some of it. The women in the tribe would go and wait at a certain place on Los Moros Creek while the men continued on. They would not wait for long, she told him, and when they returned they would have silver, which the women would carry to camp.

Grumble was sure that if she could show him the place where the women had waited, then he could find the mine. He made arrangements with her and her husband and they agreed to accompany him to the site of the fort. When they reached the village of San Saba, a week later, Grumble stayed at the hotel and they made their own camp. In the morning, the rancher stepped into the saloon to have a drink and came face to face with an old and bitter enemy. Both men drew their guns at the same time and Grumble fell to the floor dead.

The Mexican woman took this as a sign that she should talk no more and she and her husband returned to San Antonio. In the months after, other men offered to pay her well to show them to the creek she called "Los Moros" but she refused. She died a year later and with her died the best hope of ever finding the silver of San Luis de las Amarillas.

In the early 1900's, the San Saba River attracted the attention of even more amateur treasure hunters and curiosity-seekers. They explored and dug everywhere and found nothing. Piece by piece, they also carried off what remained of the ruins from the old fort until there was little left to mark the spot. The last link to the buried silver had vanished and the story was banished to the occasional back page of the newspaper and to the stuff of folklore.

But what if the Lost San Saba, the famed Lost Bowie, is not merely the creation of storytellers and cowboys? If it is genuine - and most experts believe it to be - then that means that it's still out there somewhere, waiting for the right person to stumble upon the "bars of silver stacked higher than a man on a horse".

THE LOST PADRE MINE

One of the oldest legends of Spanish treasure buried in the southwest haunts the Franklin Mountains near the border city of El Paso, Texas. These chiseled mountains hide many tales and dark secrets and not the least of which is that of the Lost Padre Mine, a fabulously wealthy gold cache that is filled with ancient treasure as well.

Men have searched for this treacherous mine almost since the day it was first hidden but it has yet to be found. According to legend, it is protected by a curse and by the spirits of three Spanish padres who were buried alive in the mountain to protect the treasures of the church from plunderers.

The legend began in 1659, a year that saw the establishment of the Mission Nuestra Senora de Guadalupe in El Paso del Norte, now Ciudad Juarez, Mexico. The mission church was constructed and the padres from the church were used to supervise the minion operation that was going on in the nearby Franklin Mountains. Each morning, seven of the priests would cross the Rio Grande and oversee the labor in the mine. The ore from the mine was transported down the mountain to the river, where it was smelted into ingots and shipped to Mexico City, then on to Spain.

The mission was completed in seven months and a large, 35-foot bell tower was added to the church. Each morning, one of the priests would enter the tower and summon the others to prayer. The tower, it was said, offered a view into the mountains and of the entrance to the gold mine.

For several years, the mission existed in the region, converting the natives to Christianity and producing several mule loads of gold each month for the Church. However, a dire message was received by the padres that the Pueblo Indians in what is now New Mexico had revolted against their Spanish masters, killing hundreds and driving the rest out of the province. Several priests who had escaped fled south toward Mexico and along the way, spread the word to other missions that the Pueblo were gathering and planned to massacre all of the Spanish in the entire region.

The priests of the Mission Nuestra Senora de Guadalupe quickly went into action. They began loading up the chalices, gold candlesticks, platters and a large store of gold ingots they had accumulated and carried it all across the river to hide it in the mine. The stories say that it took as many as 250 mule loads to carry all of the wealth and valuables from the church to the mine. Once it was all secreted in the mine shaft, the priests and laborers hauled mud from the banks of the Rio Grande and filled it in as much of the mine as possible with the thick, wet silt. Then they took great pains to disguise the entrance by covering it with rocks and boulders so that it looked like a natural part of the mountainside.

Legend also has it that three of the priests volunteered to be buried alive inside of the mine shaft so that they could protect the holy valuables of the church from thieves. It is said that their ghosts remain here still.

It was not until 1692 that the Spanish finally managed to put down the Pueblo uprising and re-take the region. When peace was restored to the Rio Grande Valley near El Paso del Norte, priests returned to open the mine again but were unable to find it. Most of the original padres from the mission had been killed in the fighting and others had returned to Spain. There was nothing left to point the way to the mine but a poorly drawn map that turned out to be inaccurate. The mission priests searched for the mine for weeks but were unable to find the entrance. Eventually, the gold mine faded in importance and the priests became involved in other activities and forgot about it completely.

In 1881, a group of men from El Paso reportedly discovered some documents in the archives of the old mission in Juarez that told of a mine in the Franklin Mountains. The men also claimed to find substantiating records of the existence of the mine in Spain as well. With this information in hand, they financed several organized expeditions into the mountains but, time after time, met with failure. As many would do after them, they left the mountains empty-handed.

The next search for what came to be dubbed the Lost Padre Mine took place in 1888. A man named Robinson claimed to have located the mine shaft by standing in the old bell tower of the mission and looking for evidence of trails leading up into the canyons of the mountain. He selected a point in a canyon that could be seen from the tower and when he arrived there, he found that a large amount of debris appeared to have been moved to cover a part of the rock face of the canyon. With great effort, Robinson removed tons of rock and according to his story, discovered the entrance to the mine. His claims managed to get him some financial backing and he hired men to come in and remove what appeared to be layers of river silt from the shaft. They worked for several days, slowly making progress, but then inexplicably, his financial backer pulled out and abandoned the effort. In a fit of anger, Robinson had his men refill the shaft with silt and again cover the opening with rocks. The mine was once more "lost".

The next "discovery" of the mine was by L.C. Criss, who announced that he had found it in 1901. With the aid of an old manuscript that he had found in Juarez, he had searched for the mine for 14 years before locating the entrance, which was covered with rocks. Once the rocks were removed, Criss brought in men to remove the river mud and with a great deal of time and effort, excavated more than 125 feet of the shaft. During the digging, they found a number of Spanish artifacts, including a spur and an ancient anvil, which was enough to convince him that he was on track.

At the end of the shaft, Criss encountered two more tunnels going in opposite directions and each of them was walled up with adobe bricks. The men tore through one of the walls and removed more dirt fill for another 20 feet or so. During this part of the excavation, Criss noted that the old shaft was not well-supported and appeared very dangerous. He told his foreman that he was going to El Paso to buy some timbers to shore up the tunnel and left instructions for everyone to stay outside until he returned. One of the workers though, apparently believing that they were close to the treasure, began digging again as soon as Criss left. Moments later, the ceiling collapsed, burying the man alive and filling most of the tunnel with fallen rock. Unable to continue and out of money, Criss abandoned the site and left El Paso, never to be heard from again.

The last public expedition took place in 1968, when a Spiritualist minister named Ray Martin, his wife, and an assistant named McKinney arrived in El Paso from California. They announced that they knew the location of the Lost Padre Mine and would start their excavations in a few days. Reverend Martin claimed that he had obtained some old Spanish documents that revealed the location of the mine, as well as an inventory of the items from the mission that the priests had hidden in the shaft.

Martin rented some heavy machinery and with a crowd of the curious and two local television crews looking on, he began excavating a trench down into the rock at a point on the mountain not far from a well-traveled road. Tons of rock were removed from the trench until it was about 15 feet deep. At this point, Martin climbed down into the hole and began using his hands to remove an accumulation of loose soil. After scraping for a few moments, the outline of a shaft became visible. McKinney joined the Reverend and they began working with shovels. It took them about two hours to remove 10 feet of the fill and they revealed what appeared to be a shaft leading into the mountain. Excited by the discovery, some of the onlookers jumped down into the trench to help with the digging, which went on for about another three hours. Finally though, a local official arrived on the scene and stated that not only was the excavation hazardous, it was also illegal since it was so close to the road. Despite pleading and argument from Reverend Martin, the digging was halted and the trench was filled back in. Despondent, Martin abandoned his dream and returned to California.

Since that time, only hobbyists and amateur treasure hunters have ventured out to the mountains to search for the Lost Padre, which is unusual considering the vast amounts of wealth that may be hidden here. If the stories of the mine are to be believed - and they do seem possible if we accept that the accounts of the shafts that have been discovered are true - then the Lost Padre Mine is still there, just waiting to be uncovered. Protected by ghosts or not, it is hard to believe that no one is still seeking it!

LOST GOLD OF DEVIL'S CANYON

The Wichita Mountains of southwestern Oklahoma are comprised of several jumbles of jagged rocks and peaks that have been the scene of death, violence and madness over the course of several centuries. The rugged vastness of the range made it a perfect fortress for the Comanche, Kiowa and Wichita Indians and they found abundant game and water here, as well as a natural barrier against the encroaching white settlers. The Spanish came here first and while they were eventually driven out by the Indians, they managed to remove a vast fortune in silver and gold before they retreated.

According to both history and legend, much of that gold was found in a place dubbed Devil's Canyon - a forbidding gorge located at the western end of the Wichita Mountain range. The canyon is flanked by Flat Top Mountain and Soldier's Peak, which keeps it almost perpetually in the shade, lending a dark and ominous atmosphere to the rocky, brush-choked canyon floor. The Native Americans believed that the Devil himself dwelt in this canyon and so it's no surprise that in more recent times, stories of ghosts have come to be told as well. This eerie place is believed to be haunted by the spirits of those who died here and they remain to watch over the gold that lies hidden in the cliffs and rocks. Somewhere in this canyon, among the rocks and the bones of the men who were killed trying to find it, is an old Spanish mine that would make its discoverer wealthy beyond his wildest dreams.

Should he survive to spend the loot, that is....

The first white men saw Devil's Canyon around 1629, when a Spanish mission was established by Padre Juan de Salas. The priest, along with a few Indian converts, tried to grow fields of corn and beans near the mouth of the canyon, where a stream empties into the North Fork of the Red River. The mission remained for a few years but then a prolonged drought forced it to be abandoned. Juan de Salas and the other priests packed up and planned to return to Mexico - but they never arrived. They simply vanished without a trace in the desert.

The canyon remained quiet until 1650, when it was visited by a detachment of soldiers led by Captain Hernan Martin and adventurer Don Diego del Castillo. They searched the area for any sign of gold and silver and, encouraged by the presence of rich ore, they sent a dispatch to their superiors in Mexico City. However, no one would return to being mining the area for seven years. In 1657, a Spanish priest named Gilbert arrived at the canyon with a contingent of 100 men, including both soldiers and laborers. They began mining gold from the canyon and sank a large shaft that was over 100 feet deep into the rock of one canyon wall. Several mule loads of rich ore were taken from the mine but constant attacks by the Indians eventually forced them to close the mine and abandon the area. The mine was well-marked on maps and turned over to the authorities in Mexico City for future development.

Strangely, more than 40 years passed before the Spanish returned but when they did, they came in a detachment of more than 100 men, plus 50 soldiers to defend the miners from the Indians. Wagons were used to bring in mining equipment and the group marched inland from the ocean to the Wichita Mountains. Following a set of charts and maps, they arrived at Devil's Canyon after a journey of several weeks. When they arrived, they set up a permanent camp and built several buildings from adobe and rock, a church and a primitive smelter located in a nearby cave. As the Spaniards mined and smelted the ore, the canyon was visited several times by the Indians. When they realized that the white men were only interested in the gold, which was of no use to them, an uneasy truce was established that allowed the Spanish to remain. However, it only lasted for a short time. As the months passed, the relationship grew strained. Occasionally, the soldiers would leave the canyon to hunt and would encounter Indians. Often, violent skirmishes followed and soon the Spanish were forced to post guards around the settlement at night.

On several occasions, pack trains that were laden with gold bullion left the canyon and proceeded to a port on the gulf, where the ore was shipped to Spain. The party then returned to the canyon with more supplies. Early one winter morning, a pack train of 50 mules left Devil's Canyon and started out along the trail. As the last mule passed the final outcropping of rocks, more than 300 Indians fell upon the pack train. The miners and the soldiers from the settlement armed themselves and ran to assist their comrades but they were greatly outnumbered. The Spanish contingent, save for three men who managed to escape, were slaughtered in the canyon that morning. The area was now completely abandoned and for more than 200 years afterward, it was said that skeletons wearing pieces of Spanish armor were commonly found scattered in the rocks and brush of Devil's Canyon.

For more than five decades after the massacre, no one entered the canyon save for a few hunting parties. In 1765, a French explorer of the area made friends with the Comanche and he was told about the destruction of the Spanish company. He noted in his journals that he saw the canyon, its abandoned and ruined buildings and even the remains of the mines. Even though other travelers and explorers would follow in his wake, no one attempted to re-open the mines until the 1830's.

At that time, a party of Mexicans moved into the canyon and established a camp. The stories say that these men were led by a descendant of one of the three Spanish soldiers who survived the massacre years earlier. That man passed on maps and descriptions of great wealth to his family and in 1833, one of his grandchildren decided to use them. In the summer of 1834, the Mexicans were preparing to leave the canyon with several dozen mules that were loaded down with gold. Before they could though, they were attacked by dozens of Kiowa warriors. As the battle erupted, several of the Mexicans worked to conceal the entrance of the mine by causing a rock slide. This accomplished, they ran to the mouth of the canyon to help the others but arrived too late. The battle was over and the Mexicans had been slain. As the Kiowa went from body to body, removing scalps, the surviving men concealed themselves in the rocks and waited for a chance to escape. After taking the scalps and stripping the bodies of the dead men, the Indians turned the pack train and unloaded the ore. As the Mexicans watched, they hid it in a small cave in the canyon wall and then concealed it with rocks and debris until the entrance could no longer be seen. Once the Kiowa departed, the miners set out on foot to Mexico.

One of the survivors returned in 1850, bringing another, smaller group of men with him. On their first evening at the canyon, they set up camp just inside of the entrance and in the morning, began searching for the cache the Indians had hidden years before. As the men dug into the hillside, two young boys were sent to a trading post that was located about seven miles upriver to get supplies. When the boys were only about a half-mile from the canyon though, they hard shots and screams coming from where the men were digging. They raced back and arrived in time to see a band of Kiowa attacking the searchers. The boys turned and ran to the trading post for help but by the time they returned with a group of men, the entire search party had been killed and mutilated.

By the early 1870's, white settlers had started to move in to the Wichita

Mountains region. Several large ranches were established and the United States Army began patrolling the area in an effort to keep the settlers safe. Around this same time, a man named J. C. Settles began homesteading near Devil's Canyon. While tending his cattle, he noted the crumbling ruins of the old Spanish mission and curious, he asked a couple of the Indians who remained in the area about the site. Settles had befriended these men and several of them even worked for him on his ranch at times. One day, an older Kiowa man showed Settles the ruins and told him about the battle with the Mexicans years before. He also took the rancher back into the canyon and showed him where the miners had sunk a shaft into the canyon wall, following a large vein of gold. At the time, Settles was interested in cattle, not in mining, but several years later, he did make an effort to locate the site again. He found an ancient mine shaft with a huge boulder wedged into the entrance. With great difficulty, he managed to blast it from the opening and inside, he found a human skeleton and a coal-like substance that he couldn't identify. Without having any of the ore from the mine assayed, Settles abandoned it and never returned.

As the years passed, more and more people became interested in the story of the Lost Spanish Mine in Devil's Canyon and came searching for it. Prospectors and curiosity-seekers dug in the rock and hammered at the stone canyon walls and all of them went away disappointed. In 1900, an elderly Kiowa woman was seen hiking near Devil's Canyon, looking for specific landmarks. When questioned, she claimed that when she was a young girl, she had accompanied the band of Kiowa that had attacked and killed the Mexican miners in 1834. She had helped to conceal the pack loads of gold after the battle and was now searching for it. She never found the cache but some claim that they have...

In the years that followed, there was a new surge of interest in the Lost Spanish Mine and the gold cache. There was a brief flurry of prospecting and mining here around 1906 and one man claimed that he had discovered an 85-pound nugget of gold in Devil's Canyon. There were few other success stories though and eventually, interest died. Legends and lore took the place of truth and soon tales were told of ghosts and of a layer of human skeletons that guarded the gold.

This aspect of the lost treasure legend got several men excited back in the late 1960's. One day in 1967, a young boy was hiking in the canyon and came upon several human skeletons that had been exposed by heavy rains the previous week. He found the grisly collection of bones lying among rocks and mud along the canyon wall. Thinking that he had stumbled upon some old and abandoned graveyard, he didn't investigate any further, but he did mention it to some friends two years later. On hearing the story, a group of men who were familiar with the legends of Devil's Canyon and believed the skeletons might mark the location of treasure, hiked into the gorge. They spent several days trying to locate the bones but too much time had passed and they were unsuccessful.

Since that time, there have been no further discoveries that might lead to the discovery of either the Spanish mine or the cache of gold that was hidden by the Kiowa. Today, Devil's Canyon is a part of Quartz Mountain State Park and is frequently visited by hikers, rock collectors and the curious. Most of them walk through this sometimes unsettling canyon without having any idea what might be buried just beneath their feet.

LOST PLUNDER OF SAMUEL MASON

The years of the late 1700's and early years of the 1800's are almost a lost time on the American frontier. In those days, the frontier regions of the country were the vast acres of land that stretched from beyond the Appalachians to the Mississippi River. The cutthroats and outlaws who roamed the region in those days are barely remembered today, despite the fact that some of them were the bloodiest killers in the history of the country.

One such man was Samuel Mason, the leader of one of our first real criminal organizations. Mason lived and died at the dawn of the Nineteenth Century and amassed a fortune in gold, silver and plunder that vanished without a trace at the time of his death. Said to have filled a kettle that was seven feet across and three feet deep, the gold coins and jewels were buried in a secret location that today is said to be haunted by the outlaw's ghost.

The first record of Samuel Mason comes from the outlaw hideout of Cave-in-Rock, which is located along the Ohio River at the southeastern edge of Illinois. The cave became the stronghold of pirates who plundered flatboats on the river and who murdered and robbed travelers. It was here, in the late 1790's, that Mason began operating a tavern and gambling parlor in the cave. He used whiskery, cards and prostitutes to lure travelers in off the river and many of these customers found themselves beaten, robbed and sometimes dead, after tying up at the crude wharf.

Cave-in-Rock, located close to the town of the same name, was a perfect place for criminal enterprises along the river. At that time, it boasted a partially concealed entrance and a wide view up and down the river. The cave is about one hundred feet deep, with a level floor and a vertical chimney that ascends to the bluff above.

Samuel Mason operated here for several years. He was said to be a man of gigantic size and possessing no conscience, he killed for both pleasure and profit.

He had an army of thieves and killers at his disposal and they paid one-third of anything they took back to Mason. In return, he often tipped them off to likely targets, offered markets for stolen goods and provided protection against outsiders and lawmen. After leaving Cave-in-Rock, Mason began operating along the Mississippi River and on the fabled Natchez Trace, a series of trails in the south that became known as a haven for thieves and pirates.

Few of the Mason gang victims ever lived to tell what happened to them and so

Cave-in-Rock along the Ohio River

there is little record of their bloody crimes, particularly in their acts of river piracy. In the era before the steamboat, hundreds of flatboats came down the Ohio and the Mississippi carrying a variety of cargo and passengers. Mason's men were not particular about the boats they attacked. One incident of note occurred in 1801 and involved a boat carrying furs that was coming downriver from St. Louis. About 20 miles above Natchez, the boat ran aground on a sandbar and while her boatmen tried to thrust her off of it with their poles, a boat approached them from the shoreline. The passengers and crew at first assumed they were going to be rescued until the craft rammed straight into the side of the stranded flatboat. A wave of knife-wielding men swept onto the wrecked vessel and massacred all of those aboard her. The furs, and the rest of the cargo and passenger's belongings, vanished into the coffers of the Mason gang.

River craft were looted in other ways as well. On stormy nights, welcoming lanterns were placed along the river banks in order to lure boats that were being tossed about in a storm to put ashore. Just before the boat would reach the bank, it would plow into a sandbar or a line of rocks. The stranded vessel would then be overrun by Mason's cutthroats.

Still another approach was one that was most frequently used by Mason's most fearsome confederates, Micajar and Wiley Harpe. The Harpe brothers were known as Big Harpe and Little Harpe and were remorseless butchers whose victims included innocent women and children. Big Harpe once admitted to smashing a newborn baby against the wall of a cave after one of his female companions had gone into labor. Years later, as he lay paralyzed from a bullet lodged in his spine, Big Harpe told a man who had already started to cut off his head as evidence to collect a reward, that he could "cut on and be damned." The Harpe's did not wait until nightfall or the cover of a storm to do their dirty work. They operated boldly in broad daylight. Their most effective methods was to appear on the riverbank and flag down passing boats, usually telling them that they had been attacked by Indians, or robbed, and needed help. When the sympathetic travelers came ashore, the Harpe's would slaughter them on the spot and raid the boat.

Some of the worst crimes carried out by Samuel Mason himself occurred along the Natchez Trace. This 600-mile stretch of road carried thousands of riders who wanted to avoid the dangers of river travel but ironically, they found other dangers waited for them in the wilderness. Mason normally carried at least two knives, a brace of pistols and a tomahawk when he operated along the Trace. He would often ride right into a camp, posing as a traveler who was afraid of journeying alone. Frequently, he would be asked to join whatever party he approached and after he determined what wealth the others were carrying, Mason would cut their throats in the night and leave the bodies on the side of the trail.

One of Mason's biggest hauls came when he assembled about 20 of his men together and attacked a pack train that his spies informed him was carrying a considerable quantity of gold coins from Kentucky to Natchez. The 12 men guarding the train were all killed and Mason managed to make off with more than $100,000.

In this way, Mason amassed a fortune during the five years or so that his criminal enterprise flourished in the west. There are many unanswered questions about how Mason disposed of the money that he had obtained. Some of it was undoubtedly spent in the brothels and gambling dens of the notorious Natchez-Under-the-Hill and some was lavished on his brothers and sons, who were also partners in crime. Even allowing for this, there still must have been huge amounts that Mason simply stashed away. He had grand plans for moving to Texas, buying a large tract of land from the Spanish and then building a stronghold from which he could plunder the settlers that he predicted would someday move west. He knew that sooner or later, he would be driven out of the region.

So what did he do with all of his plunder? There have been many tales of buried Mason treasure that has never been found. Whatever Mason may have secreted away, he never lived long enough to return for. After the United States purchased the Louisiana Territory from France, a concerted effort was made to drive out the outlaw element that had existed along the river for years. A reward was placed on Mason's head and for his capture, dead or alive, the authorities offered $10,000.

This was a grand sum in those days but the man who finally ended Mason's life did not do it for the money. He did it so that he could take over Mason's criminal enterprise. That man was one of his closest confederates, Wiley Harpe. He contrived to get Mason alone and then Little Harpe buried his tomahawk into his friend's back. He finished him off and then hacked off Mason's head. He then carried the grisly object to Natchez and placed it on the desk of the judge who had been charged with dispensing the reward. The men who were present that day all confirmed that he brought in the head of Samuel Mason but just as the judge was counting out the gold coins in payment, one of the others who were there recognized Little Harpe as an outlaw himself. Harpe made an effort to escape but he was quickly captured and hanged soon after. The deaths of Mason and Harpe brought about the end of the gang and Mason's men scattered to the winds.

From that time on, there has been speculation about the treasure that Mason buried but never returned to collect. Some said that it was stored in a limestone cave that the gang held secret meetings in - which was only known, of course, to other gang members - or in caches along the Natchez Trace, swamps along the Mississippi River or under the fireplace of one of the ramshackle buildings in Natchez-Under-the-Hill.

The biggest hoard was widely believed to have been hidden in an immense iron kettle, a vessel that was once used by plantation slaves in which to boil sugar cane into syrup. The story goes that one night shortly before his murder at the hands of Little Harpe, Mason gathered his family and his three closest friends together at a place about 20 miles east of Natchez. Here, at a spot near an artesian well, they dug a huge hole and lowered the sugar kettle into it. Then, into the kettle, they poured thousands of gold coins and a quantity of jewels that had been collected over the years. They tugged the heavy iron cover onto the kettle and then covered it with dirt. Once this was accomplished, Mason cold-bloodedly shot the three friends who had dug the hole so that no one but the Mason's would ever know where the treasure was buried. After the death of Samuel, his sons, brothers and their families departed from the region and were never heard from again.

For just that reason, many searches have been made for the lost Mason treasure, especially for the great iron kettle. Many thought that it was merely a legend, until 1927, when a man named Reber Dove bought a run-down old farm east of Natchez. He had bought the land for the artesian well that was on the property but soon after, he began to hear dark tales about the land - and about the fact that it was haunted by the ghost of Samuel Mason. Dove did not believe in ghost stories but he was taken with the idea that he might have bought the land where the Mason's had buried the iron kettle. One day, he was digging in the ground near the well and his shovel struck something hard. He began digging faster and saw what he thought might be the edge of something metal. Unfortunately, that was all that he saw because as soon as he uncovered it, wet mud sloshed over it. Dove dug furiously into the soft, wet earth but each time that he caught a glimpse of what might be the kettle, the hole would be flooded with water and mud again. The digging went on and on until Dove suddenly became aware of the fact that by disturbing the earth, he was causing the kettle to sink. The nearby well and the ancient delta system of the Mississippi worked together to make the land like quicksand and so Dove gave up before the kettle - or whatever it was - sank any deeper.

Reber Dove abandoned the project but others took over. The first to try and obtain the kettle were a group of local farmers, who fared no better than Dove. In 1939, a syndicate was formed and an engineer was brought in to study the location. It was his opinion that rather than try digging from above, an effort should be made to dig from the side and to come in under the kettle. This plan had disastrous results and by enlarging the muck-filled hole, the kettle sank even deeper.

The next major effort took place in 1955 when M.H. Bullock, a businessman from Laurel, Mississippi made a deal with the Dove family to try and dig for the kettle. Bullock and his partners brought in heavy machinery and started an enormous excavation. For a time, it appeared that they were making progress and as the pit reached a depth of 20 feet, it seemed to be drying out. However, after a terrible three-day rain, the hole filled with mud and water again. Bullock made other attempts, but each failed. The searcher's probes revealed that the object they sought was still there - but they could never catch up with it. Eventually, this excavation was also shut down. To this day, no one has yet succeeded in finding Mason's treasure or in figuring out how to retrieve the kettle - if it is indeed the treasure trove of Samuel Mason - from the old farm.

Some people around the area still believe that the ghost of Samuel Mason is on the farm, preventing those who seek it from bringing his plunder out of the ground. The only way to ever do this, they believe, is to somehow exorcize the ghost. Others offer perhaps more sage advice - that Mason undoubtedly buried his loot in other locations in the region and rather than face his wrathful spirit, the searchers should seek the lost treasure elsewhere.

THE MYSTERY OF THE YOACHUM SILVER DOLLARS

One of the most enduring legends of lost treasure to ever come out of the Ozark regions of Missouri involves the Yoachum Silver Dollars and the vanished Spanish silver mine that produced them. As both a child and an adult, I have traveled many times to the Missouri Ozarks and anyone who has ever been to the area around Branson is familiar with a place called "Silver Dollar City", an amusement park that was first started to entertain tourists who came to see famed Marvel Cave.

Those who are familiar with the history of the region know there is much more to the area than just theme parks, water slides, variety shows and country music. The region around Table Rock Lake is home to an enduring mystery and if the legends are to be believed - a vast, hidden fortune as well.

The mysterious Yoachum Silver Dollars are as much a part of the history of southwestern Missouri as the amusement park that has become their namesake. That the elusive silver dollars existed there can be no doubt, for government records clearly substantiate their existence and a few of them still exist in rare coin collections around the country. However, the origin of the silver, and the circumstances involved in the manufacturing of the dollars, remains a mystery today as the search for the coins and the strange cave from which the silver was allegedly taken continues today.

The legend began in 1541, when Spanish explorers penetrated the rugged and isolated valleys of the Ozark Mountains in search of wealth. They intended to locate gold and silver, extract the ore, smelt it and then ship it back to Spain. A large party of Spaniards explored the region and when they found some indication of promising ore, they established a small settlement in the area in which they planned to develop mines A log fortress was erected atop Breadtray Mountain, about three miles northwest of the present-day town of Lampe, Missouri, near Table Rock Lake.

While inspecting an ancient shelter cave that had been used by Indians, the Spanish discovered numerous passageways, including one that contained a thick vein of silver ore. Local Choctaw Indians were enslaved to dig the ore and smelt it into ingots. The vein was followed deep into the cavern and copious amounts of ingots were created and stacked in the passages until they could be loaded onto mules and transported to the Mississippi River. From there, they would be rafted to the Gulf of Mexico and then loaded onto ships bound for Spain.

The cruel treatment of the Indian laborers led to unrest among the local tribes and soon hunting parties sent by the Spanish left the safety of the fort - and never returned. Night time watches were doubled and then tripled but it was only a matter of time before the unrest led to greater violence. One morning, the Choctaw attacked the mine and encampment and massacred the Spanish. A few of them managed to escape but the mine was abandoned and largely forgotten. After the Spanish were driven out, the silver mine remained silent and empty, with ingots still stacked along the passageways, for more than two and a half centuries.

Choctaw history relates that the silver cave remained undisturbed until around 1809. In that year, during a violent thunderstorm, a hunting party of Choctaw sought shelter in its passages. While waiting out the storm, they ventured back into the interior of the cave and discovered the silver bars and a few human skeletons, likely victims from the massacre so many years before. The Choctaw traditionally had no use for silver, save for the fashioning of ornaments, but contact with white trappers and traders in the area had taught them that they could trade it for supplies such as blankets, weapons and horses. Legend has it that they conducted a two-day ceremony at the mouth of the cave to drive out evil spirits who resided there.

For many years after, the Choctaw made regular trips into the cave and returned with just enough silver to make jewelry and to conduct trade. They carried the silver as far as St. Louis to barter for goods they wanted.

One day, a Choctaw scout reported a party of Mexicans riding to the cave on a trail that ran alongside the White River. They were soon approached by a group of armed Choctaw warriors that halted the group. The leader of the Mexicans explained that they were searching for a silver mine that had been excavated about 200 years before and that they believed was nearby. He unrolled a map and showed it to the Indians and several of them recognized landmarks on it that could be found nearby. However, they told the Mexicans that there was no such mine and encouraged them to leave. After that, fearing that someone else might come looking for it, the Choctaw sealed the entrance to the cave and abandoned it. The cave remained closed for a number of years, until other Indians arrived in the area.

After the War of 1812, the Delaware Indians were re-located to the Ozarks. They had originally occupied lands in parts of Ohio, Indiana and Illinois but had been driven out after the war. Most of them moved onto the James River area of the Ozarks, in southwestern Missouri before 1820. Here, they were joined by some Shawnee, Kickapoo, Seneca and Pottawatomie, who had also been evicted from their lands.

This same period marked the arrival of the Yoachum family in the James River Valley. Their name has been listed in many ways over the years, including Yocum, Yokum, Yoakum and others, but most believe the accurate spelling is Yoachum.

James Yoachum was born in Kentucky in 1772 and a year later, his brother, Solomon, was born. While they were still young, their family moved to Illinois and started a farm. When James was 18 though, he abandoned his pregnant wife and farm and decided to seek his fortunes as a trapper in the Ozark Mountains. He had considerable success in this venture and returned to Illinois to get his brother and bring their families to the mountains. When he arrived back home though, he discovered that his wife had died in childbirth, leaving him a son. The boy, Jacob Levi, was raised by Solomon and his wife.

James remained in Illinois for several years but had difficulty adjusting to the restraints of farm life. He finally decided to return to the Ozarks and to trapping with the agreement that his brother and his family, as well as his son, would soon join him. On his second trip, James met and married a Delaware Indian woman named Winona and they settled near the confluence of the James and White Rivers. Historians believe the James River was later named for James Yoachum, as he developed a well-known farm along the river.

Because of family problems, Solomon's departure for the Ozarks was delayed and he was not able to join his brother on his farm until 1815. By this time, James had planted a large part of the bottoms in corn and squash and had acquired a large herd of cattle and horses. Most of his neighbors were Delaware Indians, peaceful people who traded often with the settlers. James was always generous in return and shared much of his harvest with the tribe and frequently presented fine horses to select members of the community.

One of the things that the Yoachum's noticed about their Delaware friends was that they, along with other Indians who lived nearby, often wore jewelry and ornaments of fine silver. When James inquired about the origin of it, he was told that an aged Choctaw had told the Delaware of a great fortune in silver that was hidden in a cave in the forest. When James asked if he could see the cave, the Delaware had to refuse, stating that it would violate a pact between the Choctaw and Delaware to never reveal the location of the place.

And so it remained for years, until the federal government began an Indian removal process that evicted the Native Americans and re-settled them in Indian Territory to the west, in what is now Oklahoma. The Delaware were among the tribes again forced out and while the Yoachum's bitterly protested against this, there was little that they could do but bid their companions goodbye. They brought many gifts to the Delaware, including horses, blankets and cooking utensils and in gratitude, a hasty meeting among the Delaware elders resulted in a decision to show the brothers where the silver cave was located. The men vowed to never reveal the location of the site and with one exception, carried the secret with them to their graves.

In the years that followed, whenever the Yoachum's needed money, they would leave the farm, stay gone for a few days, and then return with several of the ingots that they claimed were from stacks of hundreds in the cave.

As more and more settlers arrived in the Ozark region, and as more trading posts were established, the brothers became involved in the economy of the area. The largest local establishment was the James Fork Trading Post, which was run by a man named William Gilliss. The Yoachum's, in addition to farming, also hunted and trapped in the area and they traded their furs at Gilliss' store for coffee, sugar, flour and other staples. The trading post was owned by the business firm of Menard & Valle, which operated from the town of Ste. Genevieve on the Mississippi River. Colonel Pierre Menard, a friend to many of the Indians in the Ozarks, watched closely over the trading. He was also protective of the interests of French trappers in the region and since the Yoachum's were Americans, he told Gilliss to insist that they start paying for their supplies in cash. The exchange for Americans would no longer be furs or even gold and silver, but the American's federally issued coins and currency. The Yoachum's, although rich in silver and trade, were otherwise poor. They had no money.

In order to remedy this, James decided that the Yoachum's would make their own money. Using simple blacksmith tools, he made dies, melted down some of the silver ingots, rolled it into sheets and stamped out his own coins. The coins were slightly larger than the ones issued by the government and on one side bore the inscription "Yoachum" and the date "1822." On the other side was stamped "United States of America" and "1 Dollar".

Over a several-month period, thousands of these coins were stamped out and placed into circulation. Soon, most of the residents in this section of the Ozarks used the coins for all of their purchases. Gilliss examined the coins and judged them to be of the purest silver and he eagerly accepted them as a legitimate exchange. The Yoachum Silver Dollars soon became more available in the remote Ozark regions than official, government-issued money.

In 1845 though, something occurred to bring the Yoachum dollar to the notice of the federal government. When the former Indian lands around the James and White Rivers were opened for purchase, the government sent a surveying crew into the area to establish section lines and country boundaries. During this time, the settlers who were already here were notified that they would be required to abide by certain homestead laws by securing title to the property on which they lived. Part of the requirement was to pay a filing fee at the government office in Springfield. Dozens of James River region residents who were paying their filing fee, as well as many others who wanted to buy some of the newly offered land, arrived at the office and tried to pay with Yoachum Silver Dollars.

The agent on duty refused to accept the coins as payment, citing an 1833 regulation that required federally issued coins. He told the settlers that unless they paid in legitimate United States money, they would not have title to their land. Enraged, several of the men pointed loaded guns at the agent and told him that Yoachum money meant more to the residents of the Ozarks than government money and that if he valued his life, he would accept it. The agent nervously accepted the Yoachum dollars and presented the men with valid certificates to their land. The agent then forwarded the coins, along with an explanation for what had happened, to Washington. Once the dollars arrived, they were assayed and found to be composed of almost pure silver - and contained much more silver than government regulated coins. The authorities did not consider the coins to be counterfeit, since they had not been duplicates of federally minted coins but they were worried about the proliferation of non-federal money in the region. They wired the Springfield office and ordered the agent to confiscate all of the Yoachum dollars and to learn the location of the silver mine.

A few weeks later, the government agent found his way to James Yoachum's farm and announced that he had come to take a look at the silver mine. Needless to say, Yoachum ordered the man from his property at gunpoint. The agent left, but he returned a week later with eight additional agents, all armed and not to be intimidated. This time, he explained to Yoachum the official position of the federal government in regards to locally cast dollars and discouraged him from making and distributing the coins. Yoachum, always considered to be a law-abiding and patriotic man, replied that he had never intended to break any laws and agreed to stop making the silver dollars. He would not, however, reveal the location of the mine where the silver came from. The agents agreed to his terms and said that they would not prosecute, as long as Yoachum stopped making the coins. And the location of the old Spanish mine remained a secret.

James Yoachum died a few years later. There are two versions of how he died. One of them claims that he caught a fever and died in his sleep and the other maintains that he and his wife, Winona, were killed in a cave-in at the mine when they were retrieving some of the silver. Either way, his death came in 1848.

After James' death, Solomon decided to leave the Ozarks and to take his family to California. The gold fields were opening and he was determined to try his luck in that region. The legend states that before leaving Missouri, Solomon gave the dies that were used to cast the silver dollars to a relative who owned a grist mill in the area. Solomon loaded the family's wagon and departed, never to return to the

Ozarks again. While the fate of the remaining Yoachum's will never be known, local lore had it that they died crossing the Rocky Mountains on the way to California. With their death, the secret location of the Spanish mine was lost forever. According to Jacob, his father and uncle had sealed off the mine after the visit by the government agents so that no one would ever be able to find it. He passed this information on to his own son, Tom, who, like his father, searched for the mine for years but was unable to find it.

The legend of the Yoachum Silver Dollar has been told and re-told many times over the years and aside from the fact that there are different variations of the story, the basic facts of it are the truth. The Yoachum dollar did exist, there were thousands of them manufactured, and the silver to make them had to have come from somewhere.

While the location of the silver mine remains a mystery, some of the silver dollars have been found. In 1974, an unidentified man from St. Louis discovered a cache of 236 large silver coins while metal detecting. He described them as being two inches in diameter, roughly cast and each bearing the inscription of "Yoachum" on one side. There have been others found as well, most are in the hands of collectors now, but most agree there are many more to be discovered. In addition, treasure hunters and coin collectors have long pondered what became of the dies used to cast the dollars. They were presumed lost or destroyed until a remarkable discovery in 1983. On March 11, J.R. Blunk of Galena was digging near a riverbank that had once been on the Yoachum farm and unearthed a large mass of what he thought at first was wax. He broke it open and found two small sections of iron rod inside. When he scraped the waxy substance off one end of a rod, he found the word "Yoachum" and on the other rod, "1 Dollar".

Excited about his discovery, Blunk spent the next several months researching the story of the Yoachum Silver Dollar and turned up the names of several collectors who had samples of the original coins. He obtained a coin from one of them and on close examination, he realized that the dollar had come from one of the dies that he had found. Just to be sure, he also had it examined by a professional numismatist who confirmed Blunk's findings.

But what of the other thousands of dollars still out there? How many of them were hidden away, buried or locked in the attic when the government banned the Yoachum Silver Dollars? And more importantly, where is the lost Spanish mine that provided the silver used to make the coins? If this place could be found, it would certainly be the discovery of a lifetime. Even if a small portion of the Yoachum legend is true, then this means that there could still be hundreds (or more) of the Spanish silver ingots still stacked along the passageways of the cave. Thousands and thousands of people come to the Ozarks every year for vacations, boating, fishing and more and it's likely that the thought of lost treasure never even enters their mind --- but perhaps it should.

111. MYSTERIOUS CREATURES

UNEXPLAINED ACCOUNTS OF STRANGE CREATURES IN THE AMERICAN WILD

"Bigfoot is Dead!"

This is what newspapers all over America were telling readers back in November 2002 when a man named Ray Wallace passed away. His son, Michael, told the *Seattle Times* newspaper that his father had been "Bigfoot" and that the "reality is, Bigfoot just died". Needless to say, the media - and the debunkers of the idea that a creature like Bigfoot could even exist - went wild. Many hastily written stories followed that declared that Wallace, using a pair of crudely carved wooden feet, made phony tracks all over the Pacific Northwest and that his wife had dressed in a monkey suit and helped to hoax the controversial Patterson-Gimlin film. The answer as to whether or not strange man-like creatures could be lurking in the woods and remote regions of the American continent had just been answered. There is no Bigfoot, the newspapers said, it has been a hoax all along. But has it really?

To many, Ray Wallace was the "father" of modern Bigfoot stories but what happened at a construction site where he was a contractor was actually a minor event that involved some mysterious footprints. However, the incident occurred at a time when Americans were ready for something exciting to happen and the media pounced on the discovery of the tracks. The word "Bigfoot" was actually coined and became term that people have used ever since. No matter how you look at it though, what happened in Bluff Creek, California in 1958 did usher in the modern era of Bigfoot and created an interest in the subject that is still around today.

But what really happened - and why did the stories that came out about Ray Wallace after his death not really come as a surprise to Bigfoot researchers, despite what the media would like you to believe?

In the spring of 1957, construction began on a road near Bluff Creek. The site was run by a contractor named Ray Wallace and his brother, Wilbur. They hired 30 men that summer to work on the project and by late in the season, Wilbur Wallace reported that something had been throwing around some large, metal oil drums at the work site. When winter arrived that year, cold weather brought progress to a halt, even though only 10 miles of road had been built.

In early spring 1958, some odd tracks were discovered near the Mad River close to Korbel, California. After they were found, some of the locals believed they were bear tracks. As it happened, this was close to another work site that was managed by the Wallace brothers.

Later on that spring, work started up again on the road near Bluff Creek. A number of new men were hired, including Jerry Crew, who drove more than two hours each weekend so that he could be home with his family. Ten more miles of road were constructed, angling up across the face of a nearby mountain. On August 3, 1958, Wilbur Wallace stated that something threw a 700-pound spare tire to the bottom of a deep gully near the work site. This incident was reported later in the month, after the discovery of the footprints.

On August 27, Jerry Crew arrived for work early in the morning and found giant, manlike footprints all around his bulldozer. He was first upset by the discovery, thinking that someone was playing a practical joke on him, but then he finally decided to report what he found to Wilbur Wallace. At this point, the footprints had not been made public. This occurred on September 21, when Mrs. Jess Bemis, the wife of one of the Bluff Creek work crew, wrote a letter to Andrew Genzoli, the editor of a local newspaper. Genzoli published her husband's "Big Foot" story and caught the attention of others in the area. One of these was Betty Allen, a newswoman who wrote in a late September column that plaster casts should be made of the footprints. She had already collected accounts, talked to Native Americans and interviewed locals about hairy giants in the area and convinced Genzoli to run other stories and letters about Bigfoot. This would be the beginning of the story that would capture the imagination of America.

On October 1 and 2, Jerry Crew discovered more tracks, very similar to the first ones. In response to the new discovery, two other workers quit the job and Wilbur Wallace allegedly introduced his brother Ray to the situation for the first time, bringing him out to show him the tracks. On the day after the last tracks were found, Jerry Crew made plaster casts of the footprints, with help from his friend Bob Titmus and writer Betty Allen. He was irritated that people were making fun of him and wanted to offer the casts as some sort of evidence. On October 5, Andrew Genzoli published his now famous story detailing "Bigfoot" and it was picked up worldwide by the press services and soon the term was being used in general conversation.

In 1959, famous zoologist Ivan T. Sanderson was touring the country for a planned book on ecology and used the time to also do some investigative work on unexplained phenomena. He had long been interested in the Yeti creatures of Asia and decided to stop off in Bluff Creek for a look at the site involved in the Jerry Crew accounts. He stayed at a local hotel for a little over a week, looking at files offered by Betty Allen and talking to witnesses from the area. When he left, he was supposed to make some candid assessments about the incidents to Tom Slick, the Texas millionaire who had funded some on-site investigation into the Bigfoot encounters, as well as a search for the Yeti in Nepal. When the report was made though, what he called "various small items in the past" were left out. Sanderson was impressed by many of the people that he met, including Betty Allen and Jerry Crew, but he had some reservations about others - especially Ray Wallace.

In 2002, the media was trying hard to convince the general public that Ray Wallace was a highly respected figure in the world of Bigfoot research but in truth, he had been regarded with suspicion by such luminaries in the field as Ivan T. Sanderson, as far back as 1959. During his lifetime, Wallace claimed to see UFO's as many as 2,000 times, Bigfoot hundreds of times and also claimed to have film footage of Bigfoot a year before Jerry Crew found the footprints at the construction site. In 1959, he even claimed to have captured one! When Tom Slick offered some money for it though, Wallace failed to produce the creature. He later claimed that he told Roger Patterson where to go to film Bigfoot in 1967 but few believed this. Wallace said that he had many films of Bigfoot but each turned out to be an obvious hoax. Later, a man named Rant Mullens, who was known for perpetrating hoaxes, said that he often made large wooden footprints and gave them to Wallace, who then prepared plaster casts from them for display.

With his involvement in all sorts of questionable activities, Wallace has been regarded with suspicion by those with even a mild interest in Bigfoot for years. Ivan T. Sanderson was concerned about Wallace from the beginning and became even more worried when he received other letters about tracks being discovered in areas that turned out to be near other Wallace construction sites. He stated that everyone who did not believe the tracks were made by some sort of unknown, living entity believed that they had been made by Wallace. "He was a great 'funster'", Sanderson wrote and hinted that if there were enough problems on a work site, Wallace could get his work contracts changed and get no-cost extensions granted. Could this have been the motive for creating the phony tracks?

Unfortunately, the other things that Wallace got involved in from the 1950's until his death did not alleviate the early suspicions about him. His continued involvement with fakes and frauds and his later claim that he hoaxed the tracks to bring attention to the plight of the real Bigfoot and to keep him from "being killed by hunters", caused many to believe that the 1958 Bluff Creek tracks were a hoax. And it also appears that Wallace planted phony prints at other worksites in the region over the years as well. This seems to mean that the so-called "birth of Bigfoot" was nothing more than a clever hoax - a hoax that managed to fool people all over the country and around the world.

So then, if this is the case, does this mean that the existence of Bigfoot - a giant, hairy creature that lives in the most remote regions of America - is just a hoax too? The debunkers would certainly like you to think so. But just as they, and the media, overlooked the fact that most real-life Bigfoot researchers had already discredited Ray Wallace at the time of his death, they also overlooked the scores of reports, first-hand accounts and authentic evidence of the man-like creature that had been around for years.

My own involvement in the field of Bigfoot research is non-existent. While I have always been intrigued by the idea that such beings could exist, I have never encountered one, hunted for them, investigated case reports or took anything other than a mild, but curious, interest in them. I have occasionally run across reports of Bigfoot creatures while researching other things though and being intrigued, have sometimes included accounts of Bigfoot in my writings.

However, I think that it was my non-expert interest in Bigfoot that got me so upset in 2002 when Ray Wallace passed away. To be honest, I was alarmed by the revelation that Wallace had been involved in so many hoaxes over the years and having no other knowledge about him or that he was already a suspicious figure to those in the field, I wondered about the damage this was all going to do to Bigfoot research. Rather than jump to conclusions about the validity of Bigfoot study as a whole though, I decided to do a little research into the history of it - which is something that the media should have been doing rather than printing half-baked theories about how Bigfoot had been a hoax from the beginning.

To "discover" Bigfoot, I turned to the past. As some of my long-time readers know, most of my research into hauntings is based on history. I have always felt that the key to understanding the ghost who haunts a location is to understand where the ghost came from, or at least how the story got started. I began looking into the "history of Bigfoot" and what I found was fascinating. Bigfoot had not been "born" in 1958 but had been around for decades - even centuries. I had done some writing on the subject in the past but I had no idea just how reliable some of the past accounts had been. It was obvious that the news stories that claimed a life span for Bigfoot between 1958 and 2002 had not done their homework, as the reader will soon discover.

Before continuing though, let me make it clear that I do not consider myself to be an expert on Bigfoot research. You won't find any technical writings here that delve into Bigfoot physiology or the best ways to capture them. What I have instead tried to do instead is to make the case that the existence of Bigfoot is possible - even probable - based on the fact that these creatures have been with us throughout the history of this continent. I have tried to collect the best, and most compelling, incidents of encounters with Bigfoot in our history and have also included a few of the most interesting from "modern" times as well.

Strange things are out there "in the wild" and you'll find that this chapter of the book also veers out beyond Bigfoot and into country that is perhaps even stranger. There are wild things in the dark woods and remote regions of America, on the land and even in the air. If you have never been afraid of walking by yourself out in the forest before, you may be after you read this book!

WHERE BIGFOOT WALKS

There is no greater mystery in the annals of the unexplained in America than Sasquatch, the creature most commonly known as "Bigfoot". Reports of giant, man and ape-like monsters have been documented all over the country, although primarily in the forested regions of the Pacific Northwest. There are many tales of giant hairy figures in every state in America, although the "traditional" Bigfoot is believed to roam the vast regions of California, Oregon, Washington, Idaho and the western edge of Canada. The narrative that follows will include history and lore from a variety of locations.

Although most mainstream scientists maintain that no such creatures exist (and short of an actual specimen, their minds will not be changed), it is not inconceivable that undiscovered creatures could be roaming this wide region of mountains and forests. There are areas here that have been almost completely untouched by man and where few signs of the modern world can be found, even today. If we combine these often unexplored areas with the hundreds of eyewitness accounts and pieces of evidence left behind, then we have no choice but to at least consider the idea that these creatures may actually be real. Of course, the reader is asked to judge for himself but let's consider the history of Bigfoot in America.

According to the many eyewitnesses, Sasquatch averages around seven feet in height, sometimes taller and sometimes a little shorter. They are usually seen wandering alone and hair covers most of their bodies. Their limbs are usually powerful but are described as being proportioned more like people than like apes. However, their broad shoulders, short necks, flat faces and noses, sloped foreheads, ridged brows and cone-shaped heads make them appear more animal-like. They reportedly eat both meat and plants, are largely nocturnal and less active during cold weather. The creatures are most commonly reported as being covered in dark, auburn-colored hair, although reports of brown, black and even white and silver hair do occasionally pop up. The footprints left behind by the monsters range in size from about 12 to 22 inches long, with around 18 inches being the most common. They are normally reported to be somewhere around seven inches in width.

The stories of Sasquatch and reported man-like creatures have been part of Northwestern American history for generations. Native American legend and lore is filled with creatures that sound a lot like Bigfoot in description. One such creature was the "Wendigo". While this creature is considered by many to be the creation of horror writer Algernon Blackwood in his classic terror tale of the same name, this spirit was considered very real to many in the north woods and prairies. Many legends and stories have circulated over the years about a mysterious creature who was encountered by hunters and campers in the shadowy forests of the upper regions of Minnesota. In one variation of the story, the creature could only be seen if it faced the witness head-on, because it was so thin that it could not be seen from the side. The spirit was said to have a voracious appetite for human flesh and the many forest dwellers who disappeared over the years were said to be victims of the monster.

The American Indians had their own tales of the Wendigo, dating back so many years that most who were interviewed could not remember when the story had not been told. The Inuit Indians of the region called the creature by various names, including Wendigo, Witigo, Witiko and Wee-Tee-Go but each of them was roughly translated to mean "the evil spirit that devours mankind". Around 1860, a German explorer translated Wendigo to mean "cannibal" among the tribes along the Great Lakes.

Illustration from a 1969 SAGA magazine article about Bigfoot & Bigfoot sightings

Native American versions of the creature spoke of a gigantic spirit, over fifteen feet tall, that had once been human but had been transformed into a creature by the use of magic. Though all of the descriptions of the creature vary slightly, the Wendigo is generally said to have glowing eyes, long yellowed fangs and overly long tongues. Most have a sallow, yellowish skin but others are said to be matted with hair. They are tall and lanky and are driven by a horrible hunger. But how would a person grow to become one of these strange creatures?

According to the lore, the Wendigo is created whenever a human resorts to cannibalism to survive. In years past, such a practice was possible, although still rare, as many of the tribes and settlers in the region were cut off by the bitter snows and ice of the north woods. Unfortunately, eating another person to survive was sometimes resorted to and thus, the legend of the Wendigo was created.

But how real were these creatures? Could the legend of the Wendigo have been created merely as a "warning" against cannibalism? Or could sightings of Bigfoot-type creatures have created the stories? While this is unknown, it is believed that white settlers to the region took the stories seriously. It became enough a part of their culture that tales like those of Algernon Blackwood were penned. Real-life stories were told as well and according to the settlers' version of the legend, the Wendigo would often be seen (banshee-like) to signal a death in the community. A Wendigo allegedly made a number of appearances near a town called Rosesu in Northern Minnesota from the late 1800's through the 1920's. Each time that it was reported, an unexpected death followed and finally, it was seen no more.

Even into the last century, Native Americans actively believed in, and searched for, the Wendigo. One of the most famous Wendigo hunters was a Cree Indian named Jack Fiddler. He claimed to kill at least 14 of the creatures in his lifetime, although the last murder resulted in his imprisonment at the age of 87. In October 1907, Fiddler and his son, Joseph, were tried for the murder of a Cree Indian woman. They both pleaded guilty to the crime but defended themselves by stating that the woman had been possessed by the spirit of a Wendigo and was on the verge of transforming into one entirely. According to their defense, she had to be killed before she murdered other members of the tribe.

There are still many stories told of Wendigo's that have been seen in northern Ontario, near the Cave of the Wendigo, and around the town of Kenora, where a creature has been spotted by traders, trackers and trappers for decades. There are many who still believe that the Wendigo roams the woods and the prairies of northern Minnesota and Canada. Whether it seeks human flesh, or acts as a portent of coming doom, is anyone's guess but before you start to doubt that it exists - remember that the stories and legends of this fearsome creature have been around since before the white man walked on these shores. Like all legends, this one too was likely started for a reason.

The Yakama Indians of the Pacific Northwest had a tradition of a "Qah-lin-me", which was a devourer of people and the Hupa Indians called the man-like beasts the "Omah", a demon of the wilderness. The Nisqually tribe of western Washington had the "Tsiatko", which was a gigantic, hairy beast and the "Tenatco" was known by the Kaska. Their creatures were known to dig a hole in the ground as a place to sleep and would sometimes kidnap women and children. Most of the woodland giants in the lore of the Native Americans seem to be more aggressive than the creatures we know as Bigfoot but there is little mistaking them for something else. In fact, in 1934, author Diamond Jenness reported that the Carrier First nation told of a monster that left enormous footprints in the snow, had a face like a man, was very tall and was covered in long hair. This hardly seems to be coincidence when compared to "modern" version of Bigfoot.

The legend of Bigfoot-type creatures is so mired in the history of American that even the Native American term "Sasquatch" is a bit of an extraction from mythological stories. The folkloric Sasquatch (the word is the Americanized version of the Coast Salish Indian term from Canada) was introduced to the world in the writings of J.W. Burns, a schoolteacher at the Chehalis Indian Reservation near

A Native American Mask that Looks Like An Ape - An Interesting Find Considering that Apes Are not Supposed to be Found in North America. Could this be Bigfoot?

Harrison Hot Springs, British Columbia. Burns' Sasquatch was a legendary figure that he learned of through native informants and was really more man than monster. He was an intelligent "giant Indian" who was endowed with supernatural powers. Somehow, the name managed to stick for the huge beings that we would come to call Bigfoot.

WILD MEN OF THE WOODS

American legend has it that Bigfoot began to be encountered on this continent as early as the days of the first Viking visitors. Leif Erickson reportedly wrote of encountering ugly, hairy monsters with great black eyes here and in 1603, Samuel de Champlain was told of a giant, hairy beast that roamed the forests of eastern Canada. This creature was said to be much feared by the Micmac Indians of the region. In the 1790's, accounts tell of large hairy monsters in North and South Carolina and in that same decade, the creatures were being reported in the Northwest by explorers and hunters who came to the region. While exploring the British Columbia coast in 1792, naturalist Jose Mariano Mozino interviewed locals who spoke of the "Matlox", a large, hairy, human-like creature with huge feet, hooked claws and sharp teeth.

Throughout the Nineteenth Century, accounts of Bigfoot-type creatures continued to appear in newspapers and periodicals of the day. Obviously, the word "Bigfoot" had not been coined in those times and frankly, readers were not even familiar with any creature of this sort. The idea of even an "ape" was completely foreign to them, as the great apes of Africa were not discovered until later in the century. For this reason, a search through old periodicals will not reveal historical Bigfoot accounts but what did sometimes appear in newspapers of the 1800's were stories of "wild men" and beast-like creatures that were encountered, sometimes captured and occasionally killed. These reports likely thrilled readers of the day and may offer the modern researcher the first true reports of Bigfoot in America.

Likely the oldest account of a man-like creature in North America appeared in the *London Times* in January 1785. In the report, it stated that a wild man was caught in the forest, about 200 miles from Lake of the Woods, by a party of Indians. The creature was said to have been seven feet tall and covered with hair. The wild man did not speak and seemed incapable of understanding his captors. It was found beside the body of a large bear, which it had just killed. This is unfortunately the extent of the information offered and no other news apparently followed.

The oldest known Bigfoot account in American newspapers appeared in September 1818 in Ellisburgh, New York and the incident apparently occurred on August 30. The story involved a local man of good reputation that had an encounter with an animal resembling a "Wild Man of the Woods". The creature came out of the forest, looked at the man and then took flight in the opposite direction. He described it as bending forward when running, hairy, and having a narrow foot that spread wide at the toes. The newspaper article, which appeared in the *Exeter Watchman*, went on to say that hundreds of people searched for the wild man for several days but no trace of it was found.

In the late 1830's, there were reports of a "wild child" around Fish Lake in Indiana. It was said to be four feet tall and covered in chestnut hair. The creature was often seen on the shore as well as swimming in the water. No one was able to catch up with it, as it ran so quickly, and made awful screeching noises. There were also reports in Pennsylvania of similar creatures, each much smaller than the typical Bigfoot creatures of modern eras. One of the creatures seen in Pennsylvania was covered in black hair but was said to have been the size of a six or seven year-old boy. Could these have been young Bigfoot, or perhaps, as authors Janet and Colin Bord have asked, a different species of creature altogether?

The Bord's also make reference to several wild men that were seen in Arkansas in the 1830's. The creatures were of gigantic stature and had been well known in St. Francis, Greene and Poinsett Counties since 1834. Two hunters had a close encounter with a wild man in Greene County in 1851 after seeing a herd of cattle that was apparently being chased. They discovered that the animals were being pursued by "an animal bearing the unmistakable likeness of humanity. He was of gigantic stature, the body being covered with hair and the head with long locks that fairly enveloped the neck and shoulders." Apparently, the wild man looked at the two hunters for a moment before running off into the forest. His tracks measured about 13 inches in length. Interestingly, the local explanation for this creature was that he was a "survivor of the earthquake disaster that desolated the region in 1811". The implication was that he was a human who had lost his sanity and home during the massive earthquake along the New Madrid Fault and had "gone native", living in the woods and growing his hair long.

Author and Bigfoot researcher John Green pointed out that some of the prospectors of the 1849 California Gold Rush were also encountering Bigfoot.

According to a correspondent, his grandfather prospected for gold around Mount Shasta in the 1850's and told stories of seeing hairy giants in the vicinity.

In the late 1860's, residents in the Arcadia Valley of Crawford County, Kansas were encountering their own wild man. The "wild man or gorilla" or "what is it?" was approaching the cabins of settlers, tearing down fences and generally wreaking havoc. The creature was described as being so near to a human form that the "men are unwilling to shoot at it"; however, it had a stooping gait, very long arms with immense hands and claws and an extremely hairy face. According to newspaper reports of the time, the settlers were divided as to whether or not the creature belonged to the human family or not and some thought it to be an ape that had escaped from a menagerie some settlements east of the valley.

In the fall of 1869, a hunter from Grayson, California wrote a letter to the Antioch Ledger and described his own experiences with a wild man in the forest. He was hunting in the mountains around Orestimba Creek and after returning to camp, found that the ashes and burned sticks from his campfire had been scattered about. He searched around the area in curiosity and a short distance away, he found "the track of a man's foot - bare and of immense size". Thinking that he would try to catch a glimpse of the odd, barefooted visitor, he took up a position on a ridge overlooking his camp and waited there for nearly two hours. Suddenly, he was surprised by a shrill whistle and looked up to see a huge figure, standing erect by his campfire.

"It was the image of a man," the hunter wrote, "but it could not have been human." The creature stood about five feet high but was very broad at the shoulders. His arms were of great length but his legs were short and his head seemed to be set upon his shoulders with no neck. He was covered with dark brown and cinnamon-colored hair that was quite long.

The wild man continued to make the odd whistling sound as he scattered about the rest of the firewood and ashes. After a few minutes, he started to leave the clearing where the camp was located but went only a short distance and returned. This time, he brought with him another similar figure, although this one was unmistakably female. The two creatures passed close to the hunter's hiding place and then disappeared into the forest.

Another wild man that was encountered in the late 1860's was seen in northern Nevada. The creature caused great excitement and unlike most Bigfoot reports, the wild man actually carried a weapon. According to accounts, an armed party started off in pursuit of it shortly after it was spotted. The searchers concluded that it had once been a "white man, but was now covered with a coat of fine, long hair". It was seen carrying a club in one hand and a slain rabbit in the other. The moment that it caught sight of its pursuers, it let out a scream like "the roar of a lion", brandished the club and attacked the men's horses. The men let loose their dogs after it, but the wild man managed to hide behind a downfall of logs, uttering terrible cries throughout the night. It was gone by the following morning, leaving only "size 9" tracks behind.

In 1870, a report appeared in the Antioch, California newspaper that spoke of a man seeing "a gorilla, a wild man, or whatever you choose to call it" in the forest. The creature's head "appeared to be set on the shoulders without a neck", which sounds remarkably similar to a modern Bigfoot report.

One wild man report from February 1876 was likely just that - a wild man. Except for the fact that the creature spotted was covered with hair, it had no other characteristics of Bigfoot. While prospecting in San Diego County, a man named Turner Helm heard a whistling sound and came face to face with a wild man. He was sitting on a large boulder and while Helm first assumed it to be an animal, he soon realized that it was a man. He was covered with coarse black hair, like that of a bear's fur, and had coarse hair and a beard that was long and thick. He was of medium size and had fine facial features, unlike those generally described for Bigfoot. Helm was startled but spoke to the man in both English and Spanish, but received no reply. The wild man looked at him for a few moments and then jumped down from the rock and vanished into the woods. Helm later stated that he and his prospecting partner had seen the man's tracks in the mountains many times, but had assumed they belonged to an Indian.

The rugged Green Mountains of Vermont have always had a reputation for strangeness. The area known as Glastonbury Mountain and it was once home to a small village of the same name. The town is long since gone and stories are told of how the residents were plagued with misfortune, disease, death and madness. It was near the vanished town that a coach full of travelers was attacked by the "Bennington Monster" in the 1800's and where, in 1892, Henry MacDowell went insane and murdered his friend, Jim Crowley. He was locked away in the Waterbury Asylum but he escaped and disappeared into the forests and rocks of Glastenbury Mountain. He was never seen again.

These legends and lore were recalled in October 1879 when two young men who were on a hunting trip south of Williamstown, Massachusetts saw a wild man. They described the creature as being about five feet tall and while he resembled a man in form and movement, he was covered with bright red hair, had a long beard and very wild eyes. When they first saw the creature, it sprang from a rocky cliff and began running toward the woods. Thinking that it was a bear or some other wild animal, one of the young men fired a shot and apparently hit it, because the creature then let out a cry of pain and rage. It turned and then started toward the hunters in a furious state. Needless to say, the two men began to run and lost their guns and ammunition on the way down the mountain. They never came back to retrieve them!

One of the strangest of the early Bigfoot reports allegedly occurred in July 1884 when several men were said to have captured a young Sasquatch along the Fraser

River, just outside of Yale, British Columbia. I remember reading this story when I was a kid in several books for "young readers" about the unexplained. I always considered it one of my favorites and always wondered what the eventual outcome of it was. In hindsight, the story was almost too good to be true and probably because it was. I was to be disappointed years later when I learned that respected Bigfoot author John Green revealed that it was likely a hoax.

The story appeared in Victoria's *Daily British Colonist* and told the story of several railroad workers, on the regular Lytton to Yale line, who found the creature lying alongside the tracks. Apparently, he had fallen from the steep bluffs and was injured, although when the train stopped, the creature jumped up, let out a sharp, barking sound and attempted to climb back up the bluff. The railroad men gave chase and managed to capture him.

They nicknamed the creature "Jacko" and described him as being "half man and half beast". He stood approximately four feet, seven inches tall and weighed about 130 pounds. He had long, dark hair and resembled a human, except for the fact that his body (except for his hands and feet) was covered with hair. His forearms were exceptionally long and he was very strong.

As no one was able to determine Jacko's identity or origin, he was eventually entrusted to the care of George Telbury, who planned to take the creature on tour or sell him to the circus. Some reports say that Jacko was on display in Yale for a time, but all trace of him later disappeared. At the time of the creature's alleged capture, newspapers reported that more than 200 people came to the jail in Yale to see him. However, another newspaper, the *British Columbian,* stated that the only "wild man" present was the head of the jail, who had "completely exhausted his patience" with the curiosity-seekers. The *Colonist,* who originally ran the story, never disputed the criticisms of the other newspaper and it likely just another of the "tall tales" that were common in the western papers of the late 1800's.

In 1885, hunters near Lebanon, Oregon encountered a wild man in the Cascade Mountains. When seen, the creature was eating raw deer flesh. Interestingly, the locals were so sure that this was a man, not a beast, that they even identified him as a missing person. The "wild man of the mountains" was said to be a man named John Mackentire, who had been lost in the forest while hunting about four years before. He and another man in his party had wandered off and were never seen again.

In the summer of 1885, a group of hunters led by a man named Fitzgerald were in the vicinity of Bald Peter in the Cascades and saw a man that they claimed resembled Mackentire. He was naked but was "as hairy as an animal and was a complete wild man." He was bent down by the river and was eating flesh from a deer that had been recently killed. The hunters approached to within a few yards before he saw them and fled. According to the account, the wild man has been seen in the area as far back as two years before by other hunters and it was believed that

Mackentire had become deranged and was now finding shelter in a cave. A group of men organized a search party to go back and look for him but no other information was ever given about the result of the expedition.

In October 1891, a wild man encounter in Michigan had dire results for the dogs used to hunt down a local creature. George Frost and W.W. Vivian ("both reputable citizens" the report added) were near the Tittabawassee River in Gladwin County when they ran into a naked man that was completely covered with hair. He was giant in proportion, standing over seven feet tall, with arms that hung down to his knees. Vivian released one of his bull dogs at the wild man but with one mighty swing of his arm, the creature struck the dog and killed it.

Another hairy wild man appeared in late November 1893 in Rockaway Beach, New York. Both this report, and the one that follows, are important in that not every "wild man" report that appeared in newspapers of the period could have been a Bigfoot sighting. Some of the accounts, like these two, are just as strange though and are perhaps even more frightening.

A series of unprovoked attacks in Rockaway Beach were made by a "wild man of large stature, weird in appearance, with fierce bloodshot eyes, long, flowing matted hair and a shaggy beard." Armed with a "large cavalry saber", the wild man wreaked havoc in a saloon and later wrenched a shotgun out of a man's hand and fired it at him. According to witness descriptions, the man was about six feet tall and weighed about 200 pounds. Unlike most of the earlier reports that we have seen, this wild man reportedly wore one shoe and a tattered oilskin jacket. The locals believed that he was a deranged sailor named James Rush, who had been driven into shore during a recent storm and had gone missing.

This was obviously not a Bigfoot, but seemed to be strangely tied into another case that occurred just five weeks later. A similar wild man terrorized the Mine Hill - Dover area of New Jersey. In early January, three young women named Bertha Hestig, Lizzie Guscott and Katie Griffin encountered a wild man near the edge of town. He stormed out of the woods completely naked and covered with cuts and bruises. With a shriek of terror at seeing the young ladies along the road, he ran back into the forest.

A few days later, two woodcutters were working near the Indian Falls clearing when their dogs began barking at a nearby rock. Thinking that a bear was nearby, the two men grabbed their axes and cautiously approached the area that seemed to be bothering the dogs. As they approached, a savage-looking figure jumped up from behind the rock. The stranger was said to be middle-aged, nearly six feet tall and weighing about 180 pounds. His face was covered with a long, unkempt beard. The wild man looked at the two woodcutters for a moment and then jumped onto the rock and began speaking loudly to himself in some sort of gibberish language. Any time that the men got too close to him, he began to run back and forth yelling frantically, "all the time working his arms as though rowing a boat". The woodcutters tried to seize the man but he picked up a club and swung it at them. The two men wisely fled and telephoned for help from a nearby store.

A search that was led by city police officers commenced and lasted throughout most of the night, but no trace of the man was found. He finally appeared again in Saturday and tried unsuccessfully to break into the home of the Russell family. On Sunday, a man named William Mullen encountered the wild man when taking a walk. He appeared in front of him on the road and the two of them looked at one another for a few moments before the wild man shrieked loudly and ran into the woods.

The search continued for the man but only prints from his bare feet were discovered, along with a brush hut and an axe that may have belonged to the strange individual. The last sighting took place at the Dover Silk Mill when several ladies who were looking out the window saw the underbrush part and a naked man walk out. Their screams brought other employees but the wild man ran back into the woods. By the time the mill workers got outside, he was long gone. The various search parties continued to look for the man but he was never found. According to reports, inquiry was made at the Morris Plains Asylum but no inmates were missing. Who this man may have been is unknown but I suppose it's possible that he could have been the same wild man who was causing problems in New York just five weeks earlier.

In May 1894, a more classic Bigfoot-type of "wild man" report was recorded in rural Kentucky. For months, people around Deep Creek had been noticing that something was stealing chickens, eggs, young pigs, lambs and food items from area farms. Finally, a man named Joseph Ewalt spotted the creature and reported that it had long white hair all over its body and wore only a piece of sheepskin for clothing. Ewalt said that a "light came from his eyes and mouth similar to fire", which may have been a bit of an embellishment on his part.

Some of the local men decided to try and capture the creature and one morning, Eph Boston and his sons saw it lurking around their barn. They described the creature the same way that Ewalt did but added that it was about six and a half feet tall and had long claws. A few moments after they spotted it, the wild man went running from the barn with three chickens in its hands. Tom Boston shot at it but missed. He and his brothers and father, along with several neighbors, tracked the creature to a nearby cave and found evidence around the entrance, in the form of bones and feathers, that the wild man was living there. They walked a short distance in the cave but an "unearthly yell" sent them running. Efforts to try and capture the beast, including smoking it out of the cave, failed.

In 1897, a wild man sighting took place near Sailor, Indiana and a man took a shot at it and seemed to hit it, but no trace of the creature was found. The sighting occurred in late April when two farmers saw a hair-covered, man-sized beast walking near the edge of a field. When the wild man saw them approaching, it dropped from two legs to four and began racing into the woods with great speed.

Also in April 1897, another wild man was seen in the woods near Stout, Ohio. While covered with hair, the creature was said to be wearing a pair of tattered pants. It attacked a young boy in the forest and then led a party of 30 men on a several hour chase before disappearing. On May 26, the same creature may have appeared near Rome, Ohio. It was described as a "wild man" and "gorilla-like" and was spotted by two men cutting timber in the forest. They chased the figure into a rocky area along the Ohio River and then it vanished.

One of the final reports of the 1800's shows a traditional Bigfoot in a less threatening role than was noted in most of the previous encounters. In 1897, a Native American fisherman reportedly discovered an emaciated Bigfoot near Tulelake, California. The man took pity on the creature and gave it his recent catch. A few weeks after the encounter, the story goes that the fisherman awoke to find several fresh deerskins neatly arranged outside of his cabin. In the following months, a nighttime visitor left firewood, pelts, berries and fruit for him to find each morning. The fisherman came to believe that it was the Bigfoot that he had helped who was leaving the gifts. Eventually, the offerings ceased and the man guessed that the creature had left the area. About a year later though, the man was bit by a rattlesnake and fell unconscious in the forest. He awoke a few hours later to find himself being carried by three large creatures, who took him to his cabin and who also wrapped his snake bite with moss, which managed to draw out the poison. The monsters left him at his door and he never saw them again.

ROOSEVELT'S BIGFOOT

In his 1893 book, *Hunting the Grizzly*, Theodore Roosevelt relates a purportedly true story of a hunter who was abducted from his campsite and killed by an eerie creature covered with hair.

Theodore Roosevelt was born on October 27, 1858, and he spent his childhood as part of a privileged family in New York City. He was the seventh generation of Roosevelt to be born in Manhattan, and the second of four children in his household. Always a sickly child afflicted with asthma, the young Roosevelt was educated at home by private tutors prior to going to Harvard College, where he excelled in boxing and academics.

After college, Roosevelt married Alice Hathaway Lee, the nineteen-year-old friend of his Harvard roommate. She hailed from a prominent New England banking family. He then enrolled in Columbia Law School, but dropped out after one year to begin a career in public service, winning election to the New York Assembly in 1882. A double tragedy struck Roosevelt in 1884, when his young wife died giving birth to their daughter. Alice and his mother died on the same day in the same house. Devastated, Roosevelt left his daughter, named Alice for her mother, in the care of his sister and fled to the Dakota Bad Lands to forget.

An Illustration from the *Louisville Courier-Journal* in Kentucky from May 1894 about a reported 'wild man' in the vicinity.

After two years out West, where he "busted" cows as a cattle rancher and chased outlaws as a frontier sheriff, Roosevelt returned to New York rejuvenated and full of energy. He ran unsuccessfully for mayor of New York City, wrote three books on his adventures in the West and campaigned for Republican presidential nominee Benjamin Harrison. When Harrison won the election, he appointed Roosevelt to the U.S. Civil Service Commission in 1889. His burgeoning career in politics would later lead him to the White House.

Roosevelt also married his childhood sweetheart, Edith Kermit Carow. In love once again, he took his little girl Alice and moved with Edith to a beautiful house at Oyster Bay, New York, which he had built for his first wife. He called the house Sagamore Hill. The happy couple soon filled the home with four boys, another girl, and little Alice.

Even during his political career though, the adventures that Roosevelt experienced in the American West left a permanent mark on him. His thirst for adventure would later lead him to act as the Police Commissioner of New York, to fight bravely in Cuba with the "Rough Riders" and, later in life, to be renowned as a big game hunter.

In 1893, when he wrote his first books about Western adventure, Roosevelt had already roamed most of the country in search of big game. He wrote: "In hunting, the finding and killing of the game is after all but part of the whole. The free, self reliant, adventurous life, with its rugged and stalwart democracy; the wild surroundings, the grand beauty of the scenery, the chance to study the ways and habits of the woodland creature - all these unite to give to the career of the wilderness hunter its peculiar charm."

And "peculiar" would be the only word to describe a story that Roosevelt saw fit to include in one of the volumes of his western accounts. In some reports, the story is included in Roosevelt's book *The Wilderness Hunter,* but the account that I have in my own collection is told in a book called *Hunting the Grizzly.* No matter where it might be found though does not make it any less strange...

"Frontiersman are not, as rule, apt to be very superstitious," Roosevelt wrote. "They lead lives too hard and practical and have too little imagination in things spiritual or supernatural.... but I once listened to a goblin story which rather impressed me. It was told by a grizzled, weather-beaten old mountain hunter named Bauman, who was born and had passed all his life on the frontier. He must have believed what he said, for he could hardly repress a shudder at certain points of the tale."

When the event occurred that Bauman related to Roosevelt, the mountain hunter was still a young man and was trapping with a partner among the mountains dividing the forks of the Salmon River from the head of the Wisdom River in Idaho. The two men worked the area for a time without much luck and then decided to try another location, where a branch of the Snake River ran through a particularly wild and lonely pass. The stream was said to be filled with beaver but was avoided by many of the Indian trappers in the region. It had been said that a lone hunter had wandered into the pass the year before and had been killed by some wild beast. The man's half-eaten remains were discovered by a party of prospectors who had passed the man's camp only the night before.

A Photograph that was taken of Roosevelt in his hunting clothes

Bauman and his friend had little concern for the story though and decided to trap the stream anyway. They rode to the foot of the pass and then left their horses tied in a meadow, because the rocky and heavily forested lands were nearly impassable for the animals. The trappers struck out on foot through the gloomy woods, finding the country dense and hard to travel through with their heavy packs and their need to bypass the stands of fallen timber and outcroppings of rock. After about four hours of walking, they found a small forest glade that offered easy access to the river.

An hour or two of daylight remained when they made camp, so they built a brush lean-to and unpacked their gear. Then they decided to take a short hike upstream and look for signs of game, only returning to camp around dusk. They were surprised to find that in their absence, something, apparently a bear, had visited the camp and had rummaged through their things. The contents of their packs had been scattered about and the lean-to had been torn down. The beast had left a number of footprints behind but the men paid little attention to them as they had much to do to rebuild the camp before darkness fell. After lighting a fire, they quickly rebuilt their shelter.

While Bauman began cooking supper, his companion studied the animal tracks more closely in the failing light. He was so intrigued by them that he lit a small stick in the fire and used the light from the burning end to follow the tracks to the edge of the clearing. When the light flickered out, he returned to the fire and took another, continuing his inspection of what appeared to be increasingly curious tracks. A few minutes later, he returned to the fire and stood next to where his friend was cooking dinner, peering out into the darkness. He suddenly spoke up. "Bauman, that bear has been walking on two legs," he said.

Bauman later recalled laughing at this, although his partner insisted that it was true. The two of them again looked at the tracks and Bauman's partner showed him that the tracks had been made by just two paws or feet. After discussing whether the prints could be those of a large person, and deciding that they could not be, the two men rolled up in their blankets and went to sleep beneath the shelter of the lean-to.

Around midnight, Bauman was suddenly awakened by a loud noise. He sat up quickly in his blankets and remembered later that he was then struck by a strong, pungent odor. The horrible smell was soon forgotten though as the ember light of the fire illuminated a large form looming at the entrance of the lean-to! Bauman grabbed for his rifle and immediately fired off a shot. Almost as soon as he squeezed the trigger, the huge shape vanished and he heard the thing crashing through the undergrowth as it ran off into the night.

Not surprisingly, the two men slept very little after this. They sat up next to the rekindled fire, waiting and watching, but heard nothing more. In the morning, they checked the traps that had been put out the night before and began finding locations for new ones. By some unspoken agreement, they stayed within close proximity to one another all day and returned together to camp as night began to fall once again.

Again as they neared the camp, they saw that the lean-to had been destroyed. The visitor from the previous day had apparently returned and had again destroyed the shelter and scattered their gear and belongings. Whatever the beast was, it had left more large, two-legged tracks in the soft earth by the river but neither man had the nerve to want to follow them.

Instead, they gathered up as much wood as they could find and built a roaring fire that lasted throughout the night, one or the other of them sitting on guard during the darkest hours. At one point in the night, both of them heard the creature approach once again, staying on the other side of the river. They heard it moving and crashing around in the forest and once it uttered a harsh, grating moan that chilled both men to the bone. However, it did not venture near the fire.

In the morning, the trappers decided that enough was enough. They were too almost too tired to tend to their work and believed that they could find just as good a location somewhere else. They discussed the strange events and decided that it would be best to pack up their gear and leave the valley by the afternoon. The men pulled their trap lines all morning, staying close together, and strangely, they found that all of the traps were empty and sprung. It looked as though they had snagged something but then the animals had been removed from the trap. Signs and tracks remained behind and the men hurried their work along even faster. Since leaving camp, they had experienced the uncomfortable sensation of being watched and followed. Occasionally, they would hear the snap or crack of a twig in the gloom of the forest, as well as the rustling of pine trees, and while they saw nothing, they became convinced that something was there.

By noon, they were within a couple of miles of the camp and there were still three beaver traps to collect from a little pond in a nearby ravine. Bauman offered to go and gather them while his friend went ahead to the camp and put their gear together. They planned to meet as soon as Bauman returned and then go down the mountain to the horses. His companion agreed and they parted ways.

On reaching the pond, Bauman found three beavers in the traps, one of which had pulled loose and had carried the trap into a beaver house. He spent the next several hours securing and preparing the animals and when he started back to the camp, he experienced a sinking feeling as he saw how low the sun was beginning to dip in the sky. As he finally reached the clearing where the camp was located, Bauman called out to his friend but he got no reply. The camp fire had gone out and the packs lay nearby, all secured and ready to go. The woods were silent and seemed empty and Bauman called out again. Once more, he was met with silence.

The trapper looked around, at first seeing nothing, but then he glimpsed a splash of color at the edge of the camp. As he stepped forward, his eyes caught the body of his friend. He was stretched out on the ground next to the trunk of a fallen spruce and blood was sprayed liberally on the earth and woods around him. Bauman rushed over to the man and found that his body was still warm. His neck had been broken and his throat had been torn out with what looked to be huge, sharp teeth. The footprints of the beast that had been visiting the camp were marked deep in the surrounding soil and told the whole story of what had occurred.

Bauman's friend, having finished packing their gear, sat down on the log facing the fire, with his back to the woods, to await his partner. While he was waiting, the unknown assailant, which must have been lurking in the woods the entire time, came silently up behind the man and broke his neck, while burying its teeth in his throat. It had not eaten the body but had apparently tossed it around, rolling it over and over, before retreating back into the woods.

Bauman was utterly unnerved by his gruesome discovery. The creature, which they had assumed was a bear, was either something half-human or half-devil or some great beast from the stories of the Indian medicine men, who spoke of evil beings that haunted the forest depths. Regardless, Roosevelt wrote that Bauman "abandoned everything but his rifle and struck off at speed down the pass, not halting until he reached the meadows where the hobbled ponies were still grazing. Mounting, he rode onward through the night, until far beyond the reach of pursuit."

THE HISTORICAL BIGFOOT

In 1901, another account of a Sasquatch encounter appeared in the *Daily British Colonist*. In this story, a lumber man named Mike King stated that he was working alone on Vancouver Island, near Campbell River, because his Indian packers had refused to accompany him because of their fear of the "monkey men" they said lived in the forest. Late in the afternoon, he observed a "man beast" washing roots in the river and when the creature became aware of King, it cried out and ran up a nearby hill. King described it as being "covered with reddish brown hair, and his arms were peculiarly long and were used freely in climbing and brush running; while the trail showed a distinct human foot, but with phenomenally long and spreading toes".

Three years later, on December 14, 1904, the *Colonist* again featured a Sasquatch story, this time from "four credible witnesses" who saw a man-like creature on Vancouver Island. In 1907, the newspaper told of the abandonment of an Indian village due to the inhabitants being frightened away by a "monkey-like wild man who appears on the beach at night, who howls in an unearthly fashion."

In July 1924, a weird incident involving a group of Bigfoot occurred in the Mount St. Helens region of southwestern Washington. The incident involved a night long assault by unknown creatures on a cabin where four miners were staying. The men had been prospecting a claim on the Muddy, a branch of the Lewis River, about eight miles from Spirit Lake. While working in the canyon, the men occasionally saw huge footprints but had no idea what to make of them. Then one day, they saw a huge ape-like creature peering out from behind a tree and one of the men fired his gun at it. The creature was apparently struck but it ran off. Fred Beck, one of the miners, met one of the monsters at the canyon rim and shot it in the back three times. It fell down the cliff and into the canyon but they never found the body.

That night, the "apes" struck back, starting an assault on the cabin where the men were staying by knocking a heavy strip of wood out from between two logs of the cabin. After that, there were repeated poundings on the walls, door and roof. Luckily, the cabin had been constructed to withstand heavy mountain snows and the creatures were unable to break in. However, they did begin using rocks to hit the roof from above and the miners became nervous enough to barricade the doors. As the creatures began thumping around on top of the cabin, as well as battering the walls, the men fired shots through the walls and roof, but to little effect. The noises and attacks continued until nearly dawn, ending after about five hours. Even though the cabin had no windows and the men could not see what was attacking them, Beck later told Bigfoot researcher John Green that he was sure that more than two creatures had been outside.

The incident was more than enough to get the men to pack up and abandon their mine the next day. They told their story when the returned to Kelso, Washington and a party of men went back to the cabin. Big footprints were found all around it, but no creatures were discovered. There have been other sightings in the area since, but none with such dramatic results. A first-hand account of the events was later written by Fred Beck called *I Fought the Apemen of Mt. St. Helens.* The area where the events took place was later dubbed "Ape Canyon" and it still is called that today.

One of the most bizarre Bigfoot encounters in history also occurred in 1924, although it would not be reported until many years later, in 1957. It involved a man who claimed to be abducted and held captive by a party of the creatures while on a prospecting trip in British Columbia. Although such tales seem to stretch the limits of believability, those who interviewed the man years later, including esteemed investigators John Green and Ivan T. Sanderson, did not for a moment doubt his sincerity or his sanity. Primatologist John Napier remarked that the man gave a "convincing account... which does not ring false in any particular."

The same cannot be said for all alleged Bigfoot "abductions" though. In 1871, a young girl named Seraphine Long was said to have been kidnapped by a male Bigfoot and she was taken to a cave and held prisoner for a year. She eventually got sick and so her captor allowed her to leave. However, when she returned home, it was discovered that she was carrying the creature's baby! She gave birth to the child but it only lived a few days. Of course, that was the story. The reader is asked to judge the validity of it for himself but I have to confess that I have my doubts about this one.

However, it's tough to feel the same way about the ordeal of Albert Ostman, who was prospecting for gold near the Toba Inlet in British Columbia in the summer of 1924. He claimed that he was abducted by Bigfoot but his detailed accounts of the creature's habits and activities remain unique to this day - leading many to wonder if perhaps he was telling the truth after all.

Toba Inlet in British Columbia was a secluded wilderness in 1924 when Albert Ostman decided to visit there during a much-needed vacation. The construction worker and lumberjack liked to prospect for gold as a hobby and in addition to doing some hunting and fishing, he planned to search for a legendary lost gold mine that was rumored to be in the area. Ostman hired an Indian guide to take him to the head of the inlet and on the way, the Indian told him about a white man who used to come out of the area laden with gold. When Ostman asked the guide what happened to the man, the guide replied that he had disappeared and had probably been killed by Sasquatch. Ostman scoffed at the story, not believing a word of this tall tale.

When they reached the inlet, the guide helped Ostman to set up his base camp and then he departed. Ostman had paid him to return in three weeks. For the first week or so, he hunted and fished a little for food and spent quite a bit of time hiking in the woods and searching for any traces of the lost mine. He was quite casual about the search though, enjoying the outdoors and the freedom away from his work. Then one day, he returned to camp to find that his gear had been disturbed.

Nothing was missing, but it had all been moved around. Ostman assumed that a porcupine or some small animal had been looking for food. He tried to stay awake for two night to try and catch the annoying animal but each time, he fell asleep. On both mornings when he awoke, he discovered that food was missing from his pack.

Now irritated, and determined to trap the culprit, he loaded his rifle and shoved it down in his sleeping bag with his clothes and some of his personal belongings. He planned to stay awake the entire night and drive off the pesky animal. Despite his intentions though, Ostman fell asleep. Later on that night, still half asleep, Ostman awoke to find that he had been picked up, still inside his sleeping bag, and was being carried through the woods. He first assumed that he had been tied and thrown over the back of a horse, but then realized that he was pinned into his sleeping bag by two large arms. Unable to reach his rifle, or even his knife, he was trapped in the bedroll. There was no sound but the uttering of breath from the figure who carried him, the sound of powerful feet trudging through the forest and the occasional rattle of a fry pan and canned food in Ostman's pack, which the giant had also picked up from the camp.

Ostman traveled for several hours and estimated that he journeyed about 30 miles inland. At the end of this time, he was dumped onto the ground and he slowly crawled out of the bag in the darkness. His whole body ached from the trip and as he was trying to massage some feeling back into his legs, the sun came up and the prospector got his first good look at his abductors. Squatting nearby were four hairy giants, the same type of creatures that had been described to Ostman by the Indian guide.

They sat there looking at Ostman with curiosity, but did not seem threatening in the least. The two older creatures were male and female and the two younger ones were also of both sexes. The oldest male stood nearly eight feet tall and weighed an estimated 750 pounds. The oldest female was slightly smaller and had large, hanging breasts. The younger creatures were of smaller proportions than what Ostman assumed were the parents and the younger female had no breasts. All four of the Bigfoot had coarse, dark hair that covered their bodies.

Ostman later recounted that the older female seemed to object to his presence during the first day of his captivity. She chattered and grunted at the male but eventually, he seemed to win the day and was allowed to keep Ostman around. The two females avoided him as much as possible, spending their time hunting for roots, nuts and berries. The two male creatures were curious about everything the prospector did and found the contents of Ostman's pack and sleeping bag to be quite fascinating. He had with him his food, his rifle, a few pots and pans and his knife. They often looked at these items but never touched them, although the oldest creature was very interested in Ostman's snuff box and its contents. This keen interest would eventually prove to be integral in Ostman's escape.

Two days into his captivity, Ostman tried to run away. The Sasquatch lived in a small ten-acre basin that was cut between two cliff walls. A narrow break in the rock provided the only entrance. When Ostman tried to slip out of the valley, the oldest male quickly caught him and pulled him back into the basin. He considered using his rifle and trying to shoot his way out, but knew that if he did not kill the creature with the first couple of shots, the beast would surely tear him apart.

After six days, Ostman had another idea. He was becoming increasingly nervous of the creatures because he was starting to get the impression that he had been captured in order to provide a mate for the younger female. Not wanting to spend the rest of his life in captivity, he began working on a plan to break free. He knew that the elder Bigfoot was very interested in his chewing tobacco. Each day, he gave the creature a small amount of it to chew on. He wondered if there might be a way to use the Bigfoot's love of the snuff to his advantage.

On the morning of the seventh day, Ostman made a fire for the first time since he had arrived. He decided to make some coffee, which interested the two male Bigfoot. As he was eating his breakfast and drinking from the tin of coffee, he decided to try out his idea. He reached over and offered the older Bigfoot some of his snuff. He held on tightly to the box so that the creature could only take a small amount, which irritated him. He jerked the box from Ostman's hand and proceeded to devour the entire contents of it. He liked the taste so much that he literally licked clean the inside of the container.

It only took a few moments for the Bigfoot to become violently ill. Retching and coughing, the creature ran towards the stream and collapsed on all fours. At the same time, Ostman grabbed his rifle and his pack and began to run. He shot towards the narrow entrance but his escape attempt was noticed by the older female, who set off after him. He made it to the gap in the rock just seconds before she caught up with him and turning quickly, he fired a shot over her head. The creature stopped in her tracks and let out a squeal, but she did not pursue him any further.

Using his compass, Ostman managed to make his way back to civilization. After three days, he met up with a party of lumberjacks and told them that he had gotten lost while prospecting. He was sure that no one would ever believe his account of what really happened and he remained silent for more than 30 years, only telling his story in 1957.

Although Ostman has long since passed away, Bigfoot researcher John Green knew him for more than 12 years and questioned him extensively about his captivity. He had no reason to consider him a liar and neither did the police officers, primate experts and zoologists who also looked into his account. For this reason, we have only the option to consider his story, no matter how bizarre, to be true. But, of course, that remains up to the reader to decide.

Sasquatch sightings and encounters continued and were occasionally mentioned in mostly Canadian newspaper accounts. Bigfoot did not enter the American mainstream until 1958, when the now infamous tracks were discovered at

Bluff Creek. This was the time when the giant creature entered the mainstream but America's fascination with Bigfoot was only beginning. Through the remainder of the 1950's, the 1960's and the 1970's, interest in these elusive creatures reached its high point. After a cooling down period of about two decades, when only Bigfoot hunters and diehard enthusiasts were seeking information about Sasquatch, public interest is again on the rise. New attention has been given to some of the evidence that has been collected for the creature's existence, including plaster casts of footprints, possible fur, photographs and film. Let's take a look at some of that evidence and the reader can judge for himself how credible much of it actually is.

THE PATTERSON FILM

By the decade of the 1960's, Bigfoot had become firmly entrenched in the imaginations of Americans. Though scientists refused to admit that what witnesses could be seeing was actually what they claimed to see, a number of investigators had begun seeking out witnesses and venturing into the forest, hoping to catch a glimpse of one of the monsters. Books began to appear and articles began to generate even more interest with the readers of magazines like True and Saga.

Among the amateur investigators who went looking for Bigfoot was Roger Patterson, a onetime rodeo rider, hopeful documentary film maker and Bigfoot hunter. In 1967, Patterson was barely scraping by as an inventor and promoter but his interest was piqued by a 1959 *True* magazine article about Bigfoot. From them on, he devoted as much of his spare time as he could afford roaming the woods of the Pacific Northwest in search of the creature. Patterson always carried with him a motion picture camera on his expeditions, hoping that he might be able to catch one of the monsters on film.

Around 1:15 in the afternoon on October 20, 1967, Patterson and a friend, Bob Gimlin, were riding north along a dry stretch of Bluff Creek in the Six Rivers National Forest of northern California. At one point, a large pile of logs in the middle of the stream bed blocked their path and they had to maneuver their horses around to the east. As they rode along the logs, they veered left and resumed their original course, only to see something that still has investigators and researchers puzzled today.

A female Bigfoot stood up from the creek water where she had been squatting and walked away from the approaching men and horses, moving briskly and swinging her arms as she moved toward the forest. At the same time this occurred, all three horses (including the pack horse) began to panic. Patterson's horse reared up and fell over sideways onto his right leg, but managed to stagger back to its feet again. As it did, Patterson quickly reached for the 16mm camera in his saddlebag and began to follow the creature, filming as he went. Unfortunately, only 28 feet of film remained in the camera but Patterson managed to use it to record the Bigfoot's escape from three different positions.

After his return to civilization, Patterson enlisted the help of researcher John Green to get some sort of scientific confirmation of the evidence that he had captured. However, the amateur investigator was ignored and berated by the established scientific community so in 1968, he took his case to the public. After padding his film footage with a documentary-style look at other evidence gathered in the search for Bigfoot, he went on a tour of the American west, renting small theaters and auditoriums for one-night shows and lectures. Since that time, the footage has gone on to become one of the most famous, and most controversial, pieces of Bigfoot evidence ever found.

Patterson's life was cut short in 1972 when he died, nearly broke, from Hodgkin's Disease, but he swore to the end of his life that the sighting and the film were authentic. Bob Gimlin also maintained that the events really took place and that his friend's film was the genuine article. Gimlin did not start out as a believer in the creature either. He was interested but unconvinced and only came along on his buddy's expeditions out of friendship, rather than a belief that they would actually find anything. "He'd talk about it around the campfire," he said in an interview. "I didn't care, but after a time you'd find yourself looking for the doggone thing too."

The first investigator on the scene of the sighting was a man named Bob Titmus, who found tracks that matched the creature's stride depicted in the film. He made 10 casts of them and discovered that the footprints led up a small hill, where the creature had paused to look back on the men below. Patterson and Gimlin had elected to recover their horses rather than pursue the Bigfoot and risk being stranded in the wilderness.

And while Patterson died in 1972, the legacy of his film lives on. Unfortunately, it has never settled the question as to whether or not Bigfoot exists in the forests of America. Both the number of supporters and detractors of the film are many. Researchers have argued about the speed of the film, the gait of the creature, the distance of its stride and more. Most biologists and zoologists who have studied it remain noncommittal. Film experts and individuals experienced with hoaxes have been unable to find evidence that it is not authentic. For this reason, the film has never been successfully debunked.

Of course, that's not for the lack of trying though. The most recent claims against the validity of the film have stated that the Bigfoot was actually a man in a monkey suit. Some maintain that Patterson and Gimlin were knowing participants in the hoax and that they rented the suit with the idea of gaining from the resulting film financially. This is in spite of the fact that the men made very little money from it and Patterson died nearly broke. Regardless, this theory has it that Patterson and Gimlin (who were both poor rodeo riders in 1967) rented the expensive suit, transported it to an area that was nearly inaccessible by car and cleverly shot the grainy, jerky and poorly executed film.

Defenders of the film believe this is ridiculous and state that a frame by frame analysis of the footage shows a creature that does not walk like a man. Anthropologist Grover Krantz demonstrated that the human walk involves the locking of the knees but the filmed Bigfoot does not do this, which would have been very difficult for a hoaxer to do and still walk as smoothly as this creature does. In addition, after viewing the film with Bigfoot investigator Peter Byrne in 1973, the chief technician at Disney Studios stated that "the only place in the world a simulation of that quality could be created would be here, at Disney Studios, and this footage was not made here." If the Bigfoot was a fake, it was one that was very, very well done.

And while the Disney tech may have been overstating the importance of the studio, there were very few places that such a film (or a suit like that) could have been made in the late 1960's. Even the detractors grudgingly agree that Patterson and Gimlin did not have the resources to pull off a hoax of the magnitude of the film and certainly could not have paid to have a suit like this one created. Only two companies could have created a suit of that type, at that time, and both claimed that they did not do so. To make matters more mysterious, the man in the suit (if there was one) has remained silent for more than 35 years, ignoring the opportunity for financial gain by confessing.

Interestingly, a more popular theory as to who made the suit has emerged within the last few years. According to some conspiracy theorists, the Patterson Bigfoot was actually a man wearing a suit created by master makeup artist John Chambers, who created the makeup for the classic film *Planet of the Apes* with Charlton Heston. The debunkers have fixed on Chambers for a couple of reasons, including his award-winning makeup effects for the movie and also for the fact that the movie finished filming on August 10, 1967, just a couple of months before Patterson's encounter. The idea is that Patterson could have easily rented one of the surplus monkey suits for his own purposes.

Even though this seems somewhat plausible, the theory has its problems as well. For one thing, the Bigfoot in Patterson's film looks nothing like the apes that were created for the movie. The apes in *Planet of the Apes* were not suits but were mostly facial makeup. Were they clever? Yes, but the Bigfoot in Patterson's film does not resemble these apes at all. The idea that Chambers may have created the Bigfoot suit was apparently the result of director John Landis joking about it to some friends at a party. As anyone who knows anything about Hollywood knows, you can't take every rumor you hear seriously in that town. To make matters worse, Chambers himself repeatedly denied the claims until his death. He told interviewers that he was "good but not that good" in response to the story and it has been a general consensus that Chambers enjoyed people thinking that he "might" have made the suit because it bolstered his skills as an artist. The truth is that it's very unlikely that he made it. In spite of this, the story lives on.

To this day, the debate continues to rage. Many Bigfoot experts believe that it is valid footage of an unknown creature but just as many people laugh when the subject is brought up. While I see that it might be possible for Chambers to have created the suit and helped to perpetrate a hoax, I really have to ask if it's plausible? I have no hard evidence to back up my own opinion that the film is genuine. I see both sides of the argument and have followed the debate for quite some time but for myself, I see nothing here to convince me that this is a suit. Based on the time period, I don't think that enough information had been made available to the general public for someone to have imitated a creature in the way that the Bigfoot moves in the Patterson film. Just because Chambers "could" have made the suit does not mean that he did.

PRINTS, HAIR AND RECORDINGS

As the reader can well imagine, there have been literally thousands of fraudulent footprints, photos and film that have been "discovered" since Bigfoot entered the mainstream. While much of the alleged evidence that appears is dubious at best, other Bigfoot prints and samples have managed to defy easy explanation.

In 1969, a series of 1,089 tracks were discovered near Bossburg, Washington and were analyzed by researchers. They measured 17 1/2 inches long and about seven inches wide and seemed to indicate that the creature that left them had a right clubfoot, the result, some surmised, of a childhood injury. This minor detail seemed to rule out any chance of a fraud for it's unlikely that any hoaxer would have gone to the trouble to include this in such a huge number of tracks.

And there have been hundreds (perhaps thousands) more footprints found that are not easy to explain away. The occurrence of these tracks in remote and seldom-traveled areas also seems to argue against a hoax as well. Why would someone go to the trouble of creating phony Bigfoot tracks in an area where no one would likely ever see them?

Other evidence that has been discovered consists of feces and hair samples that are either associated with sightings or may have been indications of a Bigfoot's recent passing. Many of these samples seem to resist identification. But what about the body of a Bigfoot? Debunkers and skeptics say that Bigfoot cannot exist for if it did, then we would have found the corpse of one by now. Jeffrey Meldrum, an associate professor of Anthropology at Idaho State University, disagrees. "Think about it," he said in an interview. "It's rare, reproduces infrequently, and if it's like other apes, it may live for 50 years. It's at the top of the food chain, so death most likely comes from natural causes. When an animal is ill or feeble, it'll hide somewhere safe, which makes it more difficult to find any remains. Scavengers strip the carcass and scatter the bones. Rodents chew up what's left for the calcium. Soil in the Northwest is acidic, which is conducive to plant fossilization but not to bones. They disintegrate."

Beyond the physical evidence, there have also been the recordings that have been made by Bigfoot hunters of what is alleged to be the "voice" of the creature itself. Many of the tapes have been analyzed, including one notable recording that was obtained on October 21, 1972 in California's High Sierra mountains. That night, investigators recorded a series of moans, whines, growls and grunts that were coming from the darkness. Two electronic specialists, one from the University of Wyoming and one from Rockwell International, came to the conclusion that the sounds came from "more than one speaker, one or more of which is of larger physical size than an average human male. The formant frequencies found were clearly lower than for human data, and their distribution does not indicate that they were a product of human vocalization and tape speed alteration."

One of the most recent, and perhaps most convincing, pieces of evidence to turn up has been the Skookum Cast, which was discovered in September 2000 by members of the Bigfoot Field Researchers Organization around Mount St. Helens in Washington. During a Bigfoot expedition, researchers baited a marshy plain, known as Skookum Meadow, with apples and melon hoping to attract Bigfoot. They returned the next morning to find a number of prints and many pieces of the fruit missing. They recognized both coyote and elk tracks but were unable to identify a set of anthropoid forearm, heel and butt imprints. They even found marks that had been made by hair in the muddy ground, pressed down by a huge weight. The hunters spent the next eight hours studying the signs and creating a plaster cast of what appeared to be a spot where Bigfoot had reclined.

The cast found many supporters among the most influential men in the field, including John Green, Grover Krantz and others. In June 2002, three noted anthropologists studied the cast and commented on their findings. The examiners were Darius Swindler, a professor emeritus from the University of Washington, Natural History anatomist Esteban Sarimento and Jeffrey Meldrum from Idaho State University. The presence of Sarimento marked the first interest in Bigfoot by the New York-based American Museum of Natural History. In his comments, Sarimento noted that one impression that was lined with hair marks "could have been made by a huge hindquarters." Meldrum summed things up by stating that he felt that all of the evidence pointed to an eight-foot-tall creature leaving the impressions at Skookum Meadows.

As exciting as this was to Bigfoot proponents though, the real proof of the creature's existence would be not just capturing his footprints - but the creature himself. "The ultimate evidence that this thing exists," said Esteban Sarimento, "is if somebody found one and brought it back."

THE BIGFOOT HUNTERS

There have been numerous expeditions created to try and track down Bigfoot over the years and many of the men involved with these hunts have gone on to be considered as seminal figures in modern Bigfoot research.

In 1960, Texas millionaire Tom Slick organized the Pacific Northwest Bigfoot Expedition, the most formidable group of researchers working at that time. Most of the men were seasoned trackers and had spent time in the Himalayas with Slick searching for the Yeti. Despite extensive searching though, the group made little progress and when Slick died in a plane crash in 1962, the Expedition disbanded.

In 1970, Robert W. Morgan tried to continue Slick's research when he formed the American Yeti Association. The group consisted of an archaeologist, a cinematographer, at least one psychic, several biology students and George Harrison, the editor of National Wildlife. Morgan and his crew traveled to the region around Mount St. Helens and used jeeps, radios and advanced gadgets of the period in their search. Funded by the National Wildlife Association, Morgan was desperate for results and even resorted to baiting Bigfoot traps with a nude female volunteer. Eventually, after spending more than $50,000, he was forced to dissolve the association.

In 1997, Peter Byrne, the Irishman who played a prominent role in Tom Slick's 1960 expedition in the Northwest (and the 1959 expeditions to Asia), created the Bigfoot Research Project. It was financed by the Academy of Applied Science of Boston and made use of a wide range of technology, including digital global positioning units, high tech cameras, night vision equipment and motion and heat sensors. Byrne also planned to use a special biopsy dart that could be shot at a Bigfoot and that was designed to take small blood, hair and tissue samples without injuring the creature. Byrne reasoned that with this evidence, along with the other samples collected over the years, he could conclusively prove the monster's existence. Unfortunately, the team failed to spot a creature, much less shoot one with the biopsy dart. Byrne dissolved the Project and has been on hiatus ever since.

Another important figure in Bigfoot research was the late Rene Dahinden, a Canadian who conducted numerous field investigations throughout the Northwest. As a supporter of the Patterson film, Dahinden worked hard to see that it got attention from the scientific community and from the public as well. His only book, *Sasquatch* (1973), was written by Don Hunter. Sadly, due to declining health Dahinden was forced to reduce his research in 1999. He passed away in 2002.

John Green is considered one of the leading researchers in the field, although has reportedly stopped cataloguing new accounts of Bigfoot sightings. Born in Canada in 1927, Green began investigating with Tom Slick, Rene Dahinden and others during the early days of Bigfoot research. He wrote a number of books on the subject, including *Year of the Sasquatch, On the Track of the Sasquatch* and *Sasquatch: The Apes Among Us*. He chronicled many famous cases (including Albert Ostman) and reportedly has gathered more than 2,000 sightings and several hundred incidents of footprint finds.

Grover Krantz was the first real scientist to become associated with the study of Bigfoot. He once wrote that "It is tantamount to academic suicide to become associated with any of these people" and yet he did so anyway. As a professor of Anthropology at Washington State University, he paid dearly for his fascination with the mysterious creature, by way of lost promotions and professional ridicule. By the end of his life though (he died in 2002), he no longer cared. He had first been convinced that there was something "out there" after the 1969 footprints that had been found near Bossburg, Washington. He and many other researchers, including Rene Dahinden and John Green, studied the tracks that had been left behind by "Cripplefoot", as they dubbed it, and while Krantz had little hope that Bigfoot was real at that point, he was soon to change his mind. The professor managed to bring back plaster casts of 17 inch feet, the right foot of which curved like a C and had enormous bunions and splayed toes. Nobody could have faked that, Krantz realized.

He came to believe that Bigfoot may have descended from the Gigantoithecus, a huge primate that roamed southern China more than 300,000 years ago. Its bones are part of the fossil record and it may have migrated to North America by way of the Bering Strait when it was still a land bridge. He thought it possible that some remnants of these creatures may have survived.

Today, there are still many researchers out there hunting for Bigfoot, hoping to bring back remains, tracks or anything else that will prove these creatures exist. As mentioned already, the reader is asked to judge the existence of these creatures for himself for short of incredible evidence, we can only surmise that the mysterious giants are out there in the forests of the Northwest. Until one is found though, they have to remain one of the greatest of the mysteries in the annals of the unexplained in America.

THE MINNESOTA ICEMAN

Without a doubt, the story of the elusive "Minnesota Iceman" is the most compelling, the weirdest and the most mysterious tale in the annals of the unexplained in America. What was it? What happened to it? And most of all, could the figure in the ice have really been either Bigfoot or the "missing link"? Researchers are always looking for that solid proof that Bigfoot exists in the form of either a live specimen or a dead one. Did someone actually have that evidence at one time? We're likely to never know, but the story itself is nearly as compelling as the answers.

The tale really has to begin with the discovery of the Iceman by Milwaukee zoology student Terry Cullen in December 1968 at Chicago's International Livestock Exhibition and Fair. The Iceman had already appeared on the scene prior to this, but it was at this exhibition that it really entered the public spotlight. Besides that, everything that occurred before Cullen found the creature on display at the fair is definitely open to question and conjecture.

There are three different versions of the story as to how the Iceman ended up in the freezer of a Minnesota man named Frank Hansen. The convoluted history of the Iceman has only added to the mystery of the creature's authenticity over the years. According to one ridiculous version, the Iceman was a Bigfoot-type creature that tried to rape a woman named Helen Westring while she was alone on a hunting trip. According to her story, the beast grabbed her and ripped off all her clothes, but Ms. Westring fainted before the creature could rape her. When she regained consciousness, she recovered her rifle and shot the creature through the right eye. She apparently then took the body back to town and it eventually came into the hands of Frank Hansen.

Another version of the story states that the creature was not from Minnesota at all but was reportedly found (already frozen) in a block of ice in the Sea of Okhostok, near eastern Siberia. The body was found by either Russian seal hunters or Japanese fishermen, who smuggled it to Hong Kong. After that, it was purchased by an American millionaire who lived on the west coast and he in turn rented the curiosity to Air Force veteran Frank Hansen of Winona, Minnesota, who exhibited the frozen specimen. Hansen reportedly came up with this story to appease the FBI when he was questioned about transporting what he was claiming was a frozen carcass back and forth over the Canadian-American border.

The third (and "official" version) was recounted by Frank Hansen himself in the pages of *Saga Magazine* in 1970. According to Hansen, the story of the Iceman began in 1960 when he was an Air Force captain and pilot assigned to the 343rd Fighter Group in Duluth, Minnesota. During the 1960 deer hunting season, Hansen was staying at a small resort on the shores of the Whiteface Reservoir, about 60 miles from Duluth. Three other Air Force personnel, Lieutenant Roy Asfedt, Lieutenant Dave Allison and Major Lou Szrot, were also part of the hunting party.

The men left the cabin at about 6:00 on the second morning of the trip and Hansen started off for a narrow neck of swamp that he hoped would be a good location. He sat motionless on a hillside for almost two hours when a slight movement at the edge of the swamp caught his eye. He looked up to see a large doe staring at him. At that same moment, a shot was fired on the opposite side of the swamp and the deer ran in Hansen's direction. He opened fire and hit the animal just as it was reaching the edge of the trees and it fell to the ground. Hansen bolted his rifle to take another shot, but before he could, the deer was up and out of sight in the heavy brush.

Walking toward the thicket, he found large spots of blood on the grass and signs of which direction the deer had vanished into the woods. The animal had left a clear trail into the swamp and Hansen decided to follow it. He said later that he pushed along, always thinking that the wounded animal would be just around the next bend in the trail until he realized that he had been walking for almost an hour. He decided to check his bearings and then retrace his own trail out of the swamp. He knew that he would now never be able to pack the animal out of the forest, even if he did find it.

Stepping over a small cedar log, he heard a strange gurgling sound ahead. Thinking that it might be the deer, he pushed aside the brush and peered into a small clearing. There, in the center of the area, were three large creatures that he first thought were bears. Two of them were on their knees, tearing at the insides of the deer that Hansen had shot. The gurgling sound had been noises made as the creatures drank the deer's blood, Hansen reported.

The third beast was crouched about 10 feet away from the hunter, over at the edge of the clearing. When it saw Hansen watching, it immediately began to let out a weird screeching sound. It screamed with its arms raised above its head and charged right at Hansen. Without thinking, he raised his rifle and fired the chambered shell. The explosion carried the bullet into the creature's eye and it was sent spinning to the frozen ground. Apparently, the two remaining creatures ran one way and Hansen ran the other. Blind with fear, he crashed back through the swamp until he fell to the ground. Now lost, as well as terrified, he passed out for a time.

When Hansen recovered, he fired off three shots into the air (the signal for a hunter in distress) and then fired off three more. Eventually, after traveling some distance, he heard a voice calling out and he emerged out of the woods and into a hunting camp. He explained that he had become lost but never mentioned the strange creatures that he had encountered. One of the hunters said that he knew where Hansen and his friends had parked their truck that morning and offered to drive him there. When he arrived, his friends were waiting and while he good-naturedly took their ribbing about becoming lost, he never told them about what he had seen and what he had done in the swamp.

Time passed and the truth gnawed at him. What had the creature been? Was it an escaped gorilla? Was it a man dressed up for a prank? Except for the fact that it was covered with hair, the beast had seemed to be a human being. Had Hansen committed murder - or had the whole thing been the product of his fevered imagination? For the next two months after returning home, Hansen was troubled with migraine headaches and had trouble concentrating on flying and flight instruction. He knew that he had to return to the swamp, but he refused to do so unless he would be able to find his way out again. Then on November 29, the area was covered with five inches of fresh snow and Hansen returned to the region near Whiteface on December 2.

Hansen had brought along a swamp-buggy with his pickup and he drove the vehicle into the forest, re-tracing his route from hunting season. He eventually found the body of the creature, proving to himself that the encounter had been real after all. He brushed away the snow and found that the corpse had been frozen, covered with blood, and that the eye that Hansen had shot was missing. As he inspected the creature, he realized that it was not a human but what he called a "freak of nature". Even so, he did not want to leave the creature in the swamp. He feared that hunters might stumble across the corpse and summon the authorities and that the investigation that followed might lead back to Hansen. With that in mind, he left the swamp-buggy in the woods and returned to Duluth. He told his wife that the vehicle had gotten stuck and so he needed to return with a pick, shovel, ax and chainsaw to get it out. When he returned to Whiteface, Hansen chopped the body from the frozen earth and loaded it onto the rear platform of the swamp-buggy. He tied it down with cargo straps and then hauled the creature back to his truck, cutting trail as he went. He used nylon straps to then move it over to the truck bed and to cover it with tarps for the trip home.

It was almost dark when he returned to his Air Force housing in Duluth. Needless to say, his wife was almost hysterical when he told her about what had happened to him and showed her the gigantic corpse. The Hansen's had recently purchased a new freezer and because they couldn't bury the beast in the frozen ground, decided to remove the meat in the freezer and replace it with the body, at least until spring. So, after the kids had gone to bed, Hansen and his wife, Irene, hauled the body out of the truck and into the basement. The creature was now beginning to stink but they managed to hold their breath as they bent the arms and legs of the corpse and forced it into the metal box. They covered it with a blanket and left it there for over a month.

Hansen still planned to bury the corpse somewhere in the spring but after checking on its condition, saw that it was beginning to dehydrate and decay. He and Irene finally decided that the body would be better preserved if they filled the freezer with water and encased the cadaver in ice. They began to pour about 20 gallons of water into the freezer each day until it was a solid block of ice. This seemed to be the perfect plan, until the spring thaw arrived and Hansen began to wrestle with the idea of trying to thaw out the body and transport it somewhere and bury it. His plans continued to be delayed until his retirement approached and the family purchased a farm near Rollingstone, Minnesota.

Hansen realized that he could not risk hiring a moving company to transport the freezer, so he rented a truck and moved all of the furniture himself. Friends helped to move the locked, "meat packed" freezer into the truck and then into the basement of the new house. During the seven-hour ordeal, the top layer of ice began to melt and while Hansen was able to quickly re-freeze the body, he became so paranoid about the beast unthawing that he purchased a generator for the new home so that the power would never go out. He was now sure that the monster would never be discovered.

In November 1965, Hansen retired from the Air Force and joined his family on the farm. Now, with time on his hands, he began to do some reading and ran across some books and articles on the "abominable snowman". The more that he read, the more certain he was that the creature in his freezer was one of these elusive beasts.

He made a few discreet inquiries about the statute of limitations on murder in Minnesota and learned that there was no time limit. Even though he was sure the creature was not human, he decided to keep the corpse hidden in the freezer for a while longer.

A little over a year later, Hansen met a "veteran showman" who recognized his boredom with civilian life and suggested that Hansen exhibit a rare old John Deere tractor that he had acquired and had loaned to the Smithsonian Institution. It had been returned to him from Washington and he had been showing it on a limited basis. The showman suggested that Hansen take the tractor on the state fair circuit. He wouldn't make much money at it, but it would keep him busy. Hansen was pleased with the idea but had other "things" in mind. He asked his friend if the body of a hairy creature that resembled a prehistoric man would make a good attraction? The showman assured him that it would but when he asked Hansen where he would get something like that, Hansen told him that he could have a model made.

Hansen now decided to consult with his attorney concerning the legalities of displaying the creature he had killed in the woods. The lawyer didn't believe a word of the story until Hansen drove him out to the farm and showed him what was in the freezer. Not surprisingly, the attorney was stunned but advised Hansen that he could possibly get into legal trouble by displaying the body. There could be a murder charge if the creature was determined to be human, he said, and there were also laws about transporting dead bodies.

Hansen continued to press him about displaying the body as an exhibit though. The attorney considered his ideas for a moment. "You have the original body," he finally said. "The authorities will be after it because this thing is the scientific find of the century. However, it might be possible to create a model as you suggested. Maintain a record of the model's construction but show the real creature instead. If the officials pressure you, it's a small matter to produce photos of the model taken during different phases of fabrication." Hansen agreed and then came up with an even better idea. He would exhibit the model only for the first year so that the "carnies" would accept it as a bogus sideshow exhibit.

In January 1967, Hansen made sketches of the creature and then went to Hollywood to confer with some makeup artists who created special effects for the movies. He spoke with Bud Westmore, the head of makeup effects for Universal and he told Hansen that a believable model could cost as much as $20,000 to produce. He told Hansen that he didn't have time to make the model for him but if needed, he would provide technical support. Hansen then consulted with the Los Angeles County Museum and it was suggested that he contact Howard Ball, an independent artist who had created life-sized animal exhibits for the La Brea Tar Pits. Hansen hired Ball to create the model and was also told by John Chambers from Fox (the makeup master who has been accused of creating the Bigfoot suit for the Patterson film) that a small wax studio in Los Angeles could implant the hair according to

Hansen's specifications. With Chambers' introduction, Hansen hired Pete and Betty Corral, who implanted the model's hair individually with needles.

Hansen now had a model that he had spent thousands of dollars on, but no guarantee that it would make any money as an exhibit. He decided to put the final touches on the creature himself (rather than spend more money) and he and a friend from Pasadena added bloody eyes, a broken arm and blood-soaked hair to make it look as close to the original in Hansen's freezer as possible. Hansen then rented a freezer where he could encase the model in ice to get it ready for its debut on the west coast.

The exhibit debuted on May 3, 1967 as what the carnival folks called a "What is It?" show. Hansen explained that the creature had been found frozen in the Bering Straits by Japanese fishermen. He had created this cover story and stuck to it for the next two years. The tour continued until November 1967, when Hansen closed at the Louisiana State Fair and returned home to Minnesota. By March 1968, he had convinced himself that it was now safe to replace the model with the real specimen for the upcoming fair season. He had been told by carnival experts that the model was a sensational attraction but that it had too many flaws to fool anyone with an expert knowledge of anatomy. He was sure that word had gotten out that the exhibit was a fake and that he would be safe to put the real cadaver on display.

Hansen then got to work unthawing the real body so that he could cut the tendons in the arms and legs and make it look like the model. He froze it again and then prepared to hit the fair circuit. The attention that the exhibit got was different than when Hansen had been showing the model though. While most of the onlookers had been impressed with the old exhibit, the real corpse was drawing a different crowd. Now, doctors, college students and scientists were coming to examine and photograph the "missing link". At the Oklahoma State Fair, one prominent surgeon visited the exhibit on nine separate occasions, each time bringing a different colleague with him. At the Kansas State Fair, the county pathologist was so intrigued that he sent many of his associates to see the display.

Hansen was displaying the creature as the "real thing", which he maintained that it was, although he continued his cover story that the monster was actually owned by a California millionaire and that it had been recovered in the icy waters of the ocean. While the creature was drawing attention, Hansen was still able to keep its existence quiet and to maintain, despite some nagging doubts, that it was merely a carnival exhibit. However, that was all about to change.

In December 1968, college student Terry Cullen became more than a little intrigued by the exhibit that he saw at the Chicago exhibition. Like everyone else, he paid his 25 cents to see the "man left over from the Ice Age" and filed past the frozen block of ice that Hansen had secured in a refrigerated glass coffin. He was not convinced that this was some carnival sideshow and began to try unsuccessfully to interest some mainstream academics in what he had found. Finally, Cullen alerted famed naturalist and author of a book on abominable snowmen, Ivan T. Sanderson. Sanderson, who had also founded the Society for the Investigation of the Unexplained, was intrigued. As it turned out, his house guest at the time turned out to be Dr. Bernard Heuvelmans, the respected cryptozoologist and the author of *On the Track of Unknown Animals*. After hearing from Cullen, the two men immediately traveled to see first hand what Hansen was putting on display.

After seeing the frozen creature, they contacted Hansen and asked for permission to study it closer. Hansen agreed but would later admit that "this was a grave mistake on my part." Both men were very impressed with the creature, Hansen said, but neither of them made mention of publishing a scientific report about the Iceman. This was the last thing that Hansen wanted.

However, Sanderson and Heuvelmans spent three days examining the creature in Hansen's trailer. The corpse was that of an adult male with large hands and feet. Its skin was covered with dark brown hair that, for the most part, was three to four inches long. The creature had been shot through one eye and it had a gaping wound and a fracture to the left arm. In places where the ice had melted, the two investigators could smell putrefaction, leading them to believe the body was authentic. They could hardly believe what they saw. Heuvelmans would later publish a report on the creature in the February 1969 bulletin of the *Royal Institute of Natural Sciences of Belgium*. He called the creature the "Homo Pongoides" and stated that "the long search for the rumored live 'ape-man' or 'missing link' has at last been successful."

Sanderson wrote his own article for the pages of *Argosy* and it was published in May 1969. He stated that "one look was actually enough to convince us that this was -- from our point of view, at least -- the 'genuine article'. This was no phony 'Chinese' trick or 'art' work. If nothing else confirmed this, the appalling stench of rotting flesh exuding form a point in the insulation of the coffin certainly did."

Hansen's problems began with the publication of the Heuvelmans article and escalated when Sanderson's piece hit the newsstands. To make it worse, Sanderson, who was a well-known nature personality for television, mentioned the Iceman during an appearance on the *Tonight Show*. Soon, newspapers, television shows, radio stations and magazines from all over the world began trying to verify the existence of the creature. Calls came in daily and both the FBI and the Smithsonian Institution requested permission to examine the body, along with dozens of scientists who asked for blood and hair samples. Hansen refused them all. Heuvelmans had stated in this article that it appeared the creature had been shot. Because of this, newspapers began to speculate on the possibility that law enforcement officials should investigate just how Hansen had obtained the creature if, of course, it was actually real. "If the body is that of a human being, there is the question of who shot him and whether any crime was committed," said and article in the *Detroit News*.

One of Sanderson's sketches of the Iceman, showing the measurements that he was able to discern through the glass and ice. He and Heuvelmans described the creature as being covered in blood as well.
(From PURSUIT: The Journal of the Society for the Investigation of the Unexplained - April 1975)

On that note, the body of the Iceman vanished. The model was again put out in its place and Hansen kept quiet as investigators tracked down the Hollywood makeup artists who had created the fake. He now began spreading the story that the body had been returned to the possession of the California millionaire who owned it. No further examinations would be made.

According to Hansen, this was done on his attorney's advice. He told Hansen that he should substitute the model for the real thing and "take a long vacation". The actual corpse was hidden "away from the Midwest" and the model was re-frozen and put on display in its place. Debunkers quickly assured everyone that the exhibit had been a fake from the very beginning, although the original

Sanderson's sketch showing what he believed the Iceman would have looked like if seen clearly. The gaps in the drawing are portions that were too covered in ice to see clearly.
(From PURSUIT: The Journal of the Society for the Investigation of the Unexplained - April 1975)

investigators would never waver on their identification of it as something very real. Photographs that were taken of the exhibit (the model) in 1969 show at least 15 technical differences between the original that was studied by Sanderson and Heuvelmans and the replacement body. They were sure that the original exhibit had not been a fake, as was Terry Cullen. In addition to the smell noted by the later investigators, Cullen had become so intrigued by the body because he could see plant matter in the creature's teeth, along with skin shed by lice on its flesh. These were items that only would have been noticed by a scientist and would have been beyond the detail of a "carnie" hoax.

So, was the Iceman real - or an elaborate and expensive hoax? Obviously, we are never going to know for sure unless the real specimen eventually turns up somewhere. But if the whole thing was a hoax and the body never existed, then why would Hansen create such an elaborate and damning story to explain it? Was he simply trying to cash in on the model that he had created? This seems unlikely, especially based on the admissions that were paid to see whatever was in the ice block - we are not talking about huge sums of money here. The only way that Hansen could have gotten rich from the creature was by selling the genuine body, which he never did. He seemed to be more worried about criminal charges that might threaten his Air Force retirement check than about getting rich off the corpse.

The biggest question that remains in my mind is, whatever happened to the original body? According to Hansen in 1970, he had been pressed for the conditions or circumstances under which he would consider giving up the specimen for scientific evaluation. He stated that he had to be assured complete amnesty for any possible violation of federal or state laws for either the murder of the creature (if it was deemed too human) or for transporting and exhibiting the corpse. Whatever became of his requests and whether or not they were granted is unknown. As far as I know, the real body - if there was indeed a real body, as so many investigators insisted - was never seen again.

As for the fake body, the intricate model fashioned for Hansen by Hollywood, it did continue to turn up at state fairs and traveling exhibits. Many remember seeing the exhibit and it is rumored to still turn up at fairs today. I believe that I saw the model on display at the Illinois State Fair in 1982 or 1983, but I cannot be sure if it was the same exhibit. As far as I know, it has since vanished, just like Frank Hansen himself. He has kept a very low profile since about 1970 and aside from the fact that he no longer lives on his farm in Minnesota, nothing is known about his present whereabouts.

MOMO - THE MISSOURI MONSTER

One of the first "monsters" that I ever remember hearing about as a kid was "Momo", the creature that wreaked havoc in a small Missouri town during the summer that I was just six years old. I didn't hear anything about the case at the time it happened, or if I did I don't remember it, but Momo became a part of my childhood thanks to the Six Flags Over Mid-America amusement park that was located outside of St. Louis. There was a ride in the park - one of those twirling "octopus" rides that spin riders around and around while going up and down at the same time - that was called "Momo The Monster" and I used to love to ride on it. I had no idea that the ride's namesake was a hairy, foul-smelling Bigfoot creature and spent most of my childhood thinking that Momo was instead some sort of underwater, tentacled monster with octopus arms that must live in the Mississippi

River. Oh well....

Located along a stretch of Missouri's Great River Road in Pike County is the small Mississippi River town of Louisiana. This quiet, unassuming community was vaulted into the national spotlight in July 1972 when reports emerged about a hairy monster and three-toed footprints that had been seen around town. The press humorously dubbed the strange and foul-smelling creature "Momo" for "Missouri Monster" but to the local residents, the frightening encounters were anything but amusing.

The "Missouri Monster Scare" began on July 11, 1972. The first encounter with the creature occurred on the outskirts of Louisiana, Missouri, at the base of Marzolf Hill. An eight year-old boy named Terry Harrison and his brother, Walley, 5, were playing with their dog in the woods at the edge of their yard. Suddenly, an older sister, Doris,15, who was inside of the house, heard them screaming. She ran to look out of the bathroom window and saw something standing by a tree. It was "six or seven feet tall, black and hairy," she said. "It stood like a man but it didn't look like one to me." She began crying and ran into the other room to call her mother on the telephone.

Both Doris and Terry got a good look at the monster and agreed that its face could not be seen because of the mass of hair that covered its body. The creature seemed to have no neck and it was flecked with blood, likely from the dead dog that it was carrying under its arm. The smell of the creature was said to have been horrendous and it may have been this odor that made the Harrison's dog violently sick a short time after the incident. The dog's eyes grew red and it vomited for hours afterward.

At 4:00 pm, Edgar Harrison, the children's father and a deacon in the local Pentecostal Church, returned home from his job at the town waterworks. He found no monster, but he did find that the brush was beaten down where the children said that the creature had been standing. He also found faint footprints in the dust a few black hairs scattered about.

That same afternoon, a woman who lived about three blocks away from the Harrison's, Mrs. Clarence Lee, reported that she heard animal sounds outside her home. Not long afterwards, she allegedly spoke with a local farmer whose dog had disappeared. Remembering the Harrison children's report, she wondered if the monster had taken it.

Everything was quiet until three days later, on July 14. That evening, Edgar Harrison conducted a regular prayer meeting in his home and about 45 minutes after it ended, heard ringing noises that sounded as though someone was throwing rocks into the metal water reservoir on top of Marzolf Hill. The reservoir was an attraction for neighborhood children but it was unlikely that any of them would have been playing there at that hour. As he listened closely to the sounds, he heard one especially loud ring and then an animal-like growl. The sound came closer and closer and was so loud that his family came running out of the house. They urged him to leave the neighborhood but Harrison wanted to see what was making the sound.

He finally gave in to his family's pleading and as he drove down Allen Street, he met about 40 people, some of them carrying guns, who were on their way to investigate the sounds at the reservoir. For some reason, Harrison shouted "Here it comes!" and the entire crowd turned away and ran. A number of people reported hearing the strange cries and screams that night but by the time that police officers Jerry Floyd and John Whitaker arrived on the scene to investigate, they found nothing out of the ordinary.

Later that evening, Harrison and several friends explored Marzolf Hill and found an old building from which a strong and unpleasant odor lingered. Harrison described it as a "moldy, horse smell or a strong garbage smell." In the days that followed, he and others would experience the same smell around areas where the bizarre sounds were heard.

This was not the end of the odd happenings for that night either. During the early morning hours, around 5:00 a.m., Pat Howard, who lived on Third Street, stated that he saw a "dark object" crossing the road near Marzolf Hill. He said that it was running like a man when it went across the road in front of his car.

Thanks to the publicity that the monster reports were generating, Louisiana's Police Chief, Shelby Ward, organized a 20-man search party on July 19. The group included Edgar Harrison and State Conservation Officer Gus Artus and they covered Marzolf Hill and the surrounding area using two-way radios but found nothing. Some of the local residents complained that the search should have been conducted at night because by that evening, the sounds were being heard again. Mrs. George Minor reported hearing growling sounds outside on several occasions, always between 10:00 and 10:30 in the evening. The noises began as a low-pitched growl and ended with a scream.

On July 20, more investigators joined the search and again combed the area behind the Harrison house and all along Marzolf Hill. Near the tree where Doris Harrison had originally seen the monster, they could see circular spots in the brush were leaves had been stripped from the branches of nearby bushes. They also found signs that someone had been digging in the local garbage dump and Harrison showed the searchers two recent dog graves that had been uncovered and the bones scattered about. Across the top of the hill, they came upon tracks that were some distance from one another. The first was over ten inches long and five inches wide and appeared to be a footprint, while the other was only five inches long and curved. It was believed to be the mark of a hand. The prints had been pressed into the hard, dry soil (there had been no rain since around the first of the month) and the investigators guessed that it would have taken a tremendous amount of pressure to create such impressions.

The investigators then climbed the hill to the old building where Harrison and his friends had experienced the pungent odor a few evenings before. He believed that it was a hiding place for the monster. When the group got close, Harrison's dog suddenly bolted and ran away, startling everyone. Moments later, the investigators were nearly overwhelmed by the horrible smell. "That's him, boys!" Harrison exclaimed. "He's around here somewhere!"

The investigators began sweeping the surrounding woods with their flashlights but saw nothing. In the distance they could hear dogs barking furiously and the local men explained that whenever the monster was about, the neighborhood dogs would refuse to enter the woods and instead would run up and down the streets, barking and yelping. Within about five minutes, the smell had dissipated and the investigators returned to Harrison's home.

On July 21, the monster was seen again, this time on the Great River Road, which runs along the Mississippi River. Ellis Minor, who lived on the road, was sitting in front of his home late in the evening. It was very dark and suddenly, his bird dog began to growl. Minor switched on a powerful flashlight that he used for hunting and he spotted the monster about 20 feet away from him, standing in the middle of the road. He later told reporters that it had "hair as black as coal" and that he could not see its face because the hair on its head hung down to its chest. "As soon as I threw the light on it," he recalled, "it whirled and took off thataway." He did not report the sighting to the police but he did call Gust Artus, the conservation officer.

By now, national publicity was turning Louisiana into a three-ring circus. People were driving in from surrounding states, hoping to get a look at the creature. Edgar Harrison had become obsessed with finding a solution to the monster mystery. His family refused to come home again, taking up residence in a restaurant the family owned, and so his house was turned into a "monster outpost". The phones rang constantly. Meanwhile, Harrison had taken a leave of absence from his job at the waterworks to hunt the monster full time. In the company of friends and investigators, he camped out at the foot of Marzolf Hill for 21 straight nights. And while he never saw the monster, he did hear and smell it and noted that whenever the searchers were onto something, they were overwhelmed by the terrible smell. He surmised that the smell might actually be a "stink gas" that was used to distract the investigators.

During the last week of July, a series of mysterious three-toed prints appeared on the Freddie Robbins farm, about eight miles south of Louisiana. No casts were made of the prints but they were protected until investigators were able to make diagrams of them. They would turn out to be an almost exact match of prints found a few days later. More tracks were discovered on the early morning of August 3 at the farm of Mrs. and Mrs. Bill Suddarth, who lived just northwest of town. In the middle of the night, they heard a high-pitched howling in their yard and ran outside with flashlights to see what was going on. In the middle of their garden, they found four prints from a three-toed creature.

Suddarth quickly called his hunting buddy, Clyde Penrod, who drove over and made a plaster cast of the print. Penrod, who was an avid outdoorsman, was puzzled by the whole affair. With the tracks being 20 feet away from anything else, he couldn't understand how they could have been made. They began abruptly in the center of the garden and ended just as mysteriously. It looked as of the three-toed creature had just appeared in the center of the garden and then vanished. No tracks were found anywhere else on the property and there was no sign that any prankster could have made them either. This was the last encounter with the creature and perhaps it is fitting that the "monster flap" ended on such an inexplicable note.

The discovery of the strange tracks at the Suddarth farm ended the "Momo" sightings and encounters in Louisiana and the story has become little more than a remembered curiosity in the area today. There are some though, who are likely never to forget the summer of 1972. For those people, and for those with an interest in the unexplained, those days in July will always remain a mystery.

THE MURPHYSBORO MUD MONSTER

The vast reaches of forest and open fields of southern Illinois, combined with the sparse population in some areas, seem to invite weirdness that might not occur in cities and more crowded locales. In the most southern portions of the region, the Shawnee National Forest covers miles and miles of territory. The acres of forest seem almost untouched by man and some believe that strange things occasionally pass through here, unseen by human eyes.

A friend of mine, who grew up in southern Illinois, had an uncle who worked for the forestry department of the Shawnee National Forest. The uncle had the peculiar habit of driving his work truck along the unpaved back roads of the forest in the very early hours of the morning. One day, my friend asked him why he did this and his reply was nearly as mysterious as the habit itself was. "You wouldn't believe the things that you see on those roads at night," he told his nephew and that was the last time that he would ever speak of his late-night forays.

This southern portion of the state is sometimes referred to as the "Devil's Kitchen", a designation that is very telling when it comes to the question of strange phenomena in Little Egypt. As mentioned in the introduction to this book, many believe that the early explorers and the Native Americans left behind evidence of their beliefs in the unknown by the names that they gave to certain places. They were spots where the explorers, settlers and the Indians witnessed strange sights and sounds like unexplained balls of light, apparitions, screams in the night and various other unsettling types of occurrences. The Native Americans often considered such sites as "sacred" but the settlers usually believed them to be "cursed", or at least well avoided. The idea that such locations were linked to the "Devil" was the first thought that crossed the minds of the bible-reading, God-fearing folks and they began avoiding such locations and gave them names that would alert others to the potential dangers. Over the years, there have been many locations that bear a link between supernatural phenomena and a "Devil" name. In the case of the Devil's Kitchen, just about anything is possible, from ghosts reports to mystery animals, weird monster reports and more.

In the summer of 1973, the town of Murphysboro in southwestern Illinois was the site of a bizarre series of monster sightings. The enigmatic creature, now recalled as the "Murphysboro Mud Monster" or the "Big Muddy Monster" appeared without warning and then suddenly disappeared just two weeks later, seemingly without a trace. In its wake, the monster left a number of confused and frightened witnesses, baffled law enforcement officials and of course, an enduring legend.

The monster was first seen around midnight on Monday, June 25, 1973. On that humid and steamy night, a young couple, Randy Needham and Judy Johnson, were parked near a boat ramp into the Big Muddy River near Murphysboro. The night was quiet until a strange, roaring cry would shatter the stillness of the night. It came from the nearby woods and both Randy and Judy looked up to see a huge shape lumbering toward them from the shadows. Whatever it was, it walked on two legs and continued to make the horrible sound. They later described the noise as "something not human".

According to their account, the monster was about seven feet tall and covered with a matted, whitish hair. The "fur" was streaked liberally with mud from the river. As it lurched toward them, the tone of the creature's cry began to change, alarming them even further. By the time the creature approached to within 20 feet of them, they quickly left the scene. They went directly to the Murphysboro police station.

"They were absolutely terrified," former Police Chief Ron Manwaring recalled in 2003, the 30th anniversary of the sightings. The retired officer agreed to be interviewed about the case and remembered all that he could about what happened. "I'm convinced that they saw something that night.. I can't tell you what it was that they saw, whether it was a bear or something else. But something was definitely there."

A short time later, Officers Meryl Lindsay and Jimmie Nash returned to the area and surveyed the scene. Although skeptical, they were surprised to find that a number of footprints had been left in the mud. The footprints were "approximately 10-12 inches long and approximately three inches wide". At 2:00 a.m., Nash, Lindsay, a Jackson County sheriff's deputy named Bob Scott, and Randy Needham returned to the scene again. This time, they discovered more tracks and Lindsay left to go and get a camera. The others followed the new footprints, tracing their path along the river.

Suddenly, from the woods about 100 yards away, came the creature's terrifying scream. They didn't wait to see if they could spot the monster and instead, made a quick retreat for the patrol car. Needham later recalled that the sheriff's deputy was so scared that he dropped his gun into the mud. After waiting in the darkness for a little while, they got back out again and spent the rest of the night trying to track down a splashing sound they heard in the distance. Things quieted down after daylight, but the next night, the creature was back.

The first to see the monster this time was a four-year old boy named Christian Baril, who told his parents that he saw a "big white ghost in the yard". They didn't believe him, but when Randy Creath and Cheryl Ray saw an identical monster in a neighboring yard just ten minutes later, Christian's parents, and the police, quickly reconsidered the little boy's statement.

Randy and Cheryl spotted the monster at about 10:30 p.m., while sitting on the back porch of the Ray house. They heard the sound of something moving in the woods near the river and then spotted the muddy, white creature staring at them with glowing pink eyes. Cheryl would insist that the eyes were actually glowing and were not reflecting light from some other source. They estimated that it weighed at least 350 pounds, stood seven feet tall, had a roundish head and long, ape-like arms. Cheryl turned on the porch light and Randy went for a closer look. The creature seemed unconcerned and finally ambled off into the woods. Investigators would later find a trail of broken tree branches and crushed undergrowth, along with a number of large footprints. They also noticed a strong odor left in the monster's wake, but it didn't last for very long.

The officers who arrived on the scene, Jimmie Nash and Chief Ron Manwaring, quickly summoned a local man named Jerry Nellis, who had a trained German Shepherd that was often used by the police department as an attack dog and to search buildings and track suspects. The dog immediately was sent in pursuit of the monster. He followed what appeared to be a slimy trail through the weeds and then managed to track the creature through the woods and down a hill to a small pond. Eventually, the trees and undergrowth became too thick for the dog to continue and it was pulled off the track just moments after almost pulling its handler down a steep embankment. The officers began searching the area with flashlights and the dog began sniffing near the trees, hoping to pick up the scent again. He then set off toward an abandoned barn, but refused to go inside. In fact, the animal began shaking with fear and barking.

Nellis called the two officers over and they opened the barn and went inside. After a few moments, they realized that it was empty. The three men were puzzled. The dog had been trained to search buildings and Nellis could not explain why it had refused to enter the barn. A short time later, the search was called off for the night.

The Mud Monster was reported two more times that summer. On the night of July 4, traveling carnival workers stated that they spotted the creature disturbing some Shetland ponies that were being used for the holiday celebration at Riverside Park. This report actually came in on July 7 because the carnival owner was concerned that the sighting might scare away potential customers. However, he did tell the police that several of his workers noticed the ponies attempting to break loose from the trees where they had been tied up for the night. According to the police report, the workers described the monster as being seven to eight feet tall with light brown hair all over its body. It stood erect on two legs and weighed at least 300 to 400 pounds. The creature stood very close to the ponies and while it seemed curious, it did not advance on them or threaten them in any way.

Then, on July 7, Mrs. Nedra Green heard a screaming sound coming from a shed on her rural farm. She did not go out to investigate but the description of the cries matched the description given by Randy Needham, Judy Johnson and the police officers who also heard it. This was the last incident connected to the monster to occur that summer - and as far as is known, to ever occur.

As the story leaked out, it turned up in the newspapers, got posted to the wire services and soon made headlines. Even the *New York Times* sent a reporter to investigate. The story of the Big Muddy Monster was reported all around the world and soon letters came pouring into the Murphysboro Police Department from all over the country and even from as far away as South Africa. Researchers, curiosity-seekers and even scientists were pleading with the local authorities to release more information.

They received letters from hunters and trappers who offered to track down the monster and kill it or capture it. Two men from Oregon offered to do the job and wrote that they "would be willing to take on this adventure at only the cost of expenses and materials for doing so." Some wrote suggesting that the police try using bait to snare the creature. A Florida man suggested "why don't you put bread and cheese and eggs out for your creature? You would have a splendid attraction if you could have it in a little hut, to show people."

Assistant professor Leigh Van Valen, from the University of Chicago's Biology Department, also wrote a letter to Chief Manwaring. "I have heard of your creature," the letter stated, "which could be of considerable scientific interest. There have been many reports of such animals but no real specimens have been available for scientific study." Professor Van Valen went on to explain how the creature, if circumstances required shooting it, should be properly embalmed or "preserved in good condition." The professor agreed to cover the necessary expenses to procure the monster for scientific study but it wouldn't matter, for the monster would never return to Murphysboro.

There was only one other sighting that could have possibly have been the creature and it occurred in the fall of that same year, a number of miles southwest of town, near the Mississippi River. A local truck driver told police that he saw a monster that resembled the Murphysboro creature along the edge of the road. It vanished before he could get a good look at it but it did leave behind a number of large tracks in the mud. The authorities made casts of the impressions but they were unable to determine if they matched the previous footprints or were the work of a prankster. After that one last gasp, the Big Muddy Monster simply faded away.

So what was the Murphysboro Mud Monster? Local authorities admitted that they didn't know and after 30 years, no one has ever come forward with a logical explanation for the sightings. One of the police officers involved in the case said "A lot of things in life are unexplained and this is another one. We don't know what the creature is, but we do believe what these people saw was real."

According to the *St. Louis Post-Dispatch* newspaper, the Mud Monster emerged again as a possible culprit to an attack that allegedly occurred at the Rend Lake campground near Benton in August 1989. During the attack, gaping holes were left in a tent and animal blood was left behind at the scene. The attack was later determined to have been from dogs, but that didn't stop local residents from speculating about the Murphysboro Mud Monster again.

In the 1989 newspaper reports, Jerry Nellis, the dog handler in the original case stated his own theories on the famous case, which left he and the other witnesses to the events as "hunted" as the Mud Monster itself. Reporters and "monster hunters" came from everywhere asking questions about the case but Nellis maintained that "in my opinion ... we were tracking a bear."

Now, 30 years after it all happened, Randy Needham, one of the first to see the monster, disagrees. "It would be kind of naïve for us to think that we know everything that's out there," he said. He went on to admit that he never goes into the woods at night and if he goes into the woods in the daytime, "I always look for way out in case I need to leave fast."

WEREWOLVES AND THE BRAY ROAD BEAST

Perhaps the strangest question that plagues researchers and enthusiasts of the unknown is this : Is it possible that even stranger things than Bigfoot roam the dark woods and shadowy forests of America? And stranger still, could werewolves be among them?

The mythological belief in werewolves has been with us for centuries. Many historians and folklorists have pondered the origins of the belief in lycanthropy, which is really the human ability to change into not only wolves, but bears, big cats and other dangerous creatures. Of all of these transformations though, that of man into wolf is the best known. This is largely due to the Old World traditions of wolves being feared as predators by the Europeans. There are many historical accounts of wolves preying on human beings during wars and hard winters, although not all of these accounts can be taken as fact. However, the true accounts were prevalent enough that the French had a word for the wolf that has acquired a taste for human flesh, the "werewolf" or the loup-garou.

Although modern naturalists and wildlife experts would all agree that the wolf has gained an unfair reputation over the years, centuries of stories and links to the dark side have maintained most people's fears about these creatures. In northern Europe, wolf men, or berserkers, which were warriors clad in animal skins, were greatly feared for their viciousness and the slaughtering of other warriors and innocents alike. In the Baltic and Slavic regions of Europe, people worshipped a wolf deity that could be benevolent or deadly without warning.

As Christianity rose to power, the church condemned such beliefs and soon, the wolf was seen as a symbol of evil. Many debated over whether or not men really turned into wolves or if Satan merely caused witnesses to be deluded into thinking a man had changed into a wolf.

For those who claimed such powers, their delusions were frighteningly real. Many people who believed themselves to be werewolves testified, under torture and otherwise, of murdering both people and animals while in their transformed state. For this reason, many researchers today have associated being a "werewolf" with those we would deem to be murderously mentally ill. Among these were serial killers like Stubbe Peeter, who was tried in Germany in 1589 for a 25-year crime spree. During that time, he murdered adults and children, including his own son, committed cannibalism and incest and attacked animals. Peeter claimed to have made a pact with Satan, who had then given him an animal pelt that would change him into a wolf. In 1598, French authorities arrested Jacques Roulet after he was found hiding in some brush and covered with the blood of a mutilated teenaged boy. Roulet claimed that he had killed the boy while transformed into a werewolf.

With tales such as this, lycanthropy has been deemed as a serious mental disorder. But can we really place all accounts of werewolves into a category of human dysfunction? There are sightings and accounts that do exist, although few of them, that lead researchers to ponder whether or not man-wolves can actually be real. In reality, these creatures should not exist, but so much of our understanding of these creatures comes from anthropologists and folklorists (not to mention the movies) and since sensible people would never believe that a werewolf could possibly be seen - they naturally dismiss any true accounts that might surface.

This is not to say that werewolves are real - I leave such decisions for the reader to make - but there are some accounts out there that just might have you thinking twice. Remember that werewolves are only slightly less implausible than many other creatures that people claim to see (from Bigfoot to giant winged creatures) but most of us have a lot less trouble believing in the other assorted monsters said to wander the land. These accounts do not amount to trying to convince the reader that true werewolves are prowling America, but they are worthy of interest.

Strangely, the state of Wisconsin seems to have a number of werewolf sightings and the first was reported in 1936. A man named Mark Schackelman reportedly encountered a talking "wolf-man" just east of Jefferson, Wisconsin on Highway 18. As he was driving along the road one evening, he spotted a figure digging in an old Indian mound. He looked closer and saw that the figure was a strange, hair-covered creature that stood erect and stood more than six feet tall. The face of the creature boasted a muzzle and features of both an ape and a dog. Its hands were oddly formed with a twisted thumb and three fully formed fingers. The beast gave off a putrid smell that was like "decaying meat".

Schackelman returned to the site the following evening, hoping for another look, and this time, he actually heard the creature speak in what he described as being "neo human". The beast uttered a "three-syllable growling noise that sounded like ga-da-ra with the emphasis on the second syllable." Schackelman was a religious man and after spotting this obviously "evil" creature, he began to back away from it and to pray. Eventually the creature was lost to sight.

In 1964, another man, Dennis Fewless, had a similar sighting less than two miles away. Fewless was driving home around midnight from his job at the Admiral Television Corp. in Harvard, Illinois. After turning onto Highway 89 from Highway 14, his headlights caught an animal running across the road in front of him. It was dark brown in color and he estimated that it weighed between 400 and 500 pounds. He also described it as being seven or eight feet tall. It ran across the highway, jumped a barbed wire fence and vanished. Fewless returned to the spot in the daylight hours to look for footprints or other evidence but the hard, sun-dried ground offered nothing. He did find where the corn had been pushed aside as the beast entered the field though. "I was awful scared that night," Fewless later recalled.

"That was no man. It was all hairy from head to feet."

In July 1958, Mrs. Delburt Gregg of Greggton, Texas claimed to have an encounter with a werewolf, or shape shifting creature, while her husband was away from home on business. According to her account, she had pushed her bed over close to the window one warm evening, hoping to catch a breeze from outdoors. The humidity outside was gathering thunderstorms in the sky and between the rumble of thunder and the stifling heat, she had trouble getting to sleep. She tried to read for awhile and then finally snapped off the light and lay there in the darkness. After a time, she fell asleep.

She had no idea how long she had been sleeping when she was awakened by a faint scratching sound against the window screen near her face. She roused herself and was peering at the window when a flash of lightning illuminated the scene outside. To her terror and astonishment, she saw a huge, wolf-like creature in the yard. The beast was picking at the window screen with its claws and staring in with "baleful, glowing eyes". Mrs. Gregg said that when it opened its mouth, she saw a set of long, white teeth.

In seconds, Mrs. Gregg grabbed a flashlight from the side table and jumped out of bed. She said that she aimed the light at the window and flicked it on, just in time to catch another glimpse of the monstrous animal as it began to run. It fled across the yard and disappeared into a thicket of trees near the highway. Frightened but curious, she crouched near the window and watched the trees to see if she saw the animal again. A short time later, the brush began to rustle but instead of a wolf steeping out, she saw a tall man suddenly part the foliage and walk out instead. He looked around for a moment and then hurried off down the road, disappearing into the darkness.

"I closed the window and locked it," Mrs. Gregg concluded, "and I slept with a bright light on in my room the rest of that night."

In January 1970, four young people from Gallup, New Mexico encountered what may have been a Navajo "skin walker", the southwestern Native American version of a werewolf. They ran into the creature alongside the highway near Whitewater. Like the creature of Navajo legend, it moved very fast and was able to actually run alongside the speeding automobile. The teenagers inside panicked and began to drive faster and faster, finally reaching speeds in excess of 60 mph. According to their account, one of the teenagers finally took out a gun and shot at the creature. It was hit and promptly fell down at the side of the road, although it left no blood on the pavement that they could see. The young people were too frightened to go back and take a closer look.

Between July and October 1972, a number of people living near Defiance, Ohio claimed to encounter a werewolf-like creature that prowled the city and surrounding area at night. The descriptions varied the size of the creature between six and eight feet but all agreed that it was hairy and human-like, but with an oversized wolf head. Another witness added that it had "huge, hairy feet, fangs, and it ran from side to side like a caveman in the movies". It also was said to have glowing red eyes. One night, during the early morning hours, the "werewolf" crept up behind a local railroad worker and whacked him in the head with a board. Obviously, this led many to believe that the creature was not a werewolf after all, but a prankster in disguise. But then again, who knows?

In 1972, a werewolf returned to Wisconsin. One night, a woman in rural Jefferson County called the police to report an attempted break in at her home. According to an investigation conducted by the Wisconsin Department of Natural Resources, she said that the intruder was a "large, unknown animal" that had come to the house and had tried to get in the door. The creature departed but returned again a few weeks later and injured one of her farm animals. The account stated that the creature had long, dark hair, stood about eight feet tall and walked upright like a man. Its arms were long and it had claws on each hand. After trying to enter the house, the beast went out to the barn and attacked a horse that was stabled there. It left behind a deep gash on the animal that stretched from one shoulder to the other. A footprint left behind was more than a foot long. Bigfoot investigators dismissed the report, saying that a Sasquatch would never be that aggressive. But what about a werewolf?

Perhaps the most celebrated and strange werewolf reports of recent years also come from Wisconsin and involve what has been dubbed the "Bray Road Beast". The first werewolf sighting to go public occurred on October 31, 1999. A young woman named Doristine Gipson, from nearby Elkhorn, was driving along Bray Road near Delavan. As she neared the intersection of Hospital Road, she leaned over to change the station on her radio and she felt her right front tire jump off the ground as if she had hit something. Concerned, she stopped the car and got out to see what it was. Finding nothing on the roadway behind her car, she began to look around. As she peered into the darkness, she suddenly saw a dark, hairy form racing toward her. She did not see what the figure looked like from the distance at which she was standing (about 50 feet) but she did see the figure was quite bulky and she would later compare the form to someone who works out continually with weights. Startled by the oncoming form, and by the sounds of its "heavy feet", she quickly retreated to her car. She jumped in and was attempting to drive away when the beast jumped onto her trunk. Luckily, it was too wet for the creature to hang on and it fell off onto the pavement. Doristine returned to the site later on that evening with a young girl that she was taking out trick-or-treating and saw a large form on the side of the road. When she saw the creature moving, she ordered the child to lock her door and drove quickly away from the scene.

She had no idea what she had seen but wondered if perhaps it might be a bear, angry because she had struck it with her car. Regardless, she told a neighbor about the encounter the next day and showed her the scratched car. As word spread, more local people began to step forward with their own encounters with the beast, dating back to 1989.

One night in the fall of that year, 24 year-old bar manager Lorianne Endrizzi was rounding a curve on Bray Road (just a half mile from the site of the later incident) and saw what she thought was a person kneeling and hunched over on the side of the road. When she slowed down, she took a closer look at the figure on the passenger side of the car. She was no more than six feet away from it at the time. The sighting lasted for about 45 seconds and she stated that she clearly saw a beast with grayish, brown hair, fangs and pointed ears. "His face was ... long and snouty, like a wolf". She also noted that even though the car's headlights were pointed ahead down the roadway, the creature's eyes glowed with a yellowish color, just like an animal's will do when reflected in car lights. Like Doris Gipson, she also saw how wide and powerful the creature's chest and build were. She went on to add that the arms of the beast were rather strange. They were jointed as a man's would be and it seemed to be holding food with its palms upward, completely unlike any animal that she had ever heard of. The arms were muscular, "like a man who had worked out a little bit", and the creature seemed to have human-like fingers with claws on the ends. She did not notice any sort of tail but did say that its back legs were behind it, like a person would be if kneeling.

Endrizzi was completely unnerved by the sighting. She later stated in an interview that the creature "appeared to be so human-like that it was scary." He own answer to what she had seen was that it had been a "freak of nature". She had no idea what it could have been until she saw a book at the library that had an illustration of a werewolf in it. It so closely resembled what she had seen on Bray Road that her "eyes popped out" of her head.

After hearing Doris Gipson's account by way of rumor, Endrizzi contacted the Lakeland Animal Shelter and her mother contacted a local newspaper writer named Linda Godfrey, hoping that publicity might encourage other people who had encountered the creature to come forward. The story that followed was published on December 29, 1991 and while it contained basic information about the Gipson and Endrizzi sightings (using pseudonyms for the two women), it also included some scanty information on other sightings. It mentioned that chickens had been stolen and that another family who lived near Bray Road had experienced their own close encounter with the beast. Karen Bowey, who actually lived along Bowers Road, stated that her daughter Heather, age 11, had seen the creature back in 1989. They had been playing outside and thought they had spotted a large dog - until it stood up. She mentioned the odd shape of its back legs and the speed at which it could move. The county humane officer, John Frederickson, told the reporter that he believed the creature was a "coyote" but he did concede that there were a lot of people who believed that they had seen something out of the ordinary. He admitted that he was not sure what to make of it.

Predictably, large media outlets picked up the story and the witnesses began to suffer from practical jokes and laughter. Werewolf signs were planted in front yards and werewolf parties became common, even at the bar where Endrizzi worked. Monster t-shirts were sold and tourists cruised up and down Bray Road, hoping for a glimpse of the creature. As time went by though, the excitement decreased and the temper of the community began to wear thin. Despite all of the jokes and humor, there was still an undercurrent of fear in Delavan and Elkhorn. Something was going on out in the vicinity of Bray Road and soon people began to whisper about other things as well.

Just the summer before the wolf creature had been reported, a dozen or so animals had been dumped in a ditch along nearby Willow Road. John Frederickson, the humane officer from Delavan, stated that he believed several of the animals had been used in cult rituals. While Linn police chief James Jensen dismissed this idea in June 1991, Frederickson insisted that officials were missing the point. According to the officer, some of the animals had ropes tied around their back legs and their throats were slit, some were decapitated and others were dismembered in various ways. The most recently killed animal was a dog that had its chest cavity split open and its heart removed. Several of the animals matched descriptions of recently missing pets and they certainly had not been killed by passing cars. The mutilated carcasses were almost immediately covered up - literally. The site was quickly bulldozed, ending Frederickson's investigation but it did not end the whispers and rumors that followed.

Other reports began to reach Frederickson that summer as well. Rumors were passed on about humane officer imposters who pursued stray dogs. One incident also involved an unidentified man in a black uniform, driving a large black car, who attempted to intimidate a child who was home alone into giving up his black Labrador Retriever. Around this same time, there were also reports of occult graffiti being found in an abandoned house and at the local cemetery, where graves markers were also found to be covered with candle wax. The abandoned house was located just a quarter-mile off Bray Road. This led many to ponder whether the satanic activity and the Bray Road Beast were in some way connected. The strange stories and animal carcasses had been whispered about and discovered just a few months before the first sightings of the monster had been publicized -- but the beast was apparently in the vicinity long before that.

An earlier sighting of "something" was made by a dairy farmer from Elkhorn named Scott Bray, who reported seeing a "strange looking dog" in his pasture near Bray Road in September or October of 1989. He said that the beast was larger and taller than a German Shepherd and had pointed ears, a hairy tail and long gray and black hair. He added that it was built very heavy in the front, as if it had a strong chest. He followed the "dog" to a large pile of rocks but the creature had vanished.

He did find that it had left behind huge footprints though, which disappeared into the grass of the pasture.

Russell Gest of Elkhorn also reported seeing the creature about the same time as the Scott Bray sighting. He was about a block or so away from an overgrown area and when he heard weeds being rustled, he looked up to see a creature emerge from the thicket. It was standing on its hind feet and then took two "wobbly" steps forward before Gest began to run away. He looked back to see that the creature was now on all fours, but it never gave chase. After a short distance, it wandered off in the direction of Bray Road. Gest said that the creature was much larger than a German Shepherd and was covered with black and grayish hair. While standing upright, it appeared to be about five feet tall. It had an oversized dog or wolf-like head with a big neck and wide shoulders. The animal's form was mostly dog-like, leading Gest to surmise that it was some sort of dog-wolf hybrid.

Around Christmas 1990, Heather Bowey had her previously mentioned encounter. She had no idea that she had seen the same thing as Doris Gipson until she heard the young woman talking about it on the school bus. The driver, Pat Lester, who happened to be Lori Endrizzi's mother, listened to the girl's story and passed it on to Linda Godfrey. The reporter then contacted Karen Bowey, also a school bus driver, and then mentioned the sighting in the newspaper. Heather elaborated on the encounter to writer Scarlett Sankey.

The sighting occurred around 4:30 p.m. as Heather and several friends were returning home from sledding near Loveland Road (about a mile and a half southeast of the intersection of Bray and Hospital Roads). They happened to look up and see what appeared to be a large dog walking along a creek in a snow-covered cornfield. Heather estimated that it was about a block away from them. Thinking that it was a dog, the children began calling to it. The creature looked at them and then it stood up on its hind legs. She described it as being covered with long "silverfish-like- brownish" hair. The beast took four awkward steps in their direction and then dropped down on all fours and began to run at the children in what Heather later described as being "a bigger leap than dogs run." It followed the group about halfway to the Bowey home, which was about 250 yards away, before it ran off in another direction.

In March 1990, an Elkhorn dairy farmer named Mike Etten spotted something unusual along Bray Road one early morning around 2:00 a.m. In the moonlight, Etten saw a dark-haired creature that was bigger than a dog, just a short distance from the Hospital Road intersection. Whatever the creature was, it was sitting "like a raccoon sits", using its front paws to hold onto something that it was eating. As he passed by the creature, it lifted its head and looked at him. He described the head as being thick and wide, with snout that was not as long as a dog's. The body was covered with dark, thick hair and its legs were big and thick. Not being able to identify the animal, Etten assumed that it was a bear. However, when the other sightings of the Bray Road Beast were made public in 1991, he had to reconsider this assumption.

One of the last reported encounters with the creature occurred in early February 1992. It happened around 10:30 pm on Highway H, about six miles southwest of the Bray and Hospital Roads intersection. A young woman named Tammy Bray, who worked for a retirement home, was driving along when a large, dog-like animal crossed the road in front of her. She quickly punched the brakes and slid to a stop, just about the same time that the creature turned and looked at her. She described the creature as have a broad chest and pointed ears and being covered with matted brown and black fur. The narrow nose, thick neck and shining yellow eyes of the beast quickly convinced her that she was not looking at any sort of dog. Finally, it continued on, unafraid, across the road and she noted that it walked "strong in front, more slouchy, sloppy-like in the rear." Tammy drove home and hurried into the house to tell her husband, Scott Bray, that she had seen the same animal that he had earlier seen in their pasture.

The sightings eventually died out but the strangeness that seemed to envelope the region took a little longer to fade. In January 1992, just as furor over the Bray Road Beast sightings was starting to quiet down, a local "reputable businessman" told reporter Linda Godfrey that he had seen two bright lights emitting sparks and moving erratically across the sky above Delavan. Later that spring, four or five horses that were pastured near Elkhorn were found with their throats slashed. John Frederickson, who investigated, was quoted as saying that "They were almost surgical-type wounds". And then after that, things became eerily quiet.

So, what was the Bray Road Beast? Neither a coyote or the native red wolf can really match the descriptions that were given of the creature, despite humane officer John Frederickson's comments that a coyote might rear up on its hind legs before running, explaining several witnesses claims that it walked on two legs. A gray wolf would be much larger than a red wolf but are not generally found in the area. In addition, gray wolves are much narrower in the chest than the Bray Road creature was reported to be and wolves are shy of humans and despite the matching yellow eyes, would not attack a car as the creature from the Doris Gipson encounter did. The creature simply resembled no known animals, but alternately was compared to dogs, bears and wolves.

Witnesses also insisted that it was not a dog, although some suggested that it could have been a wolf-dog hybrid of some sort. But how does this explain the creature's habit of kneeling, walking on two legs and holding onto food with the flat of its paws turned upward? Also, Lori Endrizzi claimed that the animal had human-like fingers. The idea that the monster may have been a bear is also called into question. While bears do occasionally walk for short distances on two legs, they do not hold food with their palms up, do not jump onto moving cars and very rarely do they pursue or try to attack humans. So, what could it have been? If the Bray Road

Beast was real - it had to have been some sort of animal that has never been classified before.

Or more incredible to believe, a genuine werewolf! Investigator Todd Roll was quick to point out the hints that there may have been an occult connection to the Bray Road Beast. The discovery of the mutilated animal carcasses and the occult activity at the cemetery coincided with the sightings of the monster in the region. When Roll examined the occult connections to the werewolf sightings, he interviewed John Frederickson, who told him of this house deep in the woods where mutilated animals had been discovered. The owner of the property insisted that the slain animals were "part of his religion". Do we dare consider the idea that the beast was a shape shifter of some sort, blending between man and wolf?

There is also one more theory that we have to consider - that the entire thing could have been an elaborate hoax. Notwithstanding the fact that Doris Gipson's encounter took place on Halloween, there were other problems as well. The most obvious issue to cause suspicion was the relationships between all of those involved in the case. Endrizzi's mother, Pat Lester, is a central figure in the case. In addition to being one witness' mother, she was also Gipson's neighbor and drove the school bus that Gipson, Heather Bowey and Russell Gest rode. Heather's mother was also a school bus driver. Tammy Bray was a friend of Pat Lester's daughter and the wife of Scott Bray. It was also Lester who took the initiative to contact the newspaper about the sightings. However, it should be strongly pointed out that Lester never tried to influence the reports of the witnesses. It seems more likely that she was simply in a position to hear about the encounters and her interest and compassion towards those involved helped to encourage them to go public.

So, could they have been making the whole thing up? Sure, they could have been, but it doesn't seem likely, especially based on the fact that no one had anything to gain by making the sightings public, other than ridicule and embarrassment, which is hardly an incentive to make your story known.

As time has passed, the investigation into the case has grown cold and with no further sightings of the Bray Road Beast to continue the news story, the papers have fallen silent. One has to wonder if we will ever know the truth of what happened in southeastern Wisconsin between 1989 and 1992 for the mystery, at this point, remains unsolved.

THUNDERBIRDS!

For as long as I can remember, I have been fascinated with the idea of giant birds that swoop across the sky, frightening the unsuspecting, and then vanishing back into the clouds. There is no way that I can explain my interest, for I have never seen one of these strange flying beasts, other than to say that I was born and raised in Illinois. This is a state that seems to have an inordinate number of such sightings and encounters, including the famous Lawndale Thunderbird Attack, and it also the home of the legendary Piasa bird as well. Such accounts are certainly enough to have us "keep watching the sky" as we were growing up among the woods and fields of Illinois.

American Indian lore is filled with stories of strange, monster birds with enormous wingspans and the propensity to carry away human victims. They called these creatures "Thunderbirds" because the legends claimed that their flapping wings made a sound like rolling thunder. The birds have been described as having wingspans of 20 feet or more, hooked talons, razor-sharp beaks and sometimes descriptions that seem oddly close to the pterodactyls of prehistoric times.

One of the most famous of the early American legends of these giant winged creatures comes from the bluffs outside of the small Mississippi River town of Alton, Illinois. Many visitors to this historic town are often startled to see a rock painting just north of the city that portrays a pretty vicious-looking winged creature. Years ago, this rock painting was actually a petroglyph that showed two such creatures. These monsters, like the modern rendering of the paintings, were called the "Piasa" by the Illinwek Indians. The original painting existed near this location for hundreds of years and was first described in the journals of Marquette in 1673. The original painting no longer exists, having been destroyed by rock quarrying years ago, but the painting showed a winged creature with a fierce face, long claws and a serpent-like tail. The word "Piasa" was translated as the "bird that devours men" and the painting was tied to a Native American legend of a winged monster that carried off local natives and devoured them. It was eventually killed, the story stated, by a local chief.

The Piasa was always considered a folktale until a gruesome discovery was made by Professor John Russell in 1836. He discovered a cave upriver from Alton that was said to have a floor that was "one mass of human bones". Speculation continues as to whether this cave was perhaps the lair of the Piasa Bird - if it existed at all.

Aside from Indian legends though, there are many more modern accounts of Thunderbirds and winged creatures attacking and carrying off people. Such accounts should not exist and yet they do. One of the earliest reports like this I could find of someone being attacked by a giant bird took place in Tippah County, Missouri in 1868. According to the report, an eight year-old child was actually carried off by what was described by his teacher as an "eagle". It happened one day during school. The teacher's account states that "a sad tragedy occurred at my school a few days ago". He wrote that "eagles" had been very troublesome in the neighborhood, carrying off small pigs and lambs. No one thought that they would ever bother the local children until one afternoon when one of the birds swept down and picked up a boy named Jemmie Kenney and flew off with him. The other children called out but by the time the teacher ran outside to see what was going on, he could only hear the child screaming as he vanished into the sky. The teacher and the children on the playground began to cry out to raise the alarm in town and apparently, the noise frightened the bird and it dropped the boy. "But his talons had been buried in him so deeply, and the fall was so great, that he was killed."

What could this creature have really been? Could it have actually been an eagle? If so, it must have been a monstrous one because according to renowned zoologist Dr Bernard Heuvelmans, even the most powerful eagle cannot lift more than a rabbit or a lamb. Most experts insist that even the strongest birds cannot carry off a small child -- so what occurred in Missouri in 1868?

In 1882, a flock of birds resembling giant buzzards were seen by Fred Murray over Cameron County, Pennsylvania but this strange report was nothing compared to the weird Thunderbird that appeared in California and was allegedly shot down near Tombstone, Arizona in 1886. The truth behind this incident, which will be explored later in these pages, remains elusive - as does a strange photograph that is said to document one of the incidents.

In 1895, several sightings of a giant bird took place in Webster County, West Virginia. On February 7, Deputy Sheriff Rube Nihiser and his son were hunting near Owl Head Mountain when they heard screaming cries and looked up to see a "giant eagle" carrying off a deer fawn. Five days later, bear hunter Peter Swadley was attacked without warning by a similar bird and was badly hurt. He stated that his dog was carried off in the attack. The same bird was also thought to be responsible for the abduction of a 10 year-old girl named Lundy Junkins a few days before. Searchers for the missing girl followed her tracks in the snow until they suddenly turned around several times and then abruptly came to an end. The bird continued to be seen for some time after this and it was described as having a wingspan of 15-18 feet, a body the size of a man's and large eyes.

In the early 1940's, thunderbirds had returned to Pennsylvania again. In 1940, an author and local historian named Robert Lyman claimed to see a giant bird in

Pennsylvania's Black Forest. He wrote that it was standing in the center of Sheldon Road when he first spotted it, about two miles north of Coudersport. It was brownish in color and stood upright like a huge vulture. When Lyman got too close, the bird spread its wings to take off and he estimated the wingspan to be at least 25 feet.

Later in the 1940's, reports of big bird sightings began to accumulate and one series of thunderbird sightings began in April 1948. On April 4, a former Army Colonel named Walter F. Siegmund revealed that he had seen a gigantic bird in the sky above Alton, Illinois. He had been talking with a local farmer and Colonel Ralph Jackson, the head of the Western Military Academy, at the time. "I thought there was something wrong with my eyesight," he said, "but it was definitely a bird and not a glider or a jet plane. It appeared to be flying northeast... from the movements of the object and its size, I figured it could only be a bird of tremendous size."

A few days later, a farmer named Robert Price from Caledonia would see the same, or a similar, bird. He called it a "monster bird... bigger than an airplane". On April 10, another sighting would take place and this time in Overland. Mr. and Mrs. Clyde Smith and Les Bacon spotted a huge bird. They said they thought the creature was an airplane until it started to flap its wings furiously.

On April 24, the bird was back in Alton. It was sighted by E.M. Coleman and his son, James. "It was an enormous, incredible thing with a body that looked like a naval torpedo," Coleman recalled later. "It was flying at about 500 feet and cast a shadow the same size as a Piper Cub at that height." On that same day, the bird was reported across the Mississippi River in St. Louis by two city policemen. They stated that it was "as big as a small airplane". Officer Francis Hennelly added that "its wings were flapping and it was headed southwest, flying at an altitude of several hundred feet. I thought it was a large eagle but I have never seen one that big before."

On April 26, a St. Louis chiropractor named Kristine Dolezal saw the bird from her apartment window. It nearly crashed into a plane and swerved at the last minute to avoid it. The creature then flapped its wings and vanished into the clouds. The next day, the bird was reported by instructors at a flight school at the St. Louis-Lambert International Airport. On April 28, a salesman named Harry Bradford was turning onto Kingshighway, spotted the bird and then turned his auto spotlight on it. The creature circled around a time or two and then vanished northward. It was seen again by Clifford Warden and Mary and Charles Dunn on April 30.

Then, on May 5, the bird was sighted for the last time in Alton. A man named Arthur Davidson called the police that evening to report the bird flying above the city. Later on that same night, Mrs. William Stallings of St. Louis informed the authorities that she had also seen it. "It was bright, about as big as a house," she said. A number of sightings then followed in the St. Louis area, but ironically, just when the public excitement over the bird reached its peak, the sightings came to an end.

Another "big bird" was spotted in Renovo, Pennsylvania on March 27, 1957. H.M. Cranmer and a friend saw the creature go by at a height of about 500 feet. Cranmer later stated that the motion of its wings reminded him of a blue heron, except this bird was lighter and grayer in color. He later called the local American Legion to see if anyone else had reported seeing a bird of tremendous size and was told that it had also been seen over Westport, Fishdam Run and then up Two-Mile Run. The wingspread of the bird was estimated at 25-30 feet.

In May 1961, a businessman who was flying a small plane over the Hudson River Valley reported that a "big bird" buzzed his craft like a fighter jet and then continued to drift past "with scarcely a movement of wings". He added that it was of tremendous size and "for a moment, I doubted my sanity because it looked more like a pterodactyl out of the prehistoric ages."

In mid-July 1966, a bird "about as big as a Piper Cub airplane" was seen circling over Deseret, Utah. Four giant brown and gray birds were seen over Lowell, Ohio in November of that year and on December 6, a postman in Maysville, Kentucky spotted a giant birdlike creature.

In January 1976, Dr. Berthold Schwartz of Great Notch, New Jersey saw an enormous long-necked bird in the sky. He said that the creature was huge and was barely flapping its wings at all. Even though the bird was dark-colored, he commented that it seemed to give off a white light. He had no explanation for what he had seen.

Also, on January 1, 1976, a "horrible looking" black bird was seen by two children, Tracey Lawson and Jackie Davis at Harlingen, Texas. It was described as being about five feet tall, with wings bunched at the shoulders and a gray, "gorilla-like" face and red eyes. It stood on a plowed field about 100 yards away from them but Tracy was able to examine it closely with binoculars. They reported the sighting to their parents and their fathers found a number of three-toed tracks where the creature had been standing in the field. The prints were eight inches across and about one and a half inches deep in the ground. One of the men, who weighed about 170 pounds, was unable to make tracks as deep.

A week later, on January 7, the bird apparently traveled to Brownsville, Texas. Alverico Guajardo heard something hit the roof of his trailer and he went outside to see what it was. He was shocked to find a strange creature sitting on top of his home. It was about four feet tall, with black feathers, bat-like wings folded at the shoulder, a long beak and blazing red eyes. It made a horrific noises and it flew off into the darkness.

On January 11, the bird was sighted again by two ranch hands near Poteet, Texas. On January 14, Armando Grimaldo reported being attacked by a strange bird of nearly identical description at Raymondsville. He had heard the flapping of wings and a strange whistling outside of his home around 10:30 p.m. He went out to investigate and felt something come out of the dark and grab at him with large claws. When he got a look at the bird, he ran for cover. His description was close to the others but like the boys in Harlingen, did not report feathers. He said that the creature had dark, leathery skin. The creature managed to shred his shirt but his skin was not scratched.

A few days later, a big black bird with a bat-like face was seen by Libby and Dean Ford near Brownsville. They identified it as a pteranodon after looking at a book about prehistoric creatures. A similar creature was also reported on January 18 near Olmito and again on January 21 at Eagle Pass. Here, Francisco Magallenez said that he was attacked by the monster bird.

On February 24, three elementary school teachers were driving to work in San Antonio when they saw a huge bird with a 15-20 foot wingspan swoop over their cars. Patricia Bryant said that she could see the skeleton of the bird through its skin and David Renyon added that the creature glided rather than flew as its huge wings had a bony structure. Later, the teachers found the bird illustrated in an encyclopedia and captioned as a pteranodon.

More bird sightings were reported in Texas in December of that same year. On December 8, 1976, John Carroll, who owned a pig ranch in the Montalba area, spotted an enormous bird standing in a pond. He said that it was about eight feet tall, with a golden breast and a 12 inch bill. It took off and then circled around a few times to land in a nearby tree. Nervous about the safety of his pigs with this creature around, he shot at it and saw it fall a short distance away. Somehow, the body vanished and all he was able to find of it was a blood-stained feather. On December 17, a similar bird was seen about 15 miles northwest of Carroll and the witness stated that it seemed to have an injured wing. The bird was seen again at Catfish Creek on December 22 and then it was gone.

The strange birds returned to Illinois in 1977. One of the most exciting, and frightening, Illinois encounters occurred in 1977 in Lawndale, a small town in Logan County. On the evening of July 25, two giant birds appeared in the sky above Lawndale. The birds were reported several times as they circled and swooped in the sky. Finally, they headed straight down and reportedly attacked three boys who were playing in the backyard of Ruth and Jake Lowe. One of the birds grasped the shirt of ten-year-old Marlon Lowe, snagging its talons into the cloth. The boy tried in vain to fight the bird off then cried loudly for help.

The boy's cries brought Marlon's mother running outside. She later reported that she had seen the bird actually lift the boy from the ground and into the air. She screamed loudly and the bird released the child. It had carried him, at a height of about three feet, for a distance of about 35 feet. She was sure that if she had not come outside, the bird had been capable of carrying the boy away. She later stated that the bird had been bending down, trying to peck at the boy as it carried him off. Luckily, although scratched and badly frightened, Marlon was not seriously injured.

Four other adults appeared on the scene within seconds of the attack. They described the birds as being black in color, with bands of white around their necks. They had long, curved beaks and a wingspan of at least 10 feet. The two birds were last seen flying toward some trees near Kickapoo Creek.

Investigator Jerry Coleman, who lived in Decatur at the time, was able to interview the Lowe family, and the other witnesses, within hours of the incident and detailed the event. He returned to Lawndale two years later to speak to the family again and discovered that they had been harassed and bothered by media attention and by locals in the community. It was not uncommon to find dead birds on their doorstep in the morning, placed there by mean-spirited pranksters.

Marlon Lowe himself also had trouble dealing with the frightening encounter. The shock of the incident took years to wear off. Ruth Lowe had vivid memories of the event and spent years trying to identify the huge winged creatures that had almost taken her son. She spent long hours looking through books, certain that the creature had not been a turkey vulture, as an area game warden tried to convince her that it was. "I was standing at the door," she told the investigators, "and all I saw was Marlon's feet dangling in the air. There aren't any birds around here that can lift him up like that."

The Lawndale incident would not be the last sighting in Illinois that year. Three days later, a McLean County farmer named Stanley Thompson spotted a bird of the same size and description flying over his farm. He, his wife, and several friends were watching radio-controlled airplanes when the bird flew close to the models. He claimed the bird had a wingspan of again, at least 10 feet across. It dwarfed the small planes that buzzed close to it. He later told McLean County Sheriff's Sergeant Robert Boyd that the bird had about a six foot body and easily a wingspan of nine feet. Boyd commented that Thompson was a "credible witness". He had lived in the area for a long time and had no reason to make up stories. He questioned the original reports that came in but after speaking with Thompson, he had decided to investigate.

The next sighting took place near Bloomington when a mail truck driver named James Majors spotted the two birds. He was driving from Armington to Delevan when he saw them alongside of the highway. One of the birds dropped down into a field and snatched up a small animal. He believed the two birds were probably condors, but with ten foot wingspans! Majors quickly drove to the next town and then jumped out of the truck and smoked four cigarettes to regain his composure.

On July 28, Lisa Montgomery of Tremont was washing her car when she looked up and saw a giant bird crossing the sky overhead. She estimated that it had a seven foot wingspan and was black with a low tail. She said that it disappeared into the sky towards Pekin.

At 2:00 a.m. on Saturday, July 30, Dennis Turner and several friends from Downs, Illinois reported a monstrous bird perched on a telephone pole. Turner claimed that the bird dropped something near the base of the pole. When police officers investigated the sighting, they found a huge rat near the spot. Several residents of Waynesville reported seeing a black bird with an eight-foot wingspan later on that same day.

Reports of giant birds continued to come in from Bloomington and the north central Illinois area, then finally further south, from Decatur to Macon and Sullivan. On July 30, the same day the birds were reported near Bloomington, a writer and construction worker named "Texas John Huffer" filmed two large birds while fishing at Lake Shelbyville. Huffer was a resident of Tuscola and was spending the day with his son when they both spotted the birds roosting in a tree. Huffer frightened the birds with his boat horn and when they took flight, he managed to shoot over 100 feet of film. He sold a portion of the footage to a television station in Champaign for a newscast. Huffer said that the largest bird had a wingspan of over 12 feet.

After the footage aired, experts were quick to dismiss Huffer's claims, along with the accounts of everyone else who reported the birds. Officials from the Department of Conservation insisted the birds were merely turkey vultures and were nothing out of the ordinary. These claims were refuted by wildlife experts however, who stated that no turkey vultures were of the size reported by witnesses. The largest flying bird in North America is the California Condor, which has a wingspread of up to 9 feet. The Condor is also on the endangered species list and is restricted to a few areas in California.

On July 31, Mrs. Albert Dunham of rural Bloomington was on the second floor of her house when she noticed a large dark shadow passing by her window. She quickly realized that it was a giant bird and got a good look at it. Her description was almost identical to others reported at the same time, including a white ring around its neck. Her son chased the bird to a nearby landfill, but it had vanished before a local newspaper photographer could get a photo of it.

On August 11, John and Wanda Chappell saw a giant bird land in a tree near their home in Odin, Illinois. According to the witnesses, it was gray-black in color with about a 12 foot wingspan. John Chappell stated that it looked like a "prehistoric bird" and that it was likely big enough to have carried away his small daughter if it had wanted to. Wanda Chappell said that she and her husband almost didn't report the sighting because they were afraid people would think they were crazy.

And it's not surprising that they felt this way. The bird sightings of 1977 vanished from the press after the Odin, Illinois report from John and Wanda Chappell. As the notion appeared in many people's heads that these massive birds could be "turkey vultures", interest in the accounts began to fade and many were hesitant to report further sightings for fear of being laughed at, as the Lowe's in Lawndale were. The stories continued to spread of further sightings though and have not died out to this day.

On August 15, a witness who lived near Herrick, Illinois reported seeing two giant birds in a section of forest outside of town. He estimated the wingspans on the creatures to have been at least 10 feet. He followed their flight path to an abandoned barn at the edge of a field where they landed for about five minutes. After that, they vanished into the sky towards Taylorville.

On August 20, Paul Harrold reported a giant bird in the sky near Fairfield. He told me that the bird landed in a field not far from his car and remained there for a few moments before flying off again. According to his report, its wingspan was at least 12 feet in width. Harrold also stated that he was sure the bird was no vulture or buzzard, which are common in Illinois. Having lived out west for several years, he was familiar with large birds but said that he had never seen anything this big.

Another witness contacted me after seeing accounts of some Illinois big bird sightings in one of my books and said that she had also seen a huge winged creature in 1977. On November 1, she looked out the window of her home near Chester and had seen a huge bird resting in the top of a tall tree in her backyard. The bird seemed massive, much larger than anything else she had seen before, and had huge wings that it folded around itself. A few minutes later, it opened its wings and took off into the sky, gliding towards the Mississippi River. Its wingspan, she guessed, was at least 10 or 15 feet.

After that, the 1977 Illinois thunderbird sightings came to an end. But of course, the birds would be back and would not be limited to Illinois.

In September 1988, a giant bird was sighted in Brookfield, Wisconsin. A man looking out a hospital window, awaiting the birth of his son, saw a black form dipping in and out of the clouds overhead. He quickly realized that it was not a low-flying airplane but a gigantic bird. He said that it was a larger than a full-sized pickup truck but was smaller than a Piper Cub airplane. He estimated that its wingspan was 12-15 feet across. It stayed within view for some time and then vanished back into the clouds.

Another sighting occurred at Pryor Lake in Minnesota in 1988. T. Stewart had just returned from a trip to Canada and was looking out across the lake early in the morning when he saw a huge bird standing on a raft. He estimated that it was about 7-8 feet in height and had dark brown feathers. Its wingspan, he guessed, was more than twice the size of its body.

According to researcher Stan Gordon, the Black Forest region of Pennsylvania has continued to be active with giant bird sightings, just as it was back in the 1940's. In 2001, a witness in Westmoreland County saw a huge, dark-colored bird with a 10-15 foot wingspan go flapping by overhead. The bird's head was estimated to be about three feet long. It moved its wings in a frantic manner and then would glide for some distance. The bird flew about 50 feet above traffic along Route 119. The creature flew into a wooded area and then disappeared.

On June 13, 2001, a resident of Greenville, Pennsylvania reported seeing a large bird the size of a small airplane from his living room window. The bird was fully feathered and was black or very dark brown in color. The bird landed on a tree outside of the house and stayed there for about 15 minutes. When it took off and headed south, the witness was able to observe a 15-20 foot wingspan.

On July 6, a third sighting took place in Pennsylvania's Erie County. A witness named Robin Swope reported a large bird that was flying near a Greenville area mausoleum, near where she was cutting the grass. It flew near some high tension wires and she guessed it to have a 15-17 foot wingspan.

In October 2002, at least one giant winged creature was spotted several times in southwestern Alaska. Villagers in Togiak and Manokotak stated that the huge bird was about the "size of a small plane." On October 10, a heavy equipment operator named Moses Coupchiak saw the bird flying toward him from about two miles away as he worked his tractor. "At first I thought it was one of those old-time Otter planes," Coupchiak was quoted as saying. "Instead of continuing toward me, it banked to the left, and that's when I noticed it wasn't a plane." A few days later, on October 16, a giant winged creature that looked "like something out of Jurassic Park" was sighted again. A pilot spotted the bird while flying passengers to Manokotak, Alaska and calculated that its wingspan matched the length of a wing on one side of his Cessna 207, which was about 14 feet. Scientists laughed the whole thing off as "eagle sightings" but locals were unconvinced. They were familiar with larges birds, especially eagles, and the reports were, they were convinced, something very out of the ordinary.

So, what are these creatures? Some will try and convince you that the giant birds that have been seen, and on rare occasions have carried away children, are nothing more than turkey vultures or condors. In many cases though, the birds have been spotted by people who would have recognized these commonly known birds and even if they did not, only a small percentage of the anomalous reports could be so easily dismissed. Some cryptozoological researchers believe that these thunderbirds may be "Teratorns", a supposedly extinct bird that once roamed North and South America. If these prehistoric survivors are still around today, they could certainly account for the reports of the giant birds.

But could some of these winged creatures be something else altogether? Take into account the sightings in Texas in 1976 (when witnesses used guides to identify the birds they saw as pteranodons) and a sighting from the Hudson River Valley in May 1961. A businessman that was flying a small plane reported that a "big bird" buzzed his craft like a fighter jet and then continued to drift past "with scarcely a movement of wings". He added that it was of tremendous size and "for a moment, I doubted my sanity because it looked more like a pterodactyl out of the prehistoric ages."

And could this have been the case? If we take into account some of the stories and witness reports, then we have to consider that this there might be something to the idea that a handful of alleged prehistoric beasts may have survived to the modern day -- as incredible as it seems!

Could one of these impossible creatures have been killed near Tombstone, Arizona more than a hundred years ago in one of the most celebrated, and mysterious, events of this type?

THE TOMBSTONE THUNDERBIRD AND THE ELUSIVE PHOTOGRAPH

The story of the "Tombstone Thunderbird" has intrigued me as long as I can remember. Even as a child, I remember reading the story and being amazed. How, I asked myself, could what seemed to be a prehistoric creature like a pterodactyl be shot by cowboys in the 1800's? Such a thing seemed impossible but evidence existed in the form of many stories and references to the event and of course, existed in the form of a photograph. That was the really exciting part - that photograph! I still remember what it looked like today. Or do I?

You see, in more recent years, an even greater mystery has developed than whether or not a group of cowpokes shot down a "flying monster" in the Arizona desert. That mystery surrounds the elusive photograph that was taken of the incident and which many of us (myself included) believe that we saw. But if we did, where is the photo and what has become of it over the years?

One of the first accounts that was written of the Thunderbird that was allegedly killed in Tombstone was in the book *On the Old West Coast* by Major Horace Bell. I was able to track down a copy of this long out of print title and found it to be a very readable and entertaining book about Bell's adventures in California in the late 1800's. *On the Old West Coast* was published in 1930 and edited from Bell's writings by Lanier Bartlett.

Horace Bell had previously written a book called *Reminiscences of a Ranger* about his life in and journeys throughout California, Texas, Mexico and Central America. Bell had been a miner, a Ranger who pursued Joaquin Murrietta, a soldier of fortune in the forces of Benito Juarez in Mexico, an aide to General William Walker in Nicaragua, a Union officer in the Civil War and on the Texas border and finally, a newspaper editor in Los Angeles. He was considered a history writer and while he admitted to often writing stories that were "tongue in cheek", he declared that he was a truthful history writer, chronicling events as they happened. This is why the events that he wrote about in the Lake Elizabeth area - and by extension, Tombstone - are so strange to read about today.

The account in Bell's book, in a chapter entitled "Spit in the Mouth of Hell", does not start out to be about the creature that was killed in Tombstone. Bell believed that this same creature had its origins in California instead.

In October 1886, a Los Angeles, California newspaper reported on some strange events that had been occurring for years around nearby Lake Elizabeth. According to early stories from the days of the Spanish occupation of the region, the lake had long been considered a haunted place, plagued by frightening voices, shrieks, screams and groans that apparently emanated from the lake itself. After the Spanish, the Mexican settlers refused to live near the lake. They called it "La Laguna del Diablo" - the "Devil's Lake".

In the middle 1830's, Don Pedro Carrillo purchased the land around La Laguna del Diablo and built a hacienda, barn and corral by the water. He disregarded the superstitions about the place but just three months after construction on his ranch was completed, he abandoned the place. He stated that there were supernatural beings nearby and refused to live there. The land remained idle for the next two decades and even after the Americans came to the region, the lake was shunned as a cursed spot.

Some years later, Don Chico Lopez settled on the property and what occurred next was told in a manuscript by Don Guillermo Embustero y Mentiroso, who was a guest at the Lopez ranch. According to Don Guillermo, a great agitation took place during his visit. Around noon one day, Lopez's foreman, Chico Vasquez, rode up to the hacienda very upset. He told of strange happenings at the lake and everyone saddled their horses and rode out to the shore. They arrived to find the water calm and quiet and Lopez began berating his foreman for bothering them with foolishness but then stopped as a terrifying scream came from some brush at the edge of the lake. The plants whipped back and forth and the account stated that they were so close to whatever was lurking in the brush that they could smell its foul breath. The men were startled when their horses reared up and began running in fright.

As they brought their horses back under control, the men turned and looked back to the lake. Silhouetted against the sky was a large creature with enormous wings. The creature flapped them over and over again as it tried to rise from the mud. It roared and screamed and churned up the water around it. The horses and men fled in a panic. The next morning, all of the vaqueros on the ranch were mustered, armed and sent down to the lake to investigate. There was no sign of the winged monster but it was said that the smell of it still lingered in the air.

In 1883, the Lopez horses and cattle began to vanish. At first, bears or wolves were thought to be responsible but then one night, there was a terrible uproar in the corral. When the vaqueros came running, they found that ten mares and foals had been slaughtered. They said that, outlined against the sky, they saw the huge flying creature as it flapped away into the darkness. Don Chico Lopez promptly sold out and moved away from the area.

Then in 1886, the newspaper reported more strange happenings at Lake Elizabeth. The reports stated that a creature had been feeding on cattle, horses, sheep and chickens and had caused terror and excitement among the local inhabitants. On one occasion, the beast had tried to devour a large steer but as the animal bellowed and kicked, the sound attracted the attention of its owner, Don Felipe Rivera. The steer put up a fierce fight and managed to free itself. The angry creature then retreated but not before Rivera got a good look at it. He said that it was at least 45 feet long and had wings that laid flat on its back when not expanded. He pursued the monster as it started towards the lake and fired at it with his Colt revolver. Rivera said that when the bullets struck the monster's side, it sounded as if they were hitting a "great iron kettle".

But Don Felipe was nothing if not enterprising and he made immediate plans to try and capture the creature and sell it to the circus. He even signed a contract with Sells Brothers, who agreed to pay him $20,000 to deliver the beast to him alive. Don Felipe never managed to capture the creature, although it was reportedly seen several times in 1886. The creature was last seen, according to Horace Bell, winging away to the east.

"Since then," he wrote, "it has never been seen in its native valley because it was found and killed 800 miles from Lake Elizabeth, as is proved by the article that appeared in the *Epitaph*, Tombstone, Arizona." Bell then goes on to quote from the article, which he apparently saw, and provides details to the story. However, he does not say that the event occurred in 1886, as many believe. He provides a follow-up story, which is about the Tombstone article, that appeared in a Los Angeles newspaper in 1890. For this reason, it's safe to assume that the Thunderbird (if it really existed) was killed at some point between 1886 and 1890.

The article states that two ranchers sighted an enormous flying creature in the Arizona desert between Whetstone and the Huachuca Mountains. The beast resembled a huge alligator with an extremely elongated tail and an immense pair of wings. According to their story, the creature was greatly exhausted and was only able to fly a short distance at a time. The men, who were on horseback and armed with Winchester rifles, pursued the creature for several miles before getting close enough to open fire on it and wound it. The creature then turned on the cowboys but due to its exhaustion, they were able to keep far enough away from it until a few more shots could kill it.

An examination of the creature showed that it measured 92 feet in length and that its greatest diameter was about 50 inches. It had only two feet, situated a short distance in front of where the wings joined the body. The beak, as near as they could judge, was about eight feet long and its jaws were set with strong, sharp teeth. They experienced some difficulty trying to measure the wings, as they had folded up underneath the body as the monster had fallen, but eventually unrolled one of them. It was an incredible 78 feet in length, giving the beast a wingspan of about 160 feet. The wings were of a thick, nearly transparent membrane that had no feathers or hair on it. Its flesh was relatively smooth though and had been easily penetrated by their bullets.

The ranchers cut off a portion of the wing and took it with them, perhaps as proof of what they had seen. After arriving in Tombstone, they spread the word of the creature and made plans to return to the site where it had fallen and to skin it. They planned, the article stated, to offer the hide to eminent scientists for examination. They returned to the site to bring the creature back to town and here, the article ends. There are no details of the body being brought to town and no mention whatsoever of any photograph being taken.

The story of the Thunderbird was relegated to the ranks of creatures like the "jackalope" until 1963, when the story was revived. In the May 1963 issue of *Saga*, a men's magazine of the day, writer Jack Pearl recounted the story of the Tombstone Thunderbird, along with some large bird sightings of the early 1960's. Not only did he tell the story though, he went one step further and claimed that the Tombstone Epitaph had, in 1886, "published a photograph of a huge bird nailed to a wall. The newspaper said that it had been shot by two prospectors and hauled into town by wagon. Lined up in front of the bird were six grown men with their arms outstretched, fingertip to fingertip. The creature measured about 36 feet from wingtip to wingtip."

While this is a different variation of the story (and size of the creature), it seems to be referring to the same incident. Was this nothing more than a mythic legend of the west, or was there something to the story after all?

In the September 1963 issue of *Fate* magazine, a correspondent to the magazine named H.M Cranmer would state that not only was the story true, but the photo was published and had appeared in newspapers all over America. And Cranmer would not be the only one who remembered the photo. Eminent researcher Ivan T. Sanderson also remembered seeing the photo and in fact, even claimed to have once had a photocopy of it that he loaned to two associates, who lost it. The editors of *Fate* even came to believe that they may have published the photo in an earlier issue of the magazine but a search through back issues failed to reveal it. Meanwhile, the original *Epitaph* story, which again mentions no photograph, was revived in a 1969 issue of Old West, further confusing the issue as to whether the photo was real or not.

The *Epitaph* however stated that it did not exist, or if it did, it had not been in their newspaper. Responding to numerous inquiries, employees of the paper started a thorough search of back issues and files. They could find no such photo and even an extended search of other Arizona and California newspapers of the period produced no results. A number of articles that appeared in *Pursuit*, the journal for the Society for the Investigation of the Unexplained prompted a memory from W. Ritchie Benedict, who recalled seeing Ivan T. Sanderson himself display a copy of the photo on a Canadian television show "The Pierre Benton Show". Unfortunately though, no copies of the show have ever been found.

So, is the photo real? And if not, then why do so many of us with an interest in the unusual claim to remember seeing it? Who knows? In the late 1990's, author John Keel insisted that "I know I saw it! And not only that - I compared notes with a lot of other people who saw it." Like many of us, Keel believes that he saw it in one of the men's magazines (like *Saga* or *True)* that were so popular in the 1960's. Most of these magazines dealt with amazing subject matter like Bigfoot, ghosts and more. Keel also remembers the photo in the same way that most of us do - with men wearing cowboy clothing and the bird looking like a pterodactyl or some prehistoric, winged creature.

Interestingly, a reprint of the original article that appeared in Old West magazine caused a reader to remember another strange incident. He wrote to the magazine in the summer of 1970 and gave a firsthand account of a separate flying monster incident that also occurred near Tombstone. The writer had met two cowboys who told about seeing a similar creature around 1890, although they had shot at and chased the creature until their horses refused to go any further. This giant bird was not killed, brought to town or photographed. In fact, except for the fact that it was not shot down, their account sounds much closer to Bell's original report.

During the 1990's, the search for the "Thunderbird Photo" reached a point of obsession for those interested in the subject. A discussion of the matter stretched over several issues of Mark Chorvinsky's *Strange* magazine and readers who believed they had seen the photo cited sources that ranged from old books, to Western photograph collections, men's magazines, National Geographic and beyond. As for myself, I combed through literally hundreds of issues of dusty copies of True and Saga but could find nothing more than the previously mentioned article by Jack Pearl. If the photo exists, I certainly don't have it in my own collection.

So, how do we explain this weird phenomena of a photograph that so many remember seeing and yet no one can seem to find? Author Mark Hall believes that the description of the photo creates such a vivid image in the mind that many people who have a knowledge and an interest in curious and eclectic things begin to think the photo is familiar. It literally creates a "shared memory" of something that does not exist. We think we have seen it, but we actually have not.

To be honest, I can't say for sure if I agree with this or not. I can certainly see the possibility of a "memory" like this that we have created from inside of our own overcrowded minds, but then again, what if the photo does exist and it's out there, just waiting to be discovered in some dusty garage, overflowing file cabinet or musty basement. I, for one, haven't given up quite yet - and I have a feeling that I am not the only one who is still out there looking.

But are thunderbirds and mysterious flying creatures actually real? Do they fill the skies of anything other than our imaginations? If not, then what have so many people seen over the years? At this point, such creatures remain a mystery but one thing is sure, the sightings have continued over the years and occasionally an unusual report still trickles in from somewhere across America. So keep that in mind the next time that you are standing in an open field and a large, dark shadow suddenly fills the sky overhead. Was that just a cloud passing in front of the sun - or something else??

THE JERSEY DEVIL

The historic states along America's Atlantic Seaboard have given birth to hundreds of weird tales and unusual stories over the years. One of the strangest is undoubtedly that of the Jersey Devil, a being that is believed by some to be a mythical creature and by others, a real-life monster of flesh and blood. Its origins date back to when New Jersey was still a British colony and has it roots in a wild and overgrown region called the Pine Barrens.

This rugged place is one of vast forests, sandy soil and patches of swamp, where streams that are stained orange from iron ore and cedar slither through the shadows. It is a place that is often forgotten by man. The ruins of homes and buildings vanish into trees and undergrowth, leaving behind little but names that are now nothing more than crossroads in the wilderness. Among the places are Hog Walllow, Ongs Hat, Sooy Place and Mary Ann Furnace, as well as many others. They date back to the colonial days, when settlers actually attempted to farm the Barrens. The sandy soil, dense with pine and cedar, never took to crops and so the colonists moved on, taking harsh memories of the place with them.

The Pine Barrens stretch across more than 1,700 square miles of southeastern New Jersey. The region lies within one of the most densely populated states in the country and yet the desolation here is ominous. It is not difficult to travel for many miles without ever encountering a single sign of civilization. It is a place where one can easily vanish into the wild and never be seen again - and many have.

What makes the Pine Barrens different than other wild regions of America though is its unique history. At a time when the country was overwhelmingly made up of farms, the Pine Barrens supported literally dozens of industrial towns and villages. Furnaces and forges throughout the region turned out munitions for the American cause during the Revolution, during the wars with the Barbary pirates and the War of 1812. In the middle 1800's though, a better grade of iron ore was found in the west and production in the Pine Barrens went into a decline. There were efforts to keep the paper and glass works going but eventually, they proved to be unprofitable and one by one, the factories closed down. What was already a rugged area in which to live became worse with the collapse of the local industries and many moved away. Those who remained slipped deeper into poverty and they left the crumbling towns and moved into the forests and the swamps to eke out a living. The "Piney's", as they were called, remained here for generations, often in horrific destitution. They used the natural resources and worked at season jobs to survive, keeping completely to themselves until the modern roads of the Twentieth Century finally breached the isolation of the Pine Barrens once again.

It was at this time, as civilization began to encroach on this anomalous region, that stories began to filter out about a strange creature that lurked in the swamps and forests of the Barrens. As time has passed, countless stories of this monster have circulated throughout South New Jersey, changing little as they pass from one person to the next. The stories all tell of a mysterious beast that has long terrorized communities in south Jersey and eastern Pennsylvania, always returning to its lair in the Pine Barrens.

This legendary creature is known as the Jersey Devil.

The origin of the Jersey Devil is as shrouded in mystery as the very existence of the creature itself. According to one version of the legend, Mrs. Jane Leeds came from a poor family who eked out an existence in the Pine Barrens. In 1735, Mrs. Leeds discovered that she was pregnant with her 13th child. She complained to her friends and relatives that the "Devil can take the next one", and he did. When the baby was born, he was monster. He immediately took on a grotesque appearance and grew to more than 20 feet long, with a reptilian body, a horse's head, bat wings and a long, forked tail. He thrashed about the Leeds home for a bit and then vanished up the chimney to terrorize the surrounding regions.

Other versions of the story tell similar tales but often with varying birthplaces and sometimes with families other than the Leeds. Regardless of its beginnings though, the creature, or the "Jersey Devil" as he was dubbed, began haunting the Pine Barrens. As the story of the monster spread, even grown men declined to venture out at night. It was said that the beast carried off large dogs, geese, cats, small livestock and even occasional children. The children were never seen again, but the animal remains were often found. The Devil was also said to dry up the milk of cows by breathing on them and to kill off the fish in the streams, threatening the livelihood of the entire region.

In 1740, the frightened residents begged a local minister to exorcize the creature and the stories stated that the exorcism would last 100 years, however the Devil returned to the Pine Barrens on at least two occasions before the century was over. Legend has it that naval hero Commodore Stephen Decatur visited the Hanover Iron Works in the Barrens in 1800 to test the plant's cannonballs. One day on the firing range, he noticed a strange creature flying overhead. Taking aim, he fired at the monster and while some say that his shot struck it, the Devil continued on its path.

The second sighting took place a few years later and this time the Devil was seen by another respected witness. Joseph Bonaparte, the former king of Spain and the brother of Napoleon, leased a country house near Bordertown from 1816 to 1839. He reported seeing the Jersey Devil while hunting game one day in the Pine Barrens.

In 1840, as the minister warned, the Devil returned and brought terror to the region once again. It snatched sheep from their pens and preyed on children who lingered outside after sunset. Livestock vanished and was found slaughtered and glimpses of a winged monster were accompanied by chilling screams and inexplicable tracks. People all across South Jersey locked their doors and hung a lantern on the doorstep, hoping to keep the creature away.

In 1859, an article appeared in the Atlantic Monthly that testified to the fact that fear of the Jersey Devil in the regions had not diminished over the last two decades. The author of the article, W.F. Mayer, visited the Hanover Iron Works and found about 50 people living in squalor near the old mill. He found that few of them would venture out into the woods after dark.

That same year, the Jersey Devil was seen in Haddonfield and then vanished until the winter of 1873, when it was seen in Bridgeton. Throughout the 1880's, frequent reports continued to come in and in 1894, the Devil was often sighted lurking about Smithville, Long Beach Island, Brigantine Beach, Leeds Point and Haddonfield again. In 1899, after raiding Vincentown and Burrsville, the creature winged its way north and was seen along the New Jersey and New York border. A local newspaper printed the account of a man named George Saarosy, who claimed that his sheep were disturbed over several nights by horrifying screams that came from near the Lawrence Street Bridge over the Pascack River in Spring Valley, New York. Saarosy, who spotted the source of the screams, said that it resembled a "flying serpent". Those who had heard of the Jersey Devil recognized the description and even though it was far outside of its usual territory, believed that the beast had come calling.

As the turn of the last century dawned, the stories of the Jersey Devil continued to be told and the belief was strong in South Jersey that the Pine Barrens definitely contained some sort of eerie inhabitant that periodically spread chaos through the region. To many though, the Devil was little more than a legend - until that legend came to life in 1909. In that year, the Jersey Devil returned again and literally hundreds of people spotted the monster or saw his footprints. It became so bad that schools closed and people refused to go outside.

The first sighting occurred in the early morning hours of January 17. A man named Thack Cozzens of Woodbury was leaving the Woodbury Hotel when he heard a strange hissing noise and saw a blur of white cross the street. As the blur vanished into the darkness, he saw it turn and caught a flash of two, glowing white eyes. On that same morning in Bristol, Pennsylvania, within hours or even minutes of the Woodbury sighting, a man named John McOwen was awakened by the sound of his baby daughter crying. He went to calm her and heard odd noises coming from the Delaware Division Canal, which ran behind the house. He described the noises as scratching and whistling sounds and when he looked outside, he got the shock of his life. There, on the edge of the canal, was a large creature with wings that was hopping along the tow-path.

Nearby, a police officer named James Sackville spotted the monster while walking his beat that night. He was passing along a dark alley when a winged creature hopped into the street and let out a horrific scream. Sackville, who later became the chief of Bristol's Police Department, got a closer look at the monster than Cozzens or McOwen did and said that it had wings like a bird but the features of a peculiar animal. He ran toward the creature and it hopped backward in retreat. He then fired his revolver at the beast but it spread its wings and vanished into the air.

Not long after the Devil escaped from Sackville, it was spotted by E.W. Minster, the postmaster of Bristol. He stated that he awoke around 2:00 in the morning and heard an "eerie, almost supernatural" sound coming from the direction of the Delaware River. He looked out the window and saw what looked to be a "large crane" that was flying diagonally and emitting a curious glow. The creature had a long neck that was thrust forward in flight, thin wings, long back legs and shorter legs in the front. The creature let out a combination of a squawk and a whistle and then disappeared into the darkness.

Other Bristol residents found their yards covered with abnormal-looking hoof prints the following morning. Few could provide a reasonable explanation as to where they had come from.

After leaving Bristol, the Jersey Devil next turned up in Burlington, New Jersey, a city that became the center of its activities in the days to come. Late on the night of January 17, Joseph W. Lowden and his family, who lived on High Street in the middle of town, heard noises like something heavy trampling the snow in their backyard. The sounds circled the house and then scraped against the back door, as if someone was trying to open it. When they examined the yard the following morning, they found strange tracks everywhere. The snow had been scattered around their trash cans and the garbage had been half eaten. The tracks defied all explanation - and the Lowden's would not be the only ones to find them.

Hardly a yard in Burlington seemed to be untouched by them. They climbed trees, skipped from one roof top to another, trampled across fields, into streets, over fences and then vanished, as if whatever had made them simply flew away. To add to the mystery, the size of the tracks varied. Some were as large as horses hooves but others were quite small. One thing was sure though - they were frightening and a general panic gripped the town that day. Doors and windows were bolted and people refused to leave home, especially after dark. Those who did venture out went in search of the creature. Attempts to capture and kill it were made, or at least vowed, but few of them led to anything.

Reports of more tracks poured in from surrounding communities and in Jacksonville, a hunt for the Jersey Devil was organized. Strangely though, dogs refused to follow the trail left by the monster and so their masters followed the prints for nearly four miles before the tracks disappeared. Farmers set out steel traps but - and luckily for them - they never caught anything in them.

The sightings continued and no more so than they did on January 19. At around 2:00 that morning, Nelson Evans, a Gloucester City paper hanger, and his wife were awakened at their home on Mercer Street. Strange noises were coming from outside and the couple nervously peered out their window to see a large animal on the roof of their shed. They watched for a full ten minutes as the Jersey Devil stomped back and forth. They described the beast as: "about three and a half feet high, with a face like a collie and a head like a horse. It had a long neck, wings about two feet long and its back legs were like those of a crane and it had horse's hooves. It walked on its back legs and held up two short front legs with paws on them." Mrs. Nelson also added that as the creature flapped its wings, it made a muffled sound "like a wood saw makes when it strikes a rotten place." A drawing that was based on the Nelson's description appeared in the Philadelphia Evening Bulletin and became the most famous rendition of the creature.

Yet another hunt was started for the Devil that day near Gloucester. Hank White and Tom Hamilton, professional muskrat hunters, tracked the creature for close to 20 miles through the forest. They were amazed to see the tracks jump over eight-foot fences and then duck under spaces no more than eight inches high. By the time the hunt was called off, White stated that he would not venture outside of his home without a gun until the Devil had left the region.

Sightings of the monster's footprints - or hoof prints - continued all over southern New Jersey. The daughter of William Pine, from Camden, was bringing her father his dinner pail when she stumbled across a series of strange tracks in the snow. She became so frightened that she might be attacked that she fell into a dead faint. Her father and others examined the tracks and stated that they resembled those of a donkey with only two legs. One of the tracks, they said, was larger than the other, which made it seem "obviously deformed."

Early Wednesday morning, January 20, an unidentified Burlington policeman spotted the creature and said that it "had no teeth and its eyes were blazing coals". That same morning, Reverend John Pursell spotted the beast in Pemberton. He said that he had "never saw anything like it before."

Predictably, more hunts were organized that day. Haddonfield, New Jersey was the scene of two search parties, led by a Dr. Glover and a Mr. Holloway. They found many tracks in the fields and woods around town but all of the trails ended suddenly, when the creature apparently took flight. Another search party hunted the creature near Collinswood and while they found many tracks, they only got a fleeting glimpse of the Devil as it winged its way north toward Moorestown.

The Devil's only stop in Moorestown was in the Mount Carmel Cemetery, where it was spotted by John Smith of Maple Shade. Smith actually chased the creature until it vanished around a nearby gravel pit. Moments later, the Devil crossed the path of George Snyder, who had been fishing in the same gravel pit. Both he and

Smith's description of the monster matched, stating that it was three feet tall, covered in black hair, had a face like a dog's, split hooves, wings and a tail.

The Devil was seen again late that night, this time in Springside, just south of Burlington City, by a trolley car operator named Edward Davis. He was shocked when he saw a strange shape leap across the tracks in front of the trolley and then disappear into the shadows. Davis said that he shape resembled a "winged kangaroo with a long neck."

That same night, residents in Riverside, New Jersey discovered a series of strange tracks throughout the town, especially near chicken coops, buildings and even outhouses. Joseph Mans found the tracks had paced a circle around the body of his dead puppy. Mans at first attributed the dog's death to some people that he had recently given some court testimony about and told police officers that the prowler had worn what seemed to be small horse shoes on the bottom of his boots. The dog killer had "left tracks everywhere, including the rooftop." The judge that Mans had testified in front

A Newspaper Drawing of What Mr. & Mrs. Nelson reported on the roof of the shed on January 19, 1909.

of, Justice Ziegler, became interested in the investigation and came over to the house. Curious, he made a half dozen plaster casts of the footprints and when word of this got out, crowds came to his office to see the casts. It was soon realized that the dog's death had not been the work of Mans' enemies at all.

In the early morning hours of Thursday, January 21, the Jersey Devil put in a frightening appearance in Camden. Members of the Black Hawk Social Club were having a meeting around 1:00 a.m. and a Mr. Rouh was distracted by what he called an "uncanny sound" outside the back window. He turned to see a gruesome face staring in at him and he let out a scream. The other club members fled in terror but Rouh grabbed a club and waved it at the creature. It stated that it flew off, emitting "bloodcurdling sounds."

An hour later, a Public Service Railway Trolley was pulling out of Clementon and heading for Camden. It had just passed Haddon Heights when a passenger yelled out and pointed to the window. Everyone on board crowded up to the glass to see a winged creature swoop past them. The trolley traveled another 200 yards before it stopped and when it did, the Devil circled above the car, hissing loudly. A few moments later, it flew away and headed north. Within days, trolley cars began carrying armed guards on board to protect the passengers.

A short time later, the creature turned up again, this time on the road between Trenton and Ewing. William Cromley was returning home from his job as the doorkeeper at the Trent Theater in Trenton and when his horse panicked and stopped in the road, he climbed out of the buggy to see what was wrong and saw "a sight that froze the blood in his veins and caused his hair to stand upright." Confronting him on the road was a winged beast that was larger than a big dog with glowing, sparkling eyes. The beast growled at him and then spread its wings and flew off.

Not long after this sighting, Trenton City Councilman E.P. Weeden was awakened by the sound of someone trying to forcibly enter his home. Banging and crashing sounds were coming from the back door and he sprang out of bed to see what was going on. Weeden flung open the second floor window and looked out, only to see a dark shape suddenly vanish into the darkness. The movement was accompanied by the sound of beating wings and the next morning, he would find cloven tracks in the snow of his yard and on his roof.

Later that afternoon, Mrs. J.H, White was taking clothes off her line when she noticed a strange creature huddled in the corner of her yard. She screamed and fainted and her husband rushed out the back door to find his wife on the ground and the Devil close by, "spurting flames". He chased the monster with a clothesline prop and it leapt over the fence and vanished. White ran out into the alley in pursuit but soon quit the chase and returned to his wife, who was still unconscious. He called the family doctor, who spent more than an hour reviving Mrs. White from her terrifying experience.

A short time later, the Devil was seen in West Collingswood. Charles Klos and George Boggs were walking down Grant Avenue when they saw what they first thought was an ostrich perched on the roof of the fire chief's home. Concerned, the two men called in a fire alarm and when a department truck arrived, they turned their hoses on the creature. At first it fled to some distance down the street and then the beast ignored the water and charged directly at the now frightened men. As they ran for cover, the Devil suddenly spread its wings and soared over them, disappearing into the dusk.

Leaving the West Collinswood firemen behind, the Devil traveled up Mount Ephraim Avenue and attacked a dog belonging to Mrs. Mary Sorbinski in south Camden. When she heard the cry of her pet in the darkness, she dashed outside and drove the Devil away with a broom. The creature fled, but not before tearing a chunk of flesh from the dog. Mrs. Sorbinski carried her wounded pet inside and immediately called the police. By the time that patrolmen arrived, a crowd of more than 100 people was gathered at the house. The crowd was witness to the piercing screams that suddenly erupted from nearby. The police officers emptied their revolvers at the shadow that loomed against the night sky, but the Devil escaped once again.

In the days that followed, eyewitness accounts of the Jersey Devil filled the newspapers, as well as photos and reports of cloven footprints that had been found in yards, woods and parking lots. The Philadelphia Zoo offered a $10,000 reward for the capture of the Devil, but there were no takers. Many people refused to leave their homes, even in broad daylight and many schools closed down, due to a lack of students. Theaters canceled performances and even mills in Gloucester and Hainesport were shut down when workers refused to report for their shifts.

Then, as suddenly as it had come, the Devil vanished into the Pine Barrens again.

The stunning events of 1909 had come to an end. Up until that time, it was always assumed that the Jersey Devil was nothing more than a legend, an old wives' tale from the rugged regions of the Barrens. But now, the entire region had been the scene of this mythical beast's rampage - leaving hundreds of believable eyewitnesses in its wake.

The creature did not return again until 1927. A cab driver was changing a tire one night while headed for Salem. He had just finished when his car began shaking violently. He looked up to see a gigantic, winged figure pounding on the roof of his car. The driver, leaving his jack and flat tire behind, jumped into the car and quickly drove away. He reported the encounter to the Salem police.

In August 1930, berry pickers at Leeds Point and Mays Landing reported seeing the Devil, crashing through the fields and devouring blueberries and cranberries. It was reported again two weeks later to the north and then it disappeared again.

In November 1951, a group of children were allegedly cornered by the Devil at the Duport Clubhouse in Gibbstown. The creature bounded away without hurting anyone but reports claimed that it was spotted by dozens of witnesses before finally vanishing again.

Sightings continued here and there for years and then peaked once more in 1960 when bloodcurdling cries terrorized a group of people near Mays Landing. State officials tried to calm the nervous residents but no explanation could be found for the weird sounds. Policemen nailed signs and posters everywhere stating that the Jersey Devil was a hoax, but curiosity-seekers flooded into the area anyway. Harry Hunt, who owned the Hunt Brothers Circus, offered $100,000 for the capture of the beast, hoping to add it to his sideshow attractions. Needless to say, the monster was never snared.

The most recent sighting of the creature was said to have been in 1993 when a forest ranger named John Irwin was driving along the Mullica River in southern New Jersey. He was startled to find the road ahead of him blocked by the Jersey Devil. He described it as being about six-feet tall with horns and matted black fur.

Could this have been the reported Jersey Devil - or some other creature altogether? Irwin stated that he and the creature stared at one another for several minutes before the monster finally turned and ran into the forest.

Today, there are only a few, isolated sightings of the Jersey Devil. It seems as though the paved roads, electric lights and modern conventions that have come to the region over the course of two and a half centuries have driven the monster so far into hiding that it has vanished altogether. The lack of proof of the monster's existence in these modern times leads many to believe the Devil was nothing more than a creation of New Jersey folklore. But was it really?

If it was merely a myth, then how do we explain the sightings of the creature and the witness accounts from reliable persons like businessmen, police officers and even public officials? They are not easy to dismiss as hearsay or the result of heavy drinking. Could the Jersey Devil have been real after all? And if so, is it still out there in the remote regions of the Pine Barrens - just waiting to be found?

IV. PHANTOMS OF THE PINES

CHILLING TALES OF HAUNTED PLACES IN THE AMERICAN WILD

I have never had difficulty in finding ghosts. I have written about hauntings in cities, villages and small towns. They haunt old theaters, deserted graveyards, abandoned hospitals, ramshackle homes and just about anyplace else you can think of but there are few ghosts that I find to be as downright chilling as those lingering in the great outdoors. Perhaps it is my affinity for the "wild" that makes this the case or perhaps it is because I was raised on a secluded farm and always found the wide fields, remote pastures and shadowy woods to be as haunted as anything the city had to offer.

I have recounted this story before but many years ago, I stumbled across an old house in the forest that had been abandoned. The roads and paths that led back to it had long since grown over and vanished and there had been no one living there for many years. Inside of the house though, I found that everything had been left just as it had been when the owners departed. It appeared that they had simply walked away - leaving their entire lives behind. There was furniture in the living room, cooking pots in the kitchen, clothing still hanging in the closets and even several pair of shoes still lined up next to the front door. It was probably the most eerie place that I have ever been. Haunted? Perhaps not, but it certainly gave me an appreciation for the fact that strange things happen in the woods and - to paraphrase the adage about the tree that falls when no one is around to hear it - they can happen whether we know about them or not.

I remembered my own brush with a strange house in the woods after I ran across a story that circulated in the *St. Louis Globe-Democrat* newspaper back in 1890. It told of a strange experience that happened to some weekend hunters near the village of Barry, Missouri one summer night. Today, Barry is a bedroom community of Kansas City, but in those days, it was much more remote and secluded. The house where the men spent part of a very unnerving night was located in a thick stand of forest outside of town. It would be a night that none of them would forget.

The story of the hunters, who had come out to the area around Barry one weekend, was told by a member of the party, an "Uncle Billy" Newcome, a railroad worker and reliable man. He and his friends had been in the woods of Clay County for an entire day but by early evening, a storm rolled in and it began to rain. They were about two miles from Barry when the skies opened up and rather than drive back to Kansas City in the rain, and miss the next day of hunting, they decided to try and find a place to provide shelter for the night.

Back in the woods, about a quarter mile from a dirt road, one of the men spotted a stone house that was nestled back in the trees. It was broken down and crumbling and obviously had not been lived in for years. Thinking that it would at least keep the rain from their heads, the hunters examined the place and found it empty. They loaded their gear inside, after finding it dry and warm, and then the other three hunters left Billy in charge of getting a fire going while they went to a farm house down the road to inquire about buying some food for supper. The other men left and Billy soon gathered wood and started a blaze in one of the house's old stone fireplaces.

By this time, darkness had begun to fall and Billy described his surroundings as being in "half twilight, half deep shadow". The stone house was two stories tall and there were enormous fireplaces at each end of the great room on the ground floor. After getting the fire started, he sat down near one of them to wait for his friends, dry out his damp clothing and have a good smoke. "I do not know how long I had been thus occupied," he later wrote, "when I was startled by a scream of agony apparently issued from the deserted end of the room. The cry was like that of a woman in mortal distress and it kept growing louder and louder until my blood ran cold."

Billy realized that he had been dozing when the screams began and as he quickly recovered his wits, he grabbed his gun and sprang to his feet. As he hurried toward the other end of the great room, where the sound seemed to first come from, he noticed that it was getting fainter and fainter, as though moving away from him. Although sunset had plunged the room into murky darkness, he could see that no one was there. Moments later, the heard the wailing again, this time coming from the orchard behind the house. "I dashed through the side door," he said, "and ran in that direction. As I ran, could hear the screaming ahead of me, growing more muffled, until with one last despairing scream, it ended. I was brought to a standstill right at the foot of one of the largest trees in the orchard. I could see nothing, hear nothing, could find nothing and although my nerves were strung to their highest tension through excitement, no thought of the supernatural entered my head."

Billy searched through the three-acre orchard as best that he could in the fading daylight and the drizzling rain and finally returned to the house with no clues as to the source of the sound that he had heard. He was convinced, thanks to the horrific cries, that a murder had been committed somewhere close by but there was nothing he could do and no culprit or victim that he could find. He nervously settled back in before the fireplace and built the fire in the hearth up so high that the room around him was brightly lit. As soon as his companions returned, he vowed, they would make a search of the place together.

He stretched out along the stone floor and listened intently for any further noise that would indicate the presence of someone else in the house. After listening to silence for some time, the sounds strangely began again. This time, it seemed, they began right at the edge of the area where Billy was sitting. "They were low and wailing," he added, "so suggestively mournful and sad that I felt fascinated and frozen in my seat. If you have ever heard the mournful wail of a dog, just exaggerate it ten times in its intensity, and you can form some idea of the sound that was making the perspiration start out like beads on my forehead. I can't say that I was frightened but there was something so unreal about it that I felt I was bound to my seat."

The warbling cry continued and seemed to go from the first floor to a room up on the second, directly above where he was sitting. Here, it ended in one long, drawn-out sob. Just as soon as it had ended, Billy recovered himself and ran up the stairway to where he had last heard the cry. "I could find nothing. I searched all over and through the rooms," he swore. "By this time, I began to realize that there was something wrong, either with the house or with my nerves, and I bolted down the stairway, determined to go in search of my companions."

Billy snatched up his gun as he ran through the great room, out the front door and into the rain. As he started down the path to the road, he met this three friends, almost to the gate. They were returning with milk, butter, bacon and eggs that they had purchased from the farmer. Billy made his excuses for why he was outside, now embarrassed of how he had acted, and told his friends nothing of what he had heard. Instead, he returned with them to the house and soon they had the bacon and eggs cooking in the fireplace.

After they had eaten, all four of them sat down near the fireplace. Billy's friends laughed and joked and told hunting stories but he paid little attention to them as he was listening intently for a repetition of the earlier cries. Time passed though and he heard nothing. As the hour grew later, the men tossed some extra wood on the fire and prepared to lie down on their bedrolls for the night. They were enjoying a last smoke when the cries began to echo in the house once more.

This time, the moaning seemed to come from all parts of the room at the same time, as if the house was filled with weeping, wailing women. Billy's friends were as unnerved as he had been before and the four of them ran wildly through the house in search of intruders. After shouting and calling out, the men calmed down and took torches from the fire. After Billy explained what had happened while they were gone, the four of them began an organized search of the house. It did not take them long to realize that there could be no one hidden in the simple structure. Shaken and afraid, they gathered their guns and belongings and left the house, walking back out into the cold rain.

When they made it through the woods to the road, they decided to go to the farmer who had sold them the food and ask for lodging for the night. Even his barn would have been preferable to staying in the abandoned house. It was past midnight when they reached the house but the farmer gladly allowed them in. He insisted on them bedding down in his parlor and the hunters did not speak of their strange experience.

The following morning, Billy decided to ask the man about the house. The farmer was reluctant at first but then he began to speak. "There's something wrong with it and has been for nearly 25 years. For years and years, it has been offered rent free to anyone who would live in it - but every person who has tried to stay there has gotten enough of it in one night."

According to the old man, the house had been built by a Baptist minister who had owned the orchard, well and the 60 acres of land that adjoined it. The family was well off and rumored to have a lot of money. They owned a number of slaves and were well-respected in the area. Just before the Civil War, the minister had gotten sick and died and after the war started, most of the slaves had abandoned the farm. The minister's son had joined the Confederate Army and had been killed at Manassas but his mother had continued to live on in the house alone, save for two of the slaves who had stayed with her.

The story began to circulate in the area that the old lady had buried all of her gold in the orchard before the start of the war, hoping to keep the money safe from Union soldiers and Confederate guerillas in the area. One early morning, in the fall of 1863, a worker from a nearby farm passed by the house and thought that he heard screams and cries for help. Instead of going to the house though, he ran back to his farm and told his employer what he had heard. The story was dismissed and soon forgotten.

A few days later, the mangled corpse of the minister's wife was found lying under one of the largest trees in the orchard. She had been stabbed to death but had obviously been tied up and tortured before she was killed. The house had been ransacked and the ground had been turned in various places throughout the orchard as someone had searched for her gold. The slaves were never seen or heard from again.

Ever since the discovery of the woman's body, the farmer explained, the house was considered to be haunted. He told them that each night, the unquiet spirit of the minister's wife re-enacts the moments when she lost her life in an attempt to hide the secret of her buried treasure.

Billy and his companions listened closely to the tale and attested to the fact that it was the truth. They had only been in the house for a little less than six hours and there was no doubt in their minds that those six hours had been quite long enough.

AMERICA'S HAUNTED BACK ROADS

I have long been fascinated by haunted roads and highways. They are often places where horrific events and strange deaths have occurred, leaving an indelible impression behind. Like a haunted house, roads and highways frequently become haunted by the events that occur on them or alongside them. Incidents of violence, death, murder and bloody accidents can sometimes leave a memory of the past imprinted on a lonely side road or even at a busy intersection. Sometimes, these memories replay themselves over and over again or on other occasions, the spirits of the dead linger as well. Many of them, having lost their lives suddenly and without explanation, have no idea they are dead. Others, those elusive ghosts with a purpose, are still seeking answers, justice or are perhaps still trying to make it home just one last time.

In some cases, the answer to why a road may be haunted may lie in the roadway itself. Many roads were built along original trails and foot paths that were created by the Native Americans and some believe that these inhabitants forged paths here in connection to ancient ley lines or because they believed the pathways were sacred in some way. The history left behind on such roads may be explanation enough for why they have come to be considered haunted over the years.

America's roadways play host to many ghosts from the past and one of the most chilling additions to haunted highway lore is the "vanishing hitchhiker", an eerie presence that looks for rides along deserted roads and then disappears mysteriously from the passenger seat of the automobile belonging to the luckless motorist who picked her up. Such tales are rather common and can be found all over the country. I have written on many occasions in the past of phantom hitchers and haunted stretches of road and have never had a problem finding them, especially in urban areas and around great cities like Chicago.

But what of the roads that are not so well-traveled? Do they become haunted as well? Most assuredly they do and as I did, you will soon discover that there is nothing as chilling as the lone figure in your headlights on an abandoned road in the middle of nowhere. Strange tales haunt the roads in the American wild and if you go looking for them, just remember this - if your car breaks down here, there is no one to hear you calling for help.

There is an entire book that could be written on nothing more than the ghosts of America's haunted roadways and thoroughfares. In the past, I have written frequently of roadside ghosts and vanishing hitchhikers like Resurrection Mary in Chicago and scores of others. As mentioned though, it is not only the busy streets and roads of the cities that become haunted but the roadways of America's wild regions as well.

THE BLACK WOODS ROAD

Just off the Maine coast lies the tiny town of Franklin. It has the distinction of being a town that was named for Founding Father Benjamin Franklin but it has another , most ghastly distinction as well - it was the site of a horrible accident years ago that has left a ghostly impression behind.

The accident occurred along Black Woods Road (Route 182), a pleasant ribbon of pavement that runs through forests and along marshes and lakes. It is especially scenic on an early October day as the blazing leaves of the birch and maple trees contrast vividly with the deep blue waters of Tunk Lake. During the winter months, the road can be especially hazardous with many twists, turns and sudden hills. There have been many accidents along this road and a number of fatalities, including one that occurred in the early 1950's, just after the highway was paved. A young woman from Cherryfield was killed - and they say that she has never left this road.

Her name was Catherine and she lived with her family just off Black Woods Road, about 20 miles or so from Ellsworth, where she worked. She made the drive every morning, no matter what the conditions and on one cold November day, she made her final trip. As she set out that morning, after bidding her father goodbye, she cursed the icy pellets of freezing rain that were falling from the sky. Because of the bad conditions, she knew that she was going to have to take old Route 1 to work. It was safer and more populated than her usual route along Black Woods Road but it also took her much longer to get to work. By late afternoon though, the sleet and freezing rain had stopped and the sun had even come out for awhile. When Catherine left work, she debated on whether or not to take safer Route 1 home, or the shorter passage along Black Woods Road. She chose the latter and just as the sun was dipping down past the edge of the sky, her car entered the forest along the highway.

Catherine drove through the woods and past several farms before the lights of Franklin appeared. She passed the crossroads in the center of town and drove on into the rapidly falling darkness. She was anxious to get home on this cold night, as she knew her mother would have dinner waiting. Unfortunatrely though, about two miles outside of Franklin, the engine of her car suddenly began to make a strange clanking noise. The motor coughed a few times and then died. Catherine steered the car over to the bottom of a hill next to Tunk Lake and wondered what to do. She was still several miles from home and she had no idea how to fix a broken down automobile. She tried to turn the key a few times but only received a clicking sound in reply. She debated opening the hood but would have no idea what to look for and besides that, she did not even have a flashlight in her glove box.

After a moment's consideration, she realized that her only option was to make the shorter walk back towards Franklin. She could call her father from there and he could come and pick her up. Catherine put on her gloves, buttoned her coat, wrapped her scarf around her neck and then set off into the night. She would never be seen alive again.

Later on that evening, when she did not show up at her usual time, her father began searching for her along old Route 1, which he assumed she had taken to come home. He drove back and forth all night long and even contacted the local police, who knew Catherine and her family, and officers helped him to search. They eventually began looking along Black Woods Road and by morning, found her abandoned car. There was still no sign of Catherine though. The sheriff brought in some local hunting dogs and they followed her scent from the car and back towards Franklin. Within a few hours, they discovered her body in the woods. She had been struck by a passing vehicle and her body had been thrown more than a dozen feet from the highway. It looked as though she had been killed instantly.

The cause of the accident was never discovered and the hit and run driver was never caught. There was some speculation that she might have been killed by a logging truck, as there were no skid marks at the scene. Locals who drove past the spot where Catherine was killed began to talk of having an uneasy feeling as they passed that stretch of road but dismissed it as nothing more than a case of nerves. Not long after though, people began to talk....

One night, a driver who was just passing through the area was on Black Woods Road and he spotted a young woman walking at the edge of the highway. Her figure appeared in his headlights, stumbling precariously at the edge of the pavement. The man slowed his truck and then pulled over to the side to offer her a ride into town. It was a cold night, he thought, and no one should be out walking. He stopped just past where the woman was walking and opened the passenger door to let her in. When she did not appear, he craned his neck around to look back at her - but she was gone. The young woman who had been there just moments before had vanished.

The driver told his story in a diner just down the road and soon others began to tell the same tales. Logging truck drivers, passing motorists and even sheriff's deputies told of driving along the curves from Tunk Lake and seeing a woman walking along the edge of the road. Whenever they stopped to help her, she disappeared.

Then one night, a young man was speeding along Black Woods Road, heading home to Ellsworth, and he claimed to see the same young woman at the edge of the road. He was in a hurry though and didn't bother to stop. As he kept on driving, he happened to glance up in his rearview mirror and what he saw there caused him to suddenly slam on his brakes and bring his car to a shuddering, sliding stop in the middle of the highway. The young man fumbled for the door handle and then fell out of the car onto the road, breathing heavily. He peered into the back seat of the car - but it was empty. He stood there for a moment, fighting to calm himself, and tried to understand what he had seen. Just moments after passing the young woman on the road, he had looked into his mirror and saw the same young woman, her eyes glazed and her face streaked with blood, looking at him from the back seat. Terrified, he had stopped the car, only to find that the car was empty. The girl was not there.

Needless to say, the man told the story over and over again, never minding those who did not believe him and always insisting that it was the truth. After that, the story of Catherine took a different turn and it is still told to this day. According to the locals, if you are traveling down Black Woods Road at night and see a woman walking alone at the edge of the woods, you always need to stop and offer her a ride.

If you don't, she is liable to end up in the car with you anyway - and she may be unhappy that you didn't have the courtesy to try and help her.

THE RIDGEWAY PHANTOM

In the southwestern corner of Wisconsin, near the present day town of Mineral Point, lurks a strange story. It is a tale of a section of roadway that was haunted by -- - well, something truly unusual. The strange creature was dubbed the "Ridgeway Phantom" and it took its name from an old crossroads town that has since vanished into history. The spirit, which lingered around a wooded roadway, took many forms, frightening travelers as a headless man, an old woman, a ball of light and a number of spectral animals. The phantom appeared from nowhere and attacked passersby, until it came to the point that no one would travel the Ridge Road between Mineral Point and Blue Mounds alone or unarmed.

The origins of the ghost are as mysterious as its crimes and some believe that it departed when the business district of Ridgeway burned in 1910. Others don't believe this and maintain that the phantom is still out there, lurking in the forest near Mineral Point.

The story of the Ridgeway Phantom began in the early 1840's. In those days, Wisconsin was not yet a state and settlements here were few and far between. Vast forests covered the land and the lakes were filled with pristine waters, still untouched by man. In that decade, the first pioneers arrived in the southwestern part of the state and as they came, they discovered deposits of lead in the region's limestone hills. This valuable commodity was needed to produce the bullets that Americans needed to tame the rugged land and soon mines were opened and fortunes were made.

The opening of the mines attracted rugged and dangerous men who followed the fortunes of the mines around the country. The miners settled in the lead districts that surrounded the small settlements of Mineral Point, Dodgeville, Blue Mounds and other small towns.

At the height of the mining era, over 40,000 pounds of lead was hauled away each year to markets in Chicago, Galena and beyond. For this reason, roads had to be cut through the dense forests and along these rutted dirt paths, roadhouses and saloons appeared to cater to the appetites of the miners. Along the Military Ridge Road, which passed through Mineral Point and connected Blue Mounds and Dodgeville, there were 22 saloons at one point, on just 25 miles of road. Drunken fights, robbery and murder were not uncommon along the road, especially after it was learned that the miners had money to spend. They were soon joined by the criminal element, along with the gamblers and the prostitutes, all looking to use their own methods to part the men from their hard-earned wages.

For almost 20 years, wagons carrying lead for the processing mills rolled down Ridge Road. The saloons and the bordellos, as well as the thieves and murderers, thrived. It came to an end in 1857 when the Chicago & Northwestern Railroad completed a branch line into Mineral Point. Lead could then be shipped out more easily by rail and soon, traffic along the Ridge Road declined. As the wagons stopped rolling, the saloons and roadhouses began to close down. The road, which had been carved out of the forest, began to be reclaimed by the wilderness that had so reluctantly yielded it.

By the time that the railroad was in full swing, it was only a very brave man who would travel the Ridge Road alone. For years, it had been plagued by a series of strange incidents and with only a few travelers and passersby using the roadway at all, the place began to be shunned by those who knew its tales. Some dismissed the stories as merely tales of robbers and thieves but they were soon assured there were far stranger things in the woods than mere highwaymen.

At the height of the mining era, wagon masters and travelers began to tell eerie stories of a series of bizarre encounters with ghosts and phantoms along the Ridge Road. The small community of Ridgeway, located halfway between what was then called Pokerville (later Blue Mounds) and Mineral Point, was the center of the activities for what came to be called the "Ridgeway Phantom". The ghost, it was said, took on a variety of forms as it preyed on those who lived and worked along this roadway. It appeared as dogs, horses, pigs, sheep and several different human forms, including a headless horseman. The specter roamed the countryside, frightening everyone that it encountered. It terrified riders and lead haulers if they ventured out onto Ridge Road after dark, crept up on farmers who worked late in their fields and pounced on unsuspecting wayfarers as they walked through the forest. The creature became a local menace and scores of stories about the ghost and the various appearances that it took are still told today.

But how did the tales get started? And if the ghost really existed, what was it? The origins of the Ridgeway Phantom and the beginnings of the lead mines in the region occurred at about the same time. One of the seediest establishments to spring up along Ridge Road in the early 1840's was Sampson's Hotel & Saloon. Many a traveler checked into the hotel for a drink, meal and a room and never checked back out again. The Ridgeway Phantom may have been one of them. A version of the story has it that a peddler stopped at Sampson's after a long day's ride, unaware of the poor reputation of the place. He was seen entering his room but was never seen again after that. Early the next morning, his fully saddled horse tried to enter the hotel but the animal was chased off and never spotted again.

Soon after the peddler's disappearance, people began reporting the apparition of a giant black horse on the road near Sampson's. As it galloped along the roadway, they saw the torso of a headless man mounted backward on the saddle. The headless horseman often rode up on travelers and frightened them out of their wits and if anyone tried to speak to it, only unearthly groans were heard in reply. In the years that followed, the horseman assumed other forms as well and preyed on those who used the old Ridge Road.

Some accounts of the Ridgeway Phantom stem from another horrifying incident that occurred at McKillip's Saloon, an even more notorious roadhouse that was located about five miles west of Ridgeway. According to this version of the tale, two teenaged brothers, ages 14 and 15, walked into the saloon one winter day and promptly became the objects of ridicule for the drunken customers. The teasing turned to murder when one of the boys was grabbed and thrown into a blazing fireplace, where he promptly burned to death. The other boy managed to escape and was never seen again. However, the next spring, his body was found frozen to death in a nearby field.

After the deaths of the two boys, a small gray-haired lady began to be seen wandering along the road near McKillip's. She would vanish as soon as a stranger approached. Those who saw her speculated that she might be the mother or grandmother of the murdered boys, now searching for their bodies. Various descriptions of this woman can be found interwoven through the stories of the Ridgeway Phantom.

But whatever version of the ghost's origin that you care to consider, there can be little doubt that its presence made a startling impact on this region and there were many ghost stories that started because of it. It gained an infamous reputation over the years, haunting the forests along the road and even some of the buildings as well.

The long vanished Messerschmidt Hotel in Ridgeway was long believed to be haunted by the ghost. The hotel's owner, George Messerschmidt, came to the region in 1855 and became a member of the county board. The railroad was to be built from Warren, Illinois to Mineral Point and board members had decided to raise the necessary capital by issuing county bonds. Soon after Messerschmidt decided to sign the bonds, strange creaking and groaning sounds began to be heard in the hotel, making it impossible for him, and his guests, to get any sleep. Night after night, the sounds became worse, driving away his business, and wreaking havoc on his nerves. One night an eerie voice was even heard, imploring him not to sign the county bonds. He did so regardless and when the railroads came, the old Ridge Road faded into obscurity - taking the Messerschmidt Hotel with it.

A house in Ridgeway was once also reported to be the haunt of the Phantom. An old man named Peavey was the original occupant of the house and after he moved away, it burned down. Another house was built on the foundation but the new owners left after just a few days. According to their account, they left because of a large black dog that started appearing in the house each night. The dog, tired and panting, was mysteriously found under their dining room table every evening after dark. It disappeared as suddenly as it appeared.

The house was eventually moved from the original stone foundation constructed by Peavey and the dog never appeared again. The canine apparition was replaced by unusual sounds that came from the attic. Later occupants spoke of noises in the attic that seemed to be those of children playing with marbles. They would roll back and forth for several minutes and then fade away. Try as they might, the family could never explain the strange noises.

The woods near Ridge Road were reportedly the place where a man named Evan "Strangler" Lewis met his mysterious demise. Strangely, there are two different versions of his death and a large, black dog plays a role in one of them. Lewis was a well-known wrestler of tremendous size and had a fearlessness that matched his physical strength. When he was not winning bets in the wrestling ring, he supported his family as a farmer and as a livestock butcher for other area farms. It was after a day of butchering at a neighboring farm that Lewis walked the Ridge Road for the last time. He had been warned not to walk through the woods at night but Lewis laughed at the reports of the ghost. He believed that his strength and speed, not to mention the large butcher's knives that he carried, were more than enough to protect him from any so-called Phantom.

One version of the story states that Lewis was walking across a field when a white horse pulling a driverless carriage charged at him from the trees. Lewis jumped out of the way and as he rolled across the ground, the horse and carriage vanished. He then ran all of the way home, utterly terrified by what had occurred.

The second story also sent Lewis through the pasture at the edge of the forest, although this time, he found himself confronted by a huge, black dog. The creature had blazing red eyes and while Lewis tried several times to chase it away, it continued to trail after him, keeping a short distance. The dog came so close to him on several occasions that Lewis could feel its hot breath on his hand. Finally, the dog came so close that he kicked at it and missed. The dog had moved so quickly that his foot passed through air where it had been only moments before. After that, Lewis began to run. He crashed through the brush and the trees with the dog close behind. He stumbled and thrashed until he saw the lights of his home in a clearing ahead. The black animal sprang at him and Lewis turned to ward off its fangs and claws, stabbing at it with one of his knives. He tried to keep running, swinging at the dog with the knife, but the blade hit nothing but air. At last, within steps of his house, the creature simply vanished.

In both versions of the story, Lewis was dripping with sweat, shaking and exhausted from his ordeal. His family sent for the doctor and upon examining the traumatized man, the physician stated that Lewis' heart had moved nearly two inches from its original location.

Lewis died two days later, on May 8, 1874, and no medical explanation was ever determined for what killed him. And no explanation, other than the Ridgeway Phantom, was ever suggested for what he saw in the woods that night.

Black dogs have not been the only creatures associated with the Phantom. Others have included pigs, sheep and of course, horses. In addition to the encounters already mentioned, there were many others who saw horses with hooves that flashed with sparks on the roadway or who were attacked by menacing black dogs. One night, a man named Jones was returning from the home of his future wife near Dodgeville and he heard the sound of sheep bleating on the trail behind him. He stopped his horse and a herd of sheep passed on either side of the startled rider. Two silent men followed the sheep and they neither spoke nor looked at Jones. A few moments later, they vanished into the darkness. The following morning, Jones told several friends of the incident and they returned to the spot and examined the dirt road. They could find no sign of the sheep or of the men who followed them.

On another occasion, a teamster on Ridge Road encountered a similar scene but this time, the herd of animals was made up of pigs instead. Two silent men followed the noisy swine and they too vanished into the forest.

The Ridgeway Phantom was also known for the human forms that it took, especially in the later years, after the railroad had caused the trail to be nearly abandoned. Travelers often reported the sounds of eerie, wailing screams coming from the woods along the road, as well as fleeting glimpses of a white shape, darting back and forth through the trees. There are no accounts of anyone who went out to investigate what was lurking in the forest.

A young man named Jim Moore was visiting his fiancée at her home near Blue Mounds one evening. She lived in a large, two-story house that was just off the roadway and in a clearing in the woods. The young woman had an apartment on the upper floor and an outside staircase to reach it. It was nearly dark when Moore climbed up the stairs to the apartment and he paused at the top of the steps to catch his breath before he knocked. As he did so, he glanced down into the yard and at the edge of the trees, saw an old man standing there. He had never seen the man on any of his previous visits and he thought there was a little something strange about him. Moore went inside and told his girl about the man he had seen in the yard and she grew quite concerned. As the night progressed, she urged him several times to spend the night rather than walk home through the forest after dark. Moore didn't think it was proper though and he declined.

Near midnight, he left and started walking home. Suddenly, from out of the shadows, the old man appeared and began walking alongside of Jim, matching his pace stride for stride. The man did not speak a word though. He simply stared straight ahead as he walked. As Moore neared his own home, he looked over and the old man was gone.

Jim broke into a run and made it safely into his house. As he leaned against the kitchen table, trying to catch his breath, he realized that the Ridgeway Phantom had escorted him home. After that, he never walked that way to his fiancée's house again.

One night in early autumn, a young man and his new bride accepted an invitation to a party a few miles away from their home in Wakefield. As they walked along on that warm, dark night, they had only a lantern to see by and it cast a small circle in the blackness of the woods. The night was quiet and no breeze stirred the air, so it became plainly evident when the sounds of someone walking in the freshly fallen leaves caught their attention.

Thinking that it was a neighbor, also on the way to the party, the couple called out a greeting but there was no reply. Abruptly, the night air turned cold and just past the lantern's light, the young man and his wife saw a pale human figure. The lantern's glow then flickered for a moment, almost going out, and then blazed to life again. When it did, they could see that the man who had been there just moments before was gone.

They were sure that they had met up with the Ridgeway Phantom on the road that night.

In days gone by, country doctors were often called upon at night to go to isolated farms and homes to deliver babies or to tend to the sick. Doc Cutler, who took care of the people of Ridgeway for many years, took his duties as the local physician quite seriously - but he also took the stories of the Phantom quite seriously too.

Doc Cutler always avoided the Ridge Road when traveling at night. On those rare occasions when he was forced to take it, he drove his buggy as quickly as he dared on the dark roads and almost without fail, he would encounter the Ridgeway Phantom during his nocturnal travels. The ghost would often spring from the brush or appear out of the trees and climb onto the doctor's horse or cling to the back of his buggy. Cutler would often try to whip the horse to a faster gait but this did not deter the ghost. The creature would perch itself on the animals back and stare at Cutler with hollow, vacant eyes.

After one late night call, Cutler later claimed that he overtook a man who was walking at the side of the road. He asked the stranger if he wanted a ride and the man climbed into the doctor's buggy and rode along until they reached Mineral Point. As they passed the first faint lights of town, the stranger mysteriously vanished. He was there one moment and then gone the next. Doc Cutler went to his grave believing that he had offered a ride to the Ridgeway Phantom. He was convinced that the specter's affinity for him had to do with his attraction to anyone who worked with blood.

Which would turn out to be an interesting twist to a later story about a strange figure that plagued Mineral Point.

The Ridgeway Phantom did not depart from this region in 1857 with the coming of the railroad, although reports of its appearances did decline. Over the decades that followed though, the stories of strange encounters on Ridge Road did become even more frightening, perhaps because with less traffic on the road, there were fewer people around to offer assistance. The accounts may have been fewer but they were just as strange. It seemed that the ghost continued to haunt the old road for many years to come.

Some say that its demise came in 1910, when the business district in Ridgeway burned to the ground. Those who believe the specter departed at that time say that it was consumed by flame and was never heard from again - but was it really?

Ghostly tales still thrive in southwestern Wisconsin and around the town of Mineral Point as well. The Ridgeway Phantom came in so many guises that it is nearly impossible to tell whether or not the strange encounters in more recent times were linked to the anomalous creature or not. The specter may have reared its head on many occasions, perhaps even in 1981, when another chilling phantom began to be seen in Mineral Point.

In the spring of that year, Mineral Point began to have a problem with what some dubbed a "vampire". Residents were constantly calling the police to report a man who they described as having a white face, being about six feet tall, clad in a black cape and jumping out at people from dark and shadowy places. Skeptical at first, officers were soon convinced that something weird was going on by the sheer number of calls they received.

One night, March 30, an officer named Jon Pepper was on duty when he saw a man "dressed like Dracula" lurking behind some tombstones in the city cemetery. Pepper approached the man and asked him what he was doing. The figure immediately stood up and Pepper guessed him to be at least six feet, five inches tall. Whoever the strange man was, he said nothing, but immediately turned and began to run. He quickly outdistanced the officer and when the figure jumped over a four foot barbed wire fence, Pepper called off the chase. The "vampire" vanished into the darkness. Soon after, the department stationed extra officers at the cemetery and while several more sightings took place, they were unable to capture him.

Eventually, the sightings came to an end and the story of the "Mineral Point Vampire" has largely been forgotten today. Who this mysterious figure may have been remains a mystery - but could it have been the Ridgeway Phantom, making one last appearance in Mineral Point?

ZOMBIE ROAD

The city of St. Louis is unlike many other major American cities. It is a large sprawling region of suburbs and interconnected towns that make up the metropolitan city as a whole, making it an impossible place to live if you do not own an automobile. With the Mississippi River as the eastern border of St. Louis, the settlers who came here originally had nowhere to go but to the west and the city expanded in that direction. After all of these years though, and despite the amount of construction and development that has occurred, once you leave the western suburbs of St. Louis, you enter a rugged, wild region that is marked with rivers, forests and caves. Traveling west on Interstate 44, and especially along the smaller highways, you soon leave the buildings and houses behind. It is here, you will discover, that mysteries lie...

One of the oddities in this region is a place that you will no longer find on any map -- the town of Times Beach. It vanished without a trace after a dioxin scare led to an evacuation in 1985. It made national headlines at the time and I can remember traveling past the town in the years that followed, seeing the roadblocks and the empty houses and buildings, surrounded by yellow caution tape. I even have a dim memory, which must have been in the middle 1980's, of driving past and seeing men in contamination suits wandering about the town.

Times Beach was started in 1925 along the Meramec River as a promotion for the now defunct *St. Louis Star-Times* newspaper. A purchase of a building lot in the new town, which cost $67.50, also included a six-month subscription to the newspaper. In the early years, the town was mostly a summer resort area with cottages and beach homes that were built on stilts because of frequent flooding. However, the Great Depression, followed by gas rationing during World War II, combined to make the cottages impractical and the town deteriorated into a low income community. It remained a slightly seedy place until its evacuation.

In the early 1970's, the unpaved roads in town created a dust problem for Times Beach and so the city hired a waste hauler to oil the roads with waste oil. They were later paved but by then, the damage had been done. The waste hauler had gotten the oil from a subcontractor who had operated a chemical plant in Verona, Missouri had produced Agent Orange for the Vietnam War. The waste from the plant contained levels of dioxin that were some 2,000 times higher than the poisonous content in the Agent Orange. And it had been generously sprayed all over Times Beach.

The waste hauler had previously used the same type of oil to control dust in horse stables and 62 of the animals died. The owners suspected that the contractor had done something wrong but he insisted that it had just been used engine oil. The owners followed his other contracts and after more horses died, the Center for Disease Control began investigating. The Environmental Protection Agency first visited Times Beach in the summer of 1982 and by November, stories began to appear in the press about high levels of dioxin being discovered in the soil. Needless to say, panic spread through the town and every illness, every miscarriage, and every death of an animal was attributed, rightly or wrongly, to the dioxin. By 1985, Times Beach was evacuated, except for one elderly couple who refused to leave, and the site was quarantined. Legal wrangling over the case, and further investigations that seemed to show that the evacuation was unnecessary, went on for years.

The empty town, left untouched since the day the population walked away, remained hauntingly alongside the interstate until 1992, when it was finally demolished. All traces of Times Beach, aside from the memories, have since been obliterated. Today, all that remains here is acres of woods, a wild bird sanctuary and a state park that commemorates Route 66, the famous highway that stretched from Chicago, Illinois to Los Angeles, California and passed by the community.

The story of Times Beach is a strange little tale from an unusual part of Missouri but there is nothing supernatural about it. The same cannot be said for another area that is located nearby. If the stories that are told about this forgotten stretch of roadway are even partially true, then a place called "Zombie Road" just may be one of the weirdest spots in the region.

The old roadway that has been dubbed "Zombie Road" (a name by which it was known at least as far back as the 1950's) was once listed on maps as Lawler Ford Road and was constructed at some point in the late 1860's. The road, which was once merely gravel and dirt, was paved at some point years ago but it is now largely impassable by automobile. It was originally built to provide access to the Meramec and the railroad tracks located along the river.

In 1868, the Glencoe Marble Company was formed to work the limestone deposits in what is now the Rockwoods Reservation, located nearby. A sidetrack was laid from the deposits to the town of Glencoe and on to the road, crossing the property of James E. Yeatman. The side track from the Pacific Railroad switched off the main line at Yeatman Junction and at this same location, the Lawler Ford Road ended at the river. There is no record as to where the Lawler name came from but a ford did cross the river at this point into the land belonging to the Lewis family. At times, a boat was used to ferry people across the river here, which is undoubtedly why the road was placed at this location.

As time passed, the narrow road began to be used by trucks that hauled quarry stone from railcars and then later fell into disuse. Those who recall the road when it was more widely in use have told me that the narrow, winding lane, which runs through roughly two miles of dense woods, was always enveloped in a strange silence and a half-light. Shadows were always long here, even on the brightest day, and it was always impossible to see past the trees and brush to what was coming around the next curve. I was told that if you were driving and met another car, one of you would have to back up to one of the few wide places, or even the beginning of the road, in order for the other one to pass.

Strangely, even those that I talked to with no interest in ghosts or the unusual all mentioned that Zombie Road was a spooky place. I was told that one of the strangest things about it was that it never looked the same or seemed the same length twice, even on the return trip from the dead end point where the stone company's property started. "At times", one person told me, "we had the claustrophobic feeling that it would never end and that we would drive on forever into deeper darkness and silence."

Thanks to its secluded location, and the fact that it fell into disrepair and was abandoned, the Lawler Ford Road gained a reputation in the 1950's as a local hangout for area teenagers to have parties, drink beer and as a lover's lane as well. Located in Wildwood, which was formerly Ellisville, and Glencoe, the road can be reached by taking Manchester Road out west of the city to Old State Road South. By turning down Ridge Road to the Ridge Meadows Elementary School, curiosity seekers could find the road just to the left of the school. For years, it was marked with a sign but it has since disappeared. Only a chained gate marks the entrance today.

The road saw quite a lot of traffic in the early years of its popularity and occasionally still sees a traveler or two today. Most who come here now though are not looking for a party. Instead, they come looking for the unexplained. As so many locations of this type do, Lawler Ford Road also gained a reputation for being haunted. Numerous legends and stories sprang up about the place, from the typical tales of murdered boyfriends and killers with hooks for hands to more specific tales of a local killer who was dubbed the "Zombie". He was said to live in an old dilapidated shack by the river and would attack young lovers who came here looking for someplace quiet and out of the way. As time passed, the stories of this madman were told and re-told and eventually, the name of Lawler Ford Road was largely forgotten and it was replaced with "Zombie Road", by which it is still known today.

A look down Zombie Road
(Courtesy Joe Immethun)

There are many other stories as well, from ghostly apparitions in the woods to visitors who have vanished without a trace. There are also stories about a man who was killed here by a train in the 1970's and who now haunts the road and that of a mysterious old woman who yells at passersby from a house at the end of the road. There is another about a boy who fell from the bluffs along the river and died but his body was never found. His ghost is also believed to haunt the area. There are also enough tales of Native American spirits and modern-day devil worshippers here to fill another book entirely.

But is there any truth to these tales and any history that might explain how the ghost stories got started? Believe it or not, there may just be a kernel of truth to the legends of Zombie Road - and real-life paranormal experiences taking place as well.

The region around Zombie Road was once known as Glencoe. Today, it is a small village on the banks of the Meramec River and most of its residents live in houses that were once summer resort cottages, much like those that once stood at nearby Times Beach. Most of the other houses are from the era when Glencoe was a bustling railroad and quarrying community. Days of prosperity have long since passed it by though and years ago, the village was absorbed by the larger town of Wildwood.

There is no record of the first inhabitants here but they were likely the Native Americans who built the mounds that existed for centuries at the site of present-day St. Louis. The mound city that once existed here was one of the largest in North America and at its peak boasted more than 40,000 occupants. It is believed that the Meramec River and its surrounding forests was an area heavily relied upon for food and mounds have been found at Fenton and petroglyphs have been discovered along the Meramec and Big Rivers. It is also believed that the area around Glencoe, because of the game and fresh water, was a stopping point for the Indians as they made their way to the flint quarries in Jefferson Counties.

After the Mound Builders vanished from the area, the Osage, Missouri and Shawnee Indians came to the region and also used the flint quarries and hunted and fished along the Meramec River. The Shawnee had been invited into what was then the Louisiana region by the Spanish governor. Many of them settled west of St. Louis and were, for a time, major suppliers of game to the settlement. A family that lived at what later became Times Beach reported frequent visits from the Shawnee but the majority of the tribe moved further west around 1812.

Many other tribes passed through the region as they were moved out of their original lands in the east but no records exist of any of them ever staying near Glencoe. The reason for this is because the area was a pivotal point for travelers, Indian and settlers alike. The history of the region may explain why sightings and encounters of Native American ghosts have taken place along Lawler Ford Road. As we know that a ford once existed here (a shallow point in the river that was more easily navigated), it's likely that the road leading down to the river was once an Indian trail. The early settlers had a tendency to turn the already existing trails into roads and this may have been the case with the Lawler Ford Road. If the Native Americans left an impression behind here, in their travels, hunts or quests for flint, it could be the reason why Indian spirits are still encountered here today.

The first white settler in the area was Ninian Hamilton from Kentucky. He arrived near Glencoe around 1800 and obtained a settler's land grant. He built a house and trading post and became one of the wealthiest and most influential men of the period. It was mentioned that the area around Glencoe was a pivotal point in western movement. In those days, the Meramec River bottoms were heavily forested and made up of steep hills and sharp bluffs. The river flooded frequently and the fords that existed were only usable during times of low water. There were no bridges or ferries that crossed the river, except for one that was operated far to the southeast. The trappers and traders that traveled west of St. Louis, like the Indians before them, came on horseback along the ridge route that later became Manchester Road. It skirted the Meramec and was high enough so that it was not subject to flooding. Because of this, it passed directly by Hamilton's homestead and the trading post that he established here. With the well-used trail just outside of his backdoor, as well as nearby fish, game and spring water, Hamilton's post prospered.

Hamilton later built some grist mills near his trading post, which was a badly needed resource for settlers in those days. There are also legends that say that annual gatherings of fur trappers and Indian traders occurred at Hamilton's place. These rendezvous have been the subject of great debate over the years but no one knows for sure if they occurred. It is known that his post was the last one leaving St.

Louis and the first the trappers would see when returning, so it's likely they did take place.

One of the mills that Hamilton started was later replaced by a water mill for tanning by Henry McCullough, who had a tannery and shoemaking business that not only supplied the surrounding area, but also allowed him to ship large quantities of leather to his brother in the south. McCullough was also a Kentuckian and purchased his land from Hamilton. He later served as the Justice of the Peace for about 30 years and as a judge for the County Court from 1849 to 1852. He was married three times before he died in 1853 and one of his wives was a sister of Ninian Hamilton. The wife, Della Hamilton McCullough, was killed in 1876 after being struck down by a railroad car on the spur line from the Rockwoods Reservation.

It has been suggested that perhaps the death of Della Hamilton McCullough was responsible for the legend that has grown up around Zombie Road about the ghost of the person who was run over by a train. The story of the this phantom has been told for at least three decades now but there is no record of anyone being killed in modern times. In fact, the only railroad death around Glencoe is that of Henry McCullough's unfortunate wife. Could it be her ghost that has been linked to Zombie Road?

The railroads would be another vital connection to Glencoe and to the stories of Lawler Ford Road. The first lines reached the area in 1853 when a group of passengers on flat cars arrived behind the steam locomotive called the "St. Louis". A rail line had been constructed along the Meramec River, using two tunnels, and connected St. Louis to Franklin, which was later re-named Pacific, Missouri. The tiny station house at Franklin was little more than a building in the wilderness at that time but bands played and people cheered as the train pulled into the station.

Around this same time, tracks had been extended along the river, passing through what would be Glencoe. The site was likely given its name by Scottish railroad engineer James P. Kirkwood, who laid out the route. The name has its origins in Old English as "glen" meaning "a narrow valley" and "coe" meaning "grass.

Only a few remnants of the original railroad can be found today. The old lines can still be seen at the end of Zombie Road and it is along these tracks where the railroad ghost is believed to walk. There have been numerous accounts over the years of a translucent figure in white that walks up the abandoned line and then disappears. Those who claim to have seen it say that the phantom glows with bluish-white light but always disappears if anyone tries to approach it. As mentioned, the identity of this ghost remains a mystery but despite the stories of a mysterious death in the 1970's, the presence is more likely the lingering spirit of Della McCullough.

One of the passengers who made the first trip west on the rail line from St. Louis was probably James E. Yeatman. He was one of the leading citizens of St. Louis and was the founder of the Mercantile Library, president of Merchants Bank and an early proponent of extending the railroads west of the Mississippi. He was active in both business and charitable affairs in St. Louis. He was a major force behind the Western Sanitary Commission during the Civil War. This large volunteer group provided hospital boats, medical services and looked to other needs of the wounded on both sides of the conflict. The world's first hospital railroad car is attributed to this group.

After the death of Ninian Hamilton in 1856, his heirs sold his land to A.S. Mitchell, who in turn sold out to James Yeatman. He built a large frame home on the property and dubbed it "Glencoe Park". The mansion burned to the ground in 1920, while owned by Alfred Carr and Angelica Yeatman Carr, the daughter of James Yeatman. They moved into the stone guest house on the property, which also burned in 1954. It was later rebuilt and then restored and still remains in the Carr family today.

The village of Glencoe was laid out in 1854 by Woods, Christy & Co. and in 1883, it contained "a few houses and a small store, but for about a year has had no post office." At the time the town was created, Woods, Christy & Co. also erected a grist and saw mill at Glencoe that operated until about 1868. Woods, Christy & Co. had been a large dry goods company in St. Louis. There is a family tradition in the Christy family that land was traded for goods and materials by early settlers. This firm ceased operation as a dry goods company about 1856. While it is possible that some lands near Glencoe were the result of trading for supplies, the firm actually started a large lumbering operation around the village.

One of the many prominent St. Louis citizens who traveled through Glencoe during the middle and late 1800's was Winston Churchill, the American author who wrote a number of bestselling romantic novels in the early 1900's. One of his most popular, *The Crisis*, was partially set in St. Louis and partially at Glencoe. The novel, which Churchill acknowledged was based on the activities of James E. Yeatman, depicts the struggles and conflicts in St. Louis during the critical years of the Civil War. It is believed that Angelica Yeatman Carr was his model for the heroine, Miss Virginia Carvel. The first edition of the book was released in 1901 and was followed by subsequent editions. It can still be found on dusty shelves in used and antiquarian bookstores today.

In 1868, the Glencoe Marble Company was formed and the previously mentioned side track was added to the railroad to run alongside the river. The tracks ran past where the Lawler Ford Road ended and it's likely that wagons were used to haul quarry stone up the road. Before this, the road was likely nothing more than an Indian trail, although it did see other traffic in the 1860's - and perhaps even death.

During the Civil War, the city of St. Louis found itself in the predicament of being loyal to the Union in a state that was predominately dedicated to the

Confederate cause. For this reason, men who were part of what was called the Home Guard were picketed along the roads and trails leading into the city with instructions to turn back Southern sympathizers by any means necessary. As a result, Confederate spies, saboteurs and agents often had to find less trafficked paths to get in and out of the St. Louis area. One of the lesser known trails was leading to and away from the ford across the Meramec River near Glencoe. This trail would later be known as Lawler Ford Road.

As this information reached the leaders of the militia forces, troops from the Home Guard began to be stationed at the ford. The trail here led across the river and to the small town of Crescent, which was later dubbed "Rebel Bend" because of the number of Confederates who passed through it and who found sanctuary here.

After the militia forces set up lines here, the river became very dangerous to cross. However, since there were so few fords across the Meramec, many attempted to cross here anyway, often with dire results. According to the stories, a number of men died here in short battles with the Home Guard. Could this violence explain some of the hauntings that now occur along Zombie Road?

Many of the people that I have talked with about the strange happenings here speak of unsettling feelings and the sensation of being watched. While we could certainly dismiss this as nothing more than a case of the "creeps", that overwhelming near panic that I described in an earlier chapter, it becomes harder to dismiss when combined with the eerie sounds, inexplicable noises and even the disembodied footsteps that no one seems able to trace to their source. Many have spoken of being "followed" as they walk along the trail, as though someone is keeping pace with them just in the edge of the woods. Strangely though, no one is ever seen. In addition, it is not uncommon for visitors to also report the shapes and shadows of presences in the woods too. On many occasions, these shapes have been mistaken for actual people - until the hiker goes to confront them and finds that there is no one there. It's possible that the violence and bloodshed that occurred here during the Civil War has left its mark behind on this site, as it has on so many other locations across the country.

Visitors to Lawler Ford Road today will often end their journey at the Meramec River and the area here has also played a part in the legends and tales of Zombie Road. It was here at Yeatman Junction that one of the first large scale gravel operations on the Meramec River began. Gravel was taken from the banks of the Meramec and moved on rail cars into St. Louis. The first record of this operation is in the mid-1850's. Later, steam dredges were used, to be supplanted by diesel or gasoline dredges in extracting gravel from the channel and from artificial lakes dug into the south bank. This continued, apparently without interruption, until the 1970's.

The gravel quarries were used the until the demise of the gravel operation in the 1970's. The last railroad tracks were removed from around Glencoe when the spur line to the gravel pit was taken out. Some have cited the railroads as the source for some of the hauntings along Zombie Road. In addition to the wandering spirit that is believed to be Della McCullough, it is possible that some of the other restless ghosts may be those of accident victims along the rail lines. Sharp bends in the tracks at Glencoe were the site of frequent derailments and were later recalled by local residents. The Carr family had a number of photographs in their collection of these deadly accidents. It finally got so bad that service was discontinued on around the bend in the river. It has been speculated that perhaps the victims of the train accidents may still be lingering here and might explain how the area got such a reputation for tragedy and ghostly haunts.

Many visitors also claim to have had strange experiences near the old shacks and ramshackle homes located along the beach area at the end of the trail. One of the long-standing legends of the place mentions the ghost of an old woman who screams at people from the doorways of one of the old houses. However, upon investigation, the old woman is never there. The houses here date back to about 1900, when the area around Glencoe served as a resort community. The Meramec River's "clubhouse era" lasted until about 1945. Many of the cottages were then converted to year-round residences but others were simply left to decay and deteriorate in the woods. This is the origin of the old houses that are located off Zombie Road but it does not explain the ghostly old woman and the other apparitions that have been encountered here. Could they be former residents of days gone by? Perhaps this haunting on the old roadway has nothing to do with the violence and death of the past but rather with the happiness of it instead. Perhaps some of these former residents returned to their cottages after death because the resort homes were places where they knew peace and contentment in life.

When I first began researching the history and hauntings of Lawler Ford Road, I have to confess that I started with the idea that "Zombie Road" was little more than an urban legend, created from the vivid imaginations of several generations of teenagers. I never expected to discover the dark history of violence and death in the region or anything that might substantiate the tales of ghosts and supernatural occurrences along this wooded road. It was easy to find people who "believed" in the legends of Zombie Road but I never expected to be one of those who came to be convinced.

When looking for relevance in ghost stories around the St. Louis area, I usually turn to my friends Joe Immethun and his sister, Cathe Immethun-Voege, from the Ghost Hunters of St. Louis Society . Readers may remember that we explored the caves beneath the infamous Lemp Mansion together in the last book in this series, Down in the Darkness. I contacted Joe about Zombie Road and he quickly had his own story to share.

One evening, he and another investigator had gone out to Zombie Road to look around, take some photographs and hopefully, experience something ghostly. They started down the road just as darkness was starting to fall and instead of taking flashlights with them, they planned to make it down the road and back before it got too dark. Unfortunately, they estimated wrong and didn't realize how dark it would quickly become with the trees that loomed over the trail cutting off the last minutes of the day's light. By the time they made it to the end of the trail, the sun was completely gone and they were left to stumble their way back to their car in the darkness.

"We continued walking and got to the halfway point and decided to rest for just a few minutes," Joe told me. "All of a sudden an extremely loud crashing sound came from the large hill near to where we were sitting. It sounded almost like a train or a house was falling down the hill right at us. I never ran so fast in my life. As I ran I could hear the tree branches snapping and cracking under the weight of whatever it was that was coming down that hill. I did not stick around to find out what it was, but at that moment I didn't even care!"

Joe and his companion ran all of the way down the rutted roadway to their car, where they nearly collapsed, trying to catch their breath. After a few minutes, their heart rates slowed down and they decided to get some flashlights out of the trunk and go back down the road to see if they could discover what they had heard out there.

"We walked very quietly and cautiously to the point where we first heard the noise," Joe recalled. " We kept hearing voices of children playing. We thought it was coming from a nearby house but the voices kept following, never getting louder or softer. As we neared the location where we had heard the sounds we noticed a large tree lying across the road. I first thought that the tree had simply broken and fallen over and that is what we had heard, but it was not. From the top of the hill to the bottom every tree was broken, but not just broken, uprooted. I thought a car had driven off of the road above, or a very large object was pushed down the hill, but there was nothing there. We once again heard voices and ran. I don't ever remember getting a better workout than that night."

Joe could never really explain what happened that night but it left him with the nagging feeling that something is not quite right about Zombie Road. "On some nights the road is very peaceful and on others you feel like you should not be there and there is something terribly wrong," he explained. "It could be the road has so much energy because of the people who visit it. If everyone tells you a place is haunted, your mind will play tricks on you and you will believe it is haunted. However, this would not explain what we experienced that night, the voices that have been caught on tape, or the things that have been seen on the road. If the road is not haunted in a traditional sense, by spirits of the dead, I do think that it is haunted by the memories of things that happened here."

CLINTON ROAD

For anyone with an interest in the strangeness of the state of New Jersey, the starting point of their journey will always be Clinton Road. The area around this twisting, narrow roadway, which passes through a remote, wooded region near West Milford, has gained an almost legendary reputation in recent years. Although it has been regarded as an eerie place since at least the 1970's, the revival in interest is mostly thanks to Mark Moran and Mark Sceurman, the publishers of the wildly popular and entertaining WEIRD NJ magazine.

However, Mark and Mark will both tell you that they have never written a word about Clinton Road and have done nothing to create the surge in fascination with it. In the tenth issue of their magazine, they printed a few brief stories about the place that had been submitted by their readers. As soon as the stories appeared, the flood gates opened and they began to receive more than 25 years worth of strange experiences from Clinton Road and the surrounding region.

What it is about this place that strikes such a nerve with residents of North Jersey? As mentioned, Clinton Road is a long, lonely stretch of badly paved highway that passes through a desolate region of shadowy forest - but so do many other roads in New Jersey and they do not have the chilling reputation that this place does. The stories of Clinton Road contain everything from the usual urban legends to ghosts, strange creatures, mysterious lights, a haunted castle and more. Is there any truth behind the stories or are they merely the breathless tales of teenagers out looking for a good scare?

Strangely, the region around Clinton Road had a reputation for strangeness long before the highway ever existed. Earlier in the chapter, we explored the idea that perhaps historical events really can cause an area to become haunted. The questionable legends sometimes have a basis in fact that leads to stories being told and then re-told until they are hardly recognizable anymore. If we clear away some of the proverbial dust that has settled onto them however, we sometimes find that the chilling stories actually got started for a reason. As has been stated before - if even a fraction of the weird tales here are true, then Clinton Road is the most terrifying place in New Jersey.

The first hints of strangeness connected to the area around Clinton Road came in the writings of New Jersey historian J. Percy Crayon. In 1905, he wrote about this area, calling to the "Five Mile Woods". According to Crayon, "it was never advisable to pass through Five Miles Woods after dark, for... tradition tells us they were infested with bands of robbers, and counterfeiters, to say nothing of the witches that held their nightly dances and carousels at Green Island, and the ghosts that then made their appearance in such frightful forms, that it was more terrifying to the peaceful inhabitants than wild animals or even the Indians, that often passed."

When an adventurer travels through this area, one unusual site is always the stone monument that some have mistakenly referred to as a sort of ancient pyramid. In truth, this is one of the most historic sites in the region, the Clinton Furnace, and it stands near tumbling Clinton Falls. The stone tower was never used for "human sacrifices" but actually for iron-ore smelting. It was once part of the Clinton Iron Works, which was started by William Jackson in 1826. At this time, the falls were dammed and a furnace and village were built up around them. Jackson sold out an interest that he had in a rolling mill in Rockaway and moved to what was then a wild forest region to erect the furnace and a saw mill. The iron and the wood were to be carted to Dover and Rockaway for sale.

Before the furnace ever began operations, Jackson made roads and built houses and out-buildings for his men. The homes soon turned into an entire village that consisted off a forge and shop, saw and grist mills, a blacksmith shop, an anchor shop, a school that shared quarters with a wheelwright shop and church and a number of homes. Nothing remains of this vanished village today.

The Iron Works started production in 1833, under the supervision of John F. Winslow, Jackson's son-in-law. Unfortunately, the company only lasted until 1836, due to the depletion of charcoal in the surrounding area. To make matters worse, prior to the furnace ever starting up, iron ore fell one-half or more in price because of tariff legislations. Jackson had little choice but to shut the works down. The furnace was abandoned a year later but the village managed to hang on until the early 1850's. In 1900, the deserted property was purchased by the city of Newark, who added the land to the Pequannock Watershed.

Just a short distance from the furnace and village site is Clinton Falls, a roaring cascade of water that is both beautiful to look at and - if you believe the stories - a little unsettling too. The falls were first dammed by William Jackson and his men when they started the construction of the iron works. Today, the falls are spanned by a concrete bridge that carries Clinton Road. The falls have also had a wicked reputation that dates back to long before the legends of the region began. Historian J. Percy Crayon wrote of them in 1873. He stated that this was a retreat for robbers and thieves in the early days of the area and that they often hid in "some wild gorges, where rocks overhung each other as to make a safe retreat as well as a comfortable home and a desirable shelter from the store where these land pirates would divide their plunder. Clinton was thought to be a robber's paradise and the constant roar of the falls would deaden the sound of any reveille." In other words, even in those days, it was not a place that many wanted to venture after dark.

In more modern times, the bridge over Clinton Falls has garnered an altogether different reputation. It is believed to be haunted by a ghostly boy who lurks around the bridge and returns coins to those who toss them into the water. No one seems to know how this story got started but according to the tale, the ghost is that of a small boy who was hit by a car when he wandered out into the road to pick up a quarter that he saw on the pavement.

Tradition has it that if you stop your car on the bridge (some say at midnight) and toss a coin over the side, the coin will be found lying on the road the next morning. In some cases, the story is more detailed and claims have been made that when the coin is tossed into the water, a child's reflection can sometimes be seen on the surface. Each time though, no matter what version of the story you hear, the same coin returns, either on the road or often someplace where you least expect it, like in your pocket or in your car. There are also those who claim to have come around the curve in the road where the bridge is located and have seen the figure of the boy illuminated in their headlights. This is normally terrifying enough to keep any of the occupants of the automobile from getting out to toss coins into the water.

There was no more famous, or more legendary, location on Clinton Road than what was once called the Clinton or Cross Castle. Leading away from the old furnace and Clinton Falls is a path that leads past some old foundation walls and to a stone staircase. Beyond the walls is a large, mostly overgrown area that is empty save for some crumbling ruins of stone and brick. The old foundations here are now all that remain of what was once a stunning and magnificent edifice.

Cross Castle, which was actually named "Bearfort", was built in the early 1900's by Richard J. Cross. According to his son, Cross developed heart problems in 1905 and his doctor recommended that he move to a higher altitude. With this in mind, he sought out property in the northern part of New Jersey and ended up buying a section of heavily forested land. He began construction on what would be a castle-like mansion in 1907.

The mansion, or castle as it came to be called, rose to a towering three stories and had a wide concrete porch that wrapped around the front of the structure and part of the way around each side. The house contained 40 rooms, including 13 family bedrooms and seven bathrooms. The spacious living room boasted a great stone fireplace and there was a vast library, a children's playroom and a billiard room that had to have its own concrete floor to support the weight of the heavy table of the day. In addition to the house, the estate boasted 365 acres of forest, fields and farmland and Hanks Pond, a 77-acre lake. Other buildings on the property included a boathouse, carriage house, ice house, tennis courts, guest cottages, a baker's shop and several barns. It also had its own gas plant for lighting and a huge stone tank that piped water into the house and out buildings. The stone tank is one of the only structures on the property that is still intact today.

The heyday of Beaufort lasted for a tragically short period of time. Richard Cross died in 1917 and the family sold the property to the city of Newark in 1919. It was stripped of anything that could be sold and rumors have it that Newark politicians used the mansion for wild parties in the 1920's. A fire eventually destroyed most of the remaining wooden structure, leaving only the stone walls to intrigue visitors for many years to come. However, those walls, which had been sprayed with paint and picked apart by souvenir hunters, were finally demolished in 1988. The structure had been deemed unsound and fear of lawsuits finally prompted the Newark Watershed Commission to have it destroyed. The wonderful castle did not go quietly though and many mourned the destruction of a piece of the region's colorful history. But time, and vandals, had taken too much of a toll and by the time it was torn down, there was nothing left to save.

Cross Castle has been gone for many years now and yet the memories of it remain. Stories, legends and rumors persist about the evil nature of the structure and there are scores of claims about the place being haunted and used for all sorts of nefarious rituals and deeds. Many of these rumors point back to the days when it was occupied by the Cross family and blame them for the place being haunted and "tainted" with a dark atmosphere. Stories abound that the castle even contained a dungeon and when it was destroyed, the bodies that had been left there were discovered. There is no evidence of this though and in fact, the Cross family was well-respected in their day. Despite the stories, there is nothing at all to say that they were engaged in any sort of black magic ceremonies or human sacrifice.

Such tales are better left to the modern day as rumors ran rampant in the middle 1980's about would-be Satanists using the ruins of the castle for their rituals. Stories of bonfires and figures in robes began to figure into the lore of the old mansion and many claimed to have encounters that were far too close for comfort with the cultists. Discoveries of Satanic writings, the remains of fires, melted candles and animal corpses seemed to give justification to the fears of those who visited the castle ruins and quickly left. The tales even linger today and many who have visited the castle site in recent times have stumbled across "spirit circles" of stone and have found the remnants of ritual sites. Whether they have been left behind by misguided teenagers who want to pretend to be Satanists, or a local grotto of the real thing, has not been determined.

There are many other stories told of Clinton Road that continue the legends of ghosts, hauntings and strange happenings. There are reports of Bigfoot-type creatures in the woods; glowing lights that have been seen just off Clinton Road at Upper Greenwood Lake; white, streaking lights that have raced past cars on the highway; terrifying and inexplicable noises in the forest; people who have vanished without a trace; and perhaps most disconcerting, reports of being chased by a black truck that tries to force them off the road at night. Newspaper accounts carry stories of car chases that have occurred on this road that have resulted in death.

But aside from all of the rumors and legends, and leaving out the fearful reputation that plagued the region in the 1800's, could the stories that are told here have a logical explanation? Or perhaps, more likely, could they have gotten started because of events that really did occur here and were violent or deadly enough to cause people to "create" new stories to go along with them?

Ghosts or no ghosts - Clinton Road has more than its share of death. There have been many people killed on this roadway over the years because it is a dangerous road. It twists, turns, winds back and forth and is filled with potholes and sections of broken pavement. If you drive too fast, you are likely to end up on the other side of "Dead Man's Curve" , which was given that name for a reason.

During the summer months, people often go swimming in Terrance Pond, which is right off Clinton Road. An unusually

The ruins of Bearfort -- the legendary Cross Castle -- that was located along Clinton Road for many years. Only memories of this unique structure remain today.

high number of people have drowned here, further adding to the legends - and the death toll.

Serial rapist Donald Chapman raped a woman who was riding her bicycle down Clinton Road and left her for dead. He was later sent to prison, where he underwent 12 years of therapy that left him completely unrepentant. He was released in 1993, vowing to attack more women and believing that he was a failure for allowing his victims to live.

And this is not the only crime that has been connected to this area. Some believe that Clinton Road is not haunted at all but is a place where members of the New York mafia dumped bodies in order to keep from being prosecuted by the state of New York. It has been said that many of the ghost stories and reports of strange happenings here have been invented by wiseguys who are trying to keep people out of their business and away from the area. While this seems a bit on the imaginative side for the Mafia, it was said that before his arrest in 1983, Jersey mob hitman Richard "Iceman" Kuklinski claimed to have killed over 200 people and buried at least one of the victims on Clinton Road.

What all of this boils down to is that the reader is asked to decide for himself as to the legends of Clinton Road. Is it all just hype and urban legend or does something linger here along this eerie roadway through the woods of North Jersey? If you really want to know, I suggest that you visit the place for yourself. I have a feeling that it is one sidetrip that you will not soon forget.

GHOST WATERS

Ghosts and eerie places that are connected to water sources, like rivers, lakes, ponds and waterfalls, are unique in the haunted landscape of America. No one seems to know what attracts hauntings and unusual activity to water but theories seem to be endless. Those of a scientific mind believe that perhaps it is because water tends to generate and conduct energy in a way that could help ghosts to manifest. Others look for a more traditional approach and remember stories of ghosts that cannot cross running water, like the "Headless Horseman" of the classic tale. No matter how you might look at it, water has always played an important part in the history of ghostlore.

The rivers, lakes and waters of the American wild are no different from the more famous haunted places like the Mississippi River or the Great Lakes in that they too have gained their own spirits and legends over the years. To try and compile a complete archive of American haunts that are connected to water - from the ghost ships of the rivers to the myriad of haunted lighthouses on the lakes and sea coasts - would require an entire book that would be separate and complete from this one. What I have tried to do instead is to gather a sampling of some of the strangest tales and locations from the more rugged and remote corners of our wild regions.

For instance, a small tributary called Crooked Creek, which is located not far from Harrison, Arkansas is said to be haunted by the ghost of a woman named Ella Barnham who was murdered here in 1912. The killer chopped her body up into seven pieces and dropped them into the entrance of an old mine shaft. A man named Odus Davidson was later hanged for the crime but many locals insisted that he was innocent. Likely for this reason, her ghost still continues to walk here.

Clear Lake, in northern California, has been plagued for decades by reports of a weeping woman in white. The specter appears on Bloody Island and is believed to be the last survivor of an Indian massacre that took place in 1850. Modoc Indians stopped a wagon train near the shoreline and killed all of those present, save for the young girl, who escaped into the woods wearing only her nightgown. When she came back the next night to try and bury her family, the Indians captured and killed her too.

Eventually, the Indians were driven out of the region but at least one of their victims remained behind after death. Those who lived near Clear Lake began to tell stories of a "woman in white" who haunted the lakeshore, wailing and crying in a heartbreaking voice. The stories - and the encounters with her -- were so intense that they managed to drive many of the settlers out of the area.

The ghost of a woman in a black, Spanish lace dress has been known to haunt the beaches of Black Lake, located in the dunes of Sun Luis Obispo County in California. According to the legends, this woman has no face and only a dim white light shines from where her face should be. She has been dubbed "Agnes" by locals who live in the area and her apparition normally appears late in the evening, usually after midnight. Who the woman might be, no one knows, and her presence here remains a mystery.

White Woman Creek runs through the western Kansas counties of Greeley, Wichita and Scott and is believe to be haunted by a mourning figure whose world ended tragically here many years ago. In the late 1800's, a Cheyenne hunting party was attacked along the Creek by white settlers and so in return, the survivors attacked the white settlement and took away captives. The prisoners lived with the Cheyenne for one year and then were offered their freedom when the Indians decided to move further west. Some of the prisoners decided to stay with the tribe, including a young woman who married a Cheyenne chief.

Tragically, the chief was later killed by cavalry soldiers and his body was buried along the banks of the creek. When the Cheyenne left the area, the young woman refused to leave the grave of her husband and she wandered the creek until her death. The stories say that she still continues to walk here as a ghost, singing Indian death songs and many claim to have heard her weeping on the wind.

Many years ago, the small town of Bellbrook, Ohio acquired quite a reputation for stories of ghosts and haunts. In fact, it was allegedly nicknamed "Ohio's Sleepy Hollow" by local residents. Outside of town, along Little Sugar Creek Road and near Magee Park is a small river called Little Sugar Creek. It is said to be haunted by two different ghosts, with two different stories to tell.

The first ghost is that of an Englishman named James Buckley, who built a sawmill on the river, which was then known as Possum Run Creek. Buckley managed to become quite wealthy and was envied by many who lived in the area. One morning, his cabin was raided and his money disappeared. Buckley was killed in the attack and his body was dragged outside. His head was violently severed from his body and tossed a few feet away. It was here that investigators later found it, bloody and covered with mud. The murderer was never discovered and Buckley's death remains unsolved to this day. As time passed, many started to claim that his cabin was haunted and it was avoided by the people in the area. Years passed before it was finally rented to a couple from nearby Dayton. However, they quickly left when the young woman saw Buckley's ghost, with his head under his arm, standing in the doorway to the house.

It is believed that his ghost still haunts the area of the creek where the sawmill was located and many claim to have seen the ghost, holding out his arms as if asking for help.

The other ghost haunts the area of Little Sugar Creek where Magee Park is located today. She is the spirit of a young girl who died there many years ago in a tragic suicide.

In the 1880's, the influential mayor of Bellbrook seduced a young servant girl who worked for him and began an affair with her. When she found herself pregnant, he ordered her from his house and, broken-hearted, she was forced to get by as a prostitute to support herself. The girl was the main source of gossip for people in the town. They knew that she had gotten herself into trouble, but they didn't know who the father of her child was.

The baby was born early and the girl refused to tell anyone who the father was. She only left the house after dark, the baby's face covered, because it was said to resemble the father so much that she didn't dare allow it to be seen. Many believed that the girl had lost her mind as they began to see her walking along the banks of Little Sugar Creek, singing and talking to a bundle of rags that clothed her baby.

Finally, one June night, she returned to the mayor's house, hoping that if he saw the child, he might take pity on her and if he didn't accept the baby, at least he might give her something to eat. Needless to say, she never even saw him as the door was slammed in her face by a servant.

Devastated, she clutched the baby close to her and jumped off the bridge into the creek. A week later, two boys found her body washed onto the riverbank. Her arms were still tightly gripping the old shawl but the baby was gone. It is now said, that on foggy nights in June, the ghost of the servant girl walks along the banks of the creek, crying and weeping and searching for the baby that was lost to her years ago.

The town of Dublin is located in east central Indiana, lying peacefully along Highway 40. There was once a bridge that stood on Heacock Road, southeast of Dublin, that was known to residents as "Cry-Woman's Bridge". The bridge is gone now, but its ghostly reputation still lingers. The bridge is named after a woman who died here many years ago in an auto accident. She lost control of her car on a stormy night and it plunged from the entrance to the bridge and into the river below. Searchers found her body in the wreckage and they also found a baby's blanket and a pacifier in the car - but there was no sign of the infant's body.

Shortly after the fatal accident, the ghost of the woman was seen walking the bridge on rainy and foggy nights. She was said to wander back and forth, crying and moaning and begging aloud for someone to help her find her baby. Many local residents were said to have encountered her and all of them fled from the scene after hearing her mournful cries.

According to the stories, just before the old bridge was torn down, a young couple was parked in a wooded area near the bridge one night and encountered the ghostly woman. They were startled when they heard her scratching on the trunk of the car and when they saw her pale face, peering in at them and moaning for help, they quickly drove away. The story goes on to say that they later found deep scratches in the paint of the automobile's trunk.

I hope that the pages ahead can serve as a starting point for you to begin your own adventures with the "ghost waters" of the American wilderness but just remember, such waters can be rough and what you see on the surface may not be warning enough of the dangers that lie beneath.

DIANA OF THE DUNES

Around 1915, the area that is now the Dunes State Park in northern Indiana was mostly uninhabited wilderness. This wild region, spread along the shorelines of Lake Michigan, was often visited by fishermen or swimmers looking to escape the heat of the summer, but few dared venture into the miles of dense forest that hugged the shore for miles in every direction. It was the perfect place to hide for someone who was looking to escape from the bonds of society and everyday life. A person could simply vanish into this wild region and never be seen again.

And that was exactly what a young woman decided to do in the early years of the Twentieth Century. The infrequent glimpses of her, swimming nude along the lakeshore, inspired a legend of both her life - and her death.

Not long after the young woman arrived in the Dunes, stories began to spread around Chesterton, Indiana that fishermen who were along the beach at certain times of the day had been lucky enough to catch a glimpse of a naked woman swimming in the lake. The story spread that a beautiful woman was living as a hermit along the beach and her notoriety grew to a point that many compared her to the ancient Greek goddess Diana, hence the name of this legendary creature.

Those who had the opportunity to encounter her, all described her in the same way. She was small, slender and lovely, with dark hair and skin that was tanned brown from the sun. The woman, or "Diana", as they began calling her, was shy and elusive and avoided all contact with the outside world. Those who were able to get close enough to speak to her found her quite timid. She evaded their questions and offered no information about herself at all. The only thing that she wanted, she said in a quite, sweet voice, was to be to herself.

Regardless of how badly Diana wanted to remain anonymous, her fame in the surrounding communities began to spread. The mystery of her true identity and her origins seemed to make people even more curious about her. Stories of her beauty and of her reclusive ways were told and re-told, making her into a larger than life legend. And with the tales and stories running rampant, it was only understandable that "Diana of the Dunes" was going to attract visitors. Within a year of her taking up residence along the beach, the quiet of the Dunes was disturbed by scores of curiosity-seekers, all hoping to catch a glimpse of the bronzed goddess. Diana remained as elusive as ever but was eventually tracked down to an abandoned fisherman's cottage, where she had taken up residence. Most of the visitors were scared off by a wild dog that she had adopted but a few managed to speak to her, including a newspaper reporter from Chicago.

It was discovered that Diana was actually a young woman named Alice Marble Grey, the daughter of an influential Chicago family. Alice was a cultured and educated woman, who had traveled extensively. She had graduated with honors from the University of Chicago and had worked as an editorial secretary for a popular magazine about astronomy. So what could have caused this elegant career woman to abandon the comforts of society for the solitude of the lakeshore wilderness?

That question can never be answered with any authority but some have claimed that Alice came to the Dunes because of a broken love affair. It's more likely though that she left the city because her deteriorating eyesight had made her work impossible. She had sought refuge in the rough land that she had enjoyed as a child. Alice moved into the abandoned fisherman's cottage on the beach and settled into a life of peace, borrowing books from the library, walking in the woods and of course, swimming naked in the chilly waters of Lake Michigan. She was said to have kept extensive journals of her life in the Dunes, keeping away loneliness by communing with nature.

In 1920, Alice met a drifter named Paul Wilson and he moved into the cabin with her. He was an unemployed boat builder with a shaky past and though rumored to be an "unsavory character", he seemed to make Alice happy and he did much to improve the condition of Alice's ramshackle home, as well as fishing and doing odd jobs to earn money for them. His presence also seemed to help discourage the sightseers and they remained together until 1922 - when tragedy struck.

The badly burned and beaten body of a man was found on the beach by hikers and an autopsy revealed that the man had been strangled by someone with great strength. Though the body was burned too badly to allow for an identification, or provide evidence of who the killer might be, the police suspected that Wilson had a hand in the murder. He was questioned by the authorities but claimed that he was innocent, deepening the mystery with claims of seeing a "gun-toting hermit" on the beach. The "hermit" was never found but Wilson was eventually let go because there was not enough evidence to hold him.

Soon after, he and Alice moved to nearby Michigan City, Indiana, where they made a small living selling handmade furniture. Alice bore her husband two daughters but he treated her terribly, often beating her severely. Her life was less rugged that it had been at her home along the beach but it was not as happy.

In February 1925, Alice died in her home, shortly after the birth of her second daughter. The official cause of death was said to be uremic poisoning, a common complication of pregnancy in those days, but some say that her condition had been made worse by repeated blows to her back and stomach. Sadly, it was later revealed that instead of being buried in the grave plot that her family purchased for her, Alice was illegally placed in a common grave instead. Ironically, in death, she had managed to find the anonymity that she so desperately craved in life.

Paul Wilson disappeared shortly after Alice's death and years later, turned up in a California prison, serving time for auto theft. The fate of Alice's daughters is unknown but some believe that they were taken in by Alice's family in Chicago, who learned of their existence only after their beloved daughter's death. They had completely lost touch with Alice and never forgave themselves for finding her too late.

And so ended the life and legend of Alice Grey - Diana of the Dunes. Or did it?

The legends say that Alice's ghost still returns to the wild regions that she loved so much along the rugged shores of the lake. Over the years, many have claimed that they have seen the ghostly figure of a nude woman running along the sand or disappearing into the water. She never speaks when called to and normally, she simply disappears before their startled eyes.

In 1972, a park ranger who was patrolling the lakeshore one evening reported that he saw a woman emerge from the surf and stride onto the beach. She was only a dim figure on this moonlit night but he could see the water shimmering on her naked skin. The ranger approached her to explain that swimming was not allowed after dark but when he got within about ten feet of her, she abruptly vanished.

Hikers who go out into the woods beyond the lake have also told stories of seeing a strange woman wandering through the trees in front of them but she always disappears, leaving no sign that she was ever there.

The truth of such tales is unknown but I would like to think that Alice does return to the place that she loved so much and that she still walks here, the trials and pain of her lonely and sad life forgotten, at least for a time, as she strolls along her beloved beach or disappears into the waters of the lake.

DEAD WOMAN'S CROSSING

One of the strangest tales of Oklahoma is the story of a place known as "Dead

Woman's Crossing", an old river bridge that is located in a remote area near Weatherford. For years, stories circulated about a wooden bridge where the wheels of a wagon could still be heard turning if anyone was brave enough to go there late at night. For many years, people who lived in the area were familiar with the ghostly tale but always assumed that it was just a legend. Little did they know that this particular legend had a real-life murder tale behind it.

The story began on July 7, 1905 in Custer County, Oklahoma when Katy Dewitt James, a pleasant and well-liked young woman, left home and boarded a train to visit a cousin in Payne County. Although popular in the community, no one knew that Katy hid dark secrets from everyone. On the afternoon before she left Custer County, she had filed for divorce from her husband on the grounds of cruelty. This was a daring step for a woman of those times and Katy thought it best to put some distance between herself and her volatile husband. Her father, Henry, helped her to pack her things and he took her to the train himself. He watched from the platform as the train pulled out of the station. He had no idea at the time that this was the last time that he would ever see his daughter alive.

Katy never arrived at her cousin's house and as far as anyone would know, disappeared from the face of the earth. After her father did not receive word from her for several weeks, he hired a detective named Sam Bartell to look for her. Bartell attempted to trace Katy's movements but found nothing until he reached Weatherford. Questioning some of the locals, he discovered that a woman matching Katy's description had stayed with a woman that she had met on the train. The woman was known to people in Weatherford as a "Mrs. Ham". She was a prostitute who owned a boarding house just off the main streets in the downtown area. Her real name was Fannie Norton.

According to what Bartell could find out, Katy and her child had stayed the night of July 7 in the home of William Moore, Fannie Norton's brother-in-law. On the morning of July 8, the two women and the baby had been seen leaving town in a buggy. Norton had mentioned to a worker at the livery stable that they would be back in about three hours. He overheard Norton telling Katy that they were going to Hydro, a nearby town, and would come back soon. The same stable hand reported that Norton had actually returned a little over two hours later and she had come back alone.

Bartell stayed on the trail and set off toward Hydro, questioning people along the way about any sightings of two women and a baby who had recently passed that way. Finally, he ran across a woman who had seen the buggy pass by. She added that she had seen them enter a field near Deer Creek and then pass back the same way about 45 minutes later. When the buggy came back, only a women fitting Norton's description was in the buggy and she had the baby with her.

The detective continued to visit farms around the area and found more people who had encountered Fanny Norton on July 8. She had apparently driven the buggy to a farm near Deer Creek and had left the baby with a small boy, telling him to give the baby to his mother to care for until she returned. Bartell was relieved to discover that the little girl was alive and well and still being cared for by the family. He immediately sent word to Henry Dewitt to let him know that he had found his granddaughter. Unfortunately, Bartell was given some startling information by the family. The woman who had been caring for the baby brought him the dress that the child had been wearing on the day that Norton had abandoned her. It was covered with blood. She also told him that her son had distinctly remembered seeing what also appeared to be blood splashed all over the side of the buggy when Norton had given him the baby.

Now worried, Bartell once again picked up Norton's trail and followed her across the state to Shawnee, where local police arrested her in a room that she had rented from the local butcher and his wife. When questioned as to the whereabouts of Katy James, she told a rambling, far-fetched tale about Katy meeting a man while out on the buggy ride and going away with him. Neither Bartell nor the police detectives were convinced by her story and did not believe that Katy would have abandoned her child with a woman that she hardly knew. Norton vehemently denied killing Katy however and she wept bitterly, allegedly because no one would believe her.

Later that evening, during a break in her interrogation, Bartell was out in the hallway talking to a reporter and Norton began to vomit. Heaving and gasping for air, she collapsed onto the floor and never recovered. It was determined that she had taken some sort of poison and the doctor did not believe that she had long to live. He was right -- Fannie Norton died early the next morning, never confessing about what had happened to Katy. Her death was ruled a suicide and since her body was unclaimed, she was buried in an unmarked grave in the Shawnee city cemetery.

The only clue as to where Katy might be was now lost but Sam Bartell refused to give up the search. Various rewards were posted by Henry Dewitt and even by the territorial governor. The search went on for more than a month before Katy was found. On August 31, a Weatherford man named G.W. Cornell came forward to collect the reward. He and his sons found her body while fishing along Deer Creek. The remains were badly decomposed but the hair matched that of Katy's, her clothing was still recognizable and a gold ring was still on the corpse's finger. Her skull had been severed from the body and was lying a short distance away, close to where her hat was found under a pile of mud and debris.

Once the corpse was examined, a bullet hole was discovered behind the woman's right ear. It was believed to have come from the revolver that was found a short distance downstream - a revolver that Fannie Norton's attorney positively identified as belonging to his late client. Investigators surmised that Norton had shot Katy while she was sitting in the buggy and then Katy had pitched forward, falling down into the creek bed below. The area was secluded enough that no one had seen anything or had heard the shot.

At the inquest, Katy's estranged husband, Martin Luther James, was called to testify. He was sarcastic on the stand and had never expressed any sorrow or concern about his wife and daughter's disappearance, or Katy's death. For this reason, many suspected him of having a hand in Katy's murder but there was no evidence of it and he had an alibi for his whereabouts at the time of her death. A grand jury later indicted Norton for murder, with robbery being the motive, but she had been dead for some weeks by the time the proceedings came to a conclusion.

Because a divorce decree had not been granted before her death, Martin James became the administrator of her rather substantial estate. Her father was very well off and had set up a trust for his daughter when she was a child. She had come of age not long before and had inherited a large sum of money, as well as land holdings and a working farm. James also petitioned for custody of his daughter and she was taken away from her grandfather and given back to him. Not long after, he sold the farm, liquidated Katy's accounts and vanished with his daughter. Whatever became of Martin James remains a complete mystery.

And this is not the only lingering mystery from this case. Who was Fannie Norton and why would she have murdered a woman that she barely knew? And if she did kill Katy because she wanted to rob her, then why leave the body with a gold ring still on her finger? Most of those who have looked into the case do not believe that Fannie acted alone in the murder of Katy Dewitt James. Most believe that she was hired to kill Katy by the estranged husband, Martin James, either to keep the divorce from becoming legal, to steal her estate, or most likely, for both reasons. If Fannie was a prostitute, as most in Weatherford believed, it is thought that perhaps James met her in her professional capacity and then made arrangements for Katy's murder. What really happened remains a mystery and the case remains unsolved.

One thing that was not a mystery to those who lived near Weatherford however was the fact that the bridge and riverbed where Katy had been killed was haunted! It was said that on moonlit nights, if one stood near the bridge that a visitor could hear the sound of a woman, believed to be Katy, calling out for her child. The story went on to say that anyone who stood beneath the wooden bridge could hear the sound of buggy wheels rolling across it, the impatient stamp of horse's hooves, a sudden cracking sound and then a splash as if something had been thrown from the bridge into the water below. It likely goes without saying that when examined, there was no sign of a buggy and nothing in the river beneath it. It came to be realized that this was a spectral re-playing of Katy's last moments on earth.

The old wooden bridge at what has become known as "Dead Woman's Crossing" has since been replaced by a large concrete structure but it remains an eerie place. In more recent years, the area below the bridge has become a popular gathering place for students and teenagers, who come to party and to soak up the ambience of

The concrete bridge that spans Dead Woman's Crossing today

a real-life haunting.

For years, most believed the story of the spectral buggy and the often reported cold spots beneath the bridge - where Katy's body allegedly decomposed - was nothing more than a spooky tale that had been cooked up by college students. It was a surprise for many of these people to discover that there was a true story at the heart of the legend. Given what really happened here in 1905, we have to perhaps think again before handily dismissing some of the legends that we hear because there just may be more to them than we think.

DEVIL WATERS

In the introduction to this book, I made mention of the tendency for the early settlers and inhabitants of North America to use the word "devil" when giving names to locations they believed best avoided. Throughout the book, a number of these locations have been written about and introduced and many of them, as you will soon see, are connected to America's "ghost waters". They are often haunted - or shunned - locations that were likely considered to be outside of the normal boundary of existence centuries before.

Some of the locations, like the Devil's Tower in Wyoming, were considered to by sacred and mysterious sites by the Native Americans. When the white settlers arrived in the regions where these locations existed, they followed the course set by the Indians and dubbed the sites sacred, or at least unusual, as well. In those days however, a place that might be considered sacred to the "heathens", as the Native Americans were considered at the time, would be of the "devil" to the god-fearing explorers and pioneers. In this way, sites that we might not consider haunted or weird also ended up being named after the Devil himself.

Many other sites, however, were aptly named and with the decades of strange phenomena that has been recorded at such places, calling them after the Devil was surprisingly fitting.

The Devil's Bake Oven in Southern Illinois (located in the region of the state dubbed the "Devil's Kitchen") is one of the region's oldest haunts. The Bake Oven, which is a large, rocky hill and is located next to a craggy ridge called the Devil's Backbone, is just on the edge of a small Mississippi River town called Grand Tower. The town was once a major barge-building port on the river and at the time was home to an iron-ore foundry as well. The owner of the foundry built a large home on the Devil's Bake Oven and lived there with his young daughter. The girl fell in love with one of the workers at the foundry, a man that her father did not approve of. He soon paid the man a hefty sum to leave the area. The young woman died, poetically of a broken heart, and her ghost soon returned to haunt the hill. The house, foundry and most of the town are now gone but the specter remains. According to legend, she can sometimes be seen wandering along the river banks or crying atop the rugged ridges of the Devil's Bake Oven.

The Hockomock Swamp, another term for "devil", in Massachusetts has also long been the scene of unusual happenings. Stories of strange creatures here date back to the colonial days, when local residents feared the place was infested with demons. There have been dozens of ghost sightings and phantom animals reported here.

When my family used to summer in northern Minnesota when I was growing up, I often heard about Devil's Track Lake, which was located near the small town of Cook. The Native Americans in the region had long considered the place to be haunted. They feared that evil spirits lurked in the water and would pull down to their doom anyone who was foolish enough to risk fishing or swimming in it.

Another apparently haunted spot is Devil's Lake, near Baraboo, Wisconsin. The strange lake has a number of geological oddities about it, like strange rock formations and petrified sand waves from some sort of ancient sea. There are also three effigy Indian mounds in the shape of a bear, a cat and a bird. There have been many stories of strange creatures and spirits walking in the woods here and local author August Derleth, a follower of H.P. Lovecraft, spoke of this area of southern Wisconsin as part of the "Cthulhu power zones". In 1889, there was a report of a lake monster here and in the 1970's, campers reported several instances of a large creature that was "shaking tents". There is also a local story of an Indian woman and her lover who jumped to their deaths from a nearby bluff. The Native American folklore called it the "place of many dead".

One of the most famous Devil name places is the Devil's Hole in Death Valley, California. The site is near Wingate Pass, a mysterious place itself. For many years, there were legends of a fair-skinned people who lived underground here. These stories apparently circulated among the Indians and were later picked up by the settlers. These odd people were said to come from strange caves in Wingate Pass and even more recent stories about the place tell of explorers that have discovered eerie caverns that are illuminated by unexplained green lights.

In 1931, Dr. F. Bruce Russell announced that he had discovered a cavern near Wingate Pass that contained eight-foot-tall mummies and a number of peculiar artifacts. Russell also claimed to find many other caves in the area and he spent the next 15 years exploring them. In 1947, he was able to arrange funding for an expedition to excavate the caves and salvage the artifacts that he spoke of. Despite his excitement, he found only disdain from the other members of the scientific community. They would not accompany Russell on the expedition until he returned with the artifacts and proved they were real. Determined to succeed anyway, he set off into the desert - and he never returned.

The area of the Devil's Hole gained its public notoriety in the late 1960's, when cult leader Charles Manson was arrested here. He believed that the Devil's Hole, which is a water-filled cavern at the entrance to Wingate Pass, was a passageway to an underground civilization. He was captured here before he or any of his "family" could make it through to the other side. Since then, at least two people have drowned attempting to make it through the cave and there have been numerous reports of ghost sightings in the area.

Perhaps the most famous cursed, haunted and shunned sites in America is a place called the Devil's Hole in Niagara Falls, New York. The cave is a semi-circular precipice or chasm of some 200 feet, dropping straight down to the river below. A little distance from the brink of the hole is a natural mound, several feet in height, and about 60 feet from the top is a spring that runs straight to the river, pouring down into the hole.

Known as a place of disaster long before the white settlers arrived, the site earned its name after the Seneca Indians told early explorers that the cave was the home of a malevolent entity whose name translated into English as "evil one". The creature was believed to dwell in the cave and it was said that anyone who disturbed its rest would die. Not surprisingly, most who heard this tale dismissed it as superstitious nonsense and soon after, a long series of calamities began to involve the Devil's Hole.

One of the earliest rumors of a curse on the place can be attributed to the tragedies that afflicted the famed French explorer Robert Cavalier, who was better known as the flamboyant promoter, sieur de LaSalle. He ignored the warnings of the Seneca and entered the cave in the 1670's. His continuing expeditions were plagued with all manner of accidents, unexplained deaths and illnesses. Some believe that he was unable to escape the curse that was attached to him after entering the Devil's Hole.

LaSalle had been born into a noble French family in 1643. He came to America two decades later and took up exploration as a means of creating his fortune. His first mission, seeking the Ohio River, earned him a grant that gave him control of the fur trade south of the Great Lakes. In return for it, he agreed to explore the lower Mississippi Valley and try to discover a water passage to the Pacific Ocean.

LaSalle traveled from France to Quebec in late 1667 and left Montreal two years later. In July 1669, he crossed Lake Ontario and Lake Erie and then made a number of side trips that were not documented until around 1673, when he returned to France for a period. He returned to America in 1677 after getting permission from the King to explore the land between Florida, Mexico and Canada. He brought with him a true adventurer, his friend Henri de Tonti, an Italian soldier of fortune. He was admired and feared by the Indians, thanks to the wicked metal hook that replaced a hand that he had once lost in battle. Tonti would become LaSalle's boon companion and perhaps his anchor of sanity as well.

Not long after they arrived, LaSalle and his men constructed a fort on the Niagara River and it was at this time that he was believed to have explored the Devil's Hole. After that, nothing seemed to go right for him and this may have been how he earned the reputation that he had of being "a man of magnificent failures."

Soon after the fort was completed, LaSalle began building a ship called the "Griffon", which became the first sailing ship on the Great Lakes. He planned to use it to take his cargoes of furs to the east and then on to Europe. The vessel set sail with a full crew and a hold filled with cargo, then disappeared without a trace. It has since become known as one of the greatest mysteries of the lakes. The lore of the vanished vessel has spawned tales of murder and of course, of ghosts. One such tale is connected to Lake Solitude, a small body of water located along the eastern shore of Lake Michigan. The lake was once connected to the larger body of water, but now only a narrow stream passes between them. The stories say that the passage was closed by the sinking of the *Griffon*. The ship is believed to be hidden beneath the dark surface of the lake and the ghosts of the ship's crew are said to be haunting the shoreline.

Meanwhile, LaSalle made his first trip into the Illinois country during the dead of winter. He pioneered the St. Joseph - Kankakee River route and built a shelter called Fort Crevecoeur at present-day Peoria in 1680. It was a crude, wooden structure, but was the first building erected by the French in the west. It did not last long. While LaSalle was in Canada, preparing supplies for a journey down the Mississippi, the men who remained at the fort mutinied and destroyed the building. It was never rebuilt. To make matters worse, after he left Canada, the fort on the Niagara River was also burned to the ground. His men robbed the stores and vanished into the wilderness.

In the spring of 1682, LaSalle and Tonti made the first journey down to the mouth of the Mississippi River. When they arrived, LaSalle claimed all of the land for France and dubbed the region "Louisiana". In so doing, he created a vast territory that stretched from the Appalachians to the Rocky Mountains. As they tried to return to Canada, the expedition was beset with illness and Indian attacks and many of his men were killed.

LaSalle returned to France in 1683, but sailed to the New World again in 1684 with four ships, intending to start a colony at the mouth of the Mississippi River. King Louis had actually wanted him to travel to the Rio Grande and take over the Spanish gold mines but LaSalle lied and told him that the Mississippi was farther north than it actually was.

He departed with 200 colonists but somehow managed to miss Louisiana and land in Texas instead, after losing a vital supply ship during the ocean crossing. They landed in Matagorda Bay, where one ship ran aground. A pitched battle then took place between the colonists and local Indians, who stole supplies from the wrecked ship, and one of the ships turned and set sail back to France, leaving LaSalle and the rest of the colony stranded.

The expedition built a fort at the mouth of the Lavaca River, and explored the area. They believed that if they could find the Mississippi River, they could follow it north the French missions in the Great Lakes. Out of the 20 men that set out, 12 of them died, forcing the survivors to return to the fort in October 1686. A few months later, LaSalle and 17 others left 25 members of the party at the fort and set out again. They wandered the region but never came upon the Mississippi. Finally, unable to stand it any longer, a group of mutineers shot and killed LaSalle near present-day Navasota, Texas and left his body behind for the animals to eat. The mutineers made it to Montreal in 1688 but those left behind at the fort were massacred by Indians.

Over three centuries following LaSalle's death, the Devil's Hole has continued to claim victims. The area ran red with blood during the years of the French and Indian War. In the summer of 1759, Sir William Johnson landed with troops near the Niagara River and took possession of Forts Niagara and Schlosser. The two French forts were crucial to the command of trade on the upper Great Lakes. The following year, construction was started on a road that ran from what is now Lewiston to Fort Schlosser, which was about eight miles away, and was completed in 1763.

On the morning of September 17, a group of 15 wagons, which were under the escort of 24 soldiers and accompanied by the contractor who built the road and Captain Johnson, set out from Fort Niagara with supplies and ammunition intended for the garrison at Fort Schlosser. Late that morning, they stopped to rest and to water the horses and oxen in a green pasture -- just a short distance from the Devil's Hole.

As the wagon train had made slow but steady progress along the new road, it was being observed by a large group of Seneca Indians, who were allied with the French in the war of the American wilderness. Not long after the wagons departed, word reached the fort of hostile Indian activity and so a detachment of about 130 volunteers, under the command of Captain Campbell, marched from Queenston to strengthen the escort. Just as these troops reached the point where the escort had halted, a band of nearly 500 Indians appeared from their concealment behind the mound outside of the Devil's Hole. They sprang from their cover with savage yells and began to slaughter the British troops, who milled about in great confusion. The troops were unable to rally a defense and fell to the Seneca guns and blades. The men not killed outright, or driven off the precipice and into the depths of the cave, attempted to escape.

Of the men who plunged from the precipice into the Hole, a distance of about 70 or 80 feet, only one escaped with his life, a soldier named Matthews. Several trees were growing from the bottom of the hole, the tops reaching almost to the ground, and a Corporal Noble sprang into the branches. He was still hanging there when he was shot 11 times. Captain Johnson, of the escort, was killed outright, and Lieutenant Duncan, of the relief garrison, was wounded in the left arm and later died. Only 25 men survived the massacre and all of them, save for two, did so below or near the north end of the Devil's Hole, where a little sand ridge served to break their falls from the cliff.

In 1806, several men went to examine the scene of the massacre and descended into the Devil's Hole. In the bottom of the chasm, they found the skulls of several oxen "moldering and covered with moss," a portion of a wagon, bones of many of the men who were killed, swords and knives long covered by rust and even a few broken muskets. The massacre is still remembered as the time of greatest bloodshed at the Devil's Hole - and another example of the terrible curse.

In addition to the soldiers who died, legend has it that in the years that followed, many of the settlers who came to the region were also killed. In many cases they were violently thrown into the Devil's Hole, where they fell to their deaths.

The cave also claimed many victims among the Seneca tribe as well. Many battles were fought between the Native Americans and well-armed British soldiers near the Devil's Hole and dozens of the Indians lost their lives almost at the entrance to the cave. In most cases, the bodies of the dead were unceremoniously dumped into the raging waters beneath the Hole. As mentioned, the fighting between the Indians and the settlers who came later left many dead - and many more corpses "fed" to the cave.

As the years went by ,some also tied the close proximity of the Devil's Hole to at least two tragedies that affected the entire country. It could be said that despite the notorious history of the place, the builders of the Great Gorge Route Trolley allowed their carefully constructed line to pass much too close to the cave upon which great misfortune had already been blamed. After the trolley line was completed, hundreds of people passed by the entrance to the Devil's Hole on a daily basis. Most of them walked away completely unscathed, but those who were allegedly exposed to the

A vintage view of the Great Gorge Trolley as it rounds a curve near the Devil's Hole

lethal "aura" of the place often made headlines. One such person rode the trolley route past the cave in September 1901. He was President William McKinley and just hours after stepping off his trolley, he was assassinated. Coincidence? Perhaps, but those who believe in the curse of the Devil's Hole don't think so.

The worst disaster that has been connected to the Devil's Hole occurred on July 1, 1917. On this day, 12 tourists died and 24 more were injured when a trolley filled with passengers derailed and plunged into the Niagara River just at the upper end of the Whirlpool Rapids. The trolley rolled down an embankment and came to rest on several submerged rocks before tipping again and falling upside-down in the raging river. A customs officer had alerted the staff of the Great Gorge Route about a half-hour before the accident about an unstable rail bed but the trolleys were not stopped. The official cause of the accident was said to have been heavy rains that undermined the rail bed - but others blamed it on the Devil's Hole.

Since 1850, the body count around the Devil's Hole has continued to climb and averages at least one death each year and today, the bodies of those who plummet into Niagara Falls from the Devil's Hole are recovered with frightening regularity. Most of those unlucky enough to die here slip and fall to their deaths in freak accidents, although murders and suicides have also been recorded.

The number of untimely deaths that have occurred here have led to many coming to believe that several restless ghosts are haunting the site. It comes as no surprise that visitors to the cave have reported strange noises, including footsteps, moans, cries and screams, within the Devil's Hole. There have also been reports of ghosts that have been seen here as well, including several accounts of people actually seeing the re-enactments of people plunging to their deaths from the precipice. When no bodies are discovered below, it is realized that what seemed to be a tragic death occurring was really one that happened long ago.

There are those who would say that venturing to the Devil's Hole could be hazardous to your well-being and I will leave it to the reader to decide if they wish to heed those words of warning or not. If nothing else, it is a place of natural wonder and horrific tragedy and one that certainly has the potential to be haunted.

LA CHICA LOBO DEL RIO DIABLO

The brush country of Texas is home to a legend that began many years ago, quite some distance from the region where it is still remembered, and sometimes still experienced, today. This strange tale actually began in the fall of 1830 when John Dent and Will Marlo began trapping the headwaters of the Chickamauga River in Georgia. The two men enjoyed a prosperous season and got along well until the spring of 1833, when they violently argued over a division of the winter's catch.

A woman was at the heart of their quarrel and her name was Mollie Pertul. She was the daughter of another trapper and John Dent had met her and had fallen in love while trapping in the vicinity of her family's cabin. The two were soon engaged to be married. When he and Will Marlo had formed their partnership, the two trapped had agreed to sell all of their pelts and then divide the money between them. The agreement had been carried out for two seasons but now Dent insisted that he wanted to take half the hides and sell them on his own, believing that he could get more money from them that way.

After the two men came to blows in their argument, the division was made the way that Dent wanted it. Almost immediately after though, Marlo began telling people that he had been cheated. This went on for two weeks until the two friends met one another again. In the fight that followed, Dent stabbed his former partner to death. Although he was not charged with murder, Dent found that public opinion was against him and he had no choice but to leave the area. Before he did though, he went to see Mollie and he promised her that as soon as he found a place for them to live, he would return and spirit her away with him.

Months passed by and Mollie heard nothing from her lover. Then, on April 13, 1834, a year to the day after Marlo was stabbed, Mollie went out to milk the cows, as was her daily custom. After she was gone for an unusually long time, her parents went out to look for her and found that the cows had never been milked. As they searched through the barn, they found a Bowie knife with blood caked on it lying next to an empty milk pail. The knife had an unusual stag horn handle, just like the one that John Dent had carried.

Her family searched for her into the evening hours and the following morning, summoned some friends and neighbors to help. One of them, an expert tracker, found the trail of a man and a woman leading down to the Chickamauga River. A canoe had been tied there and then released. It appeared that Mollie Pertul had left with no explanation and nothing but the clothing on her back.

Six months passed and one morning, Mrs. Pertul received a letter in the mail. It was postmarked from Galveston, Texas. It read:

Dear Mother,
The Devil has a river in Texas that is all his own and it is made only for those who are grown.
　　Yours with love ---
　　Mollie

In those days, the people of Georgia were not familiar with the streams and rivers of Texas, or their names. In fact, very few people in Texas even knew about the Devil's River, which is located far to the west of San Antonio. In those days, it was only an outpost and its inhabitants spoke mostly Spanish. The Pertul's simply assumed that Dent had found himself a river in Texas to trap - and that Dent himself was the only "devil" Mollie could have become acquainted with.

Whether Dent was a "devil" or not, one of the mostly forgotten chapters in Texas history involves a small colony of Americans who settled on the Devil's River in 1834. They called their settlement Delores but it did not last for long. Indians killed most of the settlers and many of the rest drifted into Mexico. The rest of them, 14 adults and three children, attempted to go back to the United States but were attacked at Espantosa Lake, near what is now Carrizo Springs. After massacring the entire party, the Comanche threw the bodies and their wagons into the lake. To this day, the people here consider the lake to be haunted and even the name "Espantosa", which means "frightful".

John Dent and his bride had joined up with this colony. The Devil's River had plenty of beaver and so the did the Rio Grande, both above and below where the Devil's River emptied into it. He lived separate from the main group and had a truce with the Indians and a good relationship with several Mexican families who raised goats to the west in Pecos Canyon.

One day in May 1835, John Dent came riding into one of the goat ranches on a spent horse. Exhausted, he fell onto the ground in front of the home of one of the families that he did not know well. Unable to even explain to them who he was, he told them that his home was located where Dry Creek meets the Devil's River and that his wife was giving birth to a baby and she needed help. The Mexican woman agreed to go with her husband, who was already saddling their horses. Dent managed to pull himself to his feet and climb back onto his horse but then, in an incredible freak accident, lightning came out of the sky, where a storm had been gathering, and struck John Dent. Screaming, he pitched from his mount and fell, dead before his body struck the ground. Unable to believe what had just happened, the rancher summoned help from a neighbor, who recognized John Dent. When he heard why the man had come, he urged the couple to go to Mollie's assistance.

They quickly rode off but did not reach the Dent home before nightfall. They arrived early the next morning - to find only heartbreak, tragedy and death. Mollie was lying in the house, dead and alone. It appeared that she had died giving birth but no child could be found. However, scattered in the dust outside the cabin were large wolf tracks. The animals had apparently come into the house too and the Mexican couple could only assume that they had devoured the infant. In the cabin, they also found a letter, which they took along to show to the first person they found who could read English. The letter, as it later turned out, had been written by Mollie Pertul Dent to her mother in Georgia before her death. It served as the final identification for the dead woman's body.

Ten years passed and a wagon road was laid out across the new Republic of Texas to El Paso and it passed by San Felipe Springs, which is now known as Del Rio. It traveled on across the Devil's River and then into the Pecos. The road was a good one, as far as wagon roads of the day went, but remote and often dangerous. Only occasional, and well armed, travelers usually passed that way.

In 1845, a young boy who lived at San Felipe Springs reported that he had seen a pack of wolves attack a herd of goats. This was not the strange part of his story though. He claimed that with the wolves was a strange creature that was covered with hair, but looked to be a naked girl. Some Americans who were traveling through the region questioned the boy about his story but dismissed him as a liar. The story was ridiculed but it did spread among the settlements in the area.

About a year later, a Mexican woman in San Felipe Springs also reported the girl. She said that she had seen two large wolves and a naked girl eating a freshly killed goat. She got close to them before they saw her but when they looked up, they ran off. The girl at first ran on all fours but then rose up and ran on two feet, keeping in time with the wolves. The woman was sure about what she had seen and soon people in the area began keeping a lookout for the weird girl. Local Indians reported finding wolf and human tracks in sandy spots along the river and told the locals about them. They in turn recalled the disappearance of Mollie Dent's baby - and the fresh wolf tracks left behind. Could a female wolf had carried the baby away and raised it as her own?

A hunt was organized to capture the Lobo, or Wolf, Girl of the Devil's River, as they came to call her. A number of riders came together and set off along the stark, isolated border region to look for her. On the third day of the hunt, two of the riders jumped the girl in a side canyon. She was with a large wolf that cut off from her when she dodged into a crevice in the canyon wall. She cowered at first but when the men came close to her, she spat and then clawed and bit at them like a wild animal. As the men descended on her with ropes to bind her with, the wild girl began to howl and cry with a sound that resembled both the scream of a girl and the baying of a wolf. As she let out this awful scream, a huge wolf, likely the one she had been separated from, suddenly rushed at her captors. With a roar, the animal sprang at them but one of the men saw it coming and thought fast enough to draw his pistol and shoot it down. As the animal collapsed into the sand, the girl fainted dead away.

The captured creature, now securely tied, was examined more closely by the men. She was excessively hairy but had small breasts that were just starting to form and other features that showed that she was a normally developed, young female. Her hands, arms and legs were unusually muscular but not abnormal in any way.

The hunters carried the girl to a horse and after reviving, she watched them warily as she was taken to a nearby ranch for the night. Here, she was untied and placed in an isolated room for the night. The rancher's wife offered her food, water and some clothing to cover herself with but the girl cowered away from her. Snarling, she pressed herself into the darkest corner of the room and would let no one approach her. The door to the room was locked and a small window, the only other exit, was nailed shut. No sooner than was the door closed, that the girl inside of the chamber began to scream. The wild and frantic creature let forth a series of terrifying howls that carried out into the night air. The group of men who had gathered at the ranch began to feel cold chills running up and down their spines as soon, wolves out on the plains began to answer her call. They came from all sides of the ranch and their dismal and far-carrying voices were answered by animals who were farther and farther away. The men inside of the ranch house, cowboys who had lived in the region all of their lives, had never heard anything like this before, either in the sheer number of wolves assembling or in the quality of their long, deep howling.

As the girl in the room continued to cry, the men yelled at her and tried to quiet her down. The rancher's wife spoke to her soothingly. Nothing seemed to help though and she wailed louder and louder. The horde of wolves outside gathered close to the ranch, howling in unison. They bellowed out a chorus of darkness and ferocity and then paused and waited for the wild girl to answer back with her unearthly howling scream.

After a time, the pack made a rush for the corral and the barns, attacking goats, milk cows and the saddle horses. The screams and neighs of the domestic animals, accompanied by the thudding sounds of the kicking horses on the wooden stalls, brought the men out of the house and to the rescue. Ordinarily, none of the hardened range riders would have feared a wolf but these animals were acting completely unlike any of the wolves they had ever encountered before. The men kept close together as they ran into the yard, shooting into the darkness and yelling as they advanced. The onslaught of the guns made the wolves retreat.

Once the men ran out of the house though, the wolf girl somehow wrenched loose the plank that had been nailed over the window and disappeared into the night. It was assumed that she rejoined the wolves as hardly another howl was heard that night. Only the mark of bare feet within the myriad of tracks left by the wolves provided evidence that she was ever there at all. For some time after, sightings of wolves in the region were rare.

Nothing more was heard about the Wolf Girl of the Devil's River, save for rumor and legend, for nearly six years. In the meantime, gold had been discovered in California and westward travel began to increase. Around 1852, an exploring party of frontiersmen, who were searching a route to El Paso with better water than the trails that already existed, rode down to the Rio Grande at a sharp bend far above the mouth of the Devil's River.

They were almost upon the river when they saw a strange creature, sitting along the edge of a sandbar. As they looked closer, they realized that the figure was that of a clearly naked young woman with two young wolf whelps tugging at her full breasts. When the woman heard the sound of the approaching horses, she immediately sprang to her feet and snatched up the pups under each arm and ran off. She ran into the nearby breaks at full speed and vanished from sight.

After that, the Wolf Girl was rarely seen and soon only the tales of the Apache remained to show that the girl continued to live out among the wolves for years afterward. Soon, those tales also came to an end and most came to believe that the daughter of Mollie Pertul and John Dent had perished out in the wild, finally leaving the only existence that she had ever known. Years later though, strange tales began to surface that has caused many to wonder if perhaps the Wolf Girl might live on after all - at least in spirit.

In the fall of 1974, an avid bow hunter and hiker named Jim Marshall planned a weekend outing for he and two friends from Dallas in the Devil's River region. What they saw that weekend left them shaken and convinced that strange things can exist in the wild regions of Texas that have no easy explanation. "I knew the story about the wolf girl," Jim later recalled,"but I thought it was just that, a story. What we saw that evening couldn't have been just out imaginations playing tricks on us. We all three saw the same thing."

Marshall and his friends came out to the Devil's River country to hunt for javelina, the wild pigs that roam the southwestern desert areas, and to enjoy the outdoors. They camped for several days along the river and one evening they had just gotten the fire going and one of Jim's friends decided to go out and gather some more firewood. He returned just a few moments later though, his face white with shock.

They asked him what was wrong and he urged them to see for themselves. The three of them left the camp and walked down a well-used trail that led to the river banks. They stopped and looked around and just as the first man started to tell the others what he had seen, Jim looked up and saw something on the opposite shore that was watching them.

"The only way that I can describe it is that it appeared to be a girl," Jim said, "with long hair and wild eyes. Even in the darkness, we could see her. It was like she was in a haze... standing there partly bent over, digging into an ant mound. Suddenly, whatever we were seeing was gone. I don't know if it vanished or just moved quickly into the brush. I was scared and my mind started to clamp up on me."

When the three men recovered their senses, they immediately returned to their camp, packed up their tent and gear and got ready to leave. As they worked, Jim remembered, they watched all around them, lighting the area with three large lamps. They didn't want anything to sneak up on them - and they didn't stop driving until they reached Del Rio.

THE HAUNTED WILD

What is it that draws so many of us to the wild regions of America? Why do we want to walk along trails that only few people have ever set foot upon, to roam through regions of wilderness where isolated camps are rarely seen and where no settlements exist or paddle down rivers where the only maps that exist are poor ones and accounts of the place are little more than legend? Why does this feeling of wanderlust exist on our hearts, this same feeling of wanderlust that drove scores of our ancestors to leave behind the safety of hearth and home and embark on a journey to open the American West?

No one can say -- but it is likely the same feeling that exists in so many of us to search for the ghosts of these places. We look for the lingering memories of those who came before and left a little piece of themselves behind. There are those who believe that ghosts can only manifest in crowded regions, in cities or towns, or lurking in the confines of a haunted house. But this is far from the case. Ghosts dwell in the wild regions as well, out here in the haunted heart of America.

AT THE MOUNTAINS OF MADNESS

In 1931, author H.P. Lovecraft wrote a horror tale about terrifying events that occurred in the mountainous regions of the Antarctic. The great, evil beings that were encased in ice in his story were perhaps the work of fantasy but the mountainous regions of the world have often been places of terror for those courageous enough to try and conquer them.

For years, climbers all over the world have reported attacks of paralyzing and unreasoning fear, much like the "creeps" described in an earlier chapter of this book, but much more fearsome. Thanks to this, there is an impressive record of otherwise hardy outdoorsmen who have abandoned their climbs, although always for no particular reason.

In 1888, J. Normal Collie was seized by terror while climbing Scotland's Ben MacDhui mountain and retreated from his expedition. He admitted that he suddenly found himself scurrying down the mountain in absolute horror but had no idea why. In 1945, P.A. Densham, an experienced mountaineer who specialized in aircraft rescue, was on the same mountain when he sensed what he called a "presence". Then, he heard what he thought were footsteps and went to investigate. When he came to the place where he was sure the sounds had been coming from, he was suddenly gripped by an inexplicable feeling of fright. He bolted away with such urgency that he nearly plunged to his death over a cliff.

In 1910, John Bochan was scaling a mountain in the Bavarian Alps with a local forester and at the same moment, both men panicked and fled without speaking. The two men ran until they collapsed in exhaustion in a lower valley. Looking back on it, neither man could explain what had seized him - only that they had a desperate urge to get away from the place.

What it is that these men sensed? Could this "mountain madness" be the same feeling that was identified by the ancient Greeks in their own mountains centuries ago? They believed that such episodes were attributed to the presence of the Great God Pan, lurking in the shadows. The eerie experiences coined the word "panic" from the name of this goat-footed god.

Perhaps one of the greatest "haunted" mountains in America is New Hampshire's Mt. Washington, a remote and secluded place that is not only the highest point in New England but also one of the coldest places in North America. The weather conditions here are some of the worst in the world and temperatures often reach 70 degrees below zero in the winter time. Even in the summer, the temperature routinely drops below freezing and ice is commonplace.

Despite the frigid temperatures and hurricane-force winds, Mt. Washington has been a popular place to visit since the middle 1800's. Today, you can travel up to the mountain during the warmer weather months by the famous Cog Railroad, by automobile or even on foot. As tourism on the mountain began to flourish, train service was extended to the White Mountains and then a bridle path was built to the summit of the mountain. The first hotel, the Summit House, was built in 1852, just a few feet away from Mt. Washington's highest crag. The stone hotel was so successful after its first year of operation that a competing hotel, the Tip Top House, was opened the following season.

At the time the hotels were built, the only access to the summit was by foot or on horseback so it's hard to imagine how difficult and time-consuming the work must have been. Other than the stones that were abundant on the summit, all of the other materials had to be hauled by horses over nine miles of rough trails. In addition, the workers had to climb two miles to work each day from a camp further down the mountain.

The walls of the Tip Top House were built of stone that had been blasted from the mountain rock. The original roof was flat and used as an observation deck. In clear weather, a telescope was set up for visitors and they could see four states and part of Canada from this vantage point. The hotel was expanded to include 91 rooms and also played host to a daily newspaper for a time called "Among the Clouds". A weather observatory was also built to record the extreme conditions on the summit but the great fire of 1908 destroyed all of the buildings here, sparing only the Tip Top House. This hotel was expanded again but shortly after completion of the new Summit Hotel, the Tip Top House itself was also destroyed by fire. It was rebuilt though but now only served as an annex to the Summit House. Sadly though, it fell into disrepair and its long history came to an end when it was abandoned in 1968.

Years later, the Tip Top House became a state historic site and was re-opened to visitors. A restoration was completed in 1987 and offers a look at the rich history of the mountain. The Tip Top House is believed to be the oldest mountain-top hostelry still in existence in the world.

The tourists still come to Mt. Washington, but only in the seasonal months. In the winter, there is hardly a more inhospitable place on earth. The roads and the railway are useless and closed down and the only access to the top is by tractor. Once there, Mt. Washington becomes a uniquely alarming experience - completely cut off from civilization, exposed to the wind, ice and snow and utterly isolated.

Believe it or not though, there are a few hardy souls who live in these conditions over the winter. They are the year-round staff of a television transmitter and the staff of the Mt. Washington Observatory, a scientific facility that monitors the often bizarre weather conditions of the summit.

The first regular meteorological observations on Mt. Washington were conducted by the U.S. Signal Service, a precursor of the Weather Bureau, from 1870 to 1892. The Mount Washington station was the first of its kind in the world, setting an example followed in many other countries. The current observatory reoccupied the summit in 1932 and in April 1934, observers measured a wind gust of 231 mph, which remains a world record for a surface station. In spite of the hardships

The weather station and summit of Mt. Washington Today

imposed by their environment, observers regularly monitor weather under the auspices of the U.S. Weather Bureau, and conduct landmark research in short-wave radio propagation, ice physics and the constitution of clouds. The staff continues to record and disseminate weather information today. It also develops robust instrumentation for severe weather environments and conducts many types of severe weather research and testing. Of the scores of mountaintop scientific stations that eventually followed its lead, the Mt. Washington station is perhaps the only one that can be said to have remained in continuous operation with an active and expanding mission.

The staff that remains on duty here in the winter time is made up of a dedicated group of scientific individuals - which makes the incidents reported here all the more unusual. According to those who have spent time on the summit of Mt. Washington in the winter time, there is something here that cannot easily be explained. It was known to the Native Americans centuries ago and it is known to those who remain here today. Those who have encountered it can swear that it is a living thing -- not physical at all -- but they also doubt whether or not it is the traditional idea of a ghost either. Over the years, it has simply become known as "The Presence."

Many strange events have been documented on the winter time summit of Mt. Washington over the years and all of them have been attributed to the Presence. Workers in the weather station describe hearing voices and footsteps in empty rooms; doors open and close by themselves; and they have seen things that move or hang suspended in the air by their own power. The Presence has done everything from hiding things, tossing clothing about and even attacking human beings. Different people seem to experience it in different ways and all of them have their theories to explain it. The Native Americans avoided the mountain top, believing that a great spirit lurked there and the early explorers of the region stayed away for the same reason.

For the most part, dwellers on the mountain have come to believe the Presence is a benign one, watchful and curious and either sensed or sometimes glimpsed as it vanishes from the corner of the eye. Most who have experienced it do not feel that it is menacing. As William Harris said after spending more than 25 years on the mountain in the winter months stated: "If this thing wasn't friendly, it would have gotten me good - a long time ago."

But not everyone agrees with that. The late Lee Vincent, who was the director of the television transmitter on the mountain, lived on the summit for years. He made a study of the Presence and often wrote about it in his books and included accounts of experiences with it in his lectures. He maintained that the Presence became more active in the winter months -- and when something violent happens on Mt. Washington.

There has been a history of accidents and deaths on the mountain, and in the surrounding area, dating back to 1888. Since that year, that has been an annual average of at least two deaths during the turn of each calendar. The most horrific accident occurred in September 1967 when tragedy struck the cog railroad that transports visitors to the mountain top. Carrying about 75 people, the train got to Skyline Switch but did not stop. In fact, it never stopped there because the switch was always left in the straight position - but not this time. Before the crew could correct the problem, the front cog wheel lost its grip and the engine turned on its side, releasing the coach. The passenger car rolled backward, accelerating rapidly and then plunged off the wooden Long Trestle. Many of the passengers were injured in the fall and eight were killed.

To this day, the accident remains unexplained. Many have blamed it on a railroad man's negligence or perhaps a hiker who fooled with the switch mechanism, not realizing what he was doing. Whether it was malicious or an accident though, something did move that switch. And while most agree that it was human error, others have offered less tangible and more frightening explanations.

Shortly after the accident, weird things began to be reported by John Davis, a railroad employee who was working and living on the summit at the Tip Top House. He would find the safe standing open but nothing would be missing. Chairs and tables would rearrange themselves overnight and money would vanish and then reappear in different locations. No matter how closely Davis kept on eye on things, he could not discover who was doing it. The company eventually summoned the state police to investigate and officers searched the building, using dogs, and remained on watch in the old hotel overnight. They eventually gave up, finding nothing.

Meanwhile, Peter Zwirken, who was working at the Mt. Washington Observatory at the time, recalled a knocking that came at the door late one night. It was a blustery evening and a storm had kept everyone inside, which is why he and the other staff members were so surprised to hear someone outside. One of the staffers walked over and opened the door and while no one was there, he looked down and saw a heavy, bronze plaque lying on the doorstep. Zwirken and the others gathered around recognized it as a memorial to a climber who had died of exposure on the mountain. Normally, the heavy plaque was affixed to a stone that was located about a mile away from the weather station. "It had been ripped off its foundation and somehow transported to our doorstep," Zwirken said. "No mortal could have accomplished such a feat."

Lee Vincent's own strange experiences on the summit led him to try and collect other incidents of mysterious Mt. Washington phenomena. For instance, Jon Lingel, who worked for the television station, spoke of several weird experiences. One night, when he was alone in the building, he was awakened in the middle of the night by the sound of footsteps coming down the hall toward his bedroom. Wondering who would have come to visit at such a late hour, he got up and looked out in the corridor -- it was empty.

Moments later, he heard the footsteps again, this time accompanied by heavy breathing. Puzzled and now a little frightened, he returned to bed but the longer that he lay there in the dark, the more terrified he became. It was almost as if a feeling was coming over him that he could not control. He got up and locked his bedroom door but as he did so, he heard a stirring that caused him to press his ear against the wooden panel. It was the sound of a party going on downstairs! He distinctly heard music, laughter, voices and even the tinkle of glasses. Summoning his courage, he left his room to investigate but found the downstairs area to be dark, abandoned and empty. He was totally alone in the building.

It did not stay that way for long though for Lingel hurriedly packed his things and left the building, swearing that he would never sleep there again.

Lingel would not be the only one to have strange experiences. In fact, far from it. Writer Austin Stevens planned to expose the accounts from the summit of Mt. Washington as nothing more than "ghost stories" for *Yankee* Magazine, but according to editor Judson Hale, Stevens went up there to investigate and returned convinced that the men stationed at Mt. Washington in the winter time have, at times, experienced a curious, watchful and malevolent force. A photographer named Mike Micucci claimed that he was pushed while standing on a precipitation platform one day shortly after he started working there - and no one was on the platform but him.

Some will not even comment on the unnerving experiences they have had on the mountain. "All I'll say about the whole thing is," stated Marty Engstrom, a long time television weatherman, "it tells you right in the Bible that there are such things and it tells you not to mess around with them."

So, what does occur on the frigid summit of New Hampshire's Mt. Washington? No one can say for sure and even fewer can put their finger on just how they feel about the weird happenings after they occur. One of the staff members from the observatory, Will Harris, was walking alone one night when he sensed that someone was behind him. He turned around however and found that the trail was empty.

Imagination or something else?

Whatever it was, Will counted himself luckier than one of his colleagues, he believed that he had actually been chased one night by some mysterious "force". He was working in one of the pressurized chambers when he came to feel that there was something invisible in there with him. Nervousness turned to panic, until he ran out of the chamber, unable to stop shaking.

In January 2004, a report from Jeff De Rosa, a staffer at the weather observatory, was dispatched at a little after three o'clock in the morning. He had been unable to sleep after a strange experience that had occurred earlier in the evening. It read:

> Over the years there have been many tales of 'The Presence' here on the summit of Mt. Washington. Tonight, rather than snickering at these stories, I became a believer. As we were passing food around the dinner table, we heard the tower door open, then shut. OK, so the winds which are gusting to over 100 mph generated enough force to open the door that always latches shut. I'll buy it. What I don't buy though, is how 30 seconds later, the 'wind' turned the TV on to watch the evening news. At this time, we were all stuffing our faces ... the only theory is that when the temperature drops lower than 40 degrees below zero, it becomes too much for the Presence to handle, so it comes to pay us a visit. We'll accept this though, because the Presence is earning its stay. Liz and I both heard someone de-icing the tower for us ... yikes!

As you can see, those who brave a winter here have a much different experience waiting for them than the tourist who comes to the mountain during the summer season. Many of them arrive with doubts about anything unusual going on here - but most of them leave with a different feeling altogether. There is something that dwells on the towering heights of Mt. Washington but what that something may be remains a mystery.

HAUNTS OF THE NORTH WOODS

The American North Woods, spanning states like Wisconsin, Minnesota and Michigan have already figured prominently into the pages of this book, but it would be remiss of me not to include a few final tales from the shadowy regions of the forests here. It is a strange area of great legends, lost towns and vanished people, blending together to create one of the most enigmatic wild regions of the country.

THE DELL HOUSE

The area around the Wisconsin Dells is likely the most popular vacation spot in the state. Unfortunately, many of the area's more scenic spots, like the towering bluffs and steep ravines of the Dells themselves, have been overshadowed by gaudy commercial enterprises but there do remain a few secrets here. Those who travel outside of town, and away from the bright lights and the tourists, will discover the wondrous forests and the natural wonders of the region - and perhaps some ghosts as well.

The infamous Dell House was built in 1837 by a man named Allen. It stood near a place called the Narrows in a shady glen that was close to both a sandy river beach and a fresh water spring. The Dell House was not a classy establishment. It catered to the basic needs of the rough river men who came there, which included hearty food, a place to sleep, bad whiskey, gambling and women. Violence was not uncommon here and it is believed that a number of unlucky patrons probably found their final resting place to be the muddy bottom of the nearby river.

The days of the river traffic eventually faded and the Dell House closed down. By 1900, the ramshackle building had been abandoned. Adventurous tourists and local residents occasionally camped out near the site and so began the tales of ghosts and phantoms who were said to walk the ruins of the house and in the woods beyond. Campers spread tales of ghosts and mysterious sounds like cursing, laughter, breaking glass and pounding footsteps coming from the old structure. Apparitions were sometimes seen in the forest, perhaps lingering spirits of those who met a sudden and violent end at the hotel.

The history of the Dell House came to an end in 1910 when a fire burned the empty building to the ground. All that remained were the stone foundations of the inn, the fireplace and the towering brick chimney. Eventually, the ruins were engulfed by the surrounding forest. The forest glen near the Narrows still remains, although the Dell House is gone. Only a few of the crumbling stones and bricks remain but there are many who believe that the ghostly legacy of the inn lives on.

Those who have ventured out near the site after dark still claim that unusual sounds can be heard in that area of the forest and that shadowy figures still slip past the trees and disappear. The Dell House may be gone but it is far from forgotten.

GHOST OF MINNIE QUAY

Just north of Port Sanilac, on the eastern Michigan coast, lies the small community of Forester. This small village has only a few residents in the winter time, although it is filled to capacity in the summer, when travelers gather around the camp fires and spin tales of the Lake Huron coast. They speak in hushed whispers of the ghost legend of Minnie Quay, a story that has its roots not in fiction but in truth.

Along a street in Forester is an abandoned tavern with the name "Quay" and the year of "1852" lettered above the door. This house once belonged to James Quay and his wife, Mary Ann, who had come to Forester from New England. Their eldest daughter Minnie was nearly 15 years-old when she died in April of 1876. It is this young woman whose ghost is still said to walk the lake shore and the woods near Forester.

At the time of Minnie's death, Forester was a thriving town and a busy ship port for boats hauling lumber to various places on the Great Lakes. There were four long warehouses and a pier that extended out into the bay, the ruined pilings of which can still be seen today. People came from all over town and from the surrounding area to see what ships had docked and to get news from the outside world. The small town, while busier in those days than it is today, was still a remote and isolated community and to the locals, new arrivals had an almost exotic air about them, especially the young sailors who came in from the lumber ships.

Minnie Quay, like many young girls who lived in ports, fell in love with one of the sailors who visited Forester. No one knows for sure what his name was but the relationship was greatly disapproved of in town, especially by Minnie's parents. The Quay's did not want their daughter carrying on with a sailor and they forbid her to see him again.

In the spring of 1876, word reached Forester that the ship that the young man had been working on had gone down in a storm. Minnie was heart-broken, especially since she had not even been able to tell him goodbye the last time that he had been in port. A few days later, she committed suicide by plunging off the town pier and into the cold waters of Lake Huron. Minnie was buried in the Forester Cemetery on the north end of town - but most say that she does not rest in peace.

The legends say that Minnie's ghost has been seen walking along the shore of Lake Huron near Forester. She is said to cry mournfully for the spirit of her lost love, who she seeks but never finds. Over the years, several young women have reported that Minnie has beckoned to them from the icy waters as if inviting them to join her. It is even said that one girl drowned after claiming that she saw Minnie one night. Was it suicide or simply the invitation of a ghost who is lonely in her watery grave of despair?

GHOSTS OF AU SABLE

The city of Oscoda, Michigan lies just north of Saginaw Bay on the eastern side of the state. It looks out over the waters of Lake Huron and has deep ties to the past. Nearby are many legends of death and spirits. Among them are the stories of Lake Solitude, a small body of water that was once connected to Lake Huron but now only a small and narrow creek allows the waters to join. Many believe that the passage was closed by the sinking of the Griffin, a ship of the explorer LaSalle, which sank here centuries ago. The ship is said to still be hidden beneath the lake and the ghosts of the ship's crew are still haunting the nearby shores.

Also nearby are the ruins of the original Au Sable, the region's oldest settlement. It burned to the ground in 1911 and left only ruins behind but many believe it to be a very haunted spot. Tradition holds that may ghosts still walk here inexorably tied to the past. The region has a long and troubled history and recent stories tell of at least one resident ghost that still walks here in the forest that has overtaken the once thriving town.

Au Sable was first settled in 1800 by Louis Dhevalier, a French trader, who located his post on the banks of the Au Sable River near Lake Huron. As the first settler in the area, he was granted 500 acres of land on what was then called the "Riviere Aux Sables". For the first nearly two decades, Dhevalier shared the land with the Chippewa Indians, who finally ceded their territory to the government in 1819. This brought about the end of the hunting and trapping era in Au Sable and soon commerce changed to that of fishing and lumber.

The town of Au Sable, or at least the settlement that brought it about, was started at the mouth of the river in 1849. Around that time, two men, Curtis Emerson and James Eldridge, purchased land on both sides of the river, near where Benjamin Pierce had established a trading post. Using the post as a landmark, Emerson and Eldridge platted lots and began dividing them between the resident fisherman and others.

The township of Sable was organized in 1857 and changed its name to Au Sable two decades later in 1877, not long after it had been incorporated as a village. The town elected its first mayor, Henry Martin Loud, in 1899 but the town had already started to thrive long before. As far back as 1836, the region had started to attract attention for its rich forests. In that year, a sawmill was built at Van Etta Lake but the Backus Brothers were the real pioneers in the lumber business in Au Sable. They arrived in 1866 and followed by others, created an entire industry from scratch, attracting workers, ships and the businesses to supply them from all over the Upper Midwest.

The area became a rendezvous point for many rough characters. The fishermen and the men who worked in the mills were regarded as a "necessary evil", uncouth, unpolished and coarse, they nevertheless filled the pockets of the legitimate businessmen in the town. Whiskey and fish were the town staples. The early inhabitants of the settlement were Scottish, Irish, French, German and Jewish and fought amongst each other and themselves. There is one story about an Irishman who bet his brother that the latter couldn't strike alongside his fingers with a hatchet without hitting them. The Irishman lost three fingers -- but won the bet.

As times passed, order came to Au Sable. The first churches were established in the late 1860's, a newspaper was started in 1877 and the first rail line was laid into Au Sable in 1883. The rough, frontier settlement had become a real town but the boom times were never meant to last.

Fires had always been a plague to Au Sable since 1877, when the first mill and salt block were destroyed by an out of control blaze. However, on July 11, 1911, a fire that began in the nearby forest doomed the town. The flames started in the early morning hours and swept in from the surrounding woods to ravage both Au Sable and Oscoda but only one of the towns was destined to survive. Entire blocks of businesses, mills, factories and docks were lost, as well as more than 600 homes.

Five people were killed in the devastation and the entire population was turned into refugees.

Today, there is little remaining of Au Sable, save for stone foundations and forgotten remnants of brick and mortar that has been all but devoured by the forest outside of Oscoda. It is among these ruins in the forest that many believe ghosts still walk. One of them, a young woman named Leona, has been here for decades and has been encountered in the woods on several occasions.

Perhaps the best accounting of this ghost took place in 1979 when a group of local hunters came to a cabin in the nearby woods for a weekend of hunting. One of the hunters got lost and wandered away from the others, becoming quickly disoriented in the heavy forest. He spent several hours wandering and searching for signs of civilization before, exhausted and hungry, he sat down to rest. He heard the crackling of underbrush and a young woman walked out of the forest. She was dressed in a long coat, knitted cap and mittens and she smiled at him and asked him what he was doing there. After he explained that he had become lost, she offered to lead him to safety. She told him that her father owned a farm nearby and she knew the woods quite well. Before long, they had reached the road. The hunter knew his way back to the cabin and he thanked the young woman profusely. She smiled at him- and vanished.

Needless to say, the hunter was stunned and when he told his friends about it, they at first scoffed but then were convinced by his shock and sincerity. They packed up their belongings and started for home, stopping at a local restaurant for dinner and to phone their wives and tell them they were on the way home, They had a beer at the bar and the hunter told of the bartender of his experience with the young woman in the woods. He was not surprised by the tale at all -- he had heard it before.

The young woman's name had been Leona and her family had once had a farm in those woods. Back in 1929, Leona had been shot and killed by a hunter who mistook her for a deer. Since then, her spirit had been seen many times, usually leading lost people out of the forest. She had become sort of a "guardian angel" of the forest and watched over the ruins of Au Sable and over those who came to the place.

DEAD MAN'S CANYON

There are places, scattered across the haunted and wild landscape of America, with ghastly names that are discovered to be surprisingly apt by those who come after the settlers who named them. Dead Man's Canyon, located near Colorado Springs, Colorado is just such a place. Although named posthumously for a man who was slain near Little Fountain Creek, no one could have known at the time that this particular dead man planned to claim the place as his own - and return to prey on travelers who he believed were deserving of his wrath.

William Harkins was a grizzled old mountain man who operated a sawmill in the red rock area along Little Fountain Creek. He was well known to settlers in the region, usually for his gruff demeanor and quick temper, and so most avoided him unless they had lumber that needed cutting. Then one morning in the spring of 1863, his body was discovered just steps away from his cabin. An ax had been buried in his forehead. It was generally believed that a band of Mexican religious fanatics committed the crime, stole Harkin's work horse and robbed his cabin. The murder sent a shockwave through the surrounding region and a posse was soon organized to go in pursuit of the killers. They were tracked and run aground a number of miles to the south and the pursuers hanged the killers on the spot.

Despite the fact that his death was avenged though, the angry spirit of William Harkins remained behind in the canyon where his sawmill had operated. He often walked there alone or in the company of a white, spectral horse. Whenever his specter was seen, the sightings always had at least one thing in common - the ghost was terrifying and had a phantom ax protruding from its forehead. Soon, the valley along Little Fountain Creek began to be known as Dead Man's Canyon and many travelers avoided the area if possible. But not all were lucky enough to do so...

Throughout the 1860's and 1870's, muleskinners and bullwhackers often told tales of being pursued by the ghost of Dead Man's Canyon. The haunted area was part of the Cheyenne Mountain road between Colorado Springs and Canon City. The ghost attacked freighters for miles around the area, while others were plagued only in the canyon itself. On some occasions, the ghost attacked no one and only put in an appearance, as if trying to send a message.

One such unnerving report came from Captain Marshall P. Felch, who passed through the area while searching for a man who had disappeared in the Colorado gold fields. A young woman named Gertrude Osborn had written to Captain Felch to see if he could find her lover, Oliver Kimball, who had come to the California Gulch in search of gold. For more than a year, Miss Osborn and Kimball had corresponded but then his letters had suddenly ceased and she had become increasingly worried about him. Since she lived in the east, but knew Felch and his wife, who lived in Denver, she asked her family friend and her husband to go and look for the young man.

Felch had no luck finding Kimball in the California Gulch but he did learn the name of his possible mining partner, Dave Griffin. In September 1867, while the captain was in Canon City, he received a letter from his wife that stated that Gertrude had arrived at their Denver home and that he should return at once. The wife related that Miss Osborn had been experiencing terrible nightmares in which Kimball was in a terrible struggle with a man who had slashed and stabbed him. She described the scene in minute detail and Captain Felch recognized the surroundings in her dreams as Dead Man's Canyon - a place that she had never been before. And to make matters worse, Gertrude had come to believe that she would die at the same moment that her lover's body was discovered.

Felch set off right away from Canon City but was soon caught in a storm. He waited until it had passed before riding on but this caused him to arrive in Dead Man's Canyon after dark. He experienced a feeling of horrible dread as he rode along the shadowy trail and for a moment, believed that he caught the odor of rotting flesh. "Do not imagine that this occasioned me any nervousness," he later wrote. "I had too lately been in the army and slept among the dead to feel any timidity."

As Felch rode down the trail, he was finally startled by the place. Passing a dark stand of trees, a white horse emerged from them and galloped past, thundering along the trail to a dilapidated cabin. As the horse approached, it suddenly vanished and Felch knew that he had witnessed a supernatural creature. No sooner had the horse disappeared then an old man appeared from the cabin, accompanied by a dog. The man said nothing but looked at Felch and then started off up a trail into the canyon. Curious, Felch followed and then witnessed the strange vision of two men struggling. One of them fell to the ground and they both vanished. When Captain Felch looked around for his guide, and the spectral dog, he realized that they too had disappeared.

The following morning, Felch returned to the site with the son of a local rancher. As they looked through a rocky area where the Captain had seen the two men struggling, they found a patch of what appeared to be freshly turned dirt. They dug up the body of Oliver Kimball, who was wearing a watch with his name inscribed on it. Buried between his ribs was a dagger that bore the scratched letters of "D.G.", which likely belonged to his mining partner, Dave Griffin. The unfortunate young man was buried in a local cemetery and Captain Felch returned home to Denver.

When he arrived there however, his wife informed him that Gertrude Osborn had died the previous night, muttering that her "darling was found at last" and that she was going to join him. Later, the captain returned to the California Gulch and tracked down Dave Griffin, planning to turn him over to the authorities. When he told him that he had found the body of Oliver Kimball, Griffin went to his cabin and shot himself in the head.

Justice had been served.

But the ghost of William Harkins was rarely as congenial as he was to Captain Felch. Perhaps he assisted the man because he knew that the death of another undeserving person could be avenged or for some other reason that remains mysterious. On most occasions, the ghost of Dead Man's Canyon was anything but welcoming.

On a late autumn night in 1874, J.P Galloway had the misfortune to pass through Dead Man's Canyon on his way to Colorado Springs, which lay just ten miles to the north. As he rode along, he passed a red rock cliff that was surrounded by a dense thicket of scrub oak and his horse balked, refusing to take another step. Galloway looked around toward the forest on the ridge and then down to the cottonwoods near the creek but could see nothing out of the ordinary. The horse seemed to sense that something strange was nearby but his rider could see nothing. He tried to urge the horse forward but it refused to move until suddenly. a dry rustling sound disturbed the thicket behind Galloway and he whipped the horse's flank in fear. The animal bolted, pitching the man into the waters of the creek. As Galloway scrambled to his feet, he saw a dreadful figure approaching him from the gloom.

The white and transparent form of a bearded man came out of the thicket. As he swooped out of the bushes, Galloway could see an ax was embedded into the man's skull. He came straight at the rider and Galloway shot at the specter with his revolver but onward it came, roaring with insane laughter. He could only scream as the apparition passed directly through him, seizing his body with an ice cold chill, and his helpless cries echoed through the stone canyon.

The terrified screams were heard a short distance away by two men, Lawrence Poole and Adam T. Baker, who were also passing through Dead Man's Canyon. The two riders hurried to the screaming man's assistance. Seeing the phantom in pursuit of Galloway, and believing it to be a highway robber with a peculiar head adornment, Poole immediately seized his rifle and opened fire. Baker had also stopped his horse and jumped down, pulling his revolver and shooting at the ghost as well.

The ghost continued to come at Galloway, knocking him down into the rocks and again drenching him in the stream. As the other men's guns began to boom out their lethal greeting, the phantom turned in their direction and laughed. Confusion and wild shooting followed as the new arrivals realized that the bullets were passing directly through the apparition. After a few more shots were fired, the ghost turned and vanished back into the thicket, leaving Galloway to pull himself up out of the river. Dizzy and shaking, he thanked the men for their help and then fell unconscious at their feet.

Later that night in Colorado Springs, Galloway kept babbling about being attacked by a ghost. The doctor tending to him blamed his rambling and ghost stories on the man's head injury but when he heard the same tale from Poole and Baker, he could contrive no excuse. William Harkins simply refused to rest in peace.

The sightings and bizarre attacks continued on into the 1880's but then eventually, the fears that people had about this place began to be replaced by a feeling that it was all little more than a legend. Yesterday's ghosts draw their power from being remembered and in the absence of memory, they die and are left to fade away. And perhaps this is what happened to the spirit of William Larkin.

The Cheyenne Mountain road is now the paved Highway 115 to Canon City and while Harkin's cabin and his sawmill have long since vanished, the red rocks, scrub oak thickets, cottonwood trees and Little Fountain Creek still survive. Not much has changed here since the days when a ghost walked in Dead Man's Canyon but few travelers who come here remember the tales from long ago. Has the phantom faded into history - or does he still lurk here, waiting for that one unsuspecting passerby on which he can carry out his still seething revenge?

ORDEAL BY HUNGER
HISTORY AND HAUNTINGS OF THE DONNER PARTY

"In prosecuting this journey," warned an 1849 guide book to the West, "the emigrant should never forget that it is one in which time is everything." No truer words would ever be written in regards to the wagon trains that made their way to the mountains, meadows and open ranges of the American West. Time spelled success to most of them and doom to many others in the middle decades of the 1800's. Nothing had prepared most of these travelers for the ordeals of the trail. They had pictured building new homes in the bright, shining lands of the West but the strain of getting there proved to be far worse than any guidebook had hinted at.

Life on the trail was a story of an increasingly difficult adventure, of failing food and water supplies, of bone-wrenching weariness and accumulating miseries of every sort. The pioneers pushed overland, perhaps as slowly as 15 miles each day, and many of them lost sight of the vision that had set them on the road in the first place. Their vision was replaced by only tragic signs of families that had preceded them - the wolf-pawed graves of the dead, the rotting carcasses of mules and oxen, splintered wrecks of abandoned wagons and once precious household items that had been cast away like refuse once the travel became too tough. The weight of their own privations was enough, on occasion, to bring tears to the eyes of the women and to buckle the knees of the men and yet they kept going.

The long trail to the West, from the Missouri River to the West Coast, ran more than 2,000 miles, with constant detours for pasture and water. The distance in miles however, mattered less than the distance in time. It usually took about four and a half months to reach the Far West and the trip became a race against the seasons, in which timing made the difference between success and failure.

Late April or early May was the best time to depart, although the date had to be calculated with care. If the wagon train started too early in the spring, there would not be enough grass on the prairie to graze the cattle. On the other hand, a train that left after other trains had already departed would find campsites marked by trampled grass and fouled water holes. And if there was one thing that all of the guidebooks to western travel agreed on, it was not to get caught in the mountain passes when winter came to the higher elevations. Such a dilemma would bring tragedy and disaster to even the most hardened group of travelers. Time, the pioneers were assured, waits for no man and death comes on swift wings for those who do not heed its warnings.

Westward travel began as early as the 1840's. After the opening of the Oregon Territory in 1846, settlers began to look to the West as a place of new hope and bright futures. One such man was George Donner, a well-to-do farmer from Riverton, Illinois. Donner was no ordinary emigrant, hoping for free land and open range in the West. He had married three times, sired 13 children and now, at the age of 62, was headed for California on a last great adventure. Donner traveled with his third wife, Tamsen, his five youngest children and three wagons. He also brought 12 yoke of oxen, five saddle horses, numerous milk and beef cattle, several hired hands, a dog and $10,000 in bank notes that had been sewn into a quilt. His older brother, Jacob, aged 65, had a similarly affluent train. A Riverton neighbor, James Reed, who farmed and made furniture, along with his wife, mother-in-law and four children, rounded out the leadership of the expedition. Reed, aged 46, also believed in traveling first class and stocked two support wagons with an assortment of fine foods and liquors. His living wagon also came equipped with built-in beds and a stove. The Reeds, Donners and a number of other Illinois residents left Springfield, Illinois by wagon train on April 14, 1846.

The expedition was a disaster from the beginning and the Donners and Reeds made every mistake that travelers could make. Not only did they overload their wagons but they left Springfield too late in the season, at a time when they really should have been heading out from western Missouri. Then, at Fort Bridger, they decided to take an untested route to California.

The party made this decision based on a guidebook that had been published the year before by Lansford Hastings, a zealot for California settlement. He hoped to overthrow California's weak Mexican government by bringing in enough American settlers to start a revolution that would end with himself as president of the new independent republic. His guidebook, written to boost emigration, was the first step in that plan but the Donners and Reeds were completely unaware of this.

The shortcut that Hastings recommended left the main Oregon Trail at Fort Bridger, well before the usual turn to California at Fort Hall. It went directly west across the Wasatch Mountains, down into the Salt Lake Valley and across the Great Basin to join the standard California Trail along the Humboldt River, thus saving a distance of nearly 400 miles. Unbelievably, Hastings had never even taken his own shortcut before publishing the book. He had gone west on the Oregon Trail in 1842.

He never doubted his judgment though and tried the route backwards in 1846, carrying his gear and provisions on pack mules. He had no trouble and arrived at Fort Bridger a few weeks before the Donners. After arriving, he stayed a short time and persuaded a company of 200 emigrants and 66 wagons, guided by an old Indian fighter name Captain George Harlan, to follow him back to California. He was sure that wagons traveling westward would have no more trouble on the route than his mules had experienced coming to the east.

Cutting across the Wasatch Mountains, Hastings led the emigrants through the narrow gorge of the Weber River, a passage so close and treacherous that the wagons had to be pushed and dragged along the riverbed. They moved boulders and hacked away brush and when the riverbed became too narrow, they were forced to hoist the wagons onto the bluffs using block and tackle. On the average, the luckless wagon train moved at a rate of a mile or less each day.

As the wagon train managed to get beyond the mountains and into the Great Basin, the going got even worse. The wagons traveled for two days in the desert without a sign of any water or grass. Many of the oxen simply fell down and refused to get up. Others ran about with a crazed thirst and then died. A number of the wagons were abandoned but they finally made it across the trackless wastes to the Humboldt River. Unfortunately, it took them three weeks longer than the emigrants who had taken the usual route by way of Fort Hall. Rallying what resources they had, the group continued on across another dry stretch to the foot of the Sierra Nevada, hauled the wagons up and down sheer cliffs and arrived in California's Sacramento Valley as the first snow was starting to fall. Miraculously, only one pioneer died in the bungled effort.

The Donners would not be so fortunate.

When they arrived at Fort Bridger and heard that Hastings himself had started down his

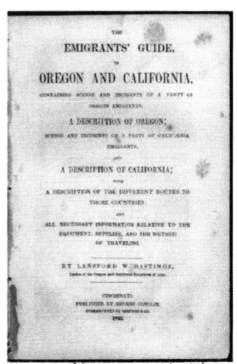

A copy of the Hastings Guidebook that doomed the Donner Party

shortcut with another wagon train, they saw no reason not to follow. By now, a large number of other pioneers had joined their expedition and on July 31, 1846, they set out with a contingent of 74 men, women and children and 20 overloaded wagons.

The party followed the wagon tracks of the earlier company into the Wasatch, where they were joined by 13 other pioneers and three wagons, bringing the total number of the party to 87. Almost immediately though, the expedition got into trouble. They lost four days trying to get through the Weber River gorge, which had been so bothersome for the Harlan party. The Donners decided that it was impassable though and turned back to try and find an alternate path over the mountains. It took them 28 days to reach the Great Salt Lake - a distance of only about 50 miles - but they relentlessly pushed on.

The desert exacted a terrible toll on the Donner party. It took them six days to travel across this wasteland, killed 100 oxen and forced many of the emigrants, including James Reed, to abandon their wagons and supplies. Legend has it that George Donner buried his money somewhere in the desert with plans to return for it, but never did. It is said to still be out there somewhere, long forgotten. By the time the group reached the Humboldt River on September 30, the Harlan party was more than 300 miles away.

Time was now running out for the expedition. Short of food, growing desperate and near the limits of their endurance, the emigrants added to their problems with constant fighting and bickering. On October 5, near the end of a hot day along the Humboldt River, aggravations boiled over. The wagons were stretched out in two units and in the rear unit was John Snyder, a young, well-liked teamster. As he pushed the wagons along, he lashed furiously at some tangled oxen. James Reed, also in the rear, ordered him to stop. Snyder's anger with the oxen shifted to Reed and he threatened the older man with his whip. Reed drew his hunting knife, a move that prompted Snyder to reverse his whip and to begin flailing at Reed with the heavy handle. As the two men grappled, Reed plunged his knife into Snyder's chest and killed him on the spot. The teamster sank to the ground and bled to death.

Those who witnessed the incident were stunned. Snyder had been well-liked and Reed, although acknowledged as one of the leaders of the expedition, was seen as arrogant and aloof. Many of the party members wanted to hang him on the spot. After further deliberation though, the company decided to expel Reed from the wagon train, forcing him to leave his wife and four children with the expedition. Reed then rode ahead to the lead unit, picked up a friend and struck out for California. After enduring days of hunger, the two men found the earlier party led by Hastings. They soon reached Sutter's Fort and began organizing an expedition to fetch Reed's family and to bring food and supplies back to the Donners. Reed was surprisingly forgiving about his ouster from the party and was more concerned with helping his friends than his own feelings.

Far back on the trail though, the emigrants were suffering and near starvation.

Two days after Reed had been expelled, an elderly man named Hardkoop had fallen far behind. By then, many of the wagons had been abandoned and Hardkoop, along with many other men, had been forced to walk across the desert. To weak to keep up and unable to find anyone who would let him ride in a wagon, he had simply given up. No one had the strength to go back and look for him and after some discussion, the emigrants decided that he was expendable and left him to die. A few days later, Patrick Breen, the father of seven children, refused a cup of water to William Eddy, who wanted it for his three year-old son and infant daughter. Threatening to kill Breen, Eddy took the water by force. Two days later, Eddy came to Mrs. Breen and a Mrs. Graves for food for famished children - and they turned him down.

Eleven weeks after leaving Fort Bridger on the Hastings shortcut, the battered remnants of the Donner party reached the meadows along the upper Truckee River, in the eastern shadows of the Sierra Nevada. It was now October 20 and far too late to attempt to cross the mountains. Early winter snows could be seen on the ridges ahead and a briskness was in the night air. The expedition believed they had no choice though and voted to push on. After grazing their emaciated cattle on the lush meadows for five days, they prepared for the final journey across the mountain range.

The trail led about 50 miles into the hills, just beyond Truckee Lake, and then climbed to its highest and most difficult point at Truckee Pass, the last major barrier between the emigrants and the Sacramento Valley. It was vital for the party to cross this pass before more snow made travel impossible.

The first three families to arrive at Truckee Lake were the Patrick Breens, the William Eddys and the Lewis Keseburgs. On October 31, they camped near the lake and in an inch of snow, made the first attempt to cross the pass. By afternoon, they were floundering in five-foot snowdrifts and could make it no further. The three families turned back to the lake and set up camp as a cold rain began to fall. The Breens moved into an abandoned cabin that had been left by earlier pioneers and waited for the other groups to arrive.

On the second day, during a pounding rain, a second group of wagons arrived at the lake. With this party came Charles T. Stanton, a diminutive bachelor who, weeks earlier, had ridden ahead to Sutter's Fort and had returned with food, mules and two Indians to serve as guides. On the morning of November 3, Stanton led another assault on the pass. The storm that had drenched the lake had brought even more snow to the higher elevations though and the wagons

James Reed

quickly bogged down. The party struggled to continue on foot, with adults carrying the children, but only Stanton and one of the Indians reached the summit of the pass. They returned when they saw that the others could not make it. That evening, another storm came up and pelted with sleet and snow, the small party spent the night around a tree that they had cut down and set on fire. When morning came, they retrieved their wagons and descended to Truckee Lake.

By this time, it was plain that they were going to have to settle in at the lake and so shelters began to be constructed. A large lean-to was erected against the old cabin - the Breens continued to claim it as their own and allow no one to share it - and two double cabins were built nearby.

Meanwhile, the far end of the wagon train had troubles of its own. They were stuck in a crude camp about five miles from the lake at Alder Creek. In this group were George Donner, his brother Jacob, their families and hired help and a widow, Mrs. Wolfinger - 21 people in all. George Donner's wagon had broken an axle and they had fallen behind trying to fix it. Even more unlucky was when Donner had gashed his hand while trying to carve a new one and while a small injury, it refused to heal. The storm that had swamped the other members of the expedition at the lake had also hit the Donner party at Alder Creek. They had erected tents and a lean-to that was covered with brush, blankets and clothing and huddled in these fragile shelters, decided to stay put.

The snow continued to fall, on and off, for the next two weeks. When it ended, the emigrants at Truckee Lake made several more attempts to get through the pass but it was to no avail. It had become painfully obvious to everyone that they were imprisoned on the back side of the California mountains and would have to remain there all winter. There were 81 people desperately trapped in the two camps and 41 of them were children.

On the western side of the mountains, James Reed and his rescue party fared no better. They were trying to make their way eastward with food and supplies from Sutter's Fort but were also being bogged down by the snow. The Indian guides had deserted with three of the pack horses and soon the remaining animals dropped from exhaustion and died in the snow. The saddle horses soon gave out as well and for awhile, the men pushed ahead on foot, with a single mule carrying the rest of the supplies. Within a day, they knew that it was useless to go on and they returned to the fort. Captain John Sutter, who had no other men to send, consoled them with the assurance that the Donner party could survive the winter on ox flesh and beef.

By December though, the conditions in both camps were grim. The oxen and cattle, which had been left to range on their own, had wandered off and had died in the deep snow. Their carcasses could not be found and it was realized that the remaining meat would not last until Christmas. A few cups of flour were hoarded to make a thin gruel for the infants and a little sugar, tea and coffee remained, but no salt. The trout in the lake had burrowed in for the winter and refused to bite. The deer had disappeared for the lower elevations but William Eddy shot a coyote one day and an owl the next. He wounded a bear on another day and when it fought him, he valiantly clubbed it to death. The meat did not go far though and the emigrants took to boiling hides and eating the glue that resulted. In one cabin, children cut up a fur rug, toasted it and ate it. At the camp on Alder Creek, water dripped continuously into the shelters and put out the fires that were supposed to keep the occupants warm.

The original attempts to make it through the pass above Truckee Meadows failed miserably -- leaving the expedition stranded for the winter

The deepening winter brought more storms, less to eat - and death. The first to die was Baylis Williams, a hired hand of the Reeds, on December 15. The shock of the young man's death sent a wave of panic through the stranded travelers at Truckee Lake. The following day, a small contingent of the strongest emigrants made another frantic effort to conquer the pass.

Ten men, five young women and two boys - an escape party that called itself "the Forlorn Hope" - set out on snowshoes that had been fashioned from rawhide and hickory oxbows from the wagons. They each carried a blanket and had among them one gun, a couple of pistols, a hatchet and finger-sized strips of meat that were meant to last for six days if each person only ate two strips, three times a day. Stanton and his two Indians led the way, accompanied by William Eddy, "Uncle Billy" Graves, Sarah and Jay Fosdick, Uncle Billy's daughter, Mary, William and Sarah Foster, Lemuel and Billy Murphy, ages 12 and 11, and the recently widowed Harriet Pike. Amanda McCutchen joined them, as she was anxious to see her husband in California, and she left her baby behind, likely in the care of Aunt Betsy Graves. Sarah Foster had left her own child and Harriet Pike had left two. It was a heartbreaking decision to do so, but it would have been impossible to carry young children through the snow. The remainder of the party included Dutch Charley

Burger, Antoine the herder, and Patrick Dolan.

The Forlorn Hope started off in single file, the leaders breaking a trail for the others. Even with the snowshoes though, they sank halfway to their knees with each step. There were also not enough snowshoes to go around, so Burger and the two Murphy boys brought up the rear, carefully stepping in the tracks left by the others. The snow rarely held them and they found themselves often stumbling and floundering in the drifts. They only made it four miles on the first day and young Billy Murphy gave out and decided to head back. Dutch Charley gave up too but no one noticed his absence for some time. They assumed that he had headed back with Billy but he actually got lost. He did make it back to the lake, but a day after the boy did.

They valiantly made it to the top of the pass and after traveling six miles, were too exhausted to go any further. The snow at their campsite was 12 feet deep but the Forlorn Hope knew how to make a fire in such conditions. The trick was to cut down two green saplings and lay them parallel on the snow a few feet apart. More green wood was placed across them to make a platform and then the fire was built on top of this. As long as someone kept the fire going all night, the travelers could stay warm in their tents, even with only one paltry blanket each.

As they climbed over the pass on December 18, they reached the open, downward slope. They traveled only short distances at a time, blinded by the glare of the sun on the snow. Stanton, the worst affected by the glare, began to fall behind. He would often wander into the camp each night after sunset. Since he was the only one among them who actually knew the trail, his misfortune affected all of them.

By now, the travelers were not only horribly starved but close to mental unbalance as well. They began to hallucinate as they dragged themselves through the snow, hearing strange sounds, eerie cries in the woods and seeing driftless shapes that appeared and then disappeared before their eyes. They began to believe that the ghosts of those who had died on the expedition already were calling to them.

On the morning of the sixth day, the last for which the party had food, Stanton sat by the campfire as the group prepared to move on. He was asked if he was coming and he answered that he was coming soon and would catch up later. The Forlorn Hope started off, guided rather uncertainly by the Indians, who had only been on the trail once and when there was no snow on the ground. As it turned out, the Indians took them in the wrong direction, which would cost them many painful days and miles, and they would not realize just how lost they were for more than a week. That night, they used up the last of the beef strips and waited for Stanton to come in to the warmth of the campfire - but he never arrived.

The next day, they traveled only about a mile when snow began to fall. They stopped and made camp and spent the day with no food, again waiting for Stanton. They waited and waited but the little man still did not come staggering in through the snow. By nightfall, they gave him up for dead. A gentleman and a hero to the very end, Stanton had sacrificed his own life rather than endanger the life of his friends by holding them back.

The following day, December 23, they climbed the barren, rocky surface of Cisco Butte, the highest point in the area, and tried to get their bearings. Without Stanton to guide them, they had to plot their own route. The easiest way appeared to be toward the south, where the mountains looked less fierce than in other directions. Unfortunately, this led them badly off the trail but they had no way of knowing this at the time. The party continued on and survived by subsisting on a half pound of bear meat that Eddy's wife had secretly placed in his pack. She had deprived herself and her children to provide extra food for the expedition.

Back at the lake, where the last of the livestock had been slaughtered and eaten, the miserable families gnawed on boiled hides and bones that had been seasoned with pepper. Margaret Reed, accustomed to the comforts of her family wealth, killed the family dog, Cash, to feed her four children. They ate everything they could from his carcass and lived on the animal for an entire week.

Meanwhile, the snowshoe party struggled down the west face of the mountain through a series of horrific snowstorms. For several days, they were totally without

The heroic Charles Stanton

food and shortly after, a series of gruesome events began - events that would earn the Donner party a unique place in the annals of the West.

The painful journey continued on Christmas Eve and another foot of snow fell. They limped along for two or three miles before finally sitting down to hold a meeting. All of the men except for Eddy wanted to give up and return to the camp at Truckee Lake but he argued that this was a foolish and suicidal plan. They had not eaten for two days and in their weakened state, would die before they made it back. Eddy, along with the women, stood firm on this and vowed to go through with the mission or die.

Finally, Patrick Dolan, a once carefree bachelor, voiced a thought that had crossed all of their minds - that one of them might die to save the rest. Dolan proposed that they draw lots to determine who might be killed so that the others could eat but William Foster opposed this plan, not wanting to take the risk that he might draw the bad lot. Eddy offered a compromise, suggesting that two of the men take revolvers and shoot it out until one of them died. This sporting proposition was also voted down. Eddy then spoke up again and offered that perhaps they should let nature take its course and continue on until someone died. After some argument, the others agreed and they staggered on into the storm for another few miles.

The night that followed this miserable day was one of disaster. First, the snow and wind made it almost impossible to get a fire started. When the flame at last caught, the travelers piled enough wood on it to make a blazing bonfire - if they had nothing to cook and eat, they could at least be warm. But one of them did not enjoy it for long. Antoine, the cattle herder, lay in an exhausted slumber near the fire and in his sleep, he flung out an arm and his hand landed in the hot coals. Eddy saw it happen but was too tired to move and help the sleeping young man. Unable to move, he thought sure that the heat from the burns would wake the man but they did not. Antoine was so bone-weary that he continued to sleep and his hand doubled up and began to roast. This was more than Eddy could bear and he flung himself forward to pull the unconscious herder from danger. Antoine soon flung out his arm again and Eddy realized that it was no use to help him, Antoine died without ever awakening from what, under normal circumstances, would have been intense pain.

Shortly after this, a terrible storm of wind, snow and hail swept down upon the camp. At the same time, the fire began to eat its way down into the snow, devouring the blazing logs, platform and all. When the supply of firewood ran out, one of the men took the party's lone hatchet and went to cut more wood. But as he chopped at a log, the head flew off of it and was lost to the depths of the snow. It was impossible to find in the darkness of the storm, even if he had managed the strength to dig for it.

One small piece of luck occurred when the fire kept burning. It was shielded from the snow by the shelter that it had melted itself into, about eight feet below the surface of the snow. The emigrants were forced to crouch around it with their feet in ice-cold melted water. They knew that the fire would soon sputter out in the water though so a few of them stood the half-burned foundation logs on end and built the fire on top of it. At this point, one of the Indians stood up to get closer to the warmth and clumsy with cold and weariness, lurched against the new platform. The rickety structure fell over and the fire hissed out in the icy pool of water they were standing in. It looked as though they were finally doomed to perish in the cold. Despair set in and everyone began to pray to God for a merciful death - except for Eddy and one or two of the women.

Eddy, always resourceful, finally persuaded his companions to try a trick that he had heard about from someone on the trail. He prodded them all out of the pit made by the fire and made them spread their blankets on the surface of the snow. They then sat on their blankets in a tight circle with the feet in the center while Eddy dragged himself across the circle and spread other blankets over them. He then slipped into the circle himself and the blankets, with the snow that fell on top of them, formed a snug, insulating tent that held in their body heat and kept them warm. It was simple enough to do but some of the emigrants were so apathetic that it took Eddy nearly an hour to bully them into position. Uncle Billy Graves had been growing weaker throughout the evening and he now told Eddy that he was dying. With his last words, he urged his daughters to eat his body when he was gone. He knew that it was the only way that they could survive.

The next day, on Christmas, Patrick Dolan also died. As a storm raged outside their tent of blankets, Dolan became delirious and began to babble incoherently. He then pulled off his boots and most of his clothing and shouted to Eddy to follow him down to the settlements - they would be there in just a few hours, he promised. With great difficulty, the others managed to overpower him and subdue him under the blankets. He thrashed about as they held him down and eventually, his energy exhausted, he became quiet. He drifted into death, his companions later said, looking as he was enjoying a calm and pleasant sleep.

On December 26, Eddy tried to start a fire under the blanket tent with gunpowder but his cold, weak hands were clumsy and a spark caused his powder horn to explode, burning his face and hands. Amanda McCutchen and Sarah Foster were also burned, but not seriously. The burns did not stop Eddy from creeping out from under the tent later that afternoon. The storm had passed by now and as he looked around, he discovered a huge, dead pine tree standing nearby. Using some scraps from the cotton lining of Harriet Pike's coat as tinder, he started a small fire with sparks from flint and steel and soon was able to set fire to the pine tree. The emigrants lay down around the burning tree to enjoy the warmth and were too weak and uncaring to dodge the big, burning limbs that began falling in their midst. Luckily, no one was injured.

As the day wore on, the survivors huddled under their blankets, close to the fire, half-crazed with hunger but unable to take that final step toward cannibalism. Finally ,that afternoon, they gave in. Unable to look one another in the eye, they began to roast and eat strips of flesh from Dolan's body. Only Eddy and the two Indians, overcome by guilt and grief, refused to take part in the feast. The others dried what they did not eat and saved it for later. Within days, Eddy and the Indians, now almost mad from a lack of food, surrendered and ate some of the meat.

The depleted survivors stayed at this site for the next four days and more death followed. Sarah Murphy Foster and Harriet Murphy Pike tried to feed a little of Dolan's flesh to their little brother, Lemuel, but he was beyond hope by this time. He grew steadily weaker and then died in the early morning hours with his head in Sarah's lap. The living members of the Forlorn Hope were not far from death themselves and looked like walking skeletons. They had resigned themselves to dying. When Eddy, hiding his own fears, tried to cheer them up, they responded only with sighs, tears and moans. But the meal of human flesh, as loathsome as it

William Eddy -- leader of the Forlorn Hope

was, had given them new strength. The women regained a bit of spirit but most of the men continued to sulk.

On December 30, the Forlorn Hope left the Camp of Death, as they called the spot, and moved on. They carried with them the dried pieces of meat that had been carved from their dead friends and relatives. Although the first taboo against eating human flesh had been broken, no one touched the meat that had been carved from his or her own kin. The group struggled down the trail, barely able to walk at all. Their feet had become so swollen that their skin had burst. They had wrapped their feet in rags to try and cushion them but the pain was so bad that the expedition could only travel short distances at a time.

On December 31, they traveled along a high-crested ridge and somehow, had accidentally blundered back onto the trail that Charley Stanton had started them on. The Indians had confessed to Eddy a few days earlier that they were lost but he chose not to tell the others, believing they had no choice but to continue on. But while the party was back on the right track, it was the most terrifying portion of the journey so far. They walked along the edges of icy, rock-strewn cliffs and crossed ravines on fragile bridges of snow. They teetered precariously on their clumsy snowshoes but their luck held out. After what seemed like an eternity of picking their way along, they reached a high point on the ridge and paused for the view. In the distance, to the west, they could see the vast, green plain of the Sacramento Valley - but their joy was dampened by the mountains and canyons that still lay in their path. Subdued, but not broken, they continued on.

Late that afternoon, they made it to the end of the ridge. Before them was a slope that plunged to a canyon bottom that was 2,000 or more feet below. They could see that the canyon on the left made a bend below them and joined the canyon on their right. Unable to continue on that day, they made camp.

New Year's Day 1847 brought the emigrants no more cheer than Christmas had - - save for the fact that there were no storms and no one died. The entire day was spent negotiating the canyon. They worked their way down the slope but squatting on their snowshoes and sliding down to the bottom, usually ending up in a snowdrift. The fierce cold had frozen the water below, the Bear River, and they were able to cross it without difficulty. Climbing up the other side of the canyon was a nightmarish task. For the first 50 feet or so, the hunger-weakened men and women had to cling to cracks in the rock to keep from tumbling back down the steep slope.

As it became less vertical, they dug their snowshoes into the snow and stair-stepped upwards, moving slowly and leaving blood from their damaged feet behind them on the trail. That night, after making camp, they ate the last of the human flesh they had brought with them.

They spent the next two days crossing a broad plateau over mostly level ground. The snow was firm enough that they could walk on it without their snowshoes but their feet could not heal while walking in the snow. To make matters worse, Jay Fosdick had become sick and his weakness forced the whole group to move slowly. One of the Indians was in even worse condition and his frostbitten toes began to drop off at the first joint.

Things began to look more encouraging on January 3. The snow remained firm and it looked like they were coming down from the upper elevations as oaks could now be seen among the conifer trees. When they camped that night, the snow was only three feet deep, which was a cause for celebration. Believing that they would no longer need their snowshoes, they toasted the rawhide strings that held them together and ate them for dinner. Eddy also cooked a pair of worn-out moccasins and shared them with the group.

They set out again the next day with no food and Fosdick was now so weak that they were only able to travel about two miles. The only good news was that they camped that night for the first time on bare ground and in a grove of oak trees. After several days without food, William Foster proposed killing the two Indians so that the rest of the party could eat. To most white Westerners, an Indian was not quite human and so no one was shocked by the suggestion except for William Eddy, who was adamantly against it. To him, the two young men were not only fellow human beings, but faithful companions. To kill them would be an unjust reward for them having brought food over the Sierra Nevada with Charley Stanton a short time before. He argued with the others and realizing that he could not change their minds, he secretly warned the two young men and horrified, they vanished into the forest.

The Forlorn Hope still had its lone rifle and a meager supply of ammunition, so Eddy became determined to take the gun and go hunting. If he had some luck, he knew, he could save the lives of his remaining companions but if not, they were no worse off. However, when he mentioned his plan to the women, they wept and begged him to stay with them, realizing that without him they would be lost. But Eddy's mind was made up and he started off the next morning. Harriet Pike threw her arms around his neck and implored him not to go. The others joined in, convinced that he was actually abandoning them and not coming back. But the once beautiful and now emaciated Mary Graves decided to accompany Eddy. She was the only one left who was strong enough to keep up with him.

They trudged through the forest for more than two miles, always keeping an eye out for a sign of deer. Eddy was an experienced hunter and when he caught sight of a place where an animal had laid for the night, he burst into tears. When he explained what he had found to Mary, she also began to weep. They continued on and, not much further into the woods, they saw a large buck. Eddy raised the gun but found to his dismay that he was too weak to aim it. As much as he tried to hold it still, the gun wavered back and forth and dipped too low to fire. He changed his grip and tried again but failed once more. He heard Mary sobbing behind him. Eddy whispered for her to be quiet and she explained, "Oh, I am afraid that you will not kill it." Then, she fell silent.

Once more, Eddy lifted the rifle to his shoulder and raised the muzzle above the deer. As his weak arms started to let it fall, he pulled the trigger with the deer in his sights. The rifle thundered and the deer leaped three feet into the air and stood still. Although Mary feared that he had missed it, Eddy knew that his aim had been true. The deer dropped its tail between its legs, a sign that it was wounded, and began to run. Eddy and Mary limped after it and then it crashed to the ground about 200 yards away. The animal was still alive when Eddy reached it and he pounced with his knife and cut the deer's throat. Mary fell to Eddy's side and the two famished survivors drank as the animal's warm blood gushed out.

They rested a bit and then rolled the carcass to a spot where they could butcher it. They built a fire, with their faces still covered with blood, and ate part of the deer's liver and organs for supper. They gorged themselves on the heavy meat and that night, for the first time in many days, they enjoyed sleep without dreams of food. During the night, Eddy fired his gun several times to alert their companions and at the camp, Fosdick heard the first crack and knew what it meant. "Eddy has killed a deer!" he weakly cried. "Now, if only I can get to him, I shall live."

But Fosdick's hopes were not meant to be. He died during the night and Sarah, his wife for less than a year, wept as she wrapped his body in their one remaining blanket and lay down on the bare ground to die herself. Somehow though, she managed to survive the frigid night and in the morning, felt better. To her horror though, she saw two of her traveling companions -- likely William and Sarah Foster, although no records ever stated for sure -- approach her campsite to make sure that she and her husband had both died during the night. They planned to help themselves to not only their flesh, but their jewelry, money and watches as well. Embarrassed at finding Sarah still alive though, they turned back to their own campsite and there met Mary and Eddy, who had emerged from the forest with venison for everyone.

As Eddy dried the remaining meat on the fire, Sarah and the two Fosters returned to Jay Fosdick's body. Sarah gave him one last kiss and then in spite of her entreaties, the Fosters, now numb to the atrocities they were committing, cut out Jay's heart and liver before her eyes and also took his arms and legs, the meatiest parts of the body. The young widow, only 22 years-old, made a little bundle of her valuables and returned to the campfire with the two people who had just callously butchered her husband. Uncaring, they skewered Jay's heart on a stick and began to roast it in the fire as Sarah looked on. When she could stand it no more, she fled to Eddy's campsite, which was a short distance away.

Over the next couple of days, the survivors made it to the north branch of the American River and crossed it. They had to climb another steep canyon wall on the other side but when they made camp that night, they were cheered by the fact that the weather was good and sat down peacefully to eat the last of the venison. Eddy made a speech, mourning their lost companions -- tactfully avoiding the fact that they had been eaten by the remaining members of the Forlorn Hope.

After supper, William Foster took Eddy aside. From the time of the first hardship experience by the group, Foster had been strangely unhelpful and weak, unable to make a decision on his own and totally dependent on Eddy. Suddenly, seized by an initiative, he wanted Eddy's approval to kill Amanda McCutchen. His excuse was that she was a nuisance and could not keep up but in truth, he had acquired a taste for flesh and deep down, his guilt over it had driven him mad.

Needless to say, Eddy was shocked and revolted. He told Foster that the young woman had a husband and children and besides that, she was one of their companions and depended on them for protection. Foster continued to argue until Eddy told him sternly that he was not going to kill her. Foster than turned to the sisters, Sarah Fosdick and Mary Graves. He pointed out that neither of the women had a child and Sarah no longer had a husband. At that, Eddy walked away from the man and returned to the fire. He loudly warned Sarah and Mary of Foster's plans for them in front of the entire company.

At that, Foster became angry and said that he did not care what Eddy said for he could do whatever he wanted. Eddy, losing patience, challenged Foster to settle their differences on the spot. He grabbed a large stick, banged it on a log to see that it was solid and then tossed it to Foster, ordering him to defend himself. Sarah Fosdick gave him her late husband's knife and Eddy went for Foster as quickly as his condition would permit. Eddy was ready to kill him when all of the women but Sarah, two of whom Foster had just proposed to kill and eat, seized Eddy and dragged him to the ground. They took his knife away but luckily, Foster just stood there in a daze and missed his chance to kill Eddy.

When Eddy recovered, he warned Foster once more that he would kill him if he ever again showed the slightest inclination to take the life of any member of the expedition. If anyone were to die, it would either be Foster or himself, he said. And they would settle the question in a fight to the death, since Foster had never been willing to draw lots, a way that Eddy believed was the only fair way of selecting a victim.

On January 8, they left the campsite and continued on. They had walked about two miles before coming on the bloody tracks of the Indian guides who had wisely deserted them some time back. Foster, now obviously deranged, vowed that he would track down the Indians and kill them. Another mile or two further on though, they found the two men on the trail, near death. Eddy wanted to let them die in peace, for they could not last more than an hour or two, but Foster, now in an almost manic state, refused to wait. He shot the two Indians in the head and then butchered their bodies. He cut the flesh from their bones and dried it over the fire.

That night, Eddy ate only dried grass, refusing to eat the flesh of the Indians. And from that night on, only Foster's wife and Harriet Pike camped with Foster. The others kept a safe distance away and one of them remained on watch at all times, afraid of what their former friend might do next.

As they continued on and passed through the forests, they saw numerous deer but Eddy was too weak that he could no longer aim the rifle at all. He was still living on nothing but handfuls of grass as he refused to touch the meat taken from his Indian companions. They all staggered as they walked and were so weakened and weary that they could only travel for a quarter mile or so before they had to stop and rest. The slightest obstacles would cause them to stumble and fall. A cold rain began to fall on the wretched wraith-like figures and did not stop.

At last, on January 12, they reached an Indian village in the foothills. The occupants, when they saw these skeletal figures, wrapped in rags, burst into tears of pity. They hurried to bring the survivors their own staple food of acorn breads but the emigrants stomachs were unable to handle it and many of them got sick. Eddy was forced to go back to easting grass. The next day, the village chief sent runners ahead to a nearby encampment and told them to take care of the travelers and to have food for them. An escort accompanied them and two Indians walked with each of the party to support them and help them along. In this way, they passed from village to village toward the white settlements.

On January 17, they reached a village and one of the men had collected a large handful of pine nuts. For some reason, after eating them, Eddy felt miraculously restored and with this new energy, he pushed his comrades on. But the others gave out after a mile and collapsed on the ground, ready to die. The Indians were greatly distressed but were unable to get them to continue.

All Eddy could think about though was his wife and children starving in the mountains and he resolved to make it through or die trying. One of the local Indians agreed to accompany him to the closest white settlement but after five miles, Eddy's strength gave out. As it happened though, another Indian passed by and Eddy prevailed on him to join them in return for some tobacco. They managed to make it another five miles before Eddy collapsed again, this time for good. His strength had completely failed but the Indians half-carried him along, dragging his bleeding feet along the ground.

At about a half hour before sunset, Eddy, starved beyond the point of recognition, came upon the home of a settler named M.D. Ritchie, who had arrived late in the fall of 1846 and had built a cabin on Johnson's ranch to winter in. Several other emigrants, who planned to claim their own spreads in the spring, lived in other winter quarters nearby. Ritchie's daughter, Harriet, heard a noise outside of the house and went to the door. There, she saw two Indians supporting a hideous-looking bundle between them. The shape lifted its head and, speaking in English, asked her for some bread. Harriet burst into tears and let the Indians bring Eddy into the house. Her family instantly put him to bed, fed him and heard his story. He remained in bed for four days, too beaten to even turn over. He had traveled 18 miles on foot that day and he had been on the trail for 31 days.

Harriet Ritchie ran immediately to the neighbors with the news of starving travelers on the trail behind Eddy. The women collected all of the bread they could spare and added sugar, tea and coffee to go with the beef that had been butchered from California's immense herds. The men rode back and forth between the cabins bearing messages and collecting food. Four men took backpacks that were loaded with as much food as they could carry and set off on foot, for they did not want to risk their horses by riding at night. They were guided by the Indians and found the remaining members of the Forlorn Hope around midnight. One man stayed up all night cooking for them. Eddy had warned the rescue party not to give them too much to eat but the survivors wept and begged for food so pathetically that they could not deny them. As a result, the gorging caused all of them to vomit.

In the morning, more men came with food, this time on horseback. They had no trouble following the trail for the last six miles was marked by Eddy's bloody footprints. The rescuers could not believe that he had covered such a distance, amazed at what had to have been a superhuman effort.

That night, the rest of the party was brought down into the California settlements. Of the 17 people who had left the lake camp a month earlier, only Eddy, Foster and five of the women had come down from the mountains alive.

A massive rescue operation was organized to try and reach the emigrants who were on the other side of the mountains at Alder Creek and Truckee Lake. On February 4, the first expedition started out and began a journey into the mountains. Eddy, whose wife and children were still at the lake, started out with the rescuers but his ordeal had left him so weak and emaciated that he was forced to turn back. Two weeks later, the relief team reached the encampment with packs filled with food. A woman staggered out from one of the cabins and cried "Are you from California or Heaven?"

The situation at the two camps was hideous. Thirteen people had died, including Eddy's wife and daughter. At the Alder Creek camp, Jake Donner and three of his hired men were dead. George Donner lay dying as the wound on his hand had become infested with gangrene. Many of those still living were on the verge of insanity. Cannibalism had become commonplace here as well. The emigrants had no other food at their disposal and after some brief objections, began eating the dead. It was almost too much for most of them to bear.

The rescuers headed back to California with 21 people, as many as they could safely take. Tamsen Donner refused to leave her dying husband and Mrs. Reed was forced to leave her son, Tommy, behind, as he was still too weak to travel. Young Patty Reed stayed behind to take care of him. "If I do not see you again, Mother, " she said, "do the best you can."

Halfway down the west side of the Sierra Nevada, the first relief party met a second band of rescuers, this one led by James Reed. After spending only a few minutes with his wife and the two children she had managed to bring with her, he continued on to the east. Reed's party gathered up 17 more survivors from the Alder Creek and lake encampments, most of them children, but almost as soon as they crossed the pass, a storm struck and snowed them in for two days and three nights. The fire they had built sank into the snow and was snuffed out and soon, the food supply was gone. Isaac Donner, who was only five years-old, died during one dark night.

When the storm finally passed, Reed tried to get the party moving again but the Breen and the Graves family refused to go on. He had to leave them behind in a crude, snowy encampment, where they remained for six days until they were found by a third relief party from California. By that time, Elizabeth Graves and her son Franklin were also dead. Parts of their bodies were found boiling in pots when the rescuers arrived and Elizabeth's infant daughter was discovered wailing next to her mother's half-eaten corpse.

In this new rescue party was William Eddy and surprisingly, William Foster. They had both recovered from their journey and Foster had also recovered from the madness that had gripped him on the trail and had repaired his friendship with Eddy. Both men had come back because they had left children behind at the lake camp and hoped to save them. Unfortunately, they were too late. When they arrived, they were informed by Lewis Keseberg, a German immigrant and member of the party, that he had eaten Eddy and Foster's sons. Grief stuck, the two men collected George Donner's children and quickly departed. Donner, unable to walk, stayed behind to die and Tamsen stayed with him. Lavina Murphy, nearly blind, stayed with Keseberg, whose wife had left with the first rescue team.

George Donner died on the night of March 29 and it was said that Tamsen went mad with grief. She ran all of the way from Alder Creek to the lake cabins to see if anyone there was left alive. On the way there, she fell into a stream and her clothing froze. Shivering and weak, she managed to make it to the cabins, where she found Keseberg. When she arrived, she was coughing and sick and burning up with fever. She told Keseberg that she had to see her children in California and she was willing to cross the mountains on foot, at that very moment, if necessary. The German realized how sick she was and put her to bed in the cabin.

When a fourth relief expedition arrived at Truckee Lake in April, the only survivor was the emaciated and spectral Keseberg. He was found lying unconscious next to a large pot that contained the liver and lungs of a young boy. He had been living on nothing but human flesh -- despite the fact that some supplies did remain from the earlier rescue parties. There were also whole cattle that had been lost in the winter storms that were now thawing in the melting snow. Their meat was untouched because, as Keseberg explained to his rescuers, the oxen meat was "too dry eating." The German's mind was obviously completely gone by now. He was eventually charged with six murders but was reunited with his wife and settled in Sacramento.

The Reeds later settled in the area outside what would become San Francisco. Margaret Reed lived in relative peace and happiness until she died in poor health, several years later.

William Eddy, the hero of the Forlorn Hope, remarried and had children in Petaluma, California.

The Donner children were left as orphans. Some of the younger Donner children were adopted by various families, while the older girls, as young as 14, married young Californians for financial support. The remaining Graves suffered a similar fate as the Donners. The more fortunate were adopted, while some had to survive without any home or family of their own. Sarah Fosdick later remarried, and she and her sister, Mary Graves, tried to support and care for their younger siblings when they could.

The various families of the Donner Party almost never saw each other after they were rescued but it's easy to understand why. They had endured a horrific experience and during the ordeal had engaged in what is still considered as one of the greatest human atrocities - cannibalism. Some of the survivors lived as unhappy recluses, while some like William and Mary Graves, Virginia Reed, and Eliza Donner published accounts describing their ordeal. Virginia Reed was even featured in a magazine in 1891.

Eventually, the cabins, shelters and bodies left behind at Alder Creek and Truckee Lake were erased by time. The chilling reminders of the Donner Party encouraged settlers to hurry along the trail for years to come, avoiding untested shortcuts, until the railroads put an end to the Oregon and California Trail. Time -- that great enemy of the Western emigrants -- defeated the physical remnants of the Donner Party's suffering but it could not erase the memories.

Of the 81 travelers who had made camp east of the pass on the night of October 31, only 47 of them survived. The area around Truckee Lake, later renamed Donner Lake, became known as a shunned and cursed place - and is it any wonder? Who could find a better place for a haunting?

As the years have passed, the legends of the lake state that the restless ghosts of the doomed expedition still wail and cry in fear and starvation here. There have been many tales told of emigrants who, not knowing what had occurred in the ruined cabins along the lakeshore, stayed the night before crossing the pass and experienced the phantoms of those who died, or were murdered, years before. These same stories tell of mournful wails and ghostly figures whose confused spirits still roam the area.

Many years after the horrible events, the ruins at the site were turned into a monument of sorts to the tragedy that occurred. The crumbling stone walls of the Murphy cabin were marked with a monument, as were the sites of the Breen and Keseberg shelters. It is near the Keseberg cabin that an inordinate amount of strange activity has been reported over the years. Many believe that it may be the ghost of Tamsen Donner who lingers here, perhaps because of the mystery surrounding her cause of death. According to Lewis Keseberg, she had come to the shelter already sick from a fever, likely caught after falling into the creek and then running through the cold woods at night. Keseberg would later admit to cannibalizing Tamsen but some believe that he may have murdered her, rather than wait for her to die. He was charged with her murder but the case never went to trial. Eliza Donner always believed Keseberg's story that her mother had died from the fever but the truth will never be known for sure.

These unanswered questions are what allegedly cause Tamsen's spirit to continue to walk. In recent years, there have been reports of an apparitions sighted here that looks like a woman dressed in white. In addition, ghost researchers have also recorded voices and sounds with recording devices that sound like a woman weeping. Could these sounds be the voice of Tamsen Donner, still crying out from the other side?

Another active site is the former location of the Murphy cabin. It is long gone now but a large stone does remain that was used as a fireplace wall. This has long been thought to be the most eerie location in what is now a state park, dedicated to the Donner Party.

A number of years ago, while living in Utah, I took a trip to Donner Lake to see where the ill-fated expedition came to an end. I had been interested in the story of the emigrants, lost in the wild, for quite some time and the promise of ghostly activity made the trip all the more inviting. As it turned out though, my night at the lakeside camp was without incident - and perhaps that was for the best.

I would be hard-pressed to think of a group of people who more deserved to rest in peace. The horrible days that they endured at the lake, and along the trail to the Sacramento Valley, were terrible enough that they should not be subjected to an endless purgatory here on earth. I would hate to think that the spirits of heroic figures like William Eddy or Charles Stanton are still lost out there, somewhere in the wilderness, forced to repeat their most hellish days over and over again.

Perhaps some ghost stories, and the ghosts who create them, just deserve to fade away.

SUGGESTIONS FOR OUTFIT

BY STEWART EDWARD WHITE
From his book THE FOREST (1903)

In replies to inquiries as to necessary outfit for camping and woods-traveling, the author furnishes the following lists ---

1. PROVISIONS PER MAN, ONE WEEK:

7 lbs, flour; 5 lbs.. Pork; 1-5 lbs. Tea; 2 lbs beans, 1 - 2 lbs. Sugar; 1-2 lbs rice; 1-2 lbs prunes and raisins; 1 pound lard; 1 pound oatmeal; baking powder; matches; soap, pepper; salt; 3 lbs. Tobacco; Weight --- a little over 20 lbs). This will last much longer if you get game and fish.

2. PACK ONE, OR ABSOLUTE NECESSITIES FOR HARD TRIP

Wear hat; suit woolen underwear; shirt; trousers; socks; silk handkerchief; cotton handkerchief; moccasins.
 Carry sweater; extra drawers; 2 extra pairs of socks; gloves (buckskin); towel; 2 extra pairs of moccasins; surgeon's plaster; laxative; pistol and cartridges; fishing tackle; blanket; rubber blanket; tent; small axe; knife; mosquito dope; compass; match box; tooth brush; comb; small whetstone; 2 tin or aluminum pails; frying pan; cup; knife, fork and spoon

Whole pack under 50 lbs. In case of two or more people, each pack would be lighter, as tent, tinware, etc. would do for both

3. PACK TWO -- FOR LUXURIES & EASY TRIPS -- EXTRA TO PACK ONE

More fishing tackle; camera, 1 more pair of socks; 1 more set of underclothes; extra sweater; wading shoes of canvas; large axe; mosquito net; mending materials; kettle; candles; more cooking utensils; extra shirt; whiskey

SELECT BIBLIOGRAPHY AND SUGGESTED READING

Allen, Robert Joseph - The Story of the Superstition Mountain & The Lost Dutchman Mine (1971)

Allen, Stewart - Forest of Disappearing Children (Fate Magazine - July 1961)

Aron, Paul - Unsolved Mysteries of American History (1997)

Ayres, Artie - Traces of Silver (1982)

Banks, Leo - Wandering Soul (Tucson Weekly - 1997)

Barnard, Barney - Superstition Mountain & Its Famed Lost Dutchman Mine (1964)

Bell, Horace - On the Old West Coast (1930)

Blackman, W. Haden - Field Guide to North American Hauntings (1998)

Blackman, W. Haden - Field Guide to North American Monsters (1998)

Bord, Janet & Colin - Alien Animals (1981)

Bord, Janet & Colin - Bigfoot Casebook (1982)

Bord, Janet & Colin - Evidence for Bigfoot & Other Man-Beasts (1984)

Brenner, Susan Woolf - Chronicles of Oklahoma (Fall 1982)

Canning, John - Great Unsolved Mysteries (1984)

Carlisle, Norman - Treasure Hunting in the USA (1977)

Churchill, Allen - They Never Came Back (1960)

Citro, Joseph A. - Passing Strange (1996)

Clark, Jerome - Unexplained! (1999)

Clark, Jerome & Loren Coleman - Swamp Slobs Invade Illinois (Fate Magazine / July 1974)

Clark, Jerome & Loren Coleman - The Unidentified (1975)

Coates, Robert - The Outlaw Years (1930)

Coleman, Loren - Bigfoot (2003)

Coleman, Loren - Curious Encounters (1985)

Coleman, Loren & Patrick Huyghe - Field Guide to Bigfoot (1999)

Coleman, Loren - Mothman & Other Curious Encounters (2002)

Coleman, Loren - Mysterious America (1983/2000)

Coleman, Loren - Mystery Animals Invade Illinois (Fate Magazine / March 1971)

Coleman, Loren & Jerome Clark - Cryptozoology A to Z (1999)

Conaster, Estee - The Stirling Legend (1972)

Coolidge, Dane - Death Valley Prospector (1937)

Crowe, Richard T. - Missouri Monster (Fate Magazine / December 1972)

Cummins, Joseph - Cannibals (2001)

Dobie, J. Frank - Coronado's Children (1930)

Downer., Deborah - Classic American Ghost Stories (1990)

Drago, Harry Sinclair - Lost Bonanzas (1966)

Dudley, Gary P. - Legend of Dudleytown (website)

Ely, Sims - Lost Dutchman Mine (1953)

Fate Magazine - Various Issues (see detailed listings)

Garner, Betty Sanders - Monster, Monster (1995)
Gentry, Kurt - The Killer Mountains (1968)
Godfrey, Linda - Beast of Bray Road (2002)
Godwin, John - This Baffling World 2 - (1968)
Gregg, Mrs. Delburt - Werewolf? (Fate Magazine - March 1960)
Green, John - On the Track of the Sasquatch (1973)
Green, John - Year of the Sasquatch (1973)
Guiley, Rosemary Ellen - Atlas of the Mysterious in North America (1995)
Guiley, Rosemary Ellen - Encyclopedia of Ghosts & Spirits (2000)
Hansen, Frank - I Killed the Ape-Man Creature of Whiteface (Saga Magazine - July 1970)
Hauck, Dennis William - Haunted Places: The National Directory (2002)
Hunt, Gerry - Bizarre America (1988)
Hunter, Don with Rene Dahinden - Sasquatch (1973)
Jameson, W.C. - Buried Treasures of the American Southwest (1989)
Jameson, W.C. - Buried Treasures of the Ozarks (1990)
Jameson, W.C. - Unsolved Mysteries of the Old West (1999)
Jennings, Gary - Treasure of the Superstition Mountains (1973)
Kolb, Ellsworth - Through the Grand Canyon from Wyoming to Mexico (1914)
Krakauer, Jon - Into the Wild (1996)
Kurland, Michael- Complete Idiot's Guide to Unsolved Mysteries (2000)
Kutz, Jack - Mysteries & Miracles of Arizona (1992)
Limburg, Peter R. - Deceived (1998)
Lovelace, Leland - Lost Mines & Hidden Treasure (1956)
Marimen, Mark - Haunted Indiana (1997)
Marrinacci, Mike - Mysterious California (1988)
Martin, Mary joy - Twilight Dwellers (2003)
Martinez, Lionel - Great Unsolved Mysteries of North America (1988)
McCloy, James F. & Ray Miller Jr. - The Jersey Devil (1976)
McCloy, James F. & Ray Miller Jr. - Phantom of the Pines (1998)
Monaco, Richard - Bizarre America 2 (1992)
Murray, Earl - Ghosts of the Old West (1988)
Nash, Jay Robert - Among the Missing (1978)
Oberding, Janice - Haunted Gold & Silver (2003)
Outdoor Illinois Magazine (October 2003)
Outside Magazine (October 2003)
Phillips, David - Legendary Connecticut (1992)
PURSUIT - Journal of the Society for the Investigation of the Unexplained (April 1975)
PURSUIT - Journal of the Society for the Investigation of the Unexplained (May 1975)
Rath, Jay - I-Files (1999)
Rath, Jay - M-Files (1998)
Rath, Jay - W-Files (1997)
Readers Digest - Great Mysteries of the Past (1991)
Readers Digest - Mysteries of the Unexplained (1982)
Readers Digest - Strange Stories, Amazing Facts (1976)

Rife, Phillip L. - Bigfoot Across America (2000)
Sanderson, Ivan T. - Abominable Snowman: Legend Come to Life (1961)
Saga Magazine (various issues)
Sankey, Scarlet - Bray Road Beast (Strange Magazine - 10) (1992)
Scott, Beth & Michael Norman - Haunted Wisconsin (2001)
Shoemaker, Michael T. - Searching for the Historical Bigfoot (Strange Magazine - 5) (1990)
Sikorsky, Robert - Quest for the Dutchman's Gold (1994)
Steiger, Brad - Strange Disappearances (1972)
Steiger, Brad & Sherry - Montezuma's Serpent (1992)
Stegner, Wallace - Mormon Country (1942)
Sterry, Iveagh & William Garages - They Found a Way (1938)
Stewart, George R. - Ordeal by Hunger (1936)
Strange Magazine - Various Issues
Taylor, Troy - Haunted Illinois (2001)
Taylor, Troy - Haunting of America (2001)
Taylor, Troy - Into the Shadows (2002)
Thompson, George A. - Some Dreams Die (1982)
Time-Life Books (editors) The Pioneers (1974)
Trento, Salvatore M. - Field Guide to Mysterious Places of Eastern North America (1997)
Trento, Salvatore M. - Field Guide to Mysterious Places of the West (1994)
Trower, John - Zombie Road Material
WEIRD NJ - Tales from Clinton Road (Mark Moran / Mark Sceurman / Joanne Austin / Chris Gethard)
White, Stewart Edward - The Forest (1903)
Young, Richard & Judy Dockery - Ghost Stories from the American Southwest ((1991)

Personal Interviews Writings & Correspondence

Cover: "The Plains Herder" by N.C. Wyeth (1908)
"A Sheep Herder of the Southwest" - Scribners Magazine (January 1909)
Collection of the First Interstate Bank of Arizona, N.A. Phoenix, Arizona

Editing & Proofreading Credit:
Kim Young / Amy Taylor
They made the pages look like they were bleeding red ink but they did a fantastic job.
Any mistakes still found are my sole responsibility

Note from the Publisher: Although Whitechapel Productions Press, Troy Taylor, and all affiliated with this book have carefully researched all sources to insure the accuracy of the information contained in this book, we assume no responsibility for errors, inaccuracies or omissions.

ABOUT THE AUTHOR

Troy Taylor is the author of 32 books about ghosts and hauntings in America, including HAUNTED ILLINOIS, THE GHOST HUNTER'S GUIDEBOOK and many others. He is also the editor of GHOSTS OF THE PRAIRIE Magazine, about the history, hauntings & unsolved mysteries of America. A number of his articles have been published here and in other ghost-related publications.

Taylor is the president of the "American Ghost Society", a network of ghost hunters, which boasts more than 600 active members in the United States and Canada. The group collects stories of ghost sightings and haunted houses and uses investigative techniques to track down evidence of the supernatural. In addition, he also hosts a National Conference each year in conjunction with the group which usually attracts several hundred ghost enthusiasts from around the country.

Along with writing about ghosts, Taylor is also a public speaker on the subject and has spoken to well over 500 private and public groups on a variety of paranormal subjects. He has appeared in literally dozens of newspaper and magazine articles about ghosts and hauntings. He has also been fortunate enough to be interviewed hundreds of times for radio and television broadcasts about the supernatural. He has also appeared in a number of documentary films like AMERICA'S MOST HAUNTED, BEYOND HUMAN SENSES, GHOST WATERS, NIGHT VISITORS, GHOSTS OF MIDDLE AMERICA, the television series MYSTERIOUS WORLDS and in one feature film, THE ST. FRANCISVILLE EXPERIMENT.

Born and raised in Illinois, Taylor has long had an affinity for "things that go bump in the night" and published his first book HAUNTED DECATUR in 1995. For seven years, he was also the host of the popular, and award-winning, "Haunted Decatur" ghost tours of the city for which he sometimes still appears as a guest host. He also hosted tours in St. Louis, St. Charles, Missouri and currently hosts the "History & Hauntings Tours" of Alton, Illinois.

In 1996, Taylor married Amy Van Lear, the Managing Director of Whitechapel Press, and they currently reside in a restored 1850's bakery in Alton. Their first child together, Margaret Opal, was born in June 2002. She joined her half siblings, Orrin and Anastasia.

ABOUT WHITECHAPEL PRODUCTIONS PRESS

Whitechapel Productions Press is a small press publisher, specializing in books about ghosts and hauntings. Since 1993, the company has been one of America's leading publishers of supernatural books. Located in Alton, Illinois, they also produce the "Ghosts of the Prairie" Internet web page and "Ghosts of the Prairie", a print magazine that is dedicated to American hauntings and unsolved mysteries. The magazine began its original run from 1997 to 2000 but was revived as a full-cover, bi-monthly magazine in 2003. Issues are available through the website or at the Alton bookstore.

In addition to publishing books and the periodical on history and hauntings, Whitechapel Press also owns and distributes the Haunted America Catalog, which features over 500 different books about ghosts and hauntings from authors all over the United States. A complete selection of these books can be browsed in person at the "History & Hauntings Book Co." Store in Alton and on our Internet website.

Visit Whitechapel Productions Press online and browse through our selection of ghostly titles, plus get information on ghosts and hauntings, haunted history, spirit photographs, information on ghost hunting and much more.
Visit the Internet web page at:

www.historyandhauntings.com

Or visit the Haunted Book Co. in Person at:

515 East Third Street
Alton, Illinois 62002
(618)-456-1086

The Alton Bookstore is home to not only Whitechapel Press and the Haunted America Catalog but is also the home base for the acclaimed History & Hauntings Ghost Tours of the city, which are hosted by Troy Taylor. The bookstore features hundreds and hundreds of titles on ghosts, hauntings and the unexplained, as well as books on American, regional and local history, the Old West, the Civil War and much more.

CPSIA information can be obtained at www.ICGtesting.com
Printed in the USA
BVOW012214071012

302231BV00001B/63/A